PUBLICATIONS OF THE GERMAN HISTORICAL INSTITUTE
WASHINGTON, D.C.

Edited by Detlef Junker
with the assistance of Daniel S. Mattern

Forced Migration and Scientific Change

THE GERMAN HISTORICAL INSTITUTE, WASHINGTON, D.C.

The German Historical Institute is a center for advanced study and research whose purpose is to provide a permanent basis for scholarly cooperation between historians from the Federal Republic of Germany and the United States. The Institute conducts, promotes, and supports research into both American and German political, social, economic, and cultural history, into transatlantic migration, especially in the nineteenth and twentieth centuries, and into the history of international relations, with special emphasis on the roles played by the United States and Germany.

Other books in the series

Hartmut Lehmann and James Sheehan, editors, *An Interrupted Past: German-Speaking Refugee Historians in the United States after 1933*

Carol Fink, Axel Frohn, and Jürgern Heideking, editors, *Genoa, Rapallo, and European Reconstruction in 1922*

David Clay Large, editor, *Contending with Hitler: Varieties of German Resistance in the Third Reich*

Larry Eugene Jones and James Retallack, editors, *Elections, Mass Politics, and Social Change in Modern Germany*

Hartmut Lehmann and Guenther Roth, editors, *Weber's Protestant Ethic: Origins, Evidence, Contexts*

Catherine Epstein, *A Past Renewed: A Catalog of German-Speaking Refugee Historians in the United States after 1933*

Hartmut Lehmann and James Van Horn Melton, editors, *Paths of Continuity: Central European Historiography from the 1930s to the 1950s*

Jeffry M. Diefendorf, Axel Frohn, and Hermann-Josef Rupieper, editors, *American Policy and the Reconstruction of West Germany, 1945–1955*

Henry Geitz, Jürgen Heideking, and Jürgen Herbst, editors, *German Influences on Education in the United States to 1917*

R. Po-chia Hsia and Hartmut Lehmann, editors, *In and Out of the Ghetto: Jewish-Gentile Relations in Late Medieval and Early Modern Germany*

Peter Graf Kielmansegg, Horst Mewes, and Elisabeth Glaser-Schmidt, editors, *Hannah Arendt and Leo Strauss: German Emigrés and American Political Thought after World War II*

Sibylle Quack, editor, *Between Sorrow and Strength: Women Refugees of the Nazi Period*

Dick Hoerder and Jörg Nagler, editors, *People in Transit: German Migrations in Comparative Perspective, 1820–1930*

Forced Migration and Scientific Change

EMIGRE
GERMAN-SPEAKING SCIENTISTS
AND SCHOLARS AFTER 1933

Edited by
MITCHELL G. ASH
and
ALFONS SÖLLNER

GERMAN HISTORICAL INSTITUTE

Washington, D.C.

CAMBRIDGE
UNIVERSITY PRESS

Published by the Press Syndicate of the University of Cambridge
The Pitt Building, Trumpington Street, Cambridge CB2 1RP
40 West 20th Street, New York, NY 10011-4211, USA
10 Stamford Road, Oakleigh, Melbourne 3166, Australia

First published 1996

Printed in the United States of America

Library of Congress Cataloging-in-Publication Data
Forced migration and scientific change : emigré German-speaking
scientists and scholars after 1933 / edited by Mitchell G. Ash
and Alfons Söllner.
    p.   cm. – (Publications of the German Historical Institute)
                      Includes index.
                ISBN 0-521-49741-8 (hc)
    1. Germans – United States – Intellectual life.   2. Germans – Great
Britain – Intellectual life.   3. Brain drain – Germany – History – 20th
century.   4. Brain drain – United States – History – 20th century.
5. Brain drain – Great Britain – History – 20th century.   6. United
States – Intellectual life – 20th century.   7. Germany – Emigration and
immigration – History – 20th century.   8. Great Britain – Intellectual
    life – 20th century.   I. Ash, Mitchell G.   II. Söllner, Alfons.
                         III Series.
                    E184.G3F3   1995
        306.4'2'08931073 – dc20   95-24894
                                                   CIP

A catalog record for this book is available from the British Library

ISBN 0-521-49741-8 Hardback

In memory of Paul K. Hoch
(1942–1993)

Contents

vii

Foreword

DONALD FLEMING

This is a salutarily disturbing book for students of the "intellectual migration" of the Hitler era, perhaps particularly for the Americans among them. It forces us to examine the assumptions that originally animated our concern with the topic – the virtually unargued premises about its claim on us. At least subliminally, we wanted to believe certain things about the topic, and took it for granted that we could.

We wanted to believe – and thought we could – that a supremely edifying morality play had been enacted in the intellectual migration. In this view, Germany had been intellectually punished for yielding to the Nazis and America and Britain intellectually rewarded for their political and civic virtues. Something like providential compensation had been at work, accomplishing a form of world-historical justice through a banished elite, avenging its wrongs by tipping the intellectual balance-of-power against Germany. Hitler had inflicted a severe injury on Germany's justifiable pride in its position as a preeminently intellectual nation; but the cunning of reason had simply fortified his enemies. An imperfect analogy, usually couched in economic rather than intellectual terms, would be the price often thought to have been paid by France for expelling the Huguenots. The moral for Americans was to renew their wavering receptivity to newcomers in view of the benefits that the refugees from Hitler had brought with them.

The moral was sound. America and Britain gained from the intellectual migration, Germany lost. But the lesson enforced by these essays is that most discussions of the topic to date have been overwhelmingly impressionistic, systematically skewed in favor of the most salient individuals and impulses, deficient in adequate quantification if any, and almost willfully uncritical, as if to keep from diluting the moral of the tale.

Part of the problem has been that most American and British students of the subject have understandably confined their researches to the receiving

end of this demographic transaction. This has almost inevitably complemented the tacit premise that everything added to the intellectual life of
America and Britain by the migrants was automatically subtracted from that
of Germany (or at least prevented from otherwise developing there) in a
zero-sum game. This assumption was rendered plausible by awareness of
the chilling effect of Hitlerism on culture in general. But Geoffrey Cocks
has already shown – what this book confirms – that psychotherapy and
psychology, which might have seemed to be prime candidates for suppres-
sion by the Nazis, actually survived the Third Reich, with basically cosmetic
emendations, because they were militarily useful. Science, even in its ideo-
logically problematical aspects, did not totally collapse in Nazi Germany.

What did occur there could not even begin to be established except by
the quantification that characterizes many of these essays. These and less
quantitative pieces yield a budget of cautions that students of the subjects
will henceforth ignore at their peril. We must never assume that the research
communities in even the most scientifically productive countries in the
most tranquil times will be equally receptive to new growing points. Indeed,
an entrenched galaxy of brilliant investigators, as in Germany on the eve of
the Nazi takeover, may actually impede the launching of new specialties.
If so, young (or paradigmatically innovative) subfields may contemplate
working abroad *without regard to any political crises or racial persecution,* though
of course the scale of this may be profoundly affected – and the motivation
for it acutely sharpened – by extra-scientific considerations. The (ultimately)
internationalizing impulse in science that facilitated such possibilities was
greatly fostered, as various essays point out, by the large-scale intervention
of the Rockefeller scientific philanthropies in Europe from the 1920s forward – identifying the most promising young scientists, giving them fellowships to America, and supplying them with invaluable American
contacts if they chose to migrate, or had to. We cannot assume that all the
younger migrants, whom Klaus Fischer shows to have been the most scientifically productive abroad, would have stayed in Germany except for
Hitler – indeed, it seems that we must *not* say this in the cardinal instance
of Max Delbrück of molecular biology fame, who never claimed to be in
an enforced exile – or that they would have found comparable opportunities
if they had stayed put in a hypothetical Germany-without-Hitler. For himself, Delbrück evidently thought not.

Conversely, it is at least arguable that American science in 1930 was
entering a period in which America would have been pulling abreast or
ahead of Germany in many fields – nuclear physics, genetics, possibly chemistry – even without the palpably accelerating factor of the German exodus.

Nothing can diminish the brilliance of the contributions that the migrants made, but they were joining a leap forward that was already in progress. The real point of the whole situation may be that the gradient of opportunities in science was predictably tilting in the direction of the United States as the richest and most powerful nation, and even without the dire tragedies of the twentieth century, many young scientists, though almost certainly fewer and far more gradually, would have been moving from Europe to America for at least part of their careers. But this would hardly qualify as the scenario for a morality play in which retribution was visited upon Germany for the Nazis' offenses.

The truly audacious thought that this book invites is that we ought to stop focusing exclusively on the Nazi era when casting accounts between Germany and the receiving countries. This would entail reframing our topic as the geographical circulation of intellectual elites in the twentieth century, antedating the Nazis and continuing after them, though accelerated, magnified, and amplified to the highest pitch of urgency in the Hitler years. The larger story would include the exodus in various stages over several decades from the Soviet Union, the pursuit of the *carrière ouverte aux talents* by Frenchmen such as Alexis Carrel and René Dubos who migrated to the United States before 1930, the flight of Spanish refugees from Franco and French refugees from Hitler, the migration to America of Enrico Fermi, Emilio Segré, and Rita Levi-Montalcini, and other Italians from 1938 forward, the exodus of Hungarians from the late 1950s, *and* the transfer across the Atlantic of German(ic) scholars such as Erwin Chargaff, Max Delbrück, and Joseph Schumpeter, whose various migrations were not enforced except by their sense of greater opportunities.

Each of these human and cultural flows, as well as the German experience in the Nazi era, requires much further research of the kind admirably embodied in this book; but now one of the ends in view should be to go beyond this by comparative studies juxtaposing different instances of the generic phenomenon. Such studies have scarcely begun, and what they would yield is hard to say in advance. But one can imagine inquiries that might profitably be pursued. Did the migrants from some cultures remain, or attempt to remain, an interacting "community" reassembled in a new environment, while migrants from other cultures speedily dispersed themselves among the receiving population?

One has the impression that the Italian refugees from Mussolini more nearly corresponded to the former pattern, and the Germanic refugees from Hitler to the latter. If so, why, and what were the respective consequences? Or did the work of the migrants rebound on the individual cultures from which they came? And if so, when, how, and by what agents (returnees or others) did the rebound occur? Apropos of returnees, did the proportion of these vary significantly as between their countries of origin, and if so, why? Many other and probably better questions could be posed, but we should certainly be looking ahead to comparative studies if only to discover new things to look for in the *individual* waves of migration by the twentieth-century intellectuals whose investigation is notably exemplified in this book.

Preface

In May 1991, an international and interdisciplinary group of scholars convened at the Wissenschaftskolleg in Berlin to discuss the impact of the forced emigration of German-speaking scholars and scientists after the Nazi takeover in 1933. The chapters in this book, combining revised and updated contributions to that conference with essays commissioned subsequently by the editors, will provide readers with new perspectives on the "intellectual migration" from Germany.

A number of individuals and institutions deserve recognition for bringing this book to fruition. First, the German Historical Institute would like to thank its former director, Hartmut Lehmann, for supporting the inclusion of this collection in our series with Cambridge University Press. He recognized immediately that the subject of forced migration and scientific change nicely complemented work already undertaken by the Institute and published in this series. The collection *An Interrupted Past: German-Speaking Refugee Historians in the United States after 1933*, edited by Hartmut Lehmann and James J. Sheehan, details the fate of German-speaking historians who fled Nazi Europe and came to the United States. Catherine Epstein's companion volume, *A Past Renewed: A Catalog of German-Speaking Refugee Historians in the United States after 1933*, documents this generation of German-speaking refugee historians with biographical sketches and bibliographical information.

Recently, the German Historical Institute published a book of essays entitled *Hannah Arendt and Leo Strauss: German Emigrés and American Political Thought after World War II*, edited by Peter Graf Kielmansegg, Horst Mewes, and Elisabeth Glaser-Schmidt, in which the careers and intellectual production of these two prominent refugee political scientists are examined. And in *Between Sorrow and Strength: Women Refugees of the Nazi Period*, editor Sibylle Quack has united the reflections of contemporary eyewitnesses with scholarly articles to explore the gender perspective of this story.

In sum, the collection follows up on general questions raised in earlier volumes in other social and natural scientific contexts, and addresses the critical issue of whether forced migration prompted or stifled scientific developments in these fields.

The Institute would also like to thank the reviewers of the draft manuscript for their constructive criticism, helpful suggestions, and supportive comments that did much to improve the essays. I would like to thank the staff of the Institute as well for their help and support in readying the manuscript for the press. Special thanks go to Bärbel Bernhardt for typing the manuscript, and to Pamela Abraham and Julia Bruggemann, two very able and cheerful interns who aided the process considerably. The series editor, Daniel S. Mattern, worked long and hard to smooth out the rough places in the authors' English prose and managed the project at the Institute from start to finish.

Finally, the German Historical Institute would like to thank the publisher and especially Frank Smith, the social science editor at Cambridge, for supporting publication of this book.

Washington, D.C.   Detlef Junker

Contributors

Mitchell G. Ash is Associate Professor of History at the University of Iowa.

Alan D. Beyerchen is Professor of History at Ohio State University.

Klaus Fischer is Professor of Philosophy of Science at the University of Trier.

Christian Fleck is associated with the Institute for Sociology at the University of Graz.

Karen J. Greenberg is the Executive Director of the Open Society Institute, New York City.

Paul K. Hoch was associated with the Hans Krebs Papers Project at the University of Sheffield. He died in 1993.

Klaus Horn is associated with the Institute for General Pedagogy at the Humboldt University in Berlin.

Claus-Dieter Krohn is Professor of History at the University of Lüneburg in Hannover.

Edith Kurzweil is University Professor of Social Thought at Adelphi University and executive editor of *Partisan Review*.

Jennifer Platt is Professor of Sociology at the University of Sussex.

Skúli Sigurdsson received his Ph.D. in history of science from Harvard University in 1991, and was Visiting Professor at the University of Hamburg in summer 1993.

Alfons Söllner is Professor of Political Theory and History of Ideas at the Technical University of Chemnitz-Zwickau.

Heinz–Elmar Tenorth is Professor of General Pedagogy at the Humboldt University in Berlin.

Paul Weindling is associated with the Wellcome Unit for the History of Medicine, University of Oxford.

Tables and Figures

TABLES

xvii

FIGURES

Introduction: Forced Migration and Scientific Change after 1933

MITCHELL G. ASH AND ALFONS SÖLLNER

The so-called "Law for the Reconstitution of the Professional Civil Service" of April 7, 1933, which authorized the dismissal or premature retirement from government service of persons who were not of "Aryan" descent or who were associated with groups considered politically undesirable in the new German state, was only the beginning of a massive, forced exodus mainly of Jewish scholars and scientists from Nazi Germany. Some particularly prescient intellectuals had already fled when the Reichstag burned in February of that year. The Nuremberg Laws of 1935, the invasion of Austria in March and the pogroms in Germany in November 1938, and finally the Nazi conquests in the rest of Europe made the emigration of scientists and scholars a mass phenomenon unprecedented in the modern history of academic life. Compared with the total of more than half a million refugees from Germany alone, the fate of approximately 2,000 academics and research scientists may seem of modest concern, but not when we remember how innovative some of these scholars and scientists were or became. Nonetheless, skeptical voices have been raised, asking among other things whether these innovations were indeed the results of emigration, or whether they might have occurred in any case. Did that "exodus of reason" in fact lead to significant scientific change, and if so, how should that change be characterized? The essays in this book attempt to provide answers to these questions, and thus to contribute to the comparative study of science in culture.

FROM A DISCOURSE OF "LOSS" AND "GAIN" TO PROCESSES AND CONTINGENCIES OF CHANGE

A certain unavoidable pathos has permeated discussion of this "intellectual migration" and its impact. Dominant in both public and academic discourse

1

during the first postwar generations, especially in West Germany, were the perspectives of political and literary exiles. Many spoke – and still speak – of this migration as an "exodus of the mind" (*Auszug des Geistes*), of the modern spirit, or – depending on the political viewpoint of the speaker – of democracy.[1] Following, and at times combining with this discourse, came studies of émigré scientists and scholars, ranging from triumphant account-ings of the émigrés' contributions to American and British science and cul-ture since the 1960s, to mournful assessments of loss in West Germany and Austria centered about the fiftieth anniversaries of the Nazi takeover in 1933 and 1938, respectively – one of many ironic aspects of those reversed ju-bilees.[2]

Stimulated in part by these efforts, younger researchers from Germany and Austria took up the subject in the 1980s, many of them funded by a major research program organized by the Deutsche Forschungsgemeinschaft (German Research Foundation). Alongside or in collaboration with Amer-ican, British, and Israeli scholars, these researchers have cast their nets more widely than before, going beyond the earlier focus on literary and political exiles and more prominent scientists and scholars to consider the careers and achievements of émigré academics and professionals in more detail.[3]

1 See, e.g., Radio Bremen, *Auszug des Geistes: Bericht über eine Sendereihe* (Bremen, 1962); Manfred Briegel and Wolfgang Frühwald, eds., *Die Erfahrung der Fremde: Kolloquium des Schwerpunktprogramms "Exilforschung" der Deutschen Forschungsgemeinschaft* (Weinheim, 1988). For an American variant of this perspective, see Anthony Heilbut, *Exiled in Paradise: German Refugee Artists and Intellectuals in America from the 1930s to the Present* (New York, 1983).

2 See, e.g., the essays by Louise W. Holborn, Herbert Marcuse, Albert Wellek, and Gerald Stourzh in *Jahrbuch für Amerikastudien* 10 (1965); Donald Fleming and Bernard Bailyn, eds., *The Intellectual Migration: Germany and America, 1930–1960* (Cambridge, Mass., 1969); Jerold C. Jackman and Carla M. Borden, eds., *The Muses Flee Hitler: Cultural Transfer and Adaptation, 1930–1945* (Washington, D.C., 1983); Horst Möller, *Exodus der Kultur* (Munich, 1984); Lewis A. Coser, *Refugee Scholars in America: Their Impact and Their Experiences* (New Haven, Conn., 1984); "Vor fünfzig Jahren: Emi-gration und Immigration von Wissenschaft," *Berichte zur Wissenschaftsgeschichte* 7 (1984); Friedrich Stadler, ed., *Vertriebene Vernunft: Emigration und Exil österreichischer Wissenschaft*, vols. 1 and 2 (Vienna and Munich, 1987, 1988); Werner E. Mosse et al., eds., *Second Chance: Two Centuries of German-Speaking Jews in the United Kingdom* (Tübingen, 1991). For an overview, see Herbert A. Strauss, "Wissenschaftsemigration als Forschungsproblem," in Strauss et al., eds., *Die Emigration der Wissen-schaften nach 1933* (Munich, 1991), 7–24.

3 On émigré professionals, see, e.g., Wolfgang Mock, *Technische Intelligenz im Exil: Vertreibung und Emigration deutschsprachiger Ingenieure nach Grossbritannien, 1933–1945* (Düsseldorf, 1986); Michael Hubenstorf, "Österreichische Ärzteemigration," in Stadler, ed., *Vertriebene Vernunft*, 1:339–415; Hans-Peter Kröner, "Die Emigration deutschsprachiger Mediziner im Nationalsozialismus," *Berichte zur Wissenschaftsgeschichte* 12 (1989), Sonderheft; Ernst C. Stiefel and Frank Mecklenburg, *Deutsche Juristen im amerikanischen Exil, 1933–1950* (Tübingen, 1991); Uwe H. Peters, *Psychiatrie im Exil: Die Emigration der dynamischen Psychiatrie aus Deutschland, 1933–1939 (Düsseldorf, 1992); The* essays on professionals in Mosse, ed., *Second Chance*; Atina Grossmann, "German Women Doctors from Berlin to New York: Maternity and Modernity in Weimar and in Exile," *Feminist Studies* 19 (1993): 65–88; and the essays on women professionals in Sybille Quack, ed., *Between Sorrow and Strength: Women Refugees of the Nazi Period* (New York, 1995). Although the situations of these émigrés had much in common with those of scientists and scholars, only cases in which sciences and professions inter-

Many of these attempts at a broader approach were stimulated by the publication of the *International Biographical Dictionary of Central European Emigrés* in 1983, which improved the basis for aggregate studies.[4] Research has since proceeded from individuals to collective biography, from the sufferings of exile to systematic comparative studies of emigration from the Central European countries as well as the émigrés' careers and impact in their new homelands, and from an exclusive focus on the contributions of a successful elite to more detailed studies of entire disciplines.

One result is that a more differentiated, in some respects more modest, picture has emerged; although earlier rhetoric and metaphors persist, it has become more difficult to be satisfied with them. The fascination with the lives and brilliant achievements of the more prominent émigrés – from physical scientists such as James Franck, Erwin Schrödinger, or Lise Meitner, to social scientists such as Paul Lazarsfeld or psychoanalysts Sigmund and Anna Freud, to the social theorists of the Frankfurt School or political thinkers such as Hannah Arendt and Leo Strauss – continues with good reason.[5] In addition to pathbreaking scientific innovations, the émigrés have given us some of the most profound and complex accounts of the cultural breaks and ironic reconstructions characteristic of modern life, as they lived through them. But continuing nearly exclusive emphasis on prestigious innovators – a common tendency in both cultural history and the history of science – diverts attention from potentially more broadly significant changes in the work and careers of less prominent researchers.

In keeping with this awareness of cultural breakage and reconstruction, there has been a turn in recent years from assessing the products or contributions of the émigrés to the processes of intellectual and cultural change that produced them. A "products" perspective has a certain historical justification in the vocabulary of the time. Even Alvin Johnson, then president of the New School for Social Research, founder of the so-called "University in Exile" and a leading advocate of rescue for émigré scholars, had no qualms about calling them "Hitler's gift to American culture." Another

   acted or overlapped, such as medical science, psychology, psychoanalysis, and pedagogy, will be considered here.

4 Herbert A. Strauss and Werner Röder, eds., *International Biographical Dictionary of Central European Emigrés, 1933–1945*, 3 vols. (Munich, 1980–83). The editors' standards of inclusion (described in vol. 1, lxxxvii ff.) limit this work's value for studies of émigré scientists and scholars to some extent. Lesser-known émigré scientists and scholars have not been included, whereas many children of émigrés who later entered these professions have been.

5 See, e.g., Patricia Rife, *Lise Meitner: Ein Leben für die Wissenschaft*, trans. Peter Jacobs (Hildesheim, 1990); Peter Gay, *Freud: A Life for Our Time* (New York, 1988); Elizabeth Young-Bruehl, *Anna Freud: A Biography* (New York, 1988); Peter Graf Kielmannsegg, Horst Mewes, and Elisabeth Glaser-Schmidt, eds., *Hannah Arendt and Leo Strauss: German Emigrés and American Political Thought after World War II* (New York, 1994).

prominent academic reportedly put it even more directly when he said, "Hitler shakes the tree and I gather the apples."[6] Today, it seems problematic to speak of the émigrés only in such terms, continuing to treat them or their research achievements now and without irony as a sort of human or intellectual capital, or as prestige objects to improve – or damage – the images of particular nations. It is surely appropriate, on the other hand, to speak of loss when the émigrés' personal experiences are in question. They lost not only their livelihoods, but personal connections to their families, their language, and not least their culture. These were, after all, the most highly acculturated Jews in Europe, for many of whom anti-Semitic discrimination came as an unbelievable shock.

More important in this context, however, is another aspect of the discourse of loss and gain – the continuing concentration on the émigrés' contributions, rather than on the processes and the sociocultural and biographical circumstances that made them possible. It is a fundamental but common error to suppose that these contributions were just what was "lost" to German-speaking culture. To inquire only about losses and gains in this sense presupposes a static view of science and of culture, as though the émigrés brought with them finished bits of knowledge, which they then inserted like building-stones into already established cultural constructs elsewhere. This error can only be reinforced by the continuing tendency – especially among German-speaking students of the subject – to ask only whether émigrés continued their previous research in their new locations, and to mourn the breakup of scientific schools or other research groups. Proceeding in this way without further reflection assumes that such research programs or groupings would necessarily have remained in place or continued working as before had their members not been forced to leave their homelands. It also ignores the fact that forced migration made possible careers that could not have happened in the smaller, more restrictive university and science systems of Central Europe, and the possibility that the pressure to respond to new circumstances may have led to innovations that might not have occurred in the same way otherwise.

Also related to the discourse of loss and gain, and equally questionable, is the widely held assumption that knowledge in the natural sciences is more "transferable" than the supposedly more language- and culture-dependent knowledge of the social sciences and the humanities. In the natural sciences the transfer of knowledge is often considered essentially unproblematic,

6   Alvin Johnson, *Pioneer's Progress: An Autobiography* (New York, 1953); Walter S. Cook, New York University Institute of Fine Arts, quoted in Wilfred McClay, "Weimar in America," *American Scholar* 55 (Winter 1985–86): 120.

with cultural factors influencing the process only indirectly, by affecting the contexts of transfer, rather than "the ideas themselves." Sociologist Sven Papcke evokes this criterion to differentiate between literary and political émigrés, whose self-concept is correctly represented by the word "exile," and émigré scientists, whom he prefers to describe as "emigrants."[7] These claims need to be examined rather than assumed. In any case, such assumptions are not well suited to help us understand or even recognize similarities in transfer or innovation processes in the natural and the social sciences.

Moreover, as biochemist Erwin Chargaff writes in his autobiography, even the modes of thought and practice of the natural sciences are not transferable without limit, for these too "live in the womb of a particular language and civilization."[8] Simply defining scientific knowledge per se as international closes off consideration of this point before it can even begin. Chargaff's remark suggests that styles of thinking about and experimenting on or with nature are not independent of the cultural contexts of their creation. Recent work on research and theoretical preferences in Europe and America in the physical and biological sciences supports the claim that there may indeed be national or even local styles in science, the conversion of which into internationally understood science or their transfer to other cultural settings is by no means easy or simple.[9]

Paul K. Hoch and Jennifer Platt have suggested that forced migration actually accelerated what they term "the denationalization of science."[10] Taking this possibility seriously would cast the *Sonderweg* debate familiar to historians of Germany in a new light. The growth of research universities and other scientific research institutes in Germany during the nineteenth and twentieth centuries was surely part of that country's "special path" into modernity; and the émigrés from Nazism learned their particular ways of doing science in those institutions. Closer study of the blendings – or clashes – of scientific cultures that occurred as a result of forced migration could thus become tests of the "specialness" of national styles in sciences, and of

---

7 Sven Papcke, "Fragen an die Exilforschung heute," *Exilforschung* 6 (1988): 19.
8 Erwin Chargaff, *Das Feuer des Heraklit: Skizzen aus einem Leben vor der Natur* (Munich, 1984), 89.
9 On physics, see Paul K. Hoch, "The Reception of Central European Refugee Physicists of the 1930s: U.S.S.R., U.K., U.S.A.," *Annals of Science* 40 (1983): 217–46; Silvan Schweber, "The Empiricist Temper Regnant: Theoretical Physics in the United States, 1920–1950," *Historical Studies in the Physical and Biological Sciences* 17 (1986): 55–98. On biology, see Jonathan Harwood, "National Styles in Science: Genetics in Germany and the United States between the World Wars," *Isis* 78 (1987): 390–414; Jonathan Harwood, *Styles of Scientific Thought: The German Genetics Community, 1900–1933* (Chicago, 1993).
10 Paul K. Hoch and Jennifer Platt, "Migration and the Denationalization of Science," in Elizabeth Crawford et al., eds., *Denationalizing Science* (Amsterdam, 1993), 133–52. H. Stuart Hughes advanced a similar thesis some years ago when he spoke of the "deprovincialization" of social thought in his *A Sea Change: The Migration of Social Thought* (New York, 1976).

their limits. National and local peculiarities are evident in the sciences, as they are in the political and social spheres. Constituting and analyzing such differences, however, is only part of the story, for German scientists and scholars had participated in international networks of scientific exchange long before 1933. Rather than focusing on national or local differences alone, it is necessary to grasp the migration of scholars and scientists after 1933 as one particularly important episode in a larger drama – the geographical circulation of intellectual elites and the resulting de- or multinationalization of knowledge in the twentieth century.

More comprehensive overviews of individual disciplines and closer analyses of scientific continuity and change in both their cognitive and social dimensions are the unifying perspectives of this book. The contributors ask and attempt to answer the following questions:

- Who were the émigrés? How uniformly distributed were they in German-speaking Europe by discipline, specialty, or locale, and who among them were given the opportunity to continue scientific or scholarly work?
- What patterns of change can be detected in more global disciplinary surveys, or in closer analyses of individuals and research groups?
- What can we learn from this episode about the interrelationships of science and culture?

DEFINING THE SUBJECTS: THE EMIGRES AS A GROUP

In order to better understand what exactly is meant by speaking of the emigration of scientists and scholars as a group phenomenon, some initial remarks about its quantitative dimensions are in order. In the autumn of 1934, officials of the newly created Reich Ministry for Education and Science prepared a list of persons dismissed or forced to retire from higher education institutions in Germany as a result of the Nazi civil service law. The list included 614 university teachers; of these, 190 were full or tenured associate professors, and 424 non-tenured associate professors and *Privatdozenten* (lecturers). Of the 575 for whom such data are given, only 80 (13.9 percent) were dismissed under Paragraph 4 of the law – that is, for political reasons. The vast majority, 384 (66.8 percent), were dismissed under Paragraph 3 – as "non-Aryans" – but a surprisingly large number, 107 (18.6 percent), came under the "rubber" Paragraph 6 ("simplification of administration"). Already at this early stage, the uneven distribution pattern of dismissals is obvious. Only three universities – Berlin, Frankfurt, and Breslau – accounted for fully 40 percent of the total (136, 69, and 43, respectively), whereas the universities of Rostock and Tübingen had as few as two each, and Erlangen only one. The numbers are thus reasonably clear indicators of the concentration of Jewish academics in Germany.[11]

As noted earlier, the Nuremberg laws, the pogroms of November 1938, and the invasions of Czechoslovakia and Austria drove still more academics from their posts and into exile. American sociologist Edward Y. Hartshorne estimated in 1937 that by that time approximately 20 percent of all German higher education faculty, including university, technical pedagogical, and commercial academy personnel, had been dismissed or forced to retire on either racial or political grounds. In the 1950s, Christian von Ferber calculated a still higher figure of more than one-third.[12] Both of these figures, particularly von Ferber's, have been challenged on methodological grounds.[13] According to an estimate by social historian Herbert Strauss, "approximately 15 percent (1,100 to 1,500) of university professors of all categories may have emigrated by 1940."[14] Adding non-university research scientists – for example, associates of the various Kaiser Wilhelm Institutes, and scholars who had begun but not yet completed their training at the time of emigration – yields the currently accepted figure of approximately 2,000.[15]

A more precise interpretation of these numbers and their meaning emerges when one considers the institutions from which the émigrés came. Klaus Fischer has attempted this for émigré physicists.[16] Of a total of 325 physicists in Germany who were "habilitated" – had earned the right to

11 "Liste der auf Grund des Gesetzes zur Wiederherstellung des Berufsbeamtentums verabschiedeten Professoren und Privatdozenten," submitted by the Reichsministerium für Erziehung, Wissenschaft und Volksbildung to the Foreign Office, December 11, 1934. Politisches Archiv des Auswärtigen Amtes, Bonn. See also Sybille Gerstengarbe, "Die erste Entlassungswelle von Hochschullehrern deutscher Hochschulen aufgrund des Gesetzes zur Wiederherstellung des Berufsbeamtentums vom 7.7.1933," *Berichte zur Wissenschaftsgeschichte* 17 (1994): 17–40. For further information on specific universities, see, e.g., Hans-Joachim Dahms, "Verluste durch Emigration: Die Auswirkungen der nationalsozialistischen 'Säuberungen' an der Universität Göttingen," *Exilforschung* 4 (1986): 165ff; Rudolf Schottlaender, *Verfolgte Berliner Wissenschaft: Ein Gedenkwerk* (Berlin, 1988); Dorothee Mussgnug, *Die vertriebenen Heidelberger Dozenten: Zur Geschichte der Ruprecht-Karls-Universität nach 1933* (Heidelberg, 1988); Eckart Krause, Ludwig Huber, and Holger Fischer, eds., *Hochschulalltag im "Dritten Reich": Die Hamburger Universität, 1933–1945* (Berlin, 1991), vol. 1.
12 Edward Y. Hartshorne, *The German Universities and National Socialism* (London, 1937); Christian von Ferber, *Die Entwicklung des Lehrkörpers der deutschen Universitäten und Hochschulen, 1864–1954* (Göttingen, 1956), 145. Horst Möller, "Wissenschaft in der Emigration–Quantitative und geographische Aspekte," *Berichte zur Wissenschaftsgeschichte* 7 (1984): 1–9, constructs an estimate similar to von Ferber's by different means.
13 Klaus Fischer, "Die Emigration von Wissenschaftlern nach 1933: Möglichkeiten und Grenzen einer Bilanzierung," *Vierteljahresschrift für Zeitgeschichte* 39 (1991): 535–49.
14 Herbert A. Strauss, "Wissenschaftsemigration als Forschungsproblem," 10.
15 For a list of émigrés from institutes of the Kaiser-Wilhelm-Gesellschaft, see Kristie Macrakis, *Surviving the Swastika: Scientific Research in Nazi Germany* (New York, 1993), 207–14.
16 Klaus Fischer, "Die Emigration deutschsprachiger Physiker nach 1933: Strukturen und Wirkungen," in Strauss et al., eds., *Die Emigration der Wissenschaften*, 28–9.

teach at a university – 50, or 15.4 percent, emigrated after 1933. This corresponds to Strauss's estimate of the proportion of all émigré scientists and scholars. More interesting still is their distribution: The 50 émigré physicists came from only 15 institutions, at which 212, or 65 percent of university physicists, taught; the other 21, generally smaller, institutions had no émigré physicists at all. The larger, generally more innovative, institutes were thus also the hardest hit.

When we realize concretely what is meant here – nearly the entire membership of the famous Göttingen institutes of physics and mathematics, for example – then we must acknowledge that the qualitative dimensions of loss were as significant in some disciplines as the quantitative. Data for psychology tell much the same story. Of the 308 members of the German Society for Psychology who lived or taught in German-speaking countries, 45 (14.6 percent) emigrated; among them, however, were the directors of four of the five largest and internationally best-known psychological institutes and 22 academics ranked associate professor or higher.[17] Nazism's racist policies thus left noticeable quantitative gaps in Germany's scientific institutions, but the qualitative losses were often still more significant. Not for nothing does Alan Beyerchen speak, in a deliberately ironic reference to Martin Heidegger's inaugural address as rector in Freiburg, of the "self-decapitation" (*Selbstenthauptung*) of German culture, rather than Heidegger's proclaimed "self-fulfillment" (*Selbstbehauptung*) of the German university.[18]

And yet that is not the whole story. As recent research on science under Nazism has shown, emigration rates were not the same for all disciplines; successors were found often enough for those dismissed academics who emigrated; and the science that replaced their work cannot be dismissed simply as Nazified ideology disguised as science – although there surely was plenty of that. Studies of the dismissal and emigration of medical scientists from Berlin, for example, present a highly differentiated picture, from complete destruction in the case of Magnus Hirschfeld's Institute for Sexual Research to nearly complete continuity in university and extra-academic institutes concerned with public health and population policy.[19] In his study of the professionalization of psychology under Nazism, Ulfried Geuter shows that after the introduction of a professional certificate for psycholo-

17 Mitchell G. Ash, "Disziplinentwicklung und Wissenschaftstransfer–deutschsprachige Psychologen in der Emigration," *Berichte zur Wissenschaftsgeschichte* 7 (1984): 208–9.
18 Alan Beyerchen, "Anti-Intellectualism and the Cultural Decapitation of Germany under the Nazis," in Jackman and Borden, eds., *The Muses Flee Hitler*, 29–44.
19 See the essays by Rolf Winau, Michael Hubenstorf, and Sigrid Stöckel in Wolfram Fischer et al., eds., *Exodus von Wissenschaften aus Berlin* (Berlin, 1994).

gists in 1941 made it necessary to create and staff full professorships in the field in all German universities, by 1942 there were more professors of psychology in German-speaking institutions of higher education than there had been ten years earlier.[20] Ute Deichmann's study of biologists under Hitler shows that funding for basic research in genetics did not diminish, but increased, in the Nazi period. Herbert Mehrtens and Helmuth Trischler note a shift to "technoscience" – technology-oriented basic research – before and during World War II in fields as disparate as mathematics and aerodynamics, a shift that paralleled trends in the West. Finally, Michael Neufeld's study of the German rocketry project at Peenemünde clearly shows that despite the mass emigration of Jewish scientists and technicians, neither personnel, resources, nor the will to invest them were lacking when it came to programs deemed central to Nazism's eugenical or expansionist aims – and to creating and unleashing a modern war machine to achieve them.[21]

Whether the quality of scientific work according to then-current international standards remained as high after 1933 as it had been before, and whether it is even possible to discuss the quality of science under Nazism without some sort of moral compass, are hotly contested issues at present, ones that can hardly be resolved with quantitative methods alone. Nonetheless, it now appears exaggerated to speak in any simple or general sense of an "exodus of reason" or even of modernity as such from Nazi Germany after 1933. Perhaps it will be necessary to revert to a more neutral terminology of change, reconstruction, and redirection in the sciences and technology, both in Germany and abroad, as a result of political upheaval. Whatever terms may ultimately be preferred, the quantitative and qualitative aspects of this issue need to be considered together. As will be clear subsequently, this is also true for analyses of processes of change after emigration.

DEFINING THE SUBJECTS AGAIN: PRESELECTION IN COUNTRIES OF SETTLEMENT

A second issue that requires attention before we can move on to scientific change proper is the question of who got the opportunity to continue

---

20 Ulfried Geuter, *The Professionalization of Psychology in Nazi Germany*, trans. Richard Holmes (Cambridge, 1992).
21 See Ute Deichmann, *Biologen unter Hitler: Vertreibung, Karrieren, Forschung* (Frankfurt/Main, 1992; trans. Cambridge, Mass., forthcoming); Michael Neufeld, *The Rocket and the Reich: Peenemünde and the Coming of the Ballistic Missile Era* (New York, 1995), and the essays by Herbert Mehrtens, Ute Deichmann, Helmuth Trischler, and Michael Neufeld in Monika Renneberg and Mark Walker, eds., *Science, Technology, and National Socialism* (Cambridge, 1994).

scientific work, and thus at least potentially to participate in scientific change, and why. Significant here was the presence or absence of institutional, economic, and social support available for science and scholarship in the countries to which the émigrés went. Studies of émigré scientists and professionals in Turkey, Palestine, and Latin America amply document the difficulties they faced owing to the lack of infrastructure, and also the pioneer spirit many showed in the face of such adversities.[22] For those émigrés – the vast majority – who received positions or stipends in the United States and to a lesser extent in Britain, it is important to clarify the mediating roles of influential scholars and scientists as well as the many aid organizations, disciplinary and multidisciplinary as well as humanitarian in character.

Traditional accounts of this subject understandably stress the humanitarian impulse to rescue persons in distress. Such humanitarian motives were undoubtedly present in most cases. Also important were the traditions of countries such as the United States as a nation of immigrants, and the continuing respect for German intellectual culture among segments of the educated elites in that country and in Britain. As recent research indicates, however, political and economic considerations and rhetoric were equally prominent. Important in this respect were two seemingly opposed but ultimately reconcilable impulses. The effects of the Great Depression and widespread fears of unemployment and competition for scarce resources among scientists and professionals in the host countries clearly worked against wholesale importation of academics or professionals, and encouraged careful selection among them. On the other hand, the desire of some influential academics as well as foundation and university administrators to grasp the opportunity of enriching their own discipline or institution by acquiring the émigré scholars judged to be best by their colleagues reinforced the impulse toward selectivity.[23]

A closely related pattern appears in the work of many scientists and of

22 See, e.g., Regine Erichsen, "Die Emigration deutschsprachiger Naturwissenschaftler von 1933 bis 1945 in die Türkei in ihrem sozial-und wissenschaftshistorischen Wirkungszusammenhang," in Strauss et al., eds., *Die Emigration der Wissenschaften nach 1933*, 73–104; Robert Jütte, *Die Emigration der deutschsprachigen "Wissenschaft des Judentums": Die Auswanderung jüdischer Historiker nach Palästina, 1933–1945* (Stuttgart, 1991).
23 Karen J. Greenberg, "The Mentor Within: The German Refugee Scholars of the Nazi Period and Their American Context," Ph.D. diss., Yale University, 1987; Besse Zaban Jones, "To the Rescue of the Learned: The Asylum Fellowship Plan at Harvard, 1938–1940," *Harvard Library Bulletin* 32 (1984): 204–38; Gerhard Hirschfeld, " 'The Defense of Learning and Science . . . ' Der Academic Assistance Council und die wissenschaftliche Emigration aus Nazi-Deutschland," *Exilforschung* 6 (1988): 28–43; Hirschfeld, " 'A High Tradition of Eagerness . . . ' British Non-Jewish Organizations in Support of Refugees," in Mosse et al., eds., *Second Chance*, 599–610. Other aid organizations with less elitist orientations, such as the American Friends' Service Committee, are less well researched.

aid committees organized within individual disciplines – for example, in psychology, psychoanalysis, and physics. In all of these cases, humanitarian aims competed, not always on equal terms, with institutional, disciplinary, and professional politics. In some cases, the aid committee's very existence expressed a disciplinary political agenda. When political liberals within the American Psychological Association organized the Emergency Committee in Aid of Displaced Foreign Psychologists in 1938 and 1939, for example, they hoped with the help of émigrés to increase demand for social scientists in social service work and thus contribute to social change.[24] In the case of psychoanalysis, Ernest Jones in England and Lawrence Kubie in New York secured visas, affidavits, and other papers for dozens of colleagues, but functioned simultaneously as selectors for the immigration authorities and tried to persuade émigrés once they arrived to take up practice in the provinces in order to spread the good word and reduce competition in the metropolises.[25] Last, but by no means least, Copenhagen physicist Niels Bohr worked closely with the Rockefeller Foundation and other agencies not only to select and place outstanding émigré scientists but also, by doing so, to set specific scientific agendas – an effort that played an important role in the emergence of both molecular biology and nuclear physics.[26]

IDENTIFYING PATTERNS OF CHANGE, LEVELS OF ACCULTURATION

Such patterns point to selective, even pre-selective, effects not only of influential individuals but also of local scientific and cultural milieus, which could have decisive impacts on émigrés' futures. Sociohistorical studies have made a start toward more careful examination of such impacts by employing acculturation rather than assimilation as an organizing concept.[27] This perspective avoids regarding the cultures of the so-called "host countries" as fixed entities to which émigrés had to adapt in a one-sided way, and opens

---

24 Robin E. Rider, "Alarm and Opportunity: Emigration of Mathematicians and Physicists to Britain and the United States," *Historical Studies in the Physical Sciences* 15 (1984): 107–76; Mitchell G. Ash, "Aid to Refugee Psychologists in the United States, 1933–1943: A Research Note," in Helio Carpintero and Jose Maria Peiró, eds., *Psychology in its Historical Context: Essays in Honor of Josef Brozek* (Valencia, 1985), 50–61.

25 For examples, see Margaret S. Mahler, *The Memoirs of Margaret S. Mahler*, Paul Stepansky, ed., (New York, 1987), 103; Mitchell G. Ash, "Emigré Central European Jewish Psychologists and Psychoanalysts in Great Britain," in Mosse et al., eds., *Second Chance*, esp. 112ff; Edith Kurzweil, "Psychoanalytic Science: From Oedipus to Culture," chap. 6 in this volume.

26 Finn Aaserud, *Redirecting Science: Niels Bohr, Philanthropy and the Rise of Nuclear Physics* (Cambridge, 1990), esp. chaps. 3–5.

27 For discussion of the acculturation concept, see Herbert A. Strauss, "Jewish Emigration in the Nazi Period: Some Aspects of Acculturation," in Mosse et al., eds., *Second Chance*, 80–95.

up the possibility of considering intellectual or scientific changes as inter-active processes embedded in cultural settings that are themselves fluid enough to change. But this viewpoint also raises new questions. Were sci-ence or scholarship a means to acculturation for the émigrés; or was ac-quiring membership in a culture a precondition for acceptance as a scientist or scholar in that setting?

Still-standard dualisms in science studies between "external" and "inter-nal" factors, or the "context" and "content" of science, ignore the fact that scientists are located and locate themselves in multiple contexts, local insti-tutional settings, disciplines, and broader sociocultural groupings, usually the educated elites of particular countries. When writing the history of émigré scientists and scholars, it is therefore necessary to distinguish various levels of potential acculturation and cultural interaction, rather than treating cultures as monolithic entities. Discipline membership, for example, could be an anchor of stability in the personal and career crises that befell many émigrés, but not if disciplines too were situated differently in different cul-tures. In such cases, forced migration often meant a wrenching challenge to reconstruct not only one's discourse but also one's social self and sense of cultural identity.

Mastery of a local language may have been less important in this regard than the ability or willingness to refigure one's behavior. Emigrés in Britain who were deemed insufficiently "suitable" in this respect were sometimes quite openly told that their chances would be better in America; and even those who stayed and succeeded as scientists often felt that they had never been fully accepted. In America, by contrast, acculturation was possible and even at times most successful through opposition to then-current cultural norms – for example, by emphasizing the superior theoretical sophistication and broader outlook that a European education brought with it.[28] As studies of the Frankfurt School as well as the "University in Exile" at the New School for Social Research indicate, and as Paul Weindling shows in his chapter on émigré medical scientists at Oxford in this book, local settings of varied kinds could offer supportive niches to scientists who differed from conventional norms in their countries of settlement.[29]

---

28 G. Hirschfeld, " 'The Defense of Learning and Science' "; Karen J. Greenberg, "Crossing the Boundary: German Refugee Scholars and the American Academic Tradition," in Ulrich Teichler and Herbert Wasser, eds., *German and American Universities: Mutual Influences—Past and Present*, Werkstattberichte, vol. 36 (Kassel, 1992), 67–80.

29 Martin Jay, *The Dialectical Imagination: A History of the Frankfurt School and the Institute of Social Research* (Berkeley, Calif., 1973); Rolf Wiggershaus, *Die Frankfurter Schule* (Munich, 1986); Peter M. Rutkoff and William B. Scott, *New School: A History of the New School for Social Research, 1919-1970* (New York, 1986); Paul Weindling, "The Impact of German Medical Scientists on British Medicine: A Case-Study of Oxford, 1933–1945," chap. 4 in this volume.

Another level at which behavior plays a central role in scientific change is that of the scientific workplace – the laboratory, seminar, or university department. Central here, particularly though not only in laboratory science, is what émigré chemist and philosopher of science Michael Polanyi has called "tacit knowledge" – the exchange not only of ideas but of skills and modes of working that are more easily learned by personal interaction than from books.[30] Taking up the recent trend in science studies toward "ethnomethodology" has led historians of science to consider more intensively such scientific practices and the cultural, or subcultural, beliefs and norms embodied in them. Paul K. Hoch has pointed to the central role of migration in the transmission and transformation of such practices. As early as 1937 in a general essay on the social situation of intellectual exiles, émigré social scientist Hans Speier described a range of such possibilities, from a relatively self-enclosed milieu (such as that of the Frankfurt School) to already-internationalized and institutionalized discursive realms (such as that of theoretical physics), within which the scientist or scholar simply changed location.[31] Seen from this perspective, simpler forms of science transfer were most likely, although not necessarily inevitable, where common conventions of scientific thought and practice had already become internationalized.

Yet a third level at which the acculturation concept is relevant for understanding the subtleties of scientific change is the role of science and scholarship as expressions of cultural values. As Alfons Söllner points out in this book, even the naming of disciplines – for example, *Staatsrecht* or "public law" in Germany versus "political science" in the United States – can embody cultural valuations and images. A further example from the social sciences is what Söllner calls the "politicization" of social science during World War II, as émigré social scientists worked on a wide range of projects for American intelligence agencies and developed plans for the "reeducation" of Germany. Particularly important in this period, but by no means limited to any single culture, was the shift that was already underway in the social structure and purposes of many natural and social sciences, from an emphasis on "pure" science legitimated as part of a traditional cultural identity to a complex interaction of basic research and applied science or science-based technologies, in which even basic research could acquire an

30 Michael Polanyi, *Personal Knowledge* (Chicago, 1950); Paul K. Hoch, "Migration and the Generation of Scientific Ideas," *Minerva* 25 (1987): 209–37; Hoch, "Institutional versus Intellectual Migrations in the Nucleation of New Scientific Specialties," *Studies in the History and Philosophy of Science* 18 (1987): 480–500.
31 Hans Speier, "The Social Conditions of the Intellectual Exile" (1937), reprinted in Speier, *Social Order and the Risks of War: Papers in Political Sociology* (New York, 1952), 86–94.

implicit practical orientation. Examples of this process in which émigrés were prominently involved are the atomic bomb project and the creation of computer science and technology.[32]

Whether and how scientific change can be attributed to forced migration depends in large part on what was or has been defined as science in the first place. Although the full range and variety of continuity and change is most visible in overviews or comparisons of individual disciplines, the most interesting loci of change and innovation appear to lie above as well as below the disciplinary level. On the one hand, global trends in which émigrés participated, such as the emergence of "big science" and the increasingly close linkages of basic research and technology, were already in progress before 1933 and were not confined to single disciplines. On the other hand, the processes of change themselves can often be followed in detail, or even detected, only at levels "below" that of the discipline – in single-field or more often in interdisciplinary research groups, and in the biographies of individual scientists.

In the most successful innovations, the result was a new synthesis, for example, in the interdisciplinary teams of émigrés and non-émigrés who created molecular biology, computer science, and in the social sciences, collaborative works such as *The Authoritarian Personality* (1950). This was cognitive acculturation in the full sense of the word – the mutual and socially mediated transformation of both the receiving and the giving scientific cultures and knowledges. Such innovations were not mere eclectic combinations of components but mobilizations and reconfigurations of intellectual as well as personal resources with different cultural roots for new purposes. Further analyses of such innovations will help to improve our understanding of intercultural science and technology transfer.

THE CHAPTERS IN OUTLINE

Consistent with the expanded research landscape of recent years, and with the multiple levels of acculturation just distinguished, the range of the following chapters extends from overviews of entire disciplines – presented here for the first time in English – to single case or biographical studies. In keeping with the inclusive German idea of *Wissenschaft* (scholarship), the

---

32 See, e.g., Steve J. Heims, *John von Neumann and Norbert Weiner: From Mathematics to the Technologies of Life and Death* (Cambridge, Mass., 1981).

fields discussed extend from physics to philosophical theology; however, the primary emphasis is on the natural and social sciences.[33] The essays are grouped into three sections by discipline.

The chapters in Part One consider the physical and biological sciences. Klaus Fischer (Chapter 1) analyses in-depth the theoretical and practical difficulties involved in claiming that forced migration caused significant innovations, even in acknowledged cases of scientific change in which émigrés were prominently involved. The next two chapters can be regarded as responses to Fischer's challenge. Skúli Sigurdsson (Chapter 2) considers the lives of mathematician Hermann Weyl and theoretical physicists Erwin Schrödinger and Max Born together. He emphasizes the fundamental continuities in their intellectual preoccupations over time with issues such as the unity of nature, the relation of theory and experiment, and the meaning of science; but he also shows how emigration changed both their locations in the scientific universe and the issues that acquired salience in their thinking. Alan Beyerchen (Chapter 3), in contrast, focuses on the single case of Göttingen physicist James Franck, whose change of field to photosynthesis research coincided with his emigration to the United States where he was generously funded by the Rockefeller Foundation.

Paul Weindling's chapter on émigré German medical scientists at Oxford (Chapter 4) integrates all of the levels of acculturation described previously, depicting the émigrés' reception and careers as complex interactions of institutional, scientific, and personal idiosyncrasies. In his view, precisely the upheaval of emigration, combined with the niches provided by sympathetic colleagues and Oxford's collegial university structure, facilitated movement between disciplines, the interaction of research cultures, and ultimately the creative responses of émigrés such as Hermann Blaschko, Ernst Chain, and Hans Krebs. Nonetheless, invisible barriers to full acceptance remained.

Part Two considers the role of émigrés in psychology, psychoanalysis, and pedagogy, disciplines that bridge the natural sciences, the social sciences, and the humanities. In these fields, as in medicine, the histories of sciences and those of the professions linked with them are inseparable. Mitchell Ash (Chapter 5) discusses three cases in which émigré psycholo-

33 With two exceptions (chaps. 2 and 7), the essays in this volume were first presented at a conference organized by the editors at the Wissenschaftskolleg/Institute for Advanced Study, Berlin, in May 1991. The natural sciences are less well represented in the volume than they were at the conference; two papers on natural sciences originally presented (by Herbert Mehrtens and Ute Deichmann) could not be included here for technical reasons. For recent studies of émigré historians, see Hartmut Lehmann and James J. Sheehan, eds., *An Interrupted Past: German-Speaking Refugee Historians in the United States after 1933* (New York, 1991).

gists mobilized biographical, institutional, and intellectual resources from both their past and their American situations to create new scientific and professional practices, while at the same time disagreeing with some of the core assumptions of American psychologists. Theirs was a case of acculturation by opposition; precisely because they differed from the mainstream, they were noticed and had an impact.

In her chapter on émigré psychoanalysts, Edith Kurzweil (Chapter 6) combines institutional, intellectual, and personal histories. She suggests that psychoanalytic discourse became a public medium for "processing" personal experiences of survivor guilt and loss at levels of abstraction that eased the pain of exile, and that that process in turn enriched psychoanalytic theory by focusing attention on ego functions and the problem of adaptation. These émigrés thus turned biography into theory in a manner that may have been paradigmatic for other fields as well.

In their study of émigré educationalists, Heinz–Elmar Tenorth and Klaus Horn (Chapter 7) consider a discipline that was only incompletely established yet of considerable social importance in Germany before 1933. The authors therefore define the field as a community of discourse, rather than a clearly marked institutional grouping. To discover the émigrés' impact, they investigate continuity and change in the topics chosen as well as the modes of argument employed in German pedagogical publications before and after 1933.

Part Three contains studies in the social sciences. Claus–Dieter Krohn's survey of émigré economists (Chapter 8) parallels Fischer's work on physicists and Ash's on psychologists by showing that many of these émigrés came from only a few specific centers in Germany and Austria. In addition, Krohn contrasts the different impacts and attitudes toward American culture of two groupings with diametrically opposed positions on the New Deal – macroeconomic experts from the schools mentioned, whom he terms "new classicists," concentrated mainly at the New School for Social Research, and Austrian neoclassical economists at elite universities such as Harvard.

Christian Fleck (Chapter 9) surveys émigré Austrian social scientists, focusing primarily on the members of four schools grouped around single leading figures – economist Ludwig von Mises, psychologist Karl Bühler, Austro-Marxist Max Adler, and legal theorist Hans Kelsen. Although school membership helped give these scholars a sense of identity before their emigration, their careers afterward show hardly any linear continuity. Fleck assesses the impact of the émigrés' forced departure on Austrian science and scholarship, and indicates the problems of measuring their impact as a group in their countries of settlement.

In their essay, Jennifer Platt and Paul K. Hoch (Chapter 10) challenge widely repeated assertions on the influence of the Vienna Circle of logical empiricist philosophers on Anglo-Saxon social science. They argue, in essence, that the impact of logical positivism on American sociology was limited to emblematic citations that legitimated trends already under way in any case. This skeptical position corresponds to Fischer's claims for natural scientists.

Alfons Söllner (Chapter 11) provides an in-depth account of émigrés in the field known in America as political science. He finds that émigrés concentrated in particular specialties, such as political theory and comparative politics. In these fields, émigrés of widely differing views responded to the challenges of their time with new vocabularies, exemplifying in their own ways the ideal type that Söller, following Franz Neumann, calls the political scholar.

Karen Greenberg (Epilogue) rounds out the book by considering the intellectual development of a single émigré, Paul Tillich, as an ideal type. In this case, like that of the psychologists and psychoanalysts, self-conscious interaction with – and opposition to – aspects of American culture led to productive rethinking. However, Tillich's case suggests that although acculturation may take place in several stages, the processes that produced new perspectives may occur in only one of these stages.[34]

OUTLOOK

All of the questions discussed in this book could be asked quite generally about scientists and professionals migrating from one culture to another. Indeed, some of them have become standard topics in the literature on cross-cultural technology transfer. There is a tendency at present to subsume the issues connected with this particular intellectual migration under such broader headings. This may be understandable in the light of our increasing biographical distance from the émigrés, and of the pressing current issues raised by mass migrations of highly educated people from the former communist countries and the so-called developing nations to Europe and the United States. Taken too far, however, such a move could give unwitting support to the tendency to "historicize" Nazism in the inappropriate sense of denying its uniqueness.

We already touched on this issue when we mentioned the potential

34 This result corresponds well to the memoirs reviewed in Barry Katz, "The Acculturation of Thought: Transformations of the Refugee Scholar in America," *Journal of Modern History* 63 (1991): 740–52.

implications of this topic for the *Sonderweg* debate among historians of Germany. Here we can only agree with historian David Blackbourn when he writes:

> There is much to be said for shifting our emphasis away from the *Sonderweg* and viewing the course of German history as distinctive but not *sui generis*: the particular might then help to illuminate the general rather than remaining stubbornly (and sometimes morbidly) peculiar. That would be less likely to encourage apologetics than to disarm them.[35]

Even as we attempt to raise more abstract and general issues about the emigration of scientists and scholars after 1933 and its broader implications for the history of science and culture in our time, we must continually emphasize that although this event may be comparable with other migrations of highly trained scholars and professionals both before 1933 and since 1945, it cannot be equated with them. This is in part because it was so large and so sudden, but primarily for two other reasons. First, the émigrés after 1933 rarely chose to leave on the basis of criteria comprehensible to them, but were required to make that decision after being deprived of their livelihoods and ultimately their right to live where they chose on grounds utterly foreign to their own definitions of themselves. In the end – and this is the second fundamental difference – the émigrés had no choice. Not only their economic and social existences, but ultimately their very lives were at stake.

The relatively small number of émigrés who returned to Central Europe after 1945 while still of working age shows that the overwhelming majority of them eventually came to regard emigration as a great boon, despite its hardships. If the acculturation perspective has merit, then re-migration too becomes a complex process of reconstruction or reconstitution rather than the simple transfer or re-importation of intellectual capital. The extent to which publications and occasional visits and contacts substituted for actual return, the complex processes of reconstruction that resulted, and the role of émigrés in the often-alleged Americanization or Sovietization of science and scholarship in the two German states – all remain to be researched in depth.[36]

The émigrés and their achievements continue to fascinate students of

---

35   David Blackbourn, "The Discreet Charm of the Bourgeoisie: Reappraising German History in the Nineteenth Century," in David Blackbourn and Geoff Eley, *The Peculiarities of German History* (Oxford, 1984), 292.

36   For initial studies of "re-migration," see the essays published under the heading "Exil und Re-migration" in *Exilforschung* 9 (1991). Given the need for further research, it is regrettable that the Deutsche Forschungsgemeinschaft decided to end the program that has already sponsored so much work in this field.

political and scientific culture in this century. But as the postwar era ends, long-suppressed particularisms return. In his thoughtful reflections on German unification, Wolf Lepenies notes that for some intellectuals the legacy of the émigrés has become less interesting than a renewed search for German identity: "A new *Korpsgeist* is in demand," he writes, "and old inhibitions can be given up."[37] Across the ocean, American neoconservatives like Alan Bloom have blamed the émigrés for the alleged decline of shared values and the rise of a supposedly dangerous cultural relativism in that country.[38] Such charges are particularly ironic, since it was precisely the émigrés who through their own struggles helped to broaden American – indeed, all of Western – culture and to make it more truly cosmopolitan. In a time when new nationalisms emerge and older ones return, and when the prosperous regions of the world try to erect new barriers against immigration, it is more important than ever to acknowledge and remember that heritage.

37 Wolf Lepenies, *Folgen einer unerhörten Begebenheit: Die Deutschen nach der Vereinigung* (Berlin, 1991), 81.
38 Alan Bloom, *The Closing of the American Mind* (Chicago, 1987), esp. chap. 7; see also Wilfred McClay, "Weimar in America."

PART ONE

Physical and Medical Sciences

1

Identification of Emigration-Induced Scientific Change

KLAUS FISCHER

Many emigration specialists maintain that the loss of approximately 2,000 scientists by Germany between 1933 and 1945 completely shattered that country's basis for scientific research. A reduction of a country's scientific brainpower by more than 30 percent, it is argued, could not fail to produce a disastrous effect on the content as well as the quality of research pursued within that country's scientific institutions. A plethora of purported facts, scholarly expositions, and historical documents appear to prove this point beyond reasonable doubt.[1] A comprehensive synopsis of the historical process in question is, however, unavailable. Moreover, any consolidated evaluation of its global effects on the growth, content, and international standing of the sciences in the countries of emigration and immigration will have to await further research.

The present situation in the field of emigration studies is perhaps best characterized by the following features:

- An abundance of either loosely connected or unrelated facts concerning Nobelists and other celebrated scientists profiting from the nonrandom survival of rich archival resources related to their work.
- Select records and analyses of some salient institutions, and of a few probably atypical specialties, again depending on the vicissitudes of available archival data.

---

1 For a selection of recent titles, see Herbert A. Strauss et al., eds., *Die Emigration der Wissenschaften nach 1933: Diziplingeschichtliche Studien* (Munich, 1991). In addition, see *Exilforschung: Ein internationales Jahrbuch* 6 (1988); Hans-Joachim Dahms, "Verluste durch Emigration," *Exilforschung* 4 (1986); Claus-Dieter Krohn, *Wissenschaft im Exil* (Frankfurt/Main, 1987); I. Srubar, ed., *Exil, Wissenschaft, Identität* (Frankfurt/Main, 1988); Alfons Söllner, "Vom Staatsrecht zur 'political science,' " *Politische Vierteljahresschrift* 31 (1990); Mitchell G. Ash, "Gestalt Psychology: Origins in Germany and Reception in the United States," in Claude E. Buxton, ed., *Points of View in the Modern History of Psychology* (San Diego, Calif., 1985); Robin E. Rider, "Alarm and Opportunity: Emigration of Mathematicians and Physicists to Britain and the United States, 1933–1945," *Historical Studies in the Physical Sciences* 15 (1985).

- Very occasional information about the development of personal networks, or schools of research, involving emigrants.
- Virtually nothing, except for "thin descriptions," of a testable kind concerning more universal categories of science such as disciplines, fields or specialties.

All together, such features yield a picture of too many open questions, too many extrapolations or other unfounded speculations derived from cases whose typicality is uncertain, too many isolated facts that constitute pieces of the puzzle but leave the larger picture blurry and indiscernible.

Among the questions not yet resolved is the alleged causal relation between scientific change and emigration, which deserves particular attention from the perspective of the general history of science. What types of scientific change can really be causally accounted for by invoking processes of emigration or – viewed from the perspective of the receiving countries – immigration? Alternately, for what (types of) processes of scientific change will the connection possibly turn out to be more of a modulating or modifying sort, or be altogether spurious? Accordingly, it might be legitimate to ask whether, in the face of the radically altered conditions for doing research in Germany, many scientific fields were not on the verge of disintegration anyway, not as an effect of the emigration of many of their main representatives but as a consequence of the enactment of other components of Nazi science policy, such as the introduction of the *Führerprinzip*, the *Völkischer Standpunkt*, as well as the fight against pure theory, abstraction, and "impractical" science, or even the deteriorating stature of the natural sciences, including the very idea of disinterested science as such.

All of these policies resulted in a continuous decline in the quality of German science, quite apart from the disastrous effect of the dismissal of Jewish scientists. Emigration could have aggravated, but it certainly did not initiate, this process. If there is cause and effect here, it might even be surmised that its structure is inverse to that stipulated by the staunch adherents of the thesis of "emigration-induced scientific change" (hereafter: EISC). In addition to the noncontroversial possibility that emigration might indeed have stimulated processes of scientific change in some areas, we have to consider the complementary hypothesis, that enforced and undesired scientific change can induce processes of migration and emigration, which might in turn occasion scientific change elsewhere.

The point of our initial qualification of the EISC hypothesis is not that it is false but that it is incomplete. The selection it makes among the set of causal relations determining emigration as a historical process seems somewhat unbalanced. Incorporating both proximate and distant causes of

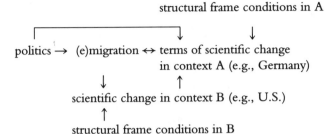

Figure 1.1 Structure of EISC causes.

EISC into a causal model may lead to a structure resembling the one shown in Figure 1.1. The main virtue of this model derives from the fact that it dispenses with the difference between migration and emigration, which in many cases looks like an artificial cleavage, while involving at least a major conceptual problem in others.[2] Many of those leaving Germany or Austria were not, strictly speaking, forced to go abroad. Some of them might have lived comfortably on their pensions in Germany. Others who were not dismissed for racial reasons might have tried to adjust at least in their overt behavior to the whims of the new rulers. These people are nevertheless called "emigrants." On the other hand, those leaving the country before 1933 are consistently classified as migrants, even if they were, using Nazi jargon, *Volljuden* (100 percent Jewish), and thus destined to be dismissed had they dared to stay. The distinction between those "migrating" and those "emigrating" from Germany between the two world wars is, to this extent, conceptually muddled, as it may obviously lead to unintended misclassifications. It makes a cleavage where none really exists, or conversely builds a single category where cases are in fact incommensurable.

After this preliminary clarification of the issue at stake here, the critical reader might wish to know more about the key term used in the previous model. What is the meaning conveyed by "scientific change"? Leaving the term without restriction as to type or degree of change might eventuate in the undesired consequence that the hypothesis is confirmed, although trivialized. Surely the hiring of an emigrant by an institution of scientific research in itself represents an instance of scientific change. After all, a concomitant shift of personal networks will inevitably occur, affecting most

2   For a discussion without undue emphasis on the distinction between migration and emigration, see Paul K. Hoch, "Migration and the Generation of New Scientific Ideas," *Minerva* 28 (1987).

certainly the flow of science-related communication. Nonetheless, being a necessary byproduct of emigration, statements referring to changes of staff size or structure as instances of EISC are not far from being empirically void or tautological.

Nontautological truth and hence empirical content presuppose some restrictions on type, quality, and amount of the outcome in order to represent what it is intended to stand for: significant and essential scientific change. What precisely significant and essential change is may of course be a matter of professional debate. I do not intend to enumerate the kinds of change regarded by historians of science as essential. The ensuing list would hardly embody more than historians' different theories of scientific development and current fashions in the philosophy of science. Nevertheless, it is surely not implausible to suppose that the historical situation of a discipline itself imposes some restrictions on the character and amount of change actually feasible. A strategy involving the dictum that only the initiation of, or participation in, "revolutionary" scientific change can satisfy the conditions of "real" change would a priori exclude emigrants working within the "colder" – that is, calmly evolving – fields of a discipline from the class of possible agents of change. Consequently, this requirement would be so strong as to render the thesis unprovable.

Another ambiguity in the EISC thesis concerns its empirical content – that is, the exact "meaning" of the thesis itself. Without further clarification it could say virtually anything, from

(A) "At least one instance of scientific change has to be causally accounted for by a case of emigration" to
(B) "Every case of emigration caused some kind of significant scientific change."

Whereas the weak thesis (A) is tautologically valid with no restrictions on the type of change being adduced, the strong thesis (B) is almost certainly wrong because it simply claims too much. To remain viable, it has to be modified in one way or another – for instance, by reformulating it thus:

(B) "Some cases of emigration caused some instances of significant scientific change."

The real problem with the reformulated version of (B) is that it is very hard to test. Every particular claim to an alleged instance of EISC can possibly be reanalyzed in a different way, yielding the same results, minus emigration. Imagine a scenario in which the emigration researcher has, in his or her own understanding, succeeded in demonstrating conclusively that emigrant "X" was the agent who transferred an idea or research practice from his native environment "A" into a foreign environment "B." Imagine also that novel scientific developments can be plausibly argued to have originated – at least in principle – from the clash or symbiotic interaction of practical and theoretical knowledge thus transferred with the knowledge entrenched in the second context. The situation turns out to be far less clearcut. For the argument to withstand criticism and prevail as an unassailable case of EISC, it must be required that virtually all elements of importance for the causal chain, terminating in the contended change, can be shown to be absolutely singular. Stated plainly, it has to be shown that there was only one road to the novel, that it could not have emerged if only a single element of the postulated concatenation were missing, and that the process of emigration was absolutely essential for the outcome.

Such a conclusive argument may be a hard thing to achieve, and an even harder one to defend. Not infrequently, new scientific ideas, as well as empirical discoveries, blossom simultaneously at several places and in different contexts, although sometimes in a slightly variant form. In many cases, results and ideas are not being transferred in conjunction with their originators or propagators but through the published literature, by letter, personal communication, gossip heard at conferences and symposia, temporal exchange of research students, and guest lectures. At an intermediate level of perceived novelty, a high degree of redundancy is inherent in the system of science, which is derived from its network-like properties. The fact of a multitude of communication pathways disseminating novel information in science independent of scientific migration attenuates most claims concerning nontrivial EISC to a degree that makes them highly controversial, if not virtually obsolete.

Although this identification problem, which is ubiquitous except in rare cases that profit from their singularity, might make the task of isolating EISC hopeless, there is a small chance of arriving at least at a plausible conjecture that has the virtue of being testable. If the emigration researcher succeeds in detecting scientific fields that should, for well-founded reasons, be specifically susceptible to EISC, then the claim of the proponents of the corresponding thesis can be reformulated in a way that is more susceptible to empirical research. In the altered version, it will no longer refer to an open set of unrelated singular empirical cases but postulate a lawful relation between emigration and nontrivial scientific change in fields characterized by certain properties. Whether such a reformulation adumbrates an abstract possibility that yields no perspective for current research, or is a result of empirical investigation, is of course the crucial point. Empirical results from different specialties of physics seem to indicate that there may be something to this speculation.

An inquiry I conducted into the literature of eleven fields of physical science yielded a nearly perfect and quite unexpected correlation between what might be called the "paradigmatic youth" of a field and the proportion of the field's literature that was written by emigrants. An explanation of this phenomenon in terms of social marginality experienced by Jewish scientists in Germany, and the motivation of socially marginal scientists moving into cognitively marginal fields such as the "frontier sciences," was given elsewhere. Since the relation between marginality and innovation was pointed out long before by Robert K. Merton and others, the cited empirical result does not contradict common theoretical assumptions.[3] Yet, the strong empirical corroboration of the "marginal innovator thesis" in the case of Jewish scientists in pre-Nazi Germany is surprising. Opinions about its range of application are mixed. Whereas it can be confirmed in the field of economics, according to Claus-Dieter Krohn, it may be invalid in biology, as Ute Deichmann has pointed out.[4] It is as yet unclear whether specific contravening factors in the development of the biology in Germany or the limited range of the hypothesis itself are responsible for Deichmann's negative result. Regarding the supposition that the marginality hypothesis is valid at least in a statistical way, the following formulation should count as an acceptable working assumption:

(C) "The emigration of scientists after 1933 caused, with a higher probability, significant scientific change within novel fields of research rather than within the established ones."

Before turning to a few case studies relevant for (C), some prerequisites and dimensions of EISC ought to be discussed in a more systematic form. To this end, it is useful to discriminate between four levels of change:

1. The personal level
2. The institutional level

3   Cf. Robert K. Merton, "Social Structure and Anomie," in Merton, *Social Theory and Social Structure* (New York, 1968). See also Shulamit Volkov, "Soziale Ursachen des Erfolgs in der Wissenschaft: Juden im Kaiserreich," *Historische Zeitschrift* 245 (1987): 332; Philip J. Pauly, *Controlling Life: Jacques Loeb and the Engineering Ideal in Biology* (Berkeley, Calif., 1990), 9. While scrutinizing the career of physicist James Franck under the lens of marginality, Alan Beyerchen came to the conclusion that this concept is indeed of explanatory value. See Beyerchen's essay in this volume.
4   Personal communication with Claus-Dieter Krohn. See also the chapter by Claus-Dieter Krohn in this volume, and Ute Deichmann, *Biologen unter Hitler: Vertreibung, Karrieren, Forschung* (Frankfurt/ Main, 1992).

3. The level of the political and cultural system
4. The cognitive (disciplinary) level

1. The Personal Level

We shall not discuss but only point out some personal requirements needed for prompting scientific change: tenacity in solving problems and overcoming obstacles, ability to withstand unfounded criticisms and to convince relevant audiences, social competence, and skill in negotiating budgets with officials. These traits are to be distinguished sharply from other behavioral properties resembling the first ones closely on the surface, although they are not generally factors of success in science, such as activism, sociability, and adaptability. Originality certainly is important, although it is an ambiguous asset. Whereas some amount of originality looks like a virtue, an abundance of it might easily turn into a vice.[5]

2. The Institutional Level

Some preconditions of EISC may sound trivial. Of course, there has to be some perceived deficiency in the agglomeration of competencies assembled at an institute before an emigrant's professional assets are given a chance to come into play. With no demand, the gifts of even the most talented emigrant remain dead capital. After having passed through that gate, the emigrant's radius of scientific action within his new environment seems to be determined mainly by the specificity of his competences, the shortage of the combination of talents represented by him within the host institution, and the complementariness of these competences with the professional interests and abilities of regular staff members, especially those of a higher rank.

The complementary condition, to give an example, was not fulfilled in the case of physicist Erwin Schrödinger's stay at Oxford University.[6] Schrödinger's competences, as well as his mode of doing physics, did not fit into the framework of contemporary Oxford physics. Both Schrödinger and Oxford proceeded in mutual scientific ignorance and parted in silent agree-

---

5 The case of Felix Ehrenhaft might exemplify the second alternative. See Paul K. Feyerabend, *Erkenntnis für freie Menschen* (Frankfurt/Main, 1980), 218.
6 For Schrödinger, see Paul K. Hoch and Edward J. Yoxen, "Schrödinger at Oxford: A Hypothetical National Cultural Synthesis that Failed," *Annals of Science* 44 (1987); Walter J. Moore, *Schrödinger: Life and Thought* (Cambridge, 1989); William McCrea, "Eamon de Valera, Erwin Schrödinger, and the Dublin Institute," in Clive W. Kilmister, ed., *Schrödinger: Centenary Celebration of a Polymath* (Cambridge, 1987).

ment after having recognized their respective errors. Only after arriving in Dublin did Schrödinger find a new professional environment sympathetic to his style of work, which had already been designed by the Irishman Eamon de Valera with an eye on the inventor of wave mechanics. Although Schrödinger's most creative period belonged to the past, he remained an unconventional and fruitful thinker. With his lectures on the philosophy of living matter, published in 1944 under the title *What Is Life?*, Schrödinger motivated some physicists to participate in the search for the physical mechanism of heredity and mutation and thus, in a sense, helped to launch the new specialty of molecular genetics. This effect was mediated through the literary pathways of science, and hardly depended on the fact of Schrödinger's emigration. Although the use of the English language might have fostered the dissemination of his ideas in the post-World War II situation, Schrödinger's departure from the German-speaking world led, on the other hand, to his rather belated acquaintance with the influential paper by Max Delbrück, Nicolaj Timoféeff-Ressovsky, and Carl Zimmer, "Über die Natur der Genmutation und der Genstruktur." This was precisely the work that stimulated Schrödinger to think about the physical foundations of life. Not until physicist Peter Ewald handed Schrödinger his own copy of the article, originally published in the *Nachrichten von der Gelehrten Gesellschaft der Wissenschaften zu Göttingen*, did Schrödinger come to know about this work.[7] In sum, it is difficult to decide whether Schrödinger's emigration acted more to accelerate or to retard the crystallization and dissemination of his biological ideas.

Schrödinger's case shows that without a symbiotically favorable milieu, the work of even a top-ranking scientist remains barren. In a stimulating context of research, on the other hand, even novices in the field of science might deploy a high degree of creativity and productivity. A case in point is physical chemist Max Perutz. Still a young student when he decided in 1936 to leave his home country, Austria, for England, Perutz succeeded in uncovering the three-dimensional conformation of hemoglobin after twenty years of relentless and tenacious work at the Cavendish Laboratory in Cambridge. Its final result secured him a Nobel prize. An application for a research grant aiming at such an achievement would have been laughed at by any referee. Perutz's success was embedded in and dependent on the congenial environment provided by the Cavendish Laboratory, whose new director, William L. Bragg, placed more emphasis on X-ray crystallography

---

7   Letter from Schrödinger to Max Born, Nov. 4, 1942; cited in Edward J. Yoxen, "Where does Schrödinger's *What is Life?* belong in the History of Molecular Biology?" *History of Science* 17 (1979): 35.

and its applications than on nuclear physics. Some outstanding nuclear physicists left the laboratory during this period, while Bragg's crystallographic
ambitions resulted in the assembling of a very fertile research group in this
field, including John C. Kendrew, John D. Bernal, and Perutz.

The interesting question is whether the results of Perutz's work might
be an instance of EISC. Depending on one's perspective, the answer to this
question might be very different. No doubt it was Perutz who furthered
the deciphering of the tertiary structure of proteins more than anyone else.
No doubt too in the period in question there was no place in Germany or
Austria where Perutz could have found an environment as advantageous
and stimulating as the Cavendish Laboratory. On the other hand, anyone
requiring that a process has to include a transfer of ideas, styles, or methods
to represent an instance of EISC, might bemoan a lack of evidence concerning any such intercultural transmission or fruitful interaction between
local cultural traditions in this case. Important as the work of Perutz was,
it stands essentially in the tradition of the British crystallographic school
represented by Henry and William L. Bragg, William T. Astbury, John D.
Bernal, Dorothy Wrinch, Kathryn Lonsdale, and Dorothy Crowfoot-
Hodgkin. With unprecedented sophistication and skill, Perutz utilized just
those methods and ideas current among British crystallographic laboratories
in the 1930s.[8]

3. The Political or Cultural Level

One of the unquestioned creeds in the historiography of science has been
until recently that twentieth-century natural science is, in an important
sense, international. On this assumption, it should not make a fundamental
difference for a chemist, astronomer, or physicist to substitute Berlin for

---

8 See Robert Olby, *The Path to the Double Helix* (London, 1974), 264; Pierre Laszlo, *Molecular Correlates
of Biological Concepts*, in *Comprehensive Biochemistry*, ed. Albert Neuburger and Laurens L. M. Deenen,
vol. 34A (Amsterdam, 1986), chaps. 22–25; Lawrence Bragg, "First Stages in the X-Ray Analysis
of Proteins," *Reports on Progress in Physics* 28 (1965); Dorothy Crowfoot, "A Review of Some Recent
X-Ray Work on Protein Crystals," *Chemical Review* 28 (1941): 215; Max F. Perutz, *Proteins and
Nucleic Acids* (Amsterdam, 1962). The development of x-ray crystallography in Germany and England is described in Herman Mark, "Kaiser Wilhelm Institut für Faserstoffchemie," in Max Planck,
ed., *25 Jahre Kaiser Wilhelm Gesellschaft* (Berlin, 1936), 2:213; Peter P. Ewald, ed., *Fifty Years of X-
Ray Diffraction* (Utrecht, 1962); Peter P. Ewald, *Kristalle und Röntgenstrahlen* (Berlin, 1923); Herman
Mark, "Über die röntgenographische Ermittlung der Struktur organischer besonders hochmole-
kularer Substanzen," *Bericht der deutschen chemischen Gesellschaft* 59 (1926): 2983; Herman Mark and
H. Philipp, "Die Struktur der Proteine im Lichte der Röntgenstrahlen," *Die Naturwissenschaften* 8
(1937): 119; John D. Bernal, "William Thomas Astbury," *Biographical Memoirs of Fellows of the Royal
Society of London* 9 (1963): 1; Dorothy M. C. Hodgkin, "John Desmond Bernal," *Biographical Memoirs
of Fellows of the Royal Society of London* 26 (1980): 17.

Copenhagen, Cambridge for Munich, or Berkeley for Rome as the site of his professional activity. It has to be conceded that this assumption sounds plausible. Compared with the norms of political life or the standards of literary criticism, the laws of nature seem to rest more on their own footing than on the whims of those who deal with them. Surely it must be admitted that this creed remains silent about a variety of observations. What, for example, are the consequences of differences in an institution's size and usable equipment? Factors such as these should certainly modulate the spectrum of problems that might be profitably researched in a certain context. Similar implications hold for the diversity of competencies assembled in a particular place and for the possible synergetic effects resulting from specific combinations or interactions of talents and interests. Because of their dependence on the idiosyncrasies inherent to a field's actual situation, synergetic effects may have the most diverse results, and thus be virtually unforeseeable and next to impossible to plan for. In the long run, infinitesimally small initial fluctuations in such factors might occasion the growth of local traditions that reproduce and even multiply via the socialization of the coming generation in the spirit of local knowledge. Different versions of the "same" basic theory might thus originate and perpetuate. The emergence of national modes of thinking is the probable result of a situation characterized by a high rate of intranational as opposed to international communication. Phenomena such as these are referred to in sociological research under the heading of the "cultural dimension of science."[9]

The cultural dimension of science purportedly accounts for these facts:

- The thriving of divergent or even incompatible research programs within one and the same discipline under a different institutional, or national, regime.
- The existence of fierce and lasting resistance against the reception of new ideas, long after they have proved their fruitfulness in other contexts.
- The emergence of divergent styles of doing research in different sites of scientific work.

For a proof of these observations, it may suffice to point to the widely diverging discussions in Germany, England, France, and the United States

9 See Bruno Latour, *Science in Action: How to Follow Scientists and Engineers through Society* (Cambridge, Mass., 1987); Bruno Latour and Steve Woolgar, *Laboratory Life* (Beverly Hills, Calif., 1979); for a critique, see Ian Hacking, "The Participant Irrealist at Large in the Laboratory," *The British Journal for the Philosophy of Science* 39 (1988): 277; David Bloor, *Knowledge and Social Imagery* (London, 1976); Andrew Pickering, *Constructing Quarks* (Edinburgh, 1984); Roy Wallis, ed., *On the Margins of Knowledge: The Social Construction of Rejected Knowledge* (Keele, 1979); Karin D. Knorr et al., eds., *The Social Process of Scientific Investigation* (Dortrecht, 1981); Joseph S. Fruton, *Constrasts in Scientific Style: Research Groups in the Chemical and Biochemical Sciences* (Philadelphia, 1990).

in the wake of the propounding of the theory of general relativity, the quantum theory, the evolutionary theory of Charles Darwin, and the theories of heredity of Gregor Mendel and Thomas H. Morgan. Minor shifts or mutations in interpretation, conceptual arrangement, method, or practical application can be located in all these cases, even if no diversity is visible on the surface.

The nature of communication channels transmitting information about an invention or innovation might also have some bearing on the speed and character of their reception. Compared with the exchange of literary information alone, both speed and quality of transmission seem to improve with a little personal persuasion. Thus, research grants by the Rockefeller Foundation as well as other donors to European scholars enabling them to lecture at American institutions, and to American students for study at Göttingen, Berlin, and Munich, might well have done more for the deployment of the new physics in the United States than the same amount of money spent for the acquisition of scientific literature. Inversely, it may be supposed that the reception and dissemination of the contents and methods of drosophila genetics in Germany improved after Curt Stern and Hans Nachtsheim spent some time at the "fly-lab" of Morgan. In case these casual observations do indicate a general phenomenon, a migration movement as massive as that arising in science after 1933 should coincide with a significant enhancement in the diffusion, assimilation, and alloying of scientific ideas. In addition, the clash of scientists utilizing different disciplinary matrices should engender a fertile concoction of competencies and ideas as well as a general upsurge of creativity and scientific change.

Plausible as this supposition looks at first glance, its practical validation proves to be more difficult than expected. In the first place, a lively exchange of students and scientific staff both among the European centers and between the European and the American centers was already characteristic for the situation before 1933.[10] Whereas prior to World War I the field of chemistry stood at the center of attention, the focus began to shift toward physics after 1918, and in particular after 1925, in accordance with the policy of the big American foundations that paid most of the bills.

Although it is true that the wave of emigrants leaving Central Europe after 1933 swept an unprecedented number of top-ranking foreign scientists into numerous countries, three questions remain unanswered:

---

10 Daniel J. Kevles, *The Physicists* (New York, 1971); Gerald Holton, "The Migration of Physicists to the United States," in Jarrell C. Jackman and Carla M. Borden, eds., *The Muses Flee Hitler* (Washington, D.C., 1983).

Can it be confirmed that with the onset of the wave of emigration after 1933 the transmission of scientific ideas underwent a kind of "quantum leap" to a higher level?

Hypothetical answer. This may be true in selected fields, in particular in those not entrenched in the respective receiving countries but well represented among immigrants. It must be adduced that for a transmission of scientific ideas to result from this constellation the receiving country has to be willing to let the immigrants pass the barriers of its institutionalized system of science – that is, it has to provide the necessary support for the new field. Both conditions, I might conjecture, were fulfilled only in rare cases such as polymer chemistry in the United States, low temperature physics in England, and a few other selected fields. It may also hold for developing countries such as Turkey and Palestine.[11] For the core fields of the natural sciences, it seems more plausible to suppose that the arrival of the immigrants acted more like an adjunct impetus than lifting the process of transmission qualitatively onto a new level.

Is it reasonable to suppose that there was a trade-off between the positive effects of immigration and other, more negative byproducts of the fascist transformation of Central Europe?

Hypothetical answer. In all likelihood, yes! Those changes concurred with a gradual withering away of the exchange programs that had characterized the international relations of science before 1933. In the 1920s, a few semesters of study at one of the most advanced Central European universities was considered mandatory for any young American or British theoretical physicists worth his salt. After 1933, this customary practice lost its rationale. For the Central European states, Nazi racial legislation proved detrimental in a twofold sense: First, many of its leading scholars were forced to leave their home institutions. Second, foreign students and scientists stayed away from formerly world-renowned places of higher learning such as Göttingen and Berlin. True, there still was scholarly influx into German universities from Italy, Russia, Japan, and the smaller countries surrounding Germany, but Western scientists mostly decided to stay away from Nazi Germany.

---

11 For polymer chemistry, see AIP-interview with Herman Mark conducted by R. S. Marvin, March 19, 1979, American Institute of Physics, New York. Information about the institutionalization of low temperature physics at the Clarendon Laboratory can be found in Nancy Arms, *A Prophet in Two Countries: The Life of E.E. Simon* (Oxford, 1966); Kurt Mendelssohn, *The World of Walter Nernst* (London, 1973); interviews with Nicholas Kurti conducted by Charles Weiner, Sept. 11, 1968, and Nov. 22, 1972, American Institute of Physics, New York. For Turkey, see Regine Erichsen, "Die Emigration deutschsprachiger Naturwissenschaftler von 1933 bis 1945 in die Türkei in ihrem sozial- und wissenschaftshistorischen Wirkungszusammenhang," in Strauss et al., eds., *Die Emigration der Wissenschaften.*

With blooming cross-Atlantic international scholarly exchange coming to a temporary halt, or rather by its unplanned redirection into a one-way stream, impulses from Central European institutions on Western scientists also diminished.[12] This is true irrespective of the fact that many of those to whom the origin of those impulses were due in the past might now be the possible recipients' next-door neighbors. Alas, the cultural context in which the physical sciences in Göttingen, Berlin, and Munich had thrived – that is, their milieu – turned out not to be transposable. In the wake of the political events that forced their main representatives to emigrate, that context was not taken abroad with them but was destroyed in situ.

Is it true that the transfer of persons can be considered a sufficient condition for the transmission of ideas?

There is a theory that motivated some researchers to affirm the last question. This theory assumes that relevant portions of the knowledge necessary for practitioners in a field of science remain uncodified and implicit. This uncodified or personal knowledge, so the argument continues, cannot be transferred by literature but only in the form of human agents entrenched in the tradition of which this knowledge is a part. Historical case studies indicate that there may be some truth to this argument, although it does not seem to embrace the whole truth. To be valid, the argument has to be reinterpreted in a statistical way to leave room for the possibility of multiple discovery and nearly parallel conceptual development, which is also exemplified in the history of science. Multiple discovery as well as the myriad cases in which scientific information is transferred by written communication show clearly that the displacement of persons is not a necessary condition for the dissemination of ideas. That it is not a sufficient condition either is demonstrated by the cases of Erwin Schrödinger in Oxford and Richard Goldschmidt in Berkeley. In Goldschmidt's case, just as in that of Schrödinger, all the conditions for a fruitful transplantation of ideas seemed to be fulfilled, except one. What was lacking was the receptivity of the context, the willingness to embrace alien ideas intruding into a cultural milieu unprepared to adopt them. Well into the 1960s, Goldschmidt remained an outsider whose influence seemed to depend more on his fitness to fulfill the role of a foil than on his positive contributions to the field of genetics.

In part, this may also be due to Goldschmidt's failure to instigate the crystallization of anything resembling a paradigmatic group. One of the

---

12 Linus Pauling, "Fifty Years of Physical Chemistry in the California Institute of Technology," *Annual Reviews of Physical Chemistry* 16 (1965): 10–11.

reasons for this was certainly rooted in his psychological constitution – his striving for intellectual independence in conjunction with an anti-dogmatic attitude nicely exemplified by his professed maxim: "I have always endeavored to keep my mind free so as to give up any hypothesis (and I cannot resist forming one on every subject) as soon as facts are shown to be opposed to it."[13] Factors of personal style and attitude notwithstanding, the main reason for the rejection of Goldschmidt's ideas was clearly intellectual, as Stephen Jay Gould remembers: "In my university classes, the name 'Goldschmidt' was always introduced as a kind of biological in-joke, and we students all laughed and snickered dutifully to prove that we were not guilty of either ignorance or heresy. . . . I do not think I exaggerated in comparing Goldschmidt with Goldstein, the object of daily 'two minute hates' in Orwell's 1984."[14]

Goldschmidt's case seems to be in no way exceptional. Others who arrived without the social capital of a high reputation failed even to make a living. This is true, for instance, in the case of the geneticist Viktor Jollos, who died in 1941 after having attempted unsuccessfully to attain a university position, leaving behind his family in utmost poverty. Jollos adhered to a token variety of genetic theory that incorporated the conception of cytoplasmic inheritance, thus colliding with the ruling dogmas of Morganism.[15] Cases such as these make it painfully obvious that the charms of the local milieu are Janus-faced: The milieu can act sympathetically to create an intellectually congenial atmosphere, but it can also erect walls that keep the unfitting individual outside.

The shipwreck of Viktor Jollos and the highly controversial position of Richard Goldschmidt stand in telling contrast to the enormous influence in America of the Jewish physiologist Jacques Loeb, who had left Germany for the United States in 1891.[16] In the United States, Loeb's mechanistic

13 Richard Goldschmidt cited in Ernst W. Caspari, "An Evaluation of Goldschmidt's Work after Twenty Years," in Leonie K. Piternick, ed., *Richard Goldschmidt: Controversial Geneticist and Creative Biologist* (Basel, 1980), 19.
14 Stephen J. Gould, "Introduction," in Richard B. Goldschmidt, *The Material Basis of Evolution* (New Haven, Conn., 1940; new edition: 1982), xv. For Goldschmidt's science, see also Richard B. Goldschmidt, *Physiological Genetics* (New York, 1938; reprint: New York, 1988); Richard B. Goldschmidt, *In and Out of the Ivory Tower* (Seattle, 1960); Leonie K. Piternick, ed., *Richard Goldschmidt*; Garland E. Allen, "Opposition to the Mendelian Chromosome Theory: The Physiological and Developmental Genetics of Richard Goldschmidt," *Journal of the History of Biology* 7 (1974): 49; Jan Sapp, *Beyond the Gene: Cytoplasmic Inheritance and the Struggle for Authority in Genetics* (New York, 1987); for a modern evaluation of Goldschmidt's science, see Niles Eldredge, *Unfinished Synthesis* (New York, 1985). The near neglect of Goldschmidt's ideas is exemplified in George W. Beadle, "Biochemical Genetics," *Chemical Review* 37 (1945).
15 See Jan Sapp, *Beyond the Gene*.
16 See Philip J. Pauly, *Controlling Life*.

conception of life was enthusiastically embraced by embryologists and physiologists, and later amalgamated with Morganism, whereas it faced stiff resistance in Germany. It is most important, however, to recognize cause and
effect in processes like these. The question is whether the rise of the mechanistic theory of life in the United States was a result of Loeb's migration,
or whether Loeb's professional success can be explained only on the assumption of an already swelling tide of American mechanistic thinking. This
is not exactly to say that all Loeb had to do was simply climb on the bandwagon, but that his thoughts dropped onto extremely fertile, or "resonat-
ing," soil. Whether a general trait of EISC is exhibited in this might be
worth some second thoughts.

4. The Disciplinary Level

By discipline, I am not referring to administrative units such as physics,
chemistry, or biology, but at least for the period in question, to socially and
cognitively coherent subunits such as x-ray crystallography, nuclear physics,
or genetics. "Specialty" and "field" are other terms used for units of a
comparable or even smaller scale. An empirical result that has some bearing
on the problem of how to focus historians' attention on those fields in which
EISC might be expected to have occurred with a higher probability than
elsewhere was briefly adverted to previously. This was the unexpected finding that the percentage of a field's literature written by scientists emigrating
from Germany after 1933 correlated in an astonishingly regular way with
what might be called the "paradigmatic youth" of that field. In the case of
physics, the spectrum begins with acoustics at the lower end, reaching an
emigrant proportion of not more than about 4 percent, and culminates with
quantum theory, where the emigrant proportion approaches 30 percent.
The rest of the fields examined in this way fell somewhere in between.[17]

I do not intend to become immersed in the problem of how to explain
this empirical regularity, beyond what has already been said. Instead, I want
to draw attention to the fact that this phenomenon might offer a chance of
finding a method to separate certain instances of EISC and non-EISC. In
view of the higher proportion of emigrants in the more recent, cognitively
"marginal" fields, the latter should exhibit a higher susceptibility to emigrant influence than the more traditional ones. Within an appropriate receiving country, a comparison of different new fields subject to immigrant

---

17 See Klaus Fischer, "Der quantitative Beitrag der nach 1933 emigrierten Naturwissenschaftler zur
    deutschsprachigen physikalischen Forschung," *Berichte zur Wissenschaftsgeschichte* 11 (1988): 83.

influx in a non-uniform way might lead to a crude evaluation of a more qualitative version of this hypothesis. The hypothesis would be corroborated in cases where there is a systematic and significant difference in the cognitive dynamics of fields that are both equally new and characterized by different proportions of immigrants.

Unfortunately, the methodological requirements for the implementation of this program are rather demanding. First, there is the problem of how to measure the cognitive dynamics of a field. Second, myriad factors beyond paradigmatic change and immigrant influx can have a bearing on the development of a field, and may thus mask the influence of the variable of primary interest. Third, it might be practically impossible to find a sufficiently large number of fields matching the specifications to install a sample with which the hypothesis can be tested. Unable to proffer an empirical solution to the third question, and without the space to tackle the rather sweeping second problem, I shall concentrate on the first point.

At least for the natural sciences, the prospects for reducing arbitrariness and uncertainty in the measurement of the state and the development of research fields have considerably improved during the last one or two decades. As several case studies have demonstrated, even to skeptical observers, quantitative techniques such as co-citation analysis can be a valuable aid when trying to prepare state descriptions of any research field characterized by a sufficiently large body of coherent, public, citable, and correctly cited knowledge.[18] Although it is true that these conditions, especially the first and last ones, are fulfilled only more or less approximately, it is important to set this objection in perspective. Granted that the validity of co-citation analysis is in general less than 100 percent, we may nonetheless suppose that, other circumstances remaining equal, a history of science aided by co-citation methods should yield a more objective and reproducible result than an analysis relying exclusively on classical qualitative methods. Co-citation analysis should thus be understood as an aid and not an alternative to the history of scientific ideas, facts, and methods. It functions like a searchlight, preventing historians from becoming lost within the wealth of facts, opinions, and publications that characterizes modern science by

---

18 See Eugene Garfield, *Citation Indexing* (New York, 1979); Stephen Cole, Jonathan R. Cole, and Lorraine Dietrich, "Measuring the Cognitive State of Scientific Disciplines," in Yehuda Elkana et al., eds., *Toward a Metric of Science* (New York, 1978); Eugene Garfield et al., "Citation Data as Science Indicators," in Garfield, *Citation Indexing*; Peter Weingart and Matthias Winterhager, *Die Vermessung der Forschung* (Frankfurt/Main, 1984); G. Nigel Gilbert, "Referencing as Persuasion," *Social Studies of Science* 7 (1977); Daniel Sullivan et al., "Co-Citation Analysis of Science: An Evaluation," *Social Studies of Science* 7 (1977); Daryl Chubin and Soumyo D. Moitra, "Content Analysis of References: Adjunct or Alternative to Citation Counting?" *Social Studies of Science* 5 (1975).

directing their attention to the foci of actual scientific controversy and to the salient symbols of a field's actual cognitive fabric.

By mapping the field in different periods of its evolution, it is possible to capture its developmental aspects to any desired level of resolution and precision permitted by the database. Different versions of the procedure allow us to focus either on the more cognitive or the more social dimensions of the disciplinary structure. In this way, the cognitive as well as the social positions of target persons and groups, and the shifts they undergo during the field's evolution, including possible contradictions between the results of the two types of analysis, can be reproduced in a way that can be controlled methodologically.

I have done a study of the kind just described for the development of the field of nuclear physics between 1921 and 1947.[19] Besides yielding a wealth of interesting details, this study vindicates both the expected divergence between the social and cognitive positions achieved by emigrants and the suspected high degree of participation of emigrant nuclear physicists in the unfolding of the field's central concepts, theories, and methods during the entire period. Alas, granted that the general dynamics of disciplinary change is captured by the procedure, the hope of solving the problem of causal agents seems premature. First, disciplinary landscapes, even if seen in temporal succession, reflect cognitive achievement as a quality that is socially acknowledged, not cognitive achievement per se. They neither necessarily depict the originators of ideas nor solve questions of who influenced whom. However, given that qualitative analysis can help in the solution of the problem of causal attribution and personal influence, we may now possess a means of identifying EISC in research fields that meet the technical requirements for the application of co-citation analysis, and have in addition the source materials needed to explore personal influences within the social network identified at least in part by co-citation methods.

It is important to keep in mind the meaning of this result. Since it is impossible to compare actual developments with hypothetical ones, it certainly does not mean that the resultant disciplinary developments could not have been nearly the same if all the emigrants had stayed in their home countries or had settled in other places. Clearly, this caveat is of a transcendental sort and for that reason not testable. On the other hand, it might be desirable to derive the strength of a hypothesis not from the implausibility of the criticism launched against it, but in a more direct way from its own empirical content. In order to corroborate the EISC hypothesis, a compar-

---

19   See Klaus Fischer, *Changing Landscapes of Nuclear Physics: A Scientometric Study* (New York, 1993).

ison of the achievements in one and the same field of different universities or laboratories strengthened in different proportions by emigrant scientists might be a useful heuristic device. Unfortunately, since a field is defined as a connected network of actors and ideas, all sorts of interactive effects and nonlinearities have to be taken into account, the more so the more rapidly a field is changing. Although the impact of emigrant scientists on the development of a discipline may be uncontroversial on the global level, this effect is not necessarily decomposed by reverting to a finer grain of analysis. The implications of this argument for the problem at hand are twofold: A high position of laboratory "X" on the achievement scale in a field characterized by a high rate of emigrant participation must not perforce be attributed to emigrant influence. Inversely, the existence of various institutions having no emigrants on the payroll but ranking high on the achievement scale cannot be turned into a compelling argument against the hypothesis that the field profited to a large extent from the work of these scientists.

The following three examples should suffice to demonstrate the entangled character of the processes purportedly involving a case of EISC. Concerning the separability of emigrant and non-emigrant induced scientific changes, the first example is ambiguous, the second supports the claim, and the third undermines it.

EXAMPLE 1: MAX DELBRÜCK AND THE RISE OF
PHAGE GENETICS[20]

During the 1930s, Max Delbrück was one of those physicists fascinated more by the fundamental enigmas of biology than with cleaning up the residual problems of quantum theory. While still working at Berlin's Kaiser Wilhelm Institute for Chemistry as one of Lise Meitner's co-workers, Delbrück was already plunging into theoretical biology. One of his first activ-

---

20 For the development of molecular biology, see E. Peter Fischer and Carol Lipson, *Thinking about Science: Max Delbrück and the Origins of Molecular Biology* (New York, 1988); Robert Olby, *The Path to the Double Helix*; Horace F. Judson, *The Eighth Day of Creation: Makers of the Revolution in Biology* (London, 1979); Franklin H. Portugal and Jack S. Cohen, *A Century of DNA: A History of the Discovery of the Structure and Function of the Genetic Substance* (Cambridge, Mass., 1977); Max Perutz, "Origins of Molecular Biology," *New Scientist*, Jan. 31, 1980, 326; John C. Kendrew, "Some Remarks on the History of Molecular Biology," in T. S. Goodwin, ed., *British Biochemistry: Past and Present* (London, 1970); John Cairns, Gunther S. Stent, and James O. Watson, eds., *Phage and the Origins of Molecular Biology* (Cold Springs Harbor, N.Y., 1966); Gunther S. Stent, *Molecular Genetics* (San Francisco, 1971); Thomas D. Brock, *The Emergence of Bacterial Genetics* (Cold Springs Harbor, N.Y., 1990); Jan Sapp, *Where the Truth Lies: Franz Moewus and the Origins of Molecular Biology* (Cambridge, 1990); Pnina G. Abir-Am, "The 'Biotheoretical Gathering' in England and the Origins of Molecular Biology (1932–38)," Ph.D. diss., Université de Montreal, 1983; Edward J. Yoxen, "The Social Impact of Molecular Biology," Ph.D. diss. Cambridge University, n.d.

ities in this field consisted of organizing an informal circle of scholars interested in discussing biological problems. The celebrated "green paper" published by Delbrück, Zimmer, and Timoféeff-Ressovsky on the nature of gene mutation and gene structure, as mentioned previously, was one of the results of this informally organized and unpaid work. But Delbrück failed in his attempts to institutionalize his new interests in a way that would have allowed him to invest the bulk of his time in his new favorite field of work. Beyond that, in Delbrück's view, most of the really exciting events in biology were taking place not in Germany but in the United States – for example, the development of drosophila genetics by the Morgan group and the crystallization of the tobacco mosaic virus (TMV) by Wendell Stanley at the Rockefeller Center for Medical Research.

At this critical juncture of his academic career, Delbrück profited from a lucky constellation of interests that he could not have foreseen. His intention to tackle problems in the foundations of biology from a physical perspective and with the conceptual and technical means of a physicist fit perfectly into the new policy of the Rockefeller Foundation. In 1937, Delbrück was awarded a Rockefeller grant, which he could use to travel to the United States to study biology at any institution of his choice.[21] After passing through several centers of genetic research, in due course becoming acquainted with Milislav Demerec, Louis Stadler, Barbara McClintock, and Wendell Stanley, Delbrück decided to stay in Pasadena with Thomas H. Morgan in order to learn drosophila genetics. This plan proved to be too ambitious, for drosophila genetics at the time had grown into a field whose complexity would have required extended study to complete even the preliminary reading necessary to imagine any novel, profitable experiment. In addition, the technical skill needed for practical work with the tiny organism was enormous. With no hope of achieving anything of worth during the months left by his grant, Delbrück was in a rather desperate mood and therefore ready to return to Germany.

At this potential turning point in his life, it was sheer luck for Delbrück to make the acquaintance of a cancer researcher named Emory Ellis, who did experiments on bacteriophage. A bacteriophage is a kind of virus that

---

21 Robert E. Kohler, "The Management of Science: The Experience of Warren Weaver and the Rockefeller Foundation Programe in Molecular Biology," *Minerva* 14 (1976); Robert E. Kohler, "Warren Weaver and the Rockefeller Foundation Program in Molecular Biology: A Case Study in the Management of Science," in Nathan Reingold, ed., *The Sciences in the American Context: New Perspectives* (Washington, D.C., 1979). For the controversy between Pnina G. Abir-Am, Ditta Bartels, and John A. Fuerst concerning the background of the molecular biology program of the Rockefeller Foundation, see articles in *Social Studies of Science* 12 (1982) and 14 (1984); in addition, see Kenneth F. Schaffner, "The Peripherality of Reductionism in the Development of Molecular Biology," *Journal of the History of Biology* 7 (1974).

reproduces by intruding into a bacterium, causing lysis or dissolution of the latter within about twenty minutes. Delbrück was fascinated. At last he had found what he had looked for in the preceding years: an organism of the simplest kind consisting of what was supposed to be a single gene, one that was in addition easy to manipulate experimentally, and with which it was possible to obtain statistically exact results with a minimal effort. In short, he thought he had found the biological analog to the hydrogen atom. Compared with bacteriophage, Morgan's drosophila failed to fulfill the first and second conditions, whereas Stanley's TMV did not match the second and the third.

The scientific community was quick to recognize the outcome of Delbrück's collaboration with Ellis. Their paper, "The Growth of Bacteriophage," marked the beginnings of phage genetics, which catalyzed the development of molecular genetics during the following years. Nonetheless, there is still room for further deliberations before evaluating the real impact of Delbrück's work. Within half a year after Delbrück and Ellis had published "The Growth of Bacteriophage" in the *Journal of General Physiology* in mid-1939, Helmut Ruska, Gustav Kausche, and Edgar Pfankuch published electron microscope photographs depicting the first steps of bacteriophage multiplication – that is, phage visibly attaching to the surface of bacteria. Two years before Thomas F. Anderson and Salvador E. Luria in the United States were in a position to replicate their findings, Ruska and his co-workers demonstrated that the viruses enter the cell not as a whole but inject only those parts that are responsible for the genetic program. This result opened up a new path of investigation, in which the focus was not on the virus as a whole but on the genetically active intruders.[22]

In this particular case, the plausibility of a re-transmission of ideas on phage genetics from American to German research is uncertain. During the late 1930s, about 150 publications on phage appeared every year, among them several on reproduction. The argument is thus not that Ruska et al., might not have in fact been stimulated by Delbrück and Ellis's paper but that such a hypothesis is redundant in view of the ubiquity of other possible stimuli. While engaged in a vigorous search for appropriate objects demonstrating the power of the electron microscope, Ernst Ruska's brother Helmut and his co-workers, among other research groups located in Berlin,

---

22 See Helmut Ruska, "Die Sichtbarmachung der bakteriophagen Lyse im Übermikroskop," *Die Naturwissenschaften* 28 (1940): 45–6; Edgar Pfankuch and Gustav A. Kausche, "Isolierung und übermikroskopische Abbildung eines Bakteriophagen," *Die Naturwissenschaften* 28 (1940): 46–7; Helmut Ruska, "Über ein neues bei der bakteriophagen Lyse autretendes Formelement," *Die Naturwissenschaften* 29 (1941): 367.

were probing the most diverse domains of microphysical reality with the new tool. They scanned viruses and bacteria as early as 1938.

In the following case, the flow of information shows up more clearly than in the case just discussed. According to the documents in the archive of the Max Planck Society, the beginnings of research on TMV in the Kaiser Wilhelm Institutes for Biology and Biochemistry must clearly be attributed to Stanley's work in the mid-1930s.[23] Once institutionalized with the aim of regaining the lead in the field from the new American frontrunners, German research on TMV moved well ahead. No later than 1939, Helmut Ruska and his crew succeeded in photographing TMV with the aid of an electron microscope. Other work on the structure of TMV done by Gerhard Schramm at the Kaiser Wilhelm Institute for Biochemistry in the early 1940s had some effect on deciphering the structure of DNA a decade later, as James Watson testifies in *The Double Helix*. The institutionalization of TMV research at the Kaiser Wilhelm Institutes might indeed score as an instance of induced scientific change. In this case, however, there was no mediation by migrants or emigrants; the transmission relied exclusively on published sources.

Delbrück seems to exemplify a case of ESIC. Among historians of science it is generally accepted that he inaugurated phage genetics in the United States. He was the one to found a flourishing school whose influence spread throughout the United States and radiated well into other countries. On a closer view, however, the case exhibits quite singular features from which one might not be able to generalize. Moreover, the fact that Delbrück was not an emigrant must also be borne in mind. Being neither Jewish nor politically endangered, he was consistent in never applying the term "emigrant" to himself. He freely admitted that political conditions in Germany were not the cause of his going abroad, and at least until the beginning of the war, would not have prevented his eventual return provided that the prospects for successful continuation of his genetics work were given. Thus, while Delbrück's case seems to be a prototypical example of the thesis that migration might induce scientific change, it is an even better example for the opposite thesis – that unfavorable conditions for scientific change can motivate scientists to migrate to a more conducive context. The causal chain leading to Delbrück's migration was not triggered by the latter's decision to go abroad on a Rockefeller grant but by the gradual realization that

23 Richard von Wettstein, "Vorschlag zur Errichtung einer Zweigstelle für Virusforschung der Kaiser Wilhelm Institute für Biochemie und Biologie," July 19, 1940, Archiv der Max-Planck-Gesellschaft, I, 1A, 2906. Gustav A. Kausche, Edgar Pfankuch, and Helmut Ruska, "Die Sichtbarmachung von pflanzlichem Virus im Übermikroskop," *Die Naturwissenschaften* 27 (1930): 29.

Germany was not the place to launch his biological research program if he wanted to have any chance at success. What the example shows is not that molecular genetics could not have emerged without the work of Delbrück, or that the state of the field at the end of the 1950s would have been very different from what it was without Delbrück's participation. It makes plausible, however, that under this assumption the course of the field's evolution would have in all probability deviated from its eventual development – with a different starting point, different problems, errors and solutions.

EXAMPLE 2: OTTO STERN AND THE MOLECULAR BEAM METHOD IN THE UNITED STATES[24]

At first glance, conditions for the transference of scientific ideas and practices were ideal in the case of Otto Stern. In 1922, in cooperation with Walter Gerlach, Stern had invented a method for measuring the quantization of space with a beam of ionized silver molecules, which was injected into an apparatus that generated a strong magnetic field. During the years prior to 1933, Stern perfected the molecular beam method with the help of numerous students from Germany and elsewhere, finally directing his attention to the magnetic moments of the proton, the neutron, and the deuteron. Since no serious competitor entered the field, Stern could act as a kind of monopolist controlling his research domain. After Stern's emigration, the Carnegie Institute of Technology, backed financially by the Buhl Foundation, offered him both a position and a laboratory to continue his research, although he was wealthy enough to live off his own means. Although all the preconditions for a prominent place in the future development of the field were fulfilled, Stern exerted only a modest influence in his new environment. The main reason for his failure to promote the molecular beam method within the American context was certainly the fact that his experimental design was quickly surpassed by an alternative instrumental setup developed by one of his former students: Isidor Rabi's resonance method. Stern stuck to the tools he was used to from his time at Hamburg University. As a consequence, he was no longer to be counted among the leading players in a field he had helped to create, and his main impact would be confined to the years prior to his emigration, for which he was awarded the Nobel prize in physics for 1943. Stern's case counts in favor of the thesis

---

24 On this, see John S. Rigden, *Rabi, Scientist and Citizen* (New York, 1987); Immanuel Estermann, "Molecular Beam Research in Hamburg, 1922–1933," in Estermann, ed., *Recent Research in Molecular Beams* (New York, 1959), 1; Immanuel Estermann, "Otto Stern," *Dictionary of Scientific Biography*, 13:40.

that emigration-induced scientific change can be separated from general scientific change, although at least in this example, only in a negative sense. In contrast to the first example, and despite the "emigration of a research program," no induced scientific change could be identified here.

EXAMPLE 3: NUCLEAR PHYSICS IN THE 1930s[25]

Nuclear physics functions as a paradigmatic example of the impact of immigration on the scientific system of a host country. As a group, immigrant nuclear physicists rank high according to scientometric criteria of excellence. The most cited nuclear physicist in the period between 1921 and 1947, Hans Bethe, was also an emigrant. Judged from the disciplinary landscapes of the field, there can be no doubt of their importance for its evolution as a cognitive unity. Nonetheless, some caveats need to be tendered. In the first place, one has to account for the anomalous fact that the very institution that had by far the largest share in the development of experimental nuclear physics and the transformation of the field into a "big science" was nearly devoid of immigrant brain power, at least before 1946. This is the Radiation Laboratory of Ernest Lawrence, who had built his first cyclotron in 1932.[26] The instrument became the prototype of ever larger and more powerful types during the next two decades, when it became the most important single piece of experimental equipment in nuclear physics. Another distracting observation for supporters of the thesis that the upsurge of nuclear physics in the United States after 1932 owed itself to emigrant influence must be seen in the fact that in the 1930s, nuclear physics was a field that thrived wherever it was at least moderately institutionally supported, irrespective of emigrant participation. This rule applies even for German institutes, although practitioners there had to cope with erratically acting authorities and the lack of any cyclotron, at least up to December 1943.

While the results of co-citation analysis make it plausible that immigrants had a disproportionately high share in the salient cognitive events of the discipline, it is again important to set this finding in perspective. In view of the demand for nuclear physicists in Germany compared with the United States, it is safe to assume that the evolution of the discipline as a whole was positively influenced by the emigration process. But this result is not

---

25   See Klaus Fischer, *Changing Landscapes of Nuclear Physics*, and the literature cited therein.
26   John L. Heilbron and Robert W. Seidel, *Lawrence and His Laboratory: A History of the Lawrence Berkeley Laboratory*, vol. 1 (Berkeley, Calif., 1989); on the rise and development of "big science" in general, see Peter Galison and Bruce Hevly, eds., *Big Science* (Stanford, Calif., 1992).

sufficient proof that the character of the field – its "disciplinary matrix" – changed as a result of emigration. Any cognitive shift indicated in the disciplinary matrix might have its origin in the interplay between the problems, facts, theories, instruments, and methods of the discipline, irrespective of the fact that some of its practitioners had changed political loyalties by emigrating from home countries. The alternative assumption – that an EISC took place – is in need of independent corroboration in each particular case.

From the end of the 1930s onward, the social organization of nuclear physics was shattered and eventually transformed by the consequences of a well-known experimental discovery: nuclear fission. Whereas this discovery, as such, had nothing to do with the process of emigration, its political and organizational consequences did. It may be a speculation, although a plausible one, that without the concentrated intelligence of so many high-ranking nuclear physicists from Germany, Italy, France, Denmark, and Hungary, nuclear weapons would not have been manufactured in the United States during World War II. In addition, immigrants played a significant role in bringing the Manhattan and Tube Alloy Projects to fruition. Speculations about how the British and American atom bomb projects may have fared without immigrant action are of little use. However, given the catalytic function of emigrant nuclear physicists such as Rudolf Peierls, Otto R. Frisch, Leo Szilard, Eugene Wigner, Edward Teller, and Albert Einstein for the creation of the projects, it seems plausible to surmise that without their activities, the enterprise would in all probability not have been launched soon enough to become relevant for the war effort.

Again, can this count as an example of scientific change brought about through immigration, or would it be more appropriate to analyze the whole process as exemplifying an important discovery of mid-twentieth century politics – that it is possible to accelerate technological progress in an unprecedented way by a new collective organization of knowledge production, in conjunction with a massive input of government money and effort? Note that the emphasis is on technological, not scientific, progress, and on the interplay of the former with organizational demands. Viktor Weisskopf may have been right in calling Los Alamos scientifically rather uninteresting, but socially very important as a melting pot of a large number of scientists coming from different countries with divergent cultural backgrounds. It is well known that the organizational dimension of the project was least amenable to emigrant influence. Big science is in no way an invention of emigrant nuclear physicists. Its principles were being deployed not exclusively in Los Alamos but also at MIT's Radiation Laboratory, where RADAR was forged into a decisive intelligence weapon. The principles of big science were utilized in similar fashion by the Germans in the rocketry project at Peenemünde, with a comparable amount of resources. If there is any sense in probing the origins of the principles of big science, it might be most profitable to concentrate on Ernest Lawrence's laboratory in Berkeley. But this owes itself to the fact that Lawrence's big machines could no longer be manipulated by a single experimenter. Seen from that perspective, big science was nobody's invention, but an unintended consequence of the growing dimension of physicists' experimental equipment.

2

Physics, Life, and Contingency: Born, Schrödinger, and Weyl in Exile

SKÚLI SIGURDSSON*

In the fall of 1930 the Zurich mathematician Hermann Weyl returned to Göttingen as successor to David Hilbert. Soon thereafter he gave a speech in which he tried to explain to Göttingen students and rationalize to himself why he had chosen to come back to Germany after seventeen years at the Swiss Federal Institute of Technology in Zurich (*Eidgenössische Technische Hochschule* or ETH), where he had been content and productive. Weyl said:

> I have returned, because I did not want to miss the contact with youth without which old age fades away into rigid loneliness, because I recognize that intellectual community is the proper site of scientific growth, and hence I acknowledge it as a serious duty to cultivate the tradition of science, and finally to embed myself again in the national community [*Volksgemeinschaft*].[1]

Weyl not only wanted to get students to escape from the relative isolation of Zurich and to return to German culture, he also had to live up to his responsibilities as a member of the Göttingen thought collective and the elite of German science and try to wear Hilbert's mantle in a manner worthy of its previous owner. That he was expected to do so can be inferred from a letter in which Arnold Sommerfeld, one of the elder statesmen of theoretical physics in Germany, congratulated him on the appointment: "I am very pleased that you have decided to go to Göttingen. The opposite would have been a great disappointment to Hilbert."[2] Moreover, with his meteoric

---

* I would like to acknowledge the support of the Alexander von Humboldt Foundation in Bonn, Germany, and the Verbund für Wissenschaftsgeschichte in Berlin. I would also like to thank Mitchell G. Ash, Liliane Beaulieu, Lorraine Daston, Klaus Hentschel, Hotze Mulder, Monika Renneberg, and John Stachel for reading earlier drafts of this essay.

1 Hermann Weyl, "Rückblick auf Zürich aus dem Jahre 1930," in Weyl, *Gesammelte Abhandlungen* (Berlin, 1968), 4:653–4.
2 Arnold Sommerfeld to Hermann Weyl, Munich, June 24, 1930, Weyl papers HS 91:757, ETH Library Archives, Zurich (hereafter ELAZ).

48

rise to academic fame in the preceding decades, Weyl had outgrown the Zurich environment. He had become the highest paid professor at the ETH, and the costs to the Swiss Board of Education were no longer commensurate with the returns on its investment. It was therefore unwilling to raise his pay further in exchange for his continued stay in Zurich.

The following years in Göttingen were a difficult period for Weyl. He was dissatisfied with the quality of scientific life, and the ominous political and economic situation in Germany weighed heavily on him. His productivity waned. By 1932, he contemplated leaving Germany, but the decision proved so taxing that in confusion and despair he declined an offer in early January 1933 from the newly founded Institute for Advanced Study in Princeton.[3] The Nazis' rise to power made him reconsider the situation, and after exploring the possibility of going to Spain he accepted a renewed offer from the Institute and emigrated to the United States with his family in October 1933. This succession of migrations marked a second rupture in Weyl's life; the first occurred in World War I. Both upheavals triggered changes in his intellectual production: the first a fanning out of interests to mathematical physics, philosophy of science, and group theory; the second a concentration on mathematics and a turning away from physics and philosophy.

In this essay I analyze the intellectual migrations of Weyl and two other émigrés, the theoretical physicists Max Born and Erwin Schrödinger. The contraction of Weyl's interests can be characterized as centering. Weyl's move to the rising center of mathematical research in Princeton consolidated his goals; as a member of a thriving mathematical community, he regained some of his creativity. Born and Schrödinger, in contrast, pursued old research programs, took up new ones, and cast their philosophical nets ever wider on the periphery of the British Isles.[4]

Here it is helpful to think in terms of collective biography. Differences abound, but similarities bind. Born, Schrödinger, and Weyl believed in unification in science and invested much time in seeking its realization, at the end of World War I and in exile. The ideal of unity was never wholly absent from the quantum mechanical project of the 1920s.[5] This essay is neither a contribution to the history of disciplines nor an analysis of the emergence of new specialties as exemplified in the work of Klaus Fischer,

3 Laura S. Porter, "From Intellectual Sanctuary to Social Responsibility: The Founding of the Institute for Advanced Study, 1930–1933," Ph.D. diss., Princeton University, 1988.
4 On center-periphery models, see Mary J. Nye, *Science in the Provinces: Scientific Communities and Provincial Leadership in France, 1860–1930* (Berkeley, Calif., 1986), 224–42.
5 Alexander Rüger, "Attitudes Towards Infinities: Responses to Anomalies in Quantum Electrodynamics, 1927–1947," *Historical Studies in the Physical and Biological Sciences* 22, no. 2 (1992): 309–37.

Paul K. Hoch, and others.[6] Rather it responds to such studies of émigré physical scientists in the 1930s by showing that emigration and the resulting changes in environment had a noticeable impact on the direction the trajectories of Born, Schrödinger, and Weyl took, and above all on the timing of changes in the orientation of research and expression of deeply held cultural and philosophical beliefs. Moreover, in exile these carriers of European culture thought about the meaning of their work and shaped the collective memory of mathematicians, physicists, and historians of science.

I begin by sketching the factors that thrust and pulled these men away from Central Europe. Then I show how Born and Schrödinger, spurred on in exile by the British physical chemist Frederick G. Donnan, grappled with the challenge of Arthur S. Eddington's philosophy of science and the bearing of modern physics on biology. Finally, I discuss these émigrés' work on and response to unified field theory, their attitudes to individual and political responsibility, and their views on the role of contingency in society and nature.

ASCENDANCY AND EXILE

Born and Weyl came of age in Göttingen under the guidance of David Hilbert, Felix Klein, and Hermann Minkowski; Schrödinger in Vienna under Franz Exner and Friedrich Hasenöhrl.[7] Born's early work was in relativity and electron theory and on the dynamics of crystal lattices; Schrödinger began studying atmospheric electricity and radioactivity, the dynamics of crystal lattices and statistical physics; Weyl's first studies dealt with problems in mathematical analysis and the theory of Riemann surfaces.

In 1913 Weyl began working in number theory. The outbreak of war the following year interrupted those plans and disturbed him profoundly. After serving in the German army he returned to Zurich in 1916, where he had been a professor since the fall of 1913. He struck gold by taking up the general theory of relativity: It was technically demanding, philosophically intriguing, and offered hopes of spiritual transcendence. Weyl moved to the forefront of modern physics with his textbook on space, time, and

6 Klaus Fischer, "Die Emigration von Wissenschaftlern nach 1933," *Vierteljahreshefte für Zeitgeschichte* 39 (1991): 535–49; Klaus Fischer, "The Identification of Emigration-Induced Scientific Change," chapter 1 of this volume; see also Paul K. Hoch, "Institutional versus Intellectual Migrations in the Nucleation of New Scientific Specialties," *Studies in the History and Philosophy of Science* 18 (1987): 481–500.

7 Armin Hermann, "Erwin Schrödinger (1887–1961)," *Dictionary of Scientific Biography* (1975), 12: 217–23; N. Kemmer and R. Schlapp, "Max Born (1882–1970)," *Biographical Memoirs of Fellows of the Royal Society* 17 (1971): 17–52; M. H. A. Newman, "Hermann Weyl (1885–1955)," *Biographical Memoirs of Fellows of the Royal Society* 3 (1957): 305–28.

matter (*Raum-Zeit-Materie*, 1918) and his unified field theory – an extension of the general theory of relativity – and achieved international fame, whereas fellow mathematicians at the ETH stayed behind in the less prominent field of mathematical analysis.[8] Heinrich Zangger, a Zurich physician and friend of both Weyl and Albert Einstein, told the president of the Swiss Board of Education that during a visit to Paris in the spring of 1920, he had often been asked about Einstein and Weyl. The physicist Paul Langevin had told Zangger that he considered Weyl the most important and promising representative of mathematical physics.[9]

Born became a professor of theoretical physics in Göttingen in 1921, and in collaboration with the Göttingen experimentalist James Franck, moved deeper into quantum physics. Born told the English physicist Ferdinand A. Lindemann in 1920 that the ideas of Niels Bohr now dominated research in Germany.[10] Einstein's sharp rejection of Weyl's unified theory, and the loss of momentum that the general theory of relativity suffered around 1920 despite public interest and front-page notoriety, contrasted with the increased ability of quantum theory to explain the structure of matter. Atomic research improved the German national self-image, which increased the attractiveness of quantum theory in the wake of military defeat.[11]

Schrödinger became a professor of theoretical physics at the University of Zurich in 1921. There his research interests shifted to quantum theory, but his previous work on the general theory of relativity enabled him to see a link between Weyl's unified field theory and Bohr's atomic theory.[12] This insight and work on statistical physics paved the way for Schrödinger's development of wave mechanics in an Alpine resort at Christmas 1925.[13] The previous summer, Werner Heisenberg had made his decisive breakthrough in the construction of matrix mechanics, which was formalized by Born, Heisenberg, and Pascual Jordan in the fall. Born utilized Schrödinger's version of the new mechanics and introduced the probabilistic interpretation of quantum mechanics in 1926. This rapid sequence of events

8   Skúli Sigurdsson, "Hermann Weyl, Mathematics and Physics, 1900–1927," Ph.D. diss., Harvard University, 1991.
9   Heinrich Zangger to Robert Gnehm, Zurich, June 3, 1920, quoted in Günther Frei and Urs Stammbach, *Hermann Weyl und die Mathematik an der ETH Zürich, 1913–1930* (Basel, 1992), 45.
10 Max Born to Ferdinand A. Lindemann, Frankfurt/Main, Sept. 26, 1920, Cherwell papers D23, Nuffield College Library, Oxford (hereafter NCLO).
11 J. L. Heilbron, *The Dilemmas of an Upright Man: Max Planck as Spokesman for German Science* (Berkeley, Calif., 1986), 92–3.
12 Erwin Schrödinger, "Über eine bemerkenswerte Eigenschaft der Quantenbahnen eines einzelnen Elektrons" (1922), in Schrödinger, *Gesammelte Abhandlungen* (Vienna, 1984), 3:14–24; V. V. Rahman and Paul Forman, "Why Was It Schrödinger Who Developed de Broeglie's Ideas?" *Historical Studies in the Physical Sciences* 1 (1969): 291–314.
13 Walter Moore, *Schrödinger: Life and Thought* (Cambridge, 1989), 194–7.

took the scientific world by storm. Heisenberg and Schrödinger received Nobel Prizes in 1932 and 1933, respectively; in 1927 Heisenberg became a professor of theoretical physics in Leipzig and Schrödinger was appointed to the chair of theoretical physics at the University of Berlin, succeeding Max Planck.

By this time, Weyl had become so removed from physics that when Born asked his advice in 1925 concerning matrix mechanics Weyl said in his reply: "But I have not calculated any further – and will not get to it in the near future 'bound [as I am] to the deep bog of philosophy.' "[14] With the ETH theoretician Peter Debye's leaving Zurich in 1927 and Schrödinger gone, Weyl lectured on the new quantum mechanics and group theory, as he had taken over teaching theoretical physics after Einstein left for Berlin in 1914.[15] This brought Weyl back to physics. In the academic year 1928–29, he was a guest professor in mathematical physics at Princeton University. This was part of an effort to establish Princeton as a center of research in mathematics and physical science.[16] Despite strong emotional bonds to Europe, Weyl might have accepted a permanent position in Princeton had his asthma not prevented him from obtaining affordable health insurance. Nevertheless, Weyl had become fascinated with the United States and its generous research facilities, and he had strengthened a network of contacts.[17]

No sooner had Weyl accepted the call to Göttingen than the Nazis scored their first decisive electoral victory in September 1930. Weyl was sensitive, as Zangger observed: "Prof. Weyl is a peculiar race mixture, at least seven parts Holstein and one part Jewish blood with the particular vasomotor irritability than one encounters relatively often in people from Holstein and Friesland."[18] Weyl was not endangered by the Nazis' prospective anti-Semitic measures but his wife was. Weyl seriously questioned his earlier

14   Hermann Weyl to Max Born, Zurich, Sept. 27, 1925, Pascual Jordan papers 965, Staatsbibliothek Preussischer Kulturbesitz, Berlin (hereafter SPKB).
15   Frei and Stammbach, *Hermann Weyl*, 26, 94.
16   William Aspray, "The Emergence of Princeton as a World Center for Mathematical Research, 1896–1939," in William Aspray and Philip Kitcher, eds., *History and Philosophy of Modern Mathematics* (Minneapolis, 1988), 346–66.
17   Oswald Veblen Hermann Weyl, Princeton, N.J., June 15, 1929, Oswald Veblen papers, Library of Congress, Manuscript Division, Washington, D.C. (hereafter LCMD/W); see also Gerald Holton, "Physics in America, and Einstein's Decision to Immigrate," in Holton, *The Advancement of Science and Its Burdens: The Jefferson Lecture and Other Essays* (Cambridge, 1986), 123–38.
18   Heinrich Zangger to Robert Gnehm, Zurich, Dec. 1, 1920, quoted in Frei and Stammbach, *Hermann Weyl*, 51; see also Heinrich A. Medicus, "The Friendship among Three Singular Men: Einstein and His Swiss Friends Besso and Zangger," *Isis* 85 (1994): 456–78.

decision, and even wanted to return to Zurich instead of staying in Göttingen, and he nearly succeeded in being his own successor at the ETH. In Göttingen there was nothing left to do but plunge into work and try to forget what was threatening; the old Hilbert seminar on the structure of matter continued by Born was one of few positive events.[19]

The early 1930s, a period of protracted economic crisis, held more surprises in store for Weyl. With state finances rapidly deteriorating, he did not receive the remuneration that he had been promised, which upset him greatly.[20] Because of this sense of betrayal, the Nazi threat, and unhappiness with the status of scientific research in Göttingen and his stifled productivity, he considered leaving and established contact with Abraham Flexner, the first director of the Princeton Institute.[21] But when Weyl's dissatisfaction and restlessness culminated in early January 1933, he went into a depression and turned down the offer from Princeton. The Göttingen mathematician Richard Courant told the Princeton mathematician Oswald Veblen:

Weyl's behavior is really extremely strange and complicated. It is only possible to understand it if one realizes that Weyl is actually in spite of his enormously broad talents an inwardly insecure person, for whom nothing is more difficult than to make a decision which will have consequences for his whole life, and who mentally is not capable of dealing with the weight of such decisions, but needs a strong support somewhere.[22]

Weyl did not find it easy to leave, given his deep attachment to the German language, but in the course of 1933 the fate of his wife and sons tipped the balance.[23] He was a very passionate person, and his acute sensitivity and eclectic interests suggest that he might be viewed as a kind of barometer, registering in detail the shifting mood and latent tendencies of his times. Thus he quickly read the signs in the German political landscape

19 Hermann Weyl to Michel Plancherel, Göttingen, Nov. 9 and 27, 1930, quoted in Frei and Stammbach, *Hermann Weyl*, 156, 158–60.
20 Hermann Weyl to Ministerialrat Dr. Windelband, Göttingen, Oct. 17 and Dec. 5, 1932, Geheimes Staatsarchiv Merseburg, Rep. 76, Sekt. 6, Tit. IV, Bd. II, Bl. 272, 296.
21 Abraham Flexner to Richard Courant, no location, Feb. 18, 1933, Oswald Veblen papers, LCMD/W.
22 Richard Courant to Oswald Veblen, Göttingen, Jan. 21, 1933, Oswald Veblen papers, LCMD/W.
23 See Hermann Weyl's resignation letter to Minister für Wissenschaft, Kunst, und Volksbildung, Zurich, Oct. 9, 1933 quoted in Norbert Schappacher, "Questions politiques dans la vie des mathématiques en Allemagne (1918–1935)," in Josiane Olff-Nathan, ed., *La science sous le Troisième Reich: victime ou alliée du Nazisme* (Paris, 1993), 81–3; see also Norbert Schappacher, "Das Mathematische Institut der Universität Göttingen, 1929–1950," in Heinrich Becker, Hans-Joachim Dahms, and Cornelia Wegeler, eds., *Die Universität Göttingen unter dem Nationalsozialismus; Das verdrängte Kapitel ihrer 250jährigen Geschichte* (Munich, 1987), 345–73.

in 1930, as a decade earlier the zeitgeist had fueled his speculations on causality and the inadequacy of determinism in physics.[24]

Neither Born nor Schrödinger had been planning to leave before Adolf Hitler came to power. But Born was Jewish and was discharged via a forced leave of absence with the Nazi restructuring of the civil service in April 1933; Schrödinger resigned in protest from the Planck chair in Berlin by asking for a study leave.[25] They both left for England at the end of the summer, Born for Cambridge, where he became a lecturer in applied mechanics, Schrödinger for Oxford, where Ferdinand A. Lindemann had arranged a lectureship for him as part of efforts to strengthen physics research.[26] But these were temporary positions; Schrödinger left in 1936 for Austria. For some time, Born entertained the possibility of returning, but in the fall of 1934, with the Nazis tightening their grip, he abandoned all hope. He told Lindemann, "Therefore, I loose [sic] any hope of my later return to Germany and must try to find some permanent post."[27]

Before going to Cambridge, Born wrote to Hilbert from the Alps with a sense of relief and told him about his progress on quantum electrodynamics. It was in the solitude of the mountains that it was possible for him to think deeply about questions of principle in physics.[28] In Cambridge he worked with the Polish émigré theoretician Leopold Infeld on nonlinear electrodynamics.[29] To the rising generation of theoretical physicists, the efforts of Born and Infeld were indicative of the crisis in quantum electrodynamics. They seemed to J. Robert Oppenheimer "full of very grave errors, useless in the quantum theoretic part, and very dubious in the classical electrodynamics."[30]

During the winter of 1935–1936, the Borns went to India, where Born lectured at the Indian Institute of Science in Bangalore at the invitation of

24 Paul Forman, "Weimar Culture, Causality, and Quantum Theory, 1918–1927: Adaptation by German Physicists and Mathematicians to a Hostile Intellectual Environment," *Historical Studies in the Physical Sciences* 3 (1971): 1–115.

25 Walter Moore, *Schrödinger*, 271–2; Ulf Rosenow, "Die Göttinger Physik unter dem Nationalsozialismus," in Becker et al., eds., *Die Universität Göttingen*, 374–409.

26 Jack Morrell, "Research in Physics at the Clarendon Laboratory, Oxford, 1919–1939," *Historical Studies in the Physical and Biological Sciences* 22, no. 2 (1992): 263–307.

27 Max Born to Ferdinand A. Lindemann, Cambridge, Nov. 14, 1934, Cherwell papers D23, NCLO; this complicates the story in Alan D. Beyerchen, *Scientists under Hitler: Politics and the Physics Community in the Third Reich* (New Haven, Conn., 1977), 21.

28 Max Born to David Hilbert, Silva Gardena, July 23, 1933, David Hilbert papers 40, Niedersächsische Staats- und Universitätsbibliothek, Göttingen; Max Born, *My Life: Recollections of a Nobel Laureate* (London, 1978), 254–64.

29 Max Born, *My Life*, 265–71; Leopold Infeld, *Quest: An Autobiography* (New York, 1980), 206–13.

30 J. Robert Oppenheimer to George E. Uhlenbeck, Feb.–March, 1934, Archive for the History of Quantum Physics (hereafter AHQP); see also Peter Galison, "The Discovery of the Muon and the Failed Revolution against Quantum Electrodynamics," *Centaurus* 26 (1983): 262–316.

the experimentalist Chandrasekhara V. Raman. Born could have obtained a position in Bangalore, but, however attractive this might have been, it came to nothing. As he wrote to Lindemann, "The situation in Europe looks pretty bad. Sometimes I think that this old continent is approaching the end of her splendid career. And then I consider staying in India."[31]

Returning to Europe the following spring, Born was offered a professorship at Moscow University by Piotr Kapitza, the experimentalist. Born recalled later:

> We were of course not very keen on going to Russia, which would mean learning a new, very complicated language, uprooting the children a second time and starting an entirely new life. Still, as we believed ourselves to have hardly a chance in England, we thought we might have to look at Moscow and its university. So we applied for Russian visas and made inquiries about the journey.[32]

The period of uncertainty came to an end in the fall of 1936. Instead of going to Russia, Born succeeded Charles G. Darwin in the Tait Chair of Natural Philosophy (theoretical physics) at the University of Edinburgh. This chair had previously been offered to Schrödinger.[33]

Since the early 1910s, the mathematician Edmund T. Whittaker and the experimentalist Charles G. Barkla had been Edinburgh's scientific luminaries. By the 1930s, however, they had lost much of their luster. Opposition to quantum theory and pursuit of a strange x-ray phenomenon took Barkla, who received the 1917 Nobel Prize (awarded in 1918), out of the mainstream of physics as swiftly as his previous research on x-rays had placed him squarely within it.[34]

In the United States the émigré physicists encountered an already thriving physics community when they arrived in the 1930s. The resonance reached a maximum in wartime efforts such as the Manhattan Project and the development of microwave radar technology at MIT's Rad Lab. In the British Isles things were different, and Born's move north to the periphery signaled that he had become a relative outsider in physics.[35]

31 Max Born to Ferdinand A. Lindemann, Bangalore, Nov. 14, 1935, Cherwell papers D23, NCLO; Max Born, *My Life*, 272–8.
32 Max Born, *My Life*, 280.
33 Walter Moore, *Schrödinger*, 318–19; G. P. Thomson, "Charles Galton Darwin (1887–1962)," *Biographical Memoirs of Fellows of the Royal Society* 9 (1963): 69–85.
34 Paul Forman, "Charles Glover Barkla (1877–1944)," *Dictionary of Scientific Biography* (1970), 1:456–9; Daniel Martin, "Edmund Taylor Whittaker (1873–1956)," *Dictionary of Scientific Biography* (1976), 14:313–16; Bruce R. Wheaton, *The Tiger and the Shark: Empirical Roots of the Wave-Particle Dualism* (Cambridge, 1983), 256–8; Brian Wynne, "C.G. Barkla and the J. Phenomenon: A Case Study in the Treatment of Deviance in Physics," *Social Studies in Science* 6 (1976): 307–47.
35 Silvan S. Schweber, "The Empiricist Temper Regnant: Theoretical Physics in the United States, 1920–1950," *Historical Studies in the Physical and Biological Sciences*, 17, no. 1 (1986): 55–98; Paul

Born did no war-related work, had little in common with his colleagues Barkla and Whittaker, and was at times overworked and discontented: "It is altogether too much for me doing all the elementary teaching, directing Ph.D. research students on dull papers about crystals, and to work on more fundamental problems, which really interest me."[36] The theoretical physicist George E. Uhlenbeck later remarked that in Edinburgh, Born "wanted to do too much." He engaged in projects such as superconductivity, theory of liquids, and field theory. "None of them panned out, really. And that bothered him."[37]

WHAT IS PHYSICS?

The move to philosophy was another sign of Born's move to the periphery – but it was encouraged by a British colleague. A constant source of incitement and support for Born during the wartime years in Edinburgh was Frederick G. Donnan. Donnan had completed his doctorate in physical chemistry with Wilhelm Ostwald in Leipzig in 1896, worked a year in Jacobus H. van't Hoff's laboratory in Berlin, and succeeded William Ramsay at University College, London, in 1913. He was interested in the phenomena of life and devoted much of his leisure time to studying recent advances in chemistry and cosmology.[38]

Donnan told Born in 1941 that there was "great need at the present – even in the midst of a terrible and bitter war – for a book on the 'philosophy' of modern physical science"; the author he had in mind was Born, who was "himself responsible for much of the present position of physical theory." Donnan had a very poor opinion of the efforts of James H. Jeans, Hyman Levy, and Herbert Dingle in this regard. The writings of Planck, Bohr, and Schrödinger corresponded to a somewhat older period, whereas the astronomer and mathematical physicist Arthur S. Eddington, "though very good in parts, tends to go off the rails, and seems to be now suffering from a definite 'idée fixe.' " Donnan had studied philosophy intensively as a young man and confessed to "a certain guilty 'hunger of the soul' in this respect." He felt that the standpoint reached by theoretical physics possessed

K. Hoch, "The Reception of Central European Refugee Physicists of the 1930s: U.S.S.R., U.K., U.S.A.," *Annals of Science* 40 (1983): 217–46.

36 Max Born to Frederick G. Donnan, Edinburgh, March 2, 1944, Bloomsbury Science Library, University College London (hereafter BSL/UCL).

37 George E. Uhlenbeck, interviewed by Thomas S. Kuhn, March 30, 1962, AHQP.

38 Francis A. Freeth, "Frederick George Donnan (1870–1956)," *Biographical Memoirs of Fellows of the Royal Society* 3 (1957): 23–39; see also Mary Jo Nye, "Chemical Explanation and Physical Dynamics: Two Research Schools at the First Solvay Chemistry Conferences, 1922–1928," *Annals of Science* 46 (1989): 460–80.

"paramount importance in a distracted world. It is indeed this very misery and distraction which cry for that enlightenment of the mind and alleviation of the spirit which true science can give."[39]

Donnan understood that Born found the times unsuitable, and in his reply he returned to Eddington: "I think part of his trouble is that he uses philosophical terms with quite unphilosophical meanings, and, like poor James Joyce, has imagined an isolated world of his own, into the lonely depths of which he gets deeper and deeper until he speaks a one-man language."[40] When Born changed his mind two years later, Donnan was delighted. Born intended to make his views known to the Durham Philosophical Society and the Pure Science Society, King's College, at Newcastle-upon-Tyne. Donnan emphasized that the lecture should be published and added: "Really, although I'm only a plain physical chemist, you have no idea how that fellow Jeans irritates me – and 'spoofs' the public."[41] Donnan felt certain nobody would find the lecture " 'trivial and dull'!" This was not "a question of 'philosophy' but of the defense of science." On reading the manuscript, he found it *"excellent,"* even *"very excellent."*[42] Donnan reassured Born that he was not being too harsh toward Eddington. "I think the young men will follow your lead, and so it is very important that this lead should be given to them. Your doing so is a great service to the young men, and they are the important ones for the future of science in the next generation."[43]

The ostensible targets of Born's lecture were the "extreme experimentalists" Philipp Lenard and Johannes Stark in Germany, who declared "experiment to be the only genuine 'Aryan' method of science."[44] The actual targets were Eddington and the astrophysicist and mathematician Edward A. Milne, who, according to Born, claimed "that to the mind well trained in mathematics and epistemology the laws of Nature are manifest without appeal to experiment." This suggests that despite the former threat of "deutsche Physik," Lenard and Stark occupied a marginal position in Born's intellectual universe, like Barkla. Born disagreed sharply with the advocates of an idealist philosophy; in the lecture he set out to show "the mutual

39 Frederick G. Donnan to Max Born, Hartlip, Kent, Jan. 7, 1941, Max Born papers 168, SPKB.

40 Frederick G. Donnan to Max Born, Hartlip, Kent, Jan. 26, 1941, Max Born papers 168, SPKB.

41 Frederick G. Donnan to Max Born, Hartlip, Kent, April 1, 1943, Max Born papers 168, SPKB; see also A. E. Woodruff, "James Hopwood Jeans (1877–1946)," *Dictionary of Scientific Biography* (1973), 7:84–6.

42 Frederick G. Donnan to Max Born, Hartlip, Kent, April 30 and May 8, 25 and 28, 1943, original emphasis, Max Born papers 168, SPKB.

43 Frederick G. Donnan to Max Born, Hartlip, Kent, May 28, 1943, Max Born papers 168, SPKB.

44 Max Born, *Experiment and Theory in Physics* (Cambridge, 1943; reprint: New York, 1956), 1–2; see also David C. Cassidy, *Uncertainty: The Life and Science of Werner Heisenberg* (New York, 1992).

relationship between theory and experiment in the actual historical development of science, and to offer a balanced opinion on the present situation and future possibilities."[45]

Born's critique of Eddington and Milne bore witness to the consensus that had been forged in the physics community in the preceding decades: Theoretical physicists occupied a niche on the border of experiment, mathematics, and philosophy. This entailed a parting of ways with neo-Kantianism, which Born had found so appealing as a neophyte in science. A major catalyst in the coming of age for philosophers of science and theoreticians raised as neo-Kantians was the spell that Einstein cast on them with his achievements in the theory of relativity and quantum physics.[46]

For the fledgling theoretical physics community, relativity theory, as a liberating force, proved to be problematical. The general theory of relativity was too mathematical, and the empirical facts few and far between. "The activity of the mathematician must, however, not carry him as far as in the theory of relativity, where the clarity of his reasoning has come to be hidden by the erection of a structure of pure speculation so vast that it is impossible to view it in its entirety." Born issued this warning when he called for continued cooperation between mathematicians and physicists in developing the new quantum theory in the winter of 1925–26. To this he added: "A single crystal can be clear, nevertheless a mass of fragments of this crystal is opaque. Even the theoretical physicist must be guided by the ideal of the closest possible contact with the world of facts. Only then do the formulas live and beget new life."[47]

Facts constituted the bedrock of certainty; Born repeated this message in the Durham-Newcastle lecture: "My advice to those who wish to learn the art of scientific prophecy is not to rely on abstract reason, but to decipher the secret language of Nature from Nature's documents, the facts of experience."[48] The attempts of Eddington and Milne to combine mathematics and philosophy without predicting new facts of experience challenged the modern order in physics and threatened to remove theoretical physics from the niche that Born and his colleagues had carved out so laboriously. Moreover, the manner in which Eddington, the proselytizer of the general theory

---

45   Max Born, *Experiment*, 1–2, see also A. Vibert Douglas, "Arthur Stanley Eddington (1882–1944)," *Dictionary of Scientific Biography* (1971), 4:277–82; and Gerald J. Whitrow, "Edward Arthur Milne (1896–1950)," *Dictionary of Scientific Biography* (1974), 9:404–6.

46   Max Born, *My Life*, 93; Max Born, "Reflections of a Physicist," in Ralph Schoenman, ed., *Bertrand Russell: Philosopher of the Century* (London, 1967), 123; see also Skúli Sigurdsson, "Einsteinian Fixations," *Annals of Science* 49 (1992): 577–83.

47   Max Born, *Problems of Atomic Dynamics* (Cambridge, Mass., 1926; reprint: Cambridge, Mass., 1970), 129.

48   Max Born, *Experiment*, 44.

of relativity, had fastened upon dimensionless constants as epistemological signposts, seemed to ridicule the importance that Heisenberg, Pauli, Born, and other theoretical physicists attached to explaining the meaning of a dimensionless number in quantum electrodynamics ($2\pi e^2/hc = 1/137$). This was the so-called fine structure constant, which had arisen in Sommerfeld's research on the fine structure of the hydrogen spectrum in 1915–16.[49]

The object of Born's extreme disdain was Eddington's derivation of the reciprocal value of the fine structure constant. From the theory of an abstract phase space of E-numbers, Eddington derived a sequence:

$$f(n) = 1/2n^2 (n^2+1)$$

This formula yields 10, 136, 666, etc., when n is either 2, 4, or 6, and in particular $f(4) = 136$. When experiments necessitated a revision of the reciprocal value of the fine structure constant from 136 to 137, Eddington "adapted his theory by adding a unit." Similarly, he obtained the ratio of proton mass to electron mass – another dimensionless number, the significance of which puzzled theoretical physicists at the time – as the ratio of the two roots of a quadratic equation. This procedure was not to Born's liking:

I cannot criticize the derivation of these expressions as I have not succeeded in understanding them. Anyhow a few coincidences of this kind, which are not true predictions but expressions of experimentally known quantities, seem to me only a weak evidence for a great theory. And there are hardly any other predictions.

As Born added in a footnote, the numbers 10 and 666 occurred in the Revelation of St. John the Divine in the Apocalypse, the last book of the Bible: "And I saw a beast coming out of the sea having $f(2)$ horns . . . and his number is $f(6)$."[50] Born asked Lindemann, now Lord Cherwell, for permission to quote his biblical allusion: "I consider Eddingtonism to be a danger for the sound development of science, and I presume you agree. As nobody else has had the courage of interfering, I thought it my duty to do it, backed by Donnan, [Ralph] Fowler and others."[51]

After the publication of Born's Durham-Newcastle lecture, Schrödinger told Donnan, "I do not like it. It's trivial. No one but a madman could seriously suggest that we *could have* concocted the present scientific picture

49 Max Born, "The Mysterious Number 137," *Proceedings of the Indian Academy of Science* 2 (1935): 533–61; Max Born, "Reciprocity and the Number 137," *Proceedings of the Royal Society of Edinburgh* 59 (1939): 219–23.
50 Max Born, *Experiment*, 36–8.
51 Max Born to Lord Cherwell (Ferdinand A. Lindemann), Edinburgh, Oct. 3, 1943, Cherwell papers D24, NCLO.

of Nature *without* experience about it." But Schrödinger had been "frequently annoyed by E.s day-dreaming." He could understand Born's reaction, although he had basic sympathy for Eddington's ideas.[52] He told
Born he was not interested in the refutation of such a silly outlook attributed
to Eddington and Milne. He had not gone much further than to tell Eddington that he would never have contemplated "these blooming E-
numbers without years and years of experimental and of 'nonaprioristic'
theoretical research work having gone before."[53] The problem was much
deeper:

> The question is, whether *after* having had all the experience about Nature we *have*
> had, it is possible to re-build it in such a way from primitive principles of thought,
> in a way which suggests that it could hardly have been different from what it was;
> in a way, to *understand it* – es aus seiner kaleidoskopartigen Mannigfaltigkeit her-
> auszuheben in die Sphäre des Klaren und Durchsichtigen. My God, but that is the
> scope of all Science – inasmuch as it forms part of Humanities, and nothing more
> does me [sic], personally, interest about it. One ought not to discourage an attempt
> in this direction, even though, in its high-flying hopes it obviously went too far
> (as Eddington's, no doubt, did).[54]

Schrödinger's attitude toward philosophy combined traditionalism and
stubborn searching. He told Born that "one must make a principle of never
feeling ultimate satisfaction, until we have reached an explanation, after
which it seems *as if* (Vaihinger) we could have foretold the actual behavior
of Nature out of the empty belly." Quantum mechanics could not have
been invented out of the belly, and Schrödinger added that we would only
really understand things once we have gained the "insight that no other
way of describing Nature is at all possible – not on account of some special
experiments, but more directly."[55]

Donnan and Schrödinger were equally critical of fashions in philosophy.
Donnan was suspicious of phenomenologists, logical positivists, and aprior-
ists of the epistemological and axiomatic schools. He told Born that he
wanted instead to hear the opinion of the creators of "present-day physical
theory."[56] Donnan delivered the same message to Schrödinger, and encouraged him to write a book on the epistemology of science. But Schrödinger declined:

52 Erwin Schrödinger to Frederick G. Donnan, Dublin, Jan. 26, 1944, original emphasis, Frederick
    G. Donnan papers, BSL/UCL.
53 Erwin Schrödinger to Max Born, Dublin, Jan. 7, 1944, Max Born papers 704, SPKB.
54 Erwin Schrödinger to Frederick G. Donnan, Dublin, Jan. 26, 1944, original emphasis, Frederick
    G. Donnan papers, BSL/UCL.
55 Erwin Schrödinger to Max Born, Dublin, April 11, 1942, Max Born papers 704, SPKB.
56 Frederick G. Donnan to Max Born, Hartlip, Kent, May 28, 1943, Max Born papers 168, SPKB.

I wish I knew a little more of the various "-ists" (Russell-Wittgenstein-Husserl etc.) you mention. I have always had a frightfully negative attitude toward modern philosophy and have read next to nothing in this direction. I have always considered it, rightly or wrongly, to be old wine in new bags. But I should have to read them, if I wanted to follow your suggestion and write an "Epistemology of Science." And probably it would also turn out to be old [Ernst] Mach-[Richard] Avenarius wine in slightly new, or at least newly mended bags! – You are quite right that most scientists are very naive realists, and if you come with anything else, they believe you have gone off your wits – or alternatively (as you said) gone senile.[57]

Aside from being critical of fads and isms in the philosophy of science, Donnan was particularly upset by the writings of Jeans on the subject. That amused Born, but he was less tolerant of other Cambridge-educated mathematical physicists such as Eddington, Milne, and Whittaker. Born confided to Donnan that Milne had received a prize from the Royal Society of Edinburgh (Whittaker was its president) probably because "the cosmology of Milne rests on the assumption of an absolute zero of time. This is taken by Whittaker, who is an ardent catholic, as a confirmation by science of a definite 'creation' of the world, as described in the bible, only a few million-million of years earlier." Born continued, "I think Milne's theory is still much worse than even Eddingtons: absolute and perfect nonsense."[58]

WHAT IS LIFE?

Schrödinger's denial of quick philosophical answers and easy satisfaction ran very deep, an attitude reinforced by his visceral objection to the finality of the Copenhagen orthodoxy in quantum theory. He spoke about the "Kopenhagen twaddle" and lamented to Donnan the disaster that Bohr's "sham philosophy" had created. Turning to biology made it possible to pursue two goals – exploring the limitations of physics based on statistical laws, while undermining Bohr's authority as an interpreter of the meaning of the new quantum physics.

Schrödinger lectured on this subject at Trinity College, Dublin, in February 1943. The resulting book, *What Is Life?* and, by implication, physics has been assigned a major role in the origin of molecular biology.[59] Evelyn

57 Erwin Schrödinger to Frederick G. Donnan, Dublin, Jan. 15, 1946, Frederick G. Donnan papers, BSL/UCL.
58 Max Born to Frederick G. Donnan, Edinburgh, May 4, 1943, Frederick G. Donnan papers, BSL/UCL; see also Andrew Warwick, "Cambridge Mathematics and Cavendish Physics: Cunningham, Campbell and Einstein's Relativity, 1905–1911: Part I: The Uses of Theory," *Studies in the History and Philosophy of Science* 23 (1992): 625–56.
59 Erwin Schrödinger, *What Is Life?: The Physical Aspect of the Living Cell and Mind and Matter* (originally published as two separate books in 1944 and 1958; reprinted together: Cambridge, 1967);

Fox Keller observes that this problem has an obsessive appeal for historians of science: "Over and over again, we return to the question of just what it was that physics contributed to molecular biology, and we still have not arrived at a fully adequate answer."[60] Forgetting molecular biology for the moment and studying this question from the perspective of Donnan and Schrödinger reveals much about the confluence of forces that affected the development of the émigrés' lives and work.

Donnan published on the phenomena of life at three stages of his life – at the end of World War I, a decade later, and on his retirement. He had also been a chief architect of the Imperial Chemical Industries's émigré support program, which funded Schrödinger's Oxford stay.[61] Schrödinger was delighted when in the mid-1930s, Donnan sent him a paper from 1918 that treated the adequacy of physical chemistry to describe the phenomena of biology. He particularly admired Donnan's "cool way" of addressing determinism. This was an instance of an odd coincidence of ideas of the most important sort. According to Schrödinger's diary, it had been in that very same year – on February 20, 1918 – that he first spoke about determinism and the statistical character of natural laws with the Vienna experimentalist Franz Exner.[62]

Leaving Graz after the Anschluss in difficult circumstances and returning briefly to Oxford, Schrödinger went to the University of Ghent, where he lectured in the winter of 1938–39. At the outbreak of World War II, he needed a transit visa from Belgium to Ireland, where he would become a member of the newly founded Institute for Advanced Studies.[63] Writing for help in acquiring a visa, Schrödinger discussed Donnan's ideas of lawfulness proper to the organic world (*Eigengesetzlichkeit*). He liked Donnan's moderate position, which admitted this as a possibility without assuming that the laws of physics were violated in organic bodies. Schrö-

James D. Watson, *The Double Helix: A Personal Account of the Discovery of the Structure of DNA* (London, 1968), 13.

60 Evelyn Fox Keller, "Physics and the Emergence of Molecular Biology: A History of Cognitive and Political Synergy," *Journal of the History of Biology* 23 (1900): 389; see also Donald Fleming, "Emigré Physicists and the Biological Revolution," *Perspectives in American History* 2 (1968): 152–89; Edward J. Yoxen, "Where Does Schrödinger's *What Is Life?* Belong in the History of Molecular Biology?" *History of Science* 17 (1979): 17–52.

61 Paul K. Hoch and Edward J. Yoxen, "Schrödinger at Oxford: A Hypothetical National Cultural Synthesis which Failed," *Annals of Science* 44 (1987): 607.

62 Erwin Schrödinger to Frederick G. Donnan, no location, Aug. 25, 1935, Frederick G. Donnan papers, BSL/UCL; see also Elisabeth Crawford, "Center-Periphery Relations in Science: The Case of Central Europe," in Crawford, *Nationalism and Internationalism in Science, 1880–1939: Four Studies of the Nobel Population* (Cambridge, 1992), 79–105.

63 Walter Moore, *Schrödinger*, 320–51.

dinger added, "Am I awake or am I dreaming? Are these the most relevant things to discuss four days after the opening of what may turn out to be the last fight of civilised mankind against the inferno? After the beginning of what may eventually be the twilight of civilization or its true dawn?"[64]

Donnan sought Born's and Schrödinger's advice in solving the integral equations that resulted from his latest attack on the problem of life. Advice flowed both ways, enriched with lavish encouragement. Donnan urged Schrödinger to consult with the Dublin professor of biochemistry E.I. Conway regarding technical questions. Schrödinger concluded a letter to Conway by stating: "Maybe, we are here in face of quite a new kind of 'lawfulness' based not at all on large numbers, but on the exact similarity of those molecules present in all cells."[65]

Schrödinger described himself as a passionate Boltzmann-Gibbs physicist, and he called the discovery of the statistical basis of the physical laws of nature the greatest physical discovery of the nineteenth century, perhaps the greatest that was ever made. Now he could confront it with the phenomena of life in a rational and nonmystical way. He was very enthusiastic that there might be such a peculiar arrangement of molecules that "the *ordinary statistical* methods do not apply, on which the ordinary laws of physics are based."[66] Schrödinger was overjoyed that his ideas about biology lined up with Donnan's earlier thoughts on the subject, for that gave him the conviction that his ideas were "substantial, and not just engendered by a lunatic theoretical physicist's brain."[67]

A resolution of the conflict between statistics and the exactness of the new quantum molecular order fueled Schrödinger's excursion into biology. Furthermore, here was a chance to score yet another point in the battle against the Copenhagen orthodoxy. He told Donnan:

I think that a few eminent scientists have puffed up some principles which have turned up in *their* science and which are intimately connected with some fundamental mistake in the methods, preceding them, puffed them up to give rise to a new philosophical aspect of subjectivisme and objectivisme. Those principles are

64 Erwin Schrödinger to Frederick G. Donnan, Sentier des Lapins, La Panne (Belgium), Sept. 7, 1939, Frederick G. Donnan papers, BSL/UCL.
65 Erwin Schrödinger to E. I. Conway, Dublin, Oct. 25, 1942, Frederick G. Donnan papers, BSL/UCL.
66 Erwin Schrödinger to Frederick G. Donnan, Dublin, Oct. 26, 1942, original emphasis, Frederick G. Donnan papers, BSL/UCL.
67 Erwin Schrödinger to Frederick G. Donnan, Dublin, Dec. 15, 1942, Frederick G. Donnan papers, BSL/UCL.

hardly properly understood as yet even *within that science.* I mean e.g. the impossibility of "measuring" at the same time the coordinate and the velocity.

The self-characterized dissenter disliked Bohr's procrustean philosophy of measurement and complementarity. He did not find Bohr's ideas on biology "very fundamental" and there was no need to kill the organism to secure information *"which is none."*[68]

Schrödinger intended to publish *What Is Life?* in Ireland first, but difficulties arose, the most serious being that the Irish publisher could not guarantee publication for both England and indirectly the United States. Schrödinger stressed the latter given the book's "outstanding importance."[69] He entrusted matters to Donnan, who, to his delight, placed the book with Cambridge University Press.[70] Donnan also arranged for this press to publish Born's Durham-Newcastle lecture. Born did not want to offend Eddington, so he pruned the manuscript of sharp remarks and wondered if it should be published inconspicuously. But he feared that if the lecture were published in the *Proceedings of the Durham Philosophical Society* it would suffer the same fate as his inaugural lecture as Tait professor at Edinburgh, which was buried and read by few.[71]

The Donnan connection adds yet another layer of complexity to the much-discussed problem of the role of physics in the emergence of molecular biology. *What Is Life?* might never have cast its spell on later generations had Donnan not encouraged Schrödinger to write it and helped to replicate and circulate it through the extensive distribution network of a major academic publisher. The Donnan connection further makes clear that emigration severed scientific contacts and links with publishers, crucial for the effective dissemination of the gospel of modern physics and mathematics, while at the same time creating new linkages. For Born, this experience was stressful, since he had cultivated extensive contacts with the publisher Ferdinand Springer while in Germany.[72]

---

68 Erwin Schrödinger to Frederick G. Donnan, Dublin, Jan. 24, 1943, original emphasis, Frederick G. Donnan papers, BSL/UCL; see also John L. Heilbron, "The Earliest Missionaries of the Copenhagen Spirit," *Revue d'Histoire des Sciences* 38 (1985): 195–230.

69 Erwin Schrödinger to Frederick G. Donnan, Dublin, Sept. 21, 1943, Frederick G. Donnan papers, BSL/UCL; see also Walter Moore, *Schrödinger*, 401–2.

70 Erwin Schrödinger to Frederick G. Donnan, Dublin, Dec. 23, 1943, also Jan. 5 and March 25, 1946, Frederick G. Donnan papers, BSL/UCL.

71 Max Born to Frederick G. Donnan, Bowness on Windermere, April 1, 1943 and Edinburgh, May 4, 15, 17, 26, and 29, 1943, Frederick G. Donnan papers, BSL/UCL; Max Born, "Some Philosophical Aspects of Modern Physics," *Proceedings of the Royal Society of Edinburgh* 57 (1937): 1–18.

72 Frank Holl, "Produktion und Distribution wissenschaftlicher Literatur, 1913–1933: Der Physiker Max Born und sein Verleger Ferdinand Springer," Ph.D. diss., Ludwig Maximilian Universität, Munich, 1992.

UNITY, RESPONSIBILITY, AND CONTINGENCY

The different relations that Born, Schrödinger, and Weyl each had to philosophy and social responsibility masks an underlying similarity. In exile, they returned repeatedly to the meaning of the science they had collectively wrought and the conflict between order and contingency. This is the background to Born's probabilistic interpretation of quantum mechanics and his critique of Eddington's and Milne's idealistic philosophies of science, and to Schrödinger's excursion into biology and his vehement opposition to Bohr's quantum philosophy.

However much he appreciated it, Schrödinger could not always heed Donnan's advice on biology. A few months before he delivered the Dublin lectures on biology and physics, the holy grail had beckoned. Referring to his discovery of wave mechanics at Christmas 1925, he told Donnan:

[T]he Good God has favored me by a Xmas-present, similar only to the one He gave me, also precisely at Xmas, in 1925. I think I am not exaggerating, if I say: He revealed to me *the* unitary theory of gravitation and electrodynamics (and *very probably* more than that, viz. the meson-field and the fields of the Dirac-type).

Schrödinger found this state of affairs quite miraculous, and would not have believed it if he "did not clearly discern the point where an insidious little intricacy of Nature let my illustrious predecessors end up with a near miss."[73]

Schrödinger was no revolutionary in physics and philosophy; what convinced him of the soundness of his field theory was the fact "that it is the straight-forward continuation of the work of Weyl-Eddington-Einstein in the years 1918–1923. It just re-adjusts a mistake, which had stopped the further development in 1923. The intimate bearing Born's 1934 theory had on the whole matter escaped everybody, including Born." He told Donnan that this was the best unified field theory one could produce on a classical basis. In December 1943, Schrödinger was still rather upbeat and added that in Edinburgh, the true quantum problem of fields was being attacked by Born and his co-worker H. W. Peng.[74]

Writing to Hedwig and Max Born the following year, Helene Weyl noted that, in spite of asthma and hay fever, Hermann Weyl had enjoyed the summer spent in the Rocky Mountains:

73 Erwin Schrödinger to Frederick G. Donnan, Dublin, Jan. 15, 1943, original emphasis, Frederick G. Donnan papers, BSL/UCL.
74 Erwin Schrödinger to Frederick G. Donnan, Dublin, Oct. 24 and Dec. 23, 1943, Frederick G. Donnan papers, BSL/UCL.

However, he has been able to work to his heart's desire, to do a lot of reading, to draw a little, and to go on long trips up to altitudes of *10 000* to *12 000* feet. The results of his research will, I expect, soon come to your knowledge. I only gathered from occasional remarks that he waged war against Birkhoff's trespasses into theory of relativity, and that he somehow joined you and Schrödinger in your [unified field] theories. Altogether I suppose, we have had as much happiness as can be had by a mathematician, who, having tasted the almost god-like pleasure of creativity in a grand manner, cannot but find ordinary mortal occupations flat, stale and unprofitable.[75]

Weyl had arrived in the United States spiritually and physically exhausted. He told a close friend three years later, "I was always in danger of losing myself, because of what was expected of me. I believe that this critical period is behind me, and now I find that I do almost as much as I have the strength for."[76] When Weyl regained some of his strength, he concentrated his efforts on relatively pure mathematics (for example, *The Classical Groups* [1939]), guiding young mathematicians and helping refugees. He suffered from asthma, and the early 1940s had been none too good in that respect. He found it increasingly difficult to do anything "beyond the limited round of my duties, beyond helping refugees to get on their feet again, and answering now and then the calls of my tyrant, mistress Mathesis."[77] Weyl emphasized the break with the past and his turning away from physics when he told a biographer of Eddington's in 1953 that "it is now more than 20 years that I ceased to follow the development of theoretical physics and the various speculative attempts at establishing a unified theory."[78]

This statement is false, for Weyl dipped into physics when he "waged war" against the Harvard mathematician George D. Birkhoff, but true insofar as he early lost faith in unified field theories and did not explore new avenues in theoretical physics after emigrating. Weyl's kind of physics – high theory – had fallen on hard times. "There was a complete deadlock in the more fundamental parts of theoretical physics," Born told Donnan in 1944, "and I think that Dirac's desperate efforts did more to accentuate than to solve it. I am pretty sure that our method is headed in the right direction." Yet illness and exhaustion prevented Born and Peng, who also worked with Schrödinger during the war, from elabo-

75   Helene Weyl to Hedwig and Max Born, Estes Park, Colorado, Sept. 10, 1944, Max Born papers 1264, SPKB.
77   Hermann Weyl to Max Born, Princeton, N.J., Dec. 9, 1942, Max Born papers 837, SPKB.
76   Hermann Weyl to Erich Hecke, April 21, 1936, Hermann Weyl papers HS 91:258, ELAZ.
78   Hermann Weyl to A. Vibert Douglas, Zurich, Oct. 31, 1953, Hermann Weyl papers HS 91:173, ELAZ.

rating a new method of field quantification, which Born thought "indeed important."[79]

Meanwhile, nuclear physics blasted ahead in the 1930s, propelled by new facts and technologies. Other parts of physics, such as solid state physics and superconductivity, prospered, but fundamental theoretical physics dealing with elementary constituents of matter and radiation was beset with grave problems and languished in the doldrums. Several young émigré theoreticians jumped on the nuclear physics bandwagon, while some of the old guard opted for unified field theory or "abandoned" physics altogether.[80]

Weyl noted on the occasion of Wolfgang Pauli's 1945 Nobel Prize the respect and genuine interest for experimental facts in all their puzzling complexity that made Pauli a physicist despite his proximity to mathematics. Weyl evinced wonder at how the theoretical physicist endured waiting for a decisive breakthrough during stagnant periods when new facts were being accumulated by the experimentalists. The mathematician had an easier lot and did not have to face the hard facts of nature. "If the mathematician cannot solve a problem, he modifies it until he can solve it; no impenetrable reality limits the freedom of his imagination."[81]

In his riposte to Birkhoff, Weyl emphasized which facts were important to a Born-Schrödinger-Weyl theorist. The fundamental fact that electric charge was not universally proportional to the inertial mass of bodies as is their gravitational mass was supported by daily experience and the most refined experiment. It had led Einstein to the conception that inertia and gravitation were one, and thus to his theory of general relativity. This fact was codified in the principle of equivalence and expressed the unity of nature.[82]

Weyl concluded his encomium for Pauli by pointing to another fact of experience that raised profound issues. Science was used both for the benefit and detriment of humankind, its technical applications were employed to build and destroy. "To what extent shall and can the theorist take responsibility for the practical consequences of his discoveries? What a beautiful theoretical edifice is quantum physics – and what a terrible thing is the

79 Max Born to Frederick G. Donnan, Edinburgh, March 2, 1933, Frederick G. Donnan papers, BSL/UCL; see, e.g., Mac Born and H. W. Peng, "Quantam Mechanics of Fields: I. Pure Fields," *Proceedings of the Royal Society of Edinburgh* 62 (1944): 40–57.

80 Roger H. Stuewer, "Nuclear Physicists in a New World: The Emigrés of the 1930s in America," *Berichte zur Wissenschaftsgeschichte* 7 (1984): 23–40.

81 Hermann Weyl, "Encomium (Wolfgang Pauli)" (1946), in Hermann Weyl, *Gesammelte Abhandlungen*, 4:266–7.

82 Hermann Weyl, "Comparison of a Degenerate Form of Einstein's with Birkhoff's Theory of Gravitation" (1944), in Weyl, *Gesammelte Abhandlungen*, 4:213.

atomic bomb!"[83] The Princeton Bicentennial Conference in 1946 gave
ample opportunity for celebration and introspection. Weyl spoke about
outstanding mathematical events of his lifetime and returned to the question
of social responsibility:

We may well envy the nineteenth century for the feeling of certainty and the
pathos with which it praised the sacrosanctity and supreme value of science and
the mind's dispassionate quest for truth and light. We are addicted to mathematical
research with no less fervor. But for us, alas!, its meaning and value are questioned
from the theoretical side by the critique of the foundations of mathematics, and
from the practical-social side by the deadly menace of its misuse.[84]

Weyl criticized the attitude that mathematicians play a nice game that
need not be taken too seriously as fundamentally unsound. The English
mathematician G.H. Hardy and Schrödinger liked to assume this pose.
Weyl stressed that real mathematics was neither useless nor harmless, as
Hardy had claimed in his melancholy wartime defense of pure mathematics.[85] Yet Hardy was not unpolitical. His devotion to the émigré cause in
the 1930s and support of internationalism in the 1920s speaks volumes for
his social responsibility and political awareness. He and Weyl were united
in helping refugees. Weyl threw himself into the rescue effort with a resolve
strengthened by his political sensitivity; for him, aiding émigrés and saving
European culture was a mission.[86] His action was not confined to the few
and eminent, but they were important to him, since he felt that the highest
form of intellectual achievement was frequently embodied and preserved
in a few individuals.[87]

It was the task of the gifted individual to synthesize. This was stressed by
Schrödinger in 1944. A truly worthwhile event in the history of human
thought was the realization that discontinuity in inanimate and living matter
was virtually the same thing. This product of the specialized research of
Planck in physics and Hugo de Vries in biology would have gone unnoticed
without synthesis. The development of science was, according to Schrö-

83   Hermann Weyl, "Encomium," 267.
84   Hermann Weyl, "Bicentennial Conference," Hermann Weyl papers HS 91a:18, ELAZ; see also
     Eugene P. Wigner, "Foreword," in *Physical Science and Human Values* (Princeton, 1947), v–vi.
85   Hermann Weyl, "Bicentennial Conference," Hermann Weyl papers HS 91a:17, ELAZ; the ref-
     erence to Hardy and Schrödinger is crossed out in this draft version; see also Godfrey H. Hardy,
     A Mathematician's Apology (Cambridge, 1940; reprinted: Cambridge, 1967).
86   Robin E. Rider, "Alarm and Opportunity: Emigration of Mathematicians and Physicists to Britain
     and the United States, 1933–1945," *Historical Studies in the Physical Sciences* 15, no. 1 (1984): 107–
     76; Nathan Reingold, "Refugee Mathematicians in the United States of America, 1933–1941:
     Reception and Reaction," *Annals of Science* 38 (1981): 313–38.
87   See José Ortega y Gasset, *The Revolt of the Masses* (New York, 1930; reprinted: New York, 1932),
     57; Fritz Stern, "Einstein's Germany," in Stern, *Dreams and Delusions: The Drama of German History*
     (New York, 1987; reprinted: New York, 1989), 25–50.

dinger, "a continual staggering between increasing specialization and attempts to regain the general outlook of a 'scientist,' nay of a *thinking human being*." This was a difficult situation, he told his listeners:

Being a highly specialized scientist myself I can assure you that the combination is not easy. *Yet we must never cease to strive for it.* The moment we sacrifice one outlook to the other, the advancement of knowledge would stop short within a very few decades.[88]

Weyl had wrestled with the question of causality in physics and the foundation of mathematics at the end of World War I. Hence he had little difficulty in accepting the novelty of the new quantum mechanics in the years 1925 to 1927. Philosophy was neither a cultural ornament nor an instrument for securing intellectual property rights, as it was partly for Born and Schrödinger; it played an active constitutive role in his scientific practice. In the 1920s philosophy of science began to branch off from Weyl's interests and to achieve an independent status. With the contraction of his research interests in the 1930s and emigration to a new linguistic environment, Weyl put philosophy aside, but he returned to it in an aesthetic and reflective mode in the late 1940s. He recognized that he had lost his earlier conviction and told Born in 1949 that his philosophical views were more uncertain than during his enthusiastic younger days.[89] In exile Weyl remained distant from the ongoing disputes concerning the foundations of mathematics (engendered by Gödel's discoveries) and the heated debates concerning the Copenhagen interpretation of quantum mechanics, whereas Born and Schrödinger entered the fray on opposite sides.

The probabilistic interpretation of quantum mechanics, for which Born received the Nobel Prize in 1954, was not of central importance to him philosophically until the late 1940s, and his understanding of its implications was often unorthodox, for example, in his work on quantum electrodynamics.[90] In the early 1940s, Born still did not see himself as a philosopher, and he told Donnan: "I am a simple physicist and I can judge general principles only according to their real usefulness in producing results."[91]

---

88 Erwin Schrödinger, "The Bearing of Physics on Heredity, Mutation, and Evolution," manuscript for a lecture in Cork, Ireland, Jan. 16, 1944, original emphasis, AHQP.
89 Hermann Weyl to Max Born, Princeton, N.J., Dec. 10, 1949, Max Born papers 837, SPKB.
90 Hermann Weyl, "Observations on Hilbert's Independence Theorem and Born's Quantization of Field Equations" (1934), in Weyl, *Gesammelte Abhandlungen*, 3:416–19; Nancy Cartwright, "Max Born and the Reality of Quantum Probabilities," in Lorenz Krüger, Gerd Gigerenzer, and Mary S. Morgan, eds., *The Probabilistic Revolution*, vol. 2: *Ideas in the Sciences* (Cambridge, Mass., 1987), 409–16.
91 Max Born to Frederick G. Donnan, Edinburgh, May 4, 1943, Frederick G. Donnan papers, BSL/UCL.

After Born's Durham–Newcastle lecture, his self-confidence grew and he became more assertive philosophically as the 1940s drew to a close, as is illustrated in his controversy with Einstein over determinism and causality. Later, Born would also assume an increasingly prominent role as a spokesman for the political responsibility of scientists.

This quest for the meaning of science is also the message of Weyl's last book, *Symmetry*. In it he tried, among other things, to understand the clash between classical unified field theory and the quantum–nuclear world order – that is, to explore the limits of deterministic physics: "If nature were all lawfulness then every phenomenon would share the full symmetry of the universal laws of nature as formulated by the theory of relativity. The mere fact that this is not so proves that *contingency* is an essential feature of the world."[92] Weyl illustrated the irreconcilable tension between order and chance by quoting the following passage:

Yet each [snow crystal] in itself – this was the uncanny, the antiorganic, the life-denying character of them all – each of them was absolutely symmetrical, icily regular in form. They were too regular, as substance adapted to life never was to this degree – the living principle shuddered at this perfect precision, found it deathly, the very marrow of death – Hans Castorp felt he understood now the reason why the builders of antiquity purposely and secretly introduced minute variation from absolute symmetry in their columnar structures.[93]

This scene from Thomas Mann's *Magic Mountain* (1924) is a portent symbol for the world that Born, Schrödinger, and Weyl left behind. In the mountains they sought release from the disease of civilization; in unified field theories and in the icy realm of crystals they sought transcendence.[94] Yet they came to realize that life and nature were not governed by a precise mathematical order, and that contingency and disorder had their place in the world. This message was reinforced by the series of political upheavals – World War I, the world economic depression, Hitler's rise to power, World War II – that unsettled their lives and eventually thrust them into exile. They lived through many migrations, not a single one in that fateful year 1933, and dealt with various themes during their long careers; the tension between order and contingency haunted them, and trying to come to terms with its meaning brought some unity and coherence to their lives.

92 Hermann Weyl, *Symmetry* (Princeton, N.J., 1952), 26, original emphasis.
93 Hermann Weyl, *Symmetry*, 64–5.
94 See also Paul Forman, "Independence, Not Transcendence, for the Historian of Science," *Isis* 82 (1991): 71–86.

3

Emigration from Country and Discipline: The Journey of a German Physicist into American Photosynthesis Research

ALAN D. BEYERCHEN

James Franck (1882–1964) was a renowned, Nobel Prize-winning director of a world-class physics institute when the National Socialists came to power. For half a century he had lived as a Jew among the Germans, and for three decades he had worked as a German among the world's scientists. His life changed irrevocably when in April 1933 he publicly resigned his university position in political protest against the policies of the new regime.

Yet in another important sense, the patterns of a lifetime could not and did not change overnight. The characteristics of personality and intellect that had made Franck so successful were not shattered. If anything, they were further fused in the crucible of dramatic change. Yet in being applied to new conditions they faced unexpected challenges. Here lies one value of the biographical approach, for the mixture of stability and instability in the life of a single person underscores the complexity of emigration at every scale of analysis.

One of the striking aspects of Franck's life was his frequent role as a mediator across social and disciplinary boundaries, especially those of German-Jewish identity and of theoretical-experimental styles of scientific research. It was not that he stood on one side reaching out to the other, but that he positioned himself in the midst of complex interactions and reached out to both sides. He was therefore accustomed to tuning his hearing to the differing vocabularies and values among his friends, acquaintances, students, co-workers, and peers. He was also accustomed to shifting his position constructively in response to the mainstream of activity around him. Both habits were to stand him in excellent stead when he was forced to depart Germany.

Franck was born in Hamburg, whose complicated tradition of cosmopolitanism and provincialism remains remarkable even today. His father was a banker, and already his name ("James" was his given name, not an Anglicization) was a sign of the strength of cosmopolitan influences in his family. Although Jewish, his formal education was secular, which for him meant embracing things modern more than it meant turning his back on his Jewish cultural heritage. As he explained in an interview late in his life:

The point is just that, my grandparents were very orthodox Jews. My parents were not orthodox Jews, but there was no doubt that we were of Jewish descent and that we wanted to remain Jews.[1]

Jewish he remained, but through cultural rather than religious affiliation. Throughout his life he declined membership in Jewish religious or social organizations, even when they sought him out.

Instead, Franck was a German of Jewish religious background – a "German citizen of the Jewish faith," as the phrase commonly put it. During student and doctoral research in physics in Berlin (1900–1906), postdoctoral research years in the physics institute of the same university (1907–1919), voluntary service in uniform during the war (1914–1918), and directorship of the second physical institute in what has often been called the "beautiful years" of the development of quantum mechanics in Göttingen (1920–1933), there was never any doubt about his commitment to things German. Yet his attitude was always that of acceptance of German identity without an assimilationist's rejection of Jewish identity.

An example of Franck's comfort with his ambiguous identity is an incident that transpired at the front during the war. He had already been decorated for bravery and was evidently exceptionally competent, for he was selected on merit to receive an officer's commission. In the same interview he recounted the discomfort of some of the officers whose ranks he would join:

Later, one of the officers in the army, when he heard that I would become an officer asked if I would do him the favor to get baptized. And I smiled and asked whether he believed that I would be a better officer if against my own conviction I would be baptized to do him a favor. And he couldn't help to say he doesn't think so, but anyway it would show that I do belong to them. I said that I feel that I belong here, whether I am an officer or not. I have not asked for it. If they want to make me an officer, it is all right with me.[2]

---

1   Interview of James Franck by Thomas Kuhn, third session, July 11, 1962, 17. This session was one of six conducted July 9–14, 1962, for the Sources for History of Quantum Physics Project. These interviews are now in the Archive for History of Quantum Physics (hereafter AHQP), deposited with the American Philosophical Society in Philadelphia and elsewhere.
2   Ibid.

This disarming smile and the unabashed question that went to the heart of the matter were typical for Franck, as was his willingness to take a stand in the face of authority. But just as typical was his firm sense of identity that others would have to accept him as he was – and they almost always did.

Franck's ability to ask the crucial question was intimately related to his skill as a keen listener and interpreter across boundaries. Perhaps at a deep level he was more comfortable living on the cultural boundary than many other German Jews (or "Germans of Jewish descent," a relationship of noun and modifier that was common at the time but from which the Holocaust has estranged us). To resolve his ambiguous identity as German would have meant abandonment and denial of his family, and to resolve it as Jewish would have meant to abandon German culture and society. The brutal clarification that came for him under the Nazis was hardly of his own choosing, and he did not believe that most other Germans wanted it either. This belief accounted in part for the manner in which he was to resign his university post in 1933.

When discussing German Jews it is commonplace to assert that their unsettled identity was an important motivation for their disproportionate success in many professions. They were outsiders in their chosen society, never fully accepted as German. Historian Fritz Stern is among those who have noted that "the need to excel was instilled by tradition and nurtured by hostility," and that "hidden wounds inspired visible achievement."[3] The result, he has suggested, was a deep ambivalence among German Jews about themselves and their place in German society.[4]

One implication of the lack of their full acceptance among Germans was that Jews were effectively permanent immigrants in German society long before the Nazis made use of this fact. Yet Franck seemed more driven by the desire to prove to his pragmatic father the value of science as a career than by an awareness of the dynamics of his status as a "marginal man" of contemporary sociological theory.[5] Furthermore, science was for Franck as inherently cosmopolitan as his own life in Hamburg or Berlin. An added personal facet was that although he took a Jewish bride in 1907, she was a Swedish pianist from Göteborg. There was little evidence of ambivalence about his cultural status – his sense of self was resilient and strong enough that he was comfortable among unsettled social boundaries. There was thus for Franck an important element of stability among the uncertainties of his life as a German Jew and Jewish German.

3 Fritz Stern, *Dreams and Delusions: The Drama of German History* (New York, 1987), 109.
4 Ibid., 111.
5 See Robert E. Park, "Human Migration and the Marginal Man," *The American Journal of Sociology* 33 (1927–28): 881–93.

Franck was also a skilled mediator and interpreter across the complex boundary between theoretical and experimental modes of research. In these dimensions, too, his identity was ambiguous. In the series of joint experiments that led to the Nobel Prize, he played theoretician to Gustav Hertz's experimentalism. In the Göttingen period, he was an experimentalist in the close relationships with his theoretician friends Max Born in Göttingen and Niels Bohr in Denmark. Later, in photosynthesis research in the United States, he once again donned the mantle of theoretician. He was famed for his ability to perceive quickly the experimental implications of theoretical issues and to clarify the meaning of new experiments for theoretical advances. Late in his life he described his contribution to the events of the Göttingen years as his ability to draw together gifted pupils and to "see early that some theoretical questions could be decided by simple experiments. In the process, a certain understanding of theory was helpful."[6]

A striking attribute of Franck's conduct of science was the interactive mode of his thought. He understood science as a social process rather than as a body of information. He kept in continual written contact with an astonishing variety of researchers elsewhere, and he received visitors and traveled widely and often. In Göttingen, in particular, the flow of scientists in and out of his laboratory and his home was virtually unceasing. Good thinking was for him a good conversation, a fact reflected in most of his publications. A tally of his scientific papers indicates that fifty-eight were independently authored, six of them had three co-authors, and ninety-five were jointly authored with another researcher.[7] Even many of the papers he wrote on his own were results of conversations, explanations, and oral negotiations of research thickets in his office or laboratory. Many of those who knew him have described how Franck would collect a conversation partner at almost any time and animatedly work through a problem in front of a blackboard. One of these was physicist Walter Elsasser, who has written that his idea of a scientist's paradise would be sitting on one end of the battered sofa in Franck's Göttingen office, with Franck on the other end and a lively discussion in between.[8] Perhaps Franck's role as an interpreter contributed to his oral mode of work, for talking allowed him to achieve

---

6 "Mein eigenes Verdienst war mehr dass ich es relativ gut verstand begabte Schüler heranzuziehen und früh zu sehen dass einige Fragen der Theorie durch einfache Experimente entschieden werden konnten. Ein gewisses Verständnis der Theorie half dabei." James Franck to Aksel Faber, n.d. [1963], Papers of James Franck in the Joseph Regenstein Library, University of Chicago, B [box] 2, F [folder] 9. See also Franck's various descriptions of the interaction of theory with experiment in the interviews by Thomas Kuhn.

7 From the list of publications in Mary Janzen Wilson, *Guide to the James Franck Papers* (Chicago, 1976), 124–33.

8 Walter Elsasser, *Memoirs of a Physicist in the Atomic Age* (New York and Bristol, 1978), 44.

a flexibility and fluidity among persons, camps, ideas, and traditions not readily attained in writing. Much like his German-Jewish identity, a certain stability was noticeable in the pattern of instability in Franck's life on the boundary between theory and experiment.

Among the most crucial continuities during the crisis of emigration was the cohesion of Franck's family. Here was both shelter and support. His father had retired in the prewar period and moved from Hamburg to Berlin to be closer to his children and grandchildren. Nothing gave James greater pleasure than to share important occasions with family members, and he was particularly pleased that his father had lived long enough to see the success he achieved with the Nobel Prize. The close-knit warmth in his family circle was one of the constants in Franck's life. It was unsurprising that he took no significant step without consultation among his family members and closest friends. By 1933, both his daughters were married to non-Jewish husbands, one of whom was an assistant in the Göttingen laboratory. The responsibility to family and the strength from loved ones was enormously sustaining among Franck and his family members in the years of exile and emigration.

Another major continuity was the financial support Franck received from the Rockefeller philanthropies. Implementing its policy of "making the peaks higher" in areas of science likely to benefit all humankind, in 1924 the International Education Board (IEB) granted $7,540 to Franck, Born, and Robert Pohl for an addition to the physics building and other matters related to hosting IEB fellows in Göttingen. In 1926 there followed a massive grant from the IEB for the mathematics and physics institutes ($275,000 for mathematics and $75,000 for physics), complemented by $375,000 from the Prussian government. In addition, a number of Franck's pupils went to the United States under IEB auspices, and a number of Rockefeller fellows arrived from America in Göttingen. In 1931, Franck received approximately $2,300 from the Rockefeller Foundation for his own research needs. And in 1932 the Trustees approved a $50,000 grant for the Institute for Inorganic Chemistry, with Franck as the primary faculty contact with the Rockefeller representatives.[9] In 1932, the scientific leaders in Berlin had convinced this foundation that Berlin should be as well supported as Göttingen. The director of a new Kaiser Wilhelm Institute for Physics was to be Franck, who would also have a post at the university. Negotiations for

---

9 The files on these projects are in the Rockefeller Archive Center in North Tarrytown, New York. A convenient summary of the totals is contained in "Report on Rockefeller Activities in Germany, June 22, 1933," Rockefeller Foundation record group, 1.1, 717 Program and Policy, box 7, folder 36.

Franck to leave Göttingen were well under way when the Nazis came to power.[10] Continued Rockefeller support for Frank abroad, first in Bohr's laboratory in Copenhagen in 1934–35 and then at Johns Hopkins University in Baltimore until 1938, was an important feature of Franck's experience of emigration.

When the Civil Service Law of April 7, 1933, was promulgated, most of Franck's friends looked to the limitations it contained (for example, exemptions for war veterans) and hoped to hold out at their positions. Franck, however, immediately recognized the import of the situation. Following intense discussion in his home, in which some of his colleagues tried to dissuade him from resigning, Franck decided to step down from his professorship on the grounds that he was opposed to the new government's policy toward Jews. In his official letter to the university administration of April 17, which he leaked to the remaining independent Göttingen newspaper, he stressed three points. One was that he wished to remain scientifically active in Germany if possible. The second was that his protest was in response to the treatment of "Germans of Jewish descent" as enemies of the fatherland. He did not refer to "Jews who were German citizens" or to "German Jews" but to Germans like himself who had a Jewish heritage. The third was the prospect of limited opportunities for his children in the German future. Formally expressing concern for the impact of events on the children was striking – how many others, had they spoken up, would have phrased things this way? Expressions of support poured into his home.[11]

Although Franck's original preference was to remain in Germany under the auspices of the Kaiser Wilhelm Society and the new Berlin institute promised by the Rockefeller Foundation, it soon became apparent that some other course would be necessary. For a time he considered seeking a post in the chemical industry, but that prospect also faded.[12] By early August, he had agreed to gain some perspective by briefly visiting the Johns Hopkins University in Baltimore, where R.W. Wood, an old friend from the Berlin years, was located. He also was courted by Bohr, who saw an

10 Fritz Haber to James Franck, Feb. 14, 1931, June 8, 1932, Nov. 22, 1932, in Franck papers, B 3, F 9.
11 A translation of the letter and a description of events is in Alan D. Beyerchen, *Scientists under Hitler: Politics and the Physics Community in the Third Reich* (London and New Haven, Conn., 1977), 15–19. There were outraged public expressions from the Nazis, of course, but the personal letters of support from strangers fill two folders in the Franck collection, with another folder of responses from friends and acquaintances, Franck papers, B 7, F 5–7.
12 James Franck to Walther Gerlach, May 3, 1933, Gerlach Nachlass, Deutsches Museum, Munich.

opportunity to support his friend in need and to use Franck's presence to secure additional funding from the Rockefeller Foundation for new initiatives in his Copenhagen laboratory. Franck was clearly relieved and pleased at the prospect of remaining close to Germany and to the home of his wife. Yet he had some reservations that were quite revealing.

In a letter to Bohr in August 1933, Franck expressed two major concerns about going to Copenhagen. The first was personal, born of his desire to gather together his children and his children's children around him – a tendency his Göttingen friend and mathematics colleague Richard Courant termed his "Abraham longings" (*Abraham-Gelüste*).[13] It would not be easy to live away from other family members. However, separation seemed temporarily unavoidable (one daughter and son-in-law were about to leave for Istanbul). Thus a second, professional reservation was more serious. He could not be sure he would produce much of scientific value and justify the expense and effort on his behalf. If Bohr wanted him to come anyway, at least he had been warned.[14]

Coming from the man who had been selected to oversee construction and operation of the newest physics institute in Germany, this seems a strange admission. Franck was well known for his quiet unpretentiousness, and perhaps this is the explanation. Perhaps he was feeling his age. Yet he was also extraordinarily self-aware and quite capable of assessing his own strengths as well as weaknesses. In view of the fact that his stay in Copenhagen from April 1934 to the summer of 1935 was indeed not terribly productive, more explanation is needed.

Usually scholars stress the importance of dislocation of those forced to leave their homeland, but in this case it may be useful to consider whether Franck's field had actually emigrated away from him. He had made his mark in science by conducting experiments of decisive importance in the context of contemporary theory. Using the simplest means possible – electrons and light – he systematically explored atoms and molecules. He always studied the energy exchange among particles, whether it was kinetic energy and light energy (the essence of the Franck-Hertz experiments) or the light energy in photochemistry (which was the focus of much of the Göttingen work) or light energy in photosynthesis. In Göttingen, the issue was not only emission and absorption of light quanta, but the progression to the increasingly complicated matters of fluorescence, phosphorescence, and

13 James Franck to Niels Bohr, Aug. 7, 1933, Franck papers, B 1, F 5. On Bohr's desire to have Franck join him, see Finn Aaserud, *Redirecting Science: Niels Bohr, Philanthropy and the Rise of Nuclear Physics* (Cambridge, 1990), 124–36.
14 Ibid.

chemiluminescence. The key principle was always study of the energy exchange.[15]

But the shape of the field of atomic physics had begun to change already at the end of the 1920s. With the spread of the quantum mechanics revolution into chemistry with the 1927 work of Walter Heitler and Fritz London, studies of chemical bonding were becoming increasingly theoretical. The synthesis of quantum mechanics with relativity by P.A.M. Dirac by the end of 1929 brought a kind of closure to the level of theory Franck was ready to follow. Many German physicists began to search for new directions in which to explore, often drawn toward the structure of the nucleus, but for others, the heyday of atomic theory was past. When Max Born wrote to a colleague at the California Institute of Technology in April 1931 concerning a possible visit there, he observed that changes in physics over the preceding few years meant that he had nothing really new to offer the Americans. In a following letter, he noted – while Franck's laboratory was still operating at full tilt in the same building as his own institute – that a contemporary physicist really needed to visit America every couple of years, because the best experiments were being conducted there, and even the American theoreticians had much to offer.[16] In contrast, during the 1920s it had been necessary for a contemporary physicist to visit Göttingen. One wonders whether such a remark from a man so close to Franck reflects discussion between them about the state and future of the kind of work that had been performed so successfully in Göttingen.

Nuclear physics was the field that attracted many of the brightest of the younger researchers who had passed through Göttingen. The 1931 Rome conference on the subject had been a sign that Enrico Fermi and his associates were in an excellent position to take the lead in this area even before the discovery of the neutron in early 1932. The Solvay conference in Belgium in 1933 and another in London in October 1934 were indications of the growing interest in the nucleus.

The other field that attracted imaginative atomic physicists on the move was biophysics. The Second International Light Congress held in Copenhagen in August 1932 offered Bohr the opportunity to present his views on the relationship between physics and biology. He opened the five-day affair with a lecture, "Light and Life," in which he stressed the differing conditions under which animate and inanimate phenomena could be studied. His primary analogy was between the indivisibility of the quantum of

15 Interview of James Franck by Thomas Kuhn, fifth session, July 13, 1962, 12–13, AHQP.
16 Max Born to Theodor von Kármán, March 27, 1931 and June 4, 1931, California Institute of Technology Archives, Theodor von Kármán papers, box 4 – Born.

action in physics and the irreducibility of life in biology, since the necessity of keeping an object alive imposes restrictions that inhibit total analysis. Perhaps the greatest effect of his talk was to induce physicist and later Nobel Prize winner Max Delbrück to become a leading advocate of his position and one of the key figures in twentieth-century molecular biology.[17]

Both nuclear physics and biology played a role in Franck's arrival in Copenhagen in April 1934. Bohr's initial response to the political crisis in Germany was to try to aid younger researchers by arranging fellowships for them from the Rockefeller Foundation and the Danish Committee for the Support of Refugee Intellectual Workers. But in 1933 a new focus on quantitative biology in the natural sciences division of the Rockefeller Foundation opened the prospect for a major infusion of funding and talent into Bohr's institute.[18] With the construction of particle accelerators in Berkeley and elsewhere in 1931–32, and the discovery of artificial radio-activity in Paris in early 1934, it seemed obvious that the emphasis of Bohr's institute should be on experimental nuclear physics. Yet the Rockefeller program stressed biology. With foundation support, Franck's task was to turn the institute in the direction of nuclear problems, while fellow refugee George Hevesy would generate a program of radioactive biomedical tracers. Bohr sought to use the talents and reputations of both men to compensate for the migration of the research forefront in physics from theory to ex-periment.[19]

Although Franck attempted to carry out his assignment, and work was a welcome diversion from worries about the political situation in Germany, he was forced to learn the vocabulary and techniques in an increasingly crowded intellectual realm. Moreover, he found that his access to equip-ment and assistance in nuclear research was limited. On the side, therefore, he soon set out with his new assistant, a young refugee molecular spec-troscopist named Hilda Levi, to study the fluorescence of green leaves.[20] This was a natural continuation of his Göttingen work, and in fact he had already published a short note on the fluorescence of leaves in which he

---

17 Abraham Pais, *Niels Bohr's Times, in Physics, Philosophy, and Polity* (Oxford, 1991), 441–2; Finn Aaserud, *Redirecting Science*, 90–7; Ernst Peter Fischer and Carol Lipson, *Thinking about Science: Max Delbrück and the Origins of Molecular Biology* (New York and London, 1988), 78–102. In general, for the physics of the period, see Abraham Pais, *Inward Bound: Of Matter and Forces in the Physical World* (Oxford, 1986).

18 See Robert E. Kohler, "The Management of Science: The Experience of Warren Weaver and the Rockefeller Foundation Program in Molecular Biology," *Minerva* 14 (Autumn 1976): 279–306; and Kohler, *Partners in Science: Foundations and Natural Scientists, 1900–1945* (Chicago, 1991), 265–303.

19 This is a major thesis of Aaserud's *Redirecting Science.*

20 Finn Aaserud, *Redirecting Science*, 149.

indicated need for an improvement of the physics in studying the effects observed. According to Levi, the reason for the green leaves was that they were readily available and that chlorophyll made a good fluorescing solution. Franck was not really interested in photosynthesis but in the energy changes characterizing the photochemistry involved. The questions that animated him were of physics, not plant physiology.[21] Eventually, two papers on the fluorescence of chlorophyll emerged from their collaboration, and the course of Franck's future work was set.[22] His efforts in nuclear physics continued to be hampered by poor facilities and the fact that his best idea was scooped by someone else who published it in *Nature*.[23]

One of the most important aspects of Franck's exile in Denmark was his inability to completely escape the need to think about politics, which resulted in his learning a very important vocabulary for an émigré. He had always found Bohr a touchstone not only in physics but other matters such as politics as well. The discussions surrounding the arrival of refugees and visitors from Germany, as well as the holding of conferences, were peppered with concerns for the future of German and European science. Franck had renounced his professorship in April 1933, and had been officially relieved of duties in early 1934. A year later, his successor had not yet been appointed, and a visitor to Göttingen noted that "Franck's institute is, of course, in a sad state as there are only one or two graduate students remaining."[24] Yet Franck still hoped developments in the Third Reich would moderate. When another visitor expressed dismay that Germans in the Saar had voted in the January 1935 plebiscite to reunite with Germany, Franck said he would have done the same thing – and then emigrated. The Nazis were a temporary phenomenon, he argued, whereas the reunification with Germany was permanent.[25] But at the same time, he had decided it was unlikely that his sons-in-law would find positions in Denmark. They – and he – would have to settle in the United States.[26]

The result of the relative quiet, the long discussions, and the continued political and professional turbulence was a deeper understanding by Franck

21 Interview with Hilda Levi by the author, Copenhagen, Nov. 12, 1980.
22 James Franck and Hilda Levi, "Zum Mechanismus der Sauerstoff-Aktivierung durch fluoreszenz-fähige Farbstoffe," *Die Naturwissenschaften* 23 (1935): 226–9; Franck and Levi, "Beitrag zur Untersuchung der Fluorescenz in Flüssigkeiten," *Zeitschrift für physikalische Chemie* B27 (1935): 409–20.
23 James Franck to Max Born, Jan. 8, 1935, copy in Franck papers, B 1, F 7. See interview of James Franck by Thomas Kuhn, sixth session, July 14, 1962, 1, AHQP.
24 Frank Spedding to G. N. Lewis, Jan. 26, 1935, University of California, Berkeley, Archives, CU-30, College of Chemistry, box 4.
25 Interview with Herbert Busemann by the author, May 10, 1972, Santa Ynez, Calif.
26 James Franck to Max Born, Jan. 8, 1935, Franck papers, B 1, F 7.

of the need for personal political action to defend his position on the German-Jewish boundary against imposed resolution. The period of introspection also underlay Franck's later concern for the social and political implications of atomic weapons and energy, manifested most obviously in the famous "Franck Report" of June 1945. In this document, Manhattan Project scientists advocated an alternative to bombing Japanese population centers and warned of an atomic arms race in the post-World War II era. The Copenhagen years furthermore framed his response to the German ambassador in 1964, to whom Franck wrote: "What has happened in our lifetime stems, I believe, from the fact that the people as a whole have left the solution of political questions chiefly to the government."[27]

Franck also experienced, for the first time, an extended immersion in the "Copenhagen spirit" around Bohr. Since the end of the World War, Franck had made much of his career testing the ideas of the theoreticians, foremost among them Bohr. Years later he considered what proximity to Bohr's genius could mean:

Bohr was so superior that some people had difficulties with him, which I never understood. Never is not right. Which I understood only after Hitler came to power, and I was one and a half years in the laboratory. Bohr did not allow me to think through whatever I did to the end. I made some experiments. And when I told Bohr about it, then he said immediately what might be wrong, what might be right. And it was so quick that after a time I felt that I am unable to think at all. . . . But to be there for a time and to learn and to see this man and to understand the greatness of him and the goodness. He is really something. Yes, a man for whom one can feel only a hero worship.[28]

Franck never lost his hero worship for Bohr, but by the summer of 1935 he was on his way to America.

When he arrived in Baltimore, he found the facilities there also lacking, and as a professor of physical chemistry he continued in the same direction as in Copenhagen, investigating the physical basis for the photochemistry of photosynthesis. His 1935 "Remarks on Photosynthesis" was the beginning of an increasingly sophisticated effort to account for all the known data on the physics of the process. With Rockefeller support for new equipment, he worked on the fluorescence of chlorophyll, whereas a small vacuum spectrograph brought from Göttingen enabled him to conduct research on the absorption spectra of water.[29] By 1937 he had worked out

27 James Franck to Ambassador K. H. Knappstein, n.d. [early 1964], Franck papers, B 3, F 8. On the "Franck Report," see Alice Kimball Smith, *A Peril and a Hope: The Scientists' Movement in America, 1945–47* (Chicago, 1965).
28 Interview with James Franck by Thomas Kuhn, fourth session, July 12, 1962, 12, AHQP.
29 James Franck, "Remarks on Photosynthesis," *Chemical Reviews* 17 (1935): 433–8.

the first of a series of tentative theories, each of which would be more complicated than the last.[30] But he decided to leave Hopkins, at least in part because of the anti-Semitic attitude of some officials there. It was a good thing for him that his instinct for the mainstream of significant problems was still intact, for his new work generated a number of options. Facilitated by T.R. Hogness, who had been a visitor to Göttingen and whose biology research group at the University of Chicago was supported by the Rockefeller Foundation, an opportunity arose to move to Chicago. Franck's research was financially underwritten by the Jewish philanthropist Samuel Fels. Moving in 1938, he set up a research laboratory and began tackling the problems of photosynthesis in earnest. Another old instinct came into play as well: He soon gathered around himself a school of pupils and assistants as distinguished as the one he had assembled in Göttingen. The Fels Fund supported Franck through his retirement to the end of his life.

Hans Gaffron, a chemist from Germany who joined Franck's prewar group in Chicago, later remarked that Franck, after resigning his chair in Göttingen, had looked around for a scientific task that was "different, important enough to be exciting, yet sufficiently familiar for him to use his skills to best advantage."[31] Franck loved to explain that he had gotten more than he had bargained for by groping toward photosynthesis – "his fate resembled that of the man who curiously puts a finger on a strip of flypaper, does not succeed in shaking it off and winds up in a terrible mess. In Franck's case, this mess was biochemistry."[32]

Biochemist Eugene Rabinowitch, who had known Franck since the Göttingen years, offered further insight into some of the difficulties of Franck's entrance into his new intellectual home. A particular challenge was how to adapt to a level of natural complexity that posed qualitatively different issues. In his memorial tribute in 1966, he noted with good humor that Franck first came at the problem "somewhere cockily."

He thought that the confusion prevailing in this field was due to lack of precise definition and controlled experimentation by biologists, and that the quantitative approach of a physicist would soon dispel it. But he did not reckon with the complexity of phenomena in live cells. Franck believed that each measurement must mean something in biology, as it does in physics, and can be used as a reliable stone in constructing a mechanism or formulating a theory. The trouble is that in

---

30 James Franck and Karl F. Herzfeld, "An Attempted Theory of Photosynthesis," *Journal of Chemical Physics* 9 (1937): 237–51.
31 Hans Gaffron, "Dinner Talk, University of Chicago," 3, text of presentation at the James Franck Memorial Symposium, University of Chicago, May 12–13, 1966, Franck papers.
32 Ibid., 4.

biology, no experiment can be "controlled" in the full sense this term has in physics, because the state and properties of a living cell depend on its whole history, and thus on more variables than can be reliably controlled.[33]

Although Franck and his group cleared away some tangled underbrush, he never extricated himself from the dense thicket of photosynthesis research. He had just finished another, more complicated version of his theory when he died in Göttingen on a visit in 1964.[34]

In one sense, Rabinowitch was indicating agreement with Bohr's conception presented in the "Light and Life" talk in 1932. It was impossible to explore the physical processes of life in a way that would satisfy a physicist without violating the inherent complexity of life that appealed to a biochemist or biologist. Franck could not escape the ambiguities of biology through simplification. That Rabinowitch was one of the co-authors of the "Franck Report" within the Manhattan Project reminds us that Franck was also unable to escape the new ambiguities in nuclear physics. Following the migration of physics into these realms while moving from country to country required continual negotiation and adaptation that placed enormous demands upon a man of Franck's age. That he kept up so well was a confirmation of his skill, insight, and commitment to change.

The story of any emigrant's life is of course unique. Franck's was characterized by certain factors that played major roles, such as his age (he was over fifty when he left Germany), the prominence conferred by his Nobel Prize, and the cohesion and support of his family. Yet an important generalization that can be adduced is that for persons with a firm identity and mature personality, the prologue to emigration is essential to understanding the phenomenon.

Franck's ambiguous yet coherent identity and mature judgment were crucial elements of his dramatically exceptional protest resignation. At the time, some of his colleagues, such as Courant, argued for remaining in one's post as a less theatrical but more pragmatic way of coping with the new regime. They argued that leaving would only play into the hands of the Nazis, who would feel empowered by resignations. Yet ultimately his colleagues' positions deteriorated, and they too had to leave. Franck understood the disproportionate effect that symbolic acts can generate, and he firmly believed that most Germans did not countenance the Nazi measures. Moreover, a principled stand against arbitrary authority and coercive so-

---

33 Eugene I. Rabinowitch, "James Franck – 1882–1984," 17, text of talk delivered at the James Franck Memorial Symposium, University of Chicago, May 12–13, 1966, Franck papers.

34 James Franck and J. L. Rosenburg, "A Theory of Light Utilization in Plant Photosynthesis," *Journal of Theoretical Biology* 7 (1964): 276–301.

cial pressure was a deeply ingrained attribute of his character, as illustrated by his response to the suggestion during the war that he undergo baptism in order to become an officer. Thus Franck's own story of emigration began with a demonstrative act of defiance and civil courage rather than with one of defeat and despair. Not all emigrants had this experience, and the difference may be significant for their subsequent sense of self.

At first, Franck expected to go into exile instead of emigration. Thus he accepted a short-term appointment in America and returned to a position in Europe that allowed him to stay near Germany and monitor events there. His cosmopolitan outlook and career as a scientist made his transition to emigrant easier than it was for many others forced out of Germany by the Nazis. His knowledge of English acquired in school and in professional visits to both England and the United States aided communication and enabled him early to contemplate moving to the United States. And his international network of personal and professional contacts greatly affected his trajectory from Göttingen through Copenhagen (Bohr) and Baltimore (Wood) to Chicago (Hogness). It was also not trivial that his Nobel Prize was a prestigious emblem that made others eager to acquire his presence at their institutions even in the midst of the economic depression.

Perhaps the greatest challenge was the need to keep abreast of developments in a discipline that had begun to leave him before he was forced to leave Germany. Atomic physics began to dissociate as a field before 1930, with researchers wandering off to quantum chemistry, nuclear physics, biophysics, and elsewhere. Franck's versatile style left him temporarily too much a theoretician for some of the new pursuits and too much an experimentalist for others. It took time amid the personal migration to find his bearings and learn the necessary vocabularies. Thus the period of relative unproductiveness in Copenhagen was not wasted. He was exposed to some of the new options, and chose as his destination neither quantum chemistry nor nuclear physics but the boundaries between physics, chemistry, and biology entailed in the study of photosynthesis.

What he might have done in these years had the Nazis not intervened is of course highly speculative. But it is unlikely that he would have opted for photochemical aspects of photosynthesis as a first choice for the focus of the planned institute in Berlin because the scale of Rockefeller support would have allowed for so much more. Since the institute would first have had to be built, however, the drain on his time would have been very large, and he might indeed have chosen a smaller photochemical project for his personal line of research. How he would have adapted to such constraints must be an open question, but raising the issue offers an expanded context for the reality that came to pass.

Part of the reality faced by emigrants in every direction from the Third Reich was the need to find the conditions that allowed for more than mere survival, so that professional adaptation was even possible. And when individual biographies are analyzed, it becomes clear that part of what needed to survive was a strong, resilient sense of self. A question that arises is whether in maintaining that sense intact, persons deform the boundaries of a field they enter as intellectual immigrants. Certainly Franck did so, bringing to photosynthesis questions and theories that stretched biochemists and biologists toward physics at the same time that he tried with varying degrees of success to adapt to their thinking. The promise of the mutual deformation of boundaries was perhaps stronger than the reality, but it was strong enough to keep the Rockefeller and other philanthropies interested.

The constant availability of foundation funding was atypical but a fact of Franck's life as a successful, world-class researcher. The steadiness of support in the turbulent transition to sustained work on photosynthesis was a matter of consistently good timing on Franck's part. It could be called luck, or it could be called his appreciation of the institutional adaptability of the international scientific enterprise. A keen sense of a changing research forefront was very much a part of what made James Franck an outstanding scientist. His ability to accept continually altered conditions and ideas on principle was a positive way of coping with the inherent plasticity of major scientific developments.

Remarkably, Franck's ability to adapt readily to instability was itself very stable over the years. His steadiness of personality was partially a function of his tested awareness of his Jewish and German heritage and identities, and his participation in science at the boundary of theory and experiment. His highly developed social skills were a crucial asset in his emigration, allowing him to adapt as needed amid the personal tragedies and collective upheaval of those years. His sense of self, of others, and of his cultures' (German, Jewish, and professional) presentation and interpretation of both were astute and noteworthy. This is the kind of complexity that must not be lost in the quest for larger-scale representations of the scholarly emigration from Nazi Germany and its consequences.

4

The Impact of German Medical Scientists on British Medicine: A Case Study of Oxford, 1933–45

PAUL WEINDLING*

Discussions of the emigration of refugee physicians and medical scientists have concentrated on a select number of outstanding researchers. Less attention has been paid to the interaction with the host academic cultures, to professional structures, and to the potential of those refused entry or career posts. Selective criteria applied at the time in the admission of emigrants have continued – with rare exceptions – to dominate the historiography of the emigration. It is all too easy to overlook the socially marginal: Certain academics came as domestic servants or gardeners, and pursued careers in fringe industrial laboratories or in general practice.[1]

Professional factors are of special importance in the medical sphere. Restrictive professional barriers were erected for the exclusion of the rank and file of clinicians.[2] Lord Dawson, president of the Royal College of Physi-

* I wish to thank the Keeper of the Archives, University of Oxford, for permission to consult documents, and the Secretary of the SPSL and Bodleian Library staff for access to the SPSL papers. I am profoundly grateful to Hermann Blaschko and Eva Glees for invaluable discussions that enriched this paper both factually and conceptually. I also wish to thank Hans R. Klein, Anthony Glees, Paul Glees, Tim Horder, and Marjory Ord for helpful comments and information. Jack Morrell commented extensively on an earlier draft. My mother contributed recollections of A.V. Hill and Benno Schlesinger.

1 Richard Klein, FLS (1892–1978), a mycologist, worked as a gardener at Nottleigh Abbey, Long Crendon, from July 1939 through July 1940, and later as a microbiologist for the Ministry of Supply and Roche Products, Ltd. Emmy Zwillinger (b. 1898?), an M.A. in pharmacy from Vienna, held a permit for household work but attempted to secure an academic position in 1939. See University Archives, Oxford (hereafter UA) PSL/4, 32. It is said that G.R. Girdlestone, the orthopaedic surgeon, found one of the Guttmanns working as a butler in North Oxford. See Robert B. Duthie and J. Mullins, *Fifty Years of the Nuffield Professorship of Orthopaedic Surgery in the University of Oxford* (Oxford, 1987), 19.

2 Paul J. Weindling, "The Contribution of Central European Jews to Medical Science and Practice in Britain: The 1930s to 1950s," in Werner E. Mosse, ed., *Second Chance: Two Centuries of German-Speaking Jews in the United Kingdom* (Tübingen, 1991), 243–54. For Scotland, see Kenneth Collins, *Go and Learn: The International Story of Jews and Medicine in Scotland* (Aberdeen, 1988), 81–97.

cians, instructed the home secretary that "the number [of German medical scientists] who could teach us anything could be counted on the fingers of one hand." While the Royal College of Physicians spoke for the elite of the medical profession, there was a rift between the profession and medical researchers.[3] Long-running tensions between scientific modernizers and the traditional professional elite explain the strong medical research lobby within the Society for the Protection of Science and Learning (SPSL) who keenly sympathized with the plight of German medical researchers. A modernizing elite of physiologically trained researchers was attempting to reform the system of medical education and professional structures. Physiologists and biochemists such as Henry Dale, A.V. Hill, and Gowland Hopkins were key figures in both the Medical Research Council and the SPSL.[4] They had enduring academic links with Germany. Dale had worked with Paul Ehrlich; Hill shared a Nobel Prize for medicine with Otto Meyerhof in 1922 for research on muscular contractions; and there were affinities between Hopkins's approach to cell chemistry and the work of Germans such as Franz Hofmeister. German biochemists, themselves a marginal group within German academia, had considerable personal and intellectual interaction with British colleagues. For example, Otto Warburg's manometric technique for measuring biological oxidation was developed from a micromanometer that Joseph Barcroft in Cambridge and J.S. Haldane in Oxford used to measure oxygen and carbon dioxide in blood samples.[5]

Although influential within scientific circles (Hill, for example, was secretary of the Royal Society), medical researchers were socially marginal to the British medical establishment. This divergence came to be expressed in the difference of opinion over the admission of professional refugees. Hill summed up the situation concerning the medical committee advising the Home Office: "[The civil servants] are terrified of the medical profession, and the most part of the medical profession – or at least the part of it that determines policy – has little regard for anything except the supposed interests of members of the profession." Hill was partisan: "I shall continue being nasty to the authorities and medical people about this."[6] It was the modernizing influence of such scientific reformers that was beginning to affect Oxford.

3 For underlying factors, see Frank Honigsbaum, *The Division in British Medicine* (London, 1979).
4 H. Dale, *The Protection of Science and Learning* (n.d., n.p.) [London, 1936].
5 Frederic L. Holmes, *Hans Krebs*, vol. 1: *The Formation of a Scientific Life, 1900–1933* (New York, 1991), 133. For Oxford's failure to secure Krebs, see Holmes, *Hans Krebs*, vol. 2: *Architect of Intermediary Metabolism, 1933–1937* (Oxford, 1993), 3–4.
6 Hill to Blaschko, June 16, 1941, Blaschko file on refugees, Wellcome Unit for the History of Medicine, Oxford.

These factors explain the relatively open situation for refugees in laboratory research, and the barriers preventing medical practice. The laboratory was a type of secular ghetto for refugee doctors and medical researchers. For the dedicated researcher (such as Hans Krebs), who had previously been burdened with routine clinical analyses, the situation was idyllic. But for others accustomed to research in a clinical context, being confined to a laboratory was a source of deep frustration. Yet superior technical skills were a pathway to obtaining academic posts. For example, expertise in Warburg's tissue slice technique was helpful in teaching biochemistry and physiology. As the Nuffield Professor of Clinical Medicine explained to the university registrar in May 1939: "We can sometimes find work for highly skilled technical assistants or for people doing highly original research work, but there is an already great competition amongst our own people for ordinary clinical posts."[7]

REFUGEES AND THE MODERNIZATION OF
OXFORD MEDICINE

I propose to investigate this situation in the key area where the disciplines of biochemistry, physiology, and pharmacology intersected through a case study of a single institution – the University of Oxford – as encapsulating the process of conflict between traditional and modern types of professional approaches to medicine.[8] There are good reasons for such a case study. Studies of the medical migration tend to be more from the German point of view, and less than from that of the receiving cultures.[9] It is artificial to analyze the complexities of British culture and medicine as a homogenous aggregate, and in this respect, any overview raises more problems than can be solved.[10] Disciplinary studies – such as Kohler's comparison of German, British, and American biochemistry – tend to see the situation in terms of national aggregates and in retrospective terms of the inevitability of certain research strategies.[11] The upheaval of emigration could facilitate movement

7   UA PSL/4, correspondence with individual scholars. The remark was made in a letter of April 18, 1939, concerning the rejection of an application on behalf of a Czechoslovak pediatrician, Otto Saxl.
8   For a sketch of Oxford from a literary perspective, see J. M. Ritchie, "Exile in Oxford," *Oxford Magazine* 83 (1992): 3–4.
9   Stephan Leibfried, "Stationen der Abwehr: Berufsverbote für Ärzte im deutschen Reich 1933–1938 und die Zerstörung des sozialen Asyls durch die organisierten Ärzteschaften des Auslands," *Bulletin des Leo Baeck Instituts* 62 (1982): 1–39. Hans-Peter Kröner, "Die Emigration deutschsprachiger Mediziner im Nationalsozialismus," *Berichte zur Wissenschaftsgeschichte* 12 [special issue] (1989).
10 This applies to my sketch "The Contribution of Central European Jews," in Mosse, *Second Chance.*
11 Robert E. Kohler, *From Medical Chemistry to Biochemistry* (Cambridge, 1982).

between disciplines – for example, of chemists into medical research. Analysis of reception throws into sharper perspective the culture of the immigrant researcher, and comparison of individual idiosyncrasies provides a corrective to generalized assumptions.

Oxford is of significance because of its social prestige. Helped by the university's decentralized structures it has incorporated a complex variety of social and intellectual attitudes, which may be taken as encapsulating processes of restructuring in academia and more broadly within British society. On the one hand, Howarth has suggested that there were pockets of innovation in institutionalizing teaching and research in the sciences.[12] On the other hand, it has been observed that antipathy to the sciences became a mark of collegiate loyalty, and Hoch and Yoxen's case-study of the physicist Erwin Schrödinger has documented the continuing existence of this "Oxford malaise" in the interwar years.[13] Can this notion of an entrenched anti-science lobby be applied to medicine? Symptomatic of Oxford's conservatism was a lack of a clinical medical school until World War II. The university responded to innovation by allowing separate spheres on its margins – for example, the women's colleges and science departments – while retaining its traditions as a teaching university with an emphasis on undergraduate tuition in the humanities. Ironically, the lack of funding for science and the traditionalism of the collegiate university forced dynamic researchers to look outside the confines of Oxford for expertise and financial resources. Thus, whereas Hoch and Yoxen have analyzed the Oxford situation from inside, I emphasize that medical research was responding to factors from outside the university.

During the 1920s the physiologist Charles Sherrington gave the university new distinction in neurophysiology, and Archibald Garrod, a pioneer of the application of Mendelism to pathology, emphasized the potential of biochemistry in clinical research. The appointment of Howard Florey (with the backing of Hopkins and Dale) as professor of pathology in 1935 gave physiology and biochemistry a further boost. During the 1930s new clinical chairs and the Nuffield Institute for Medical Research endowed by William Morris, Lord Nuffield (the motor manufacturer), gave an impetus to proposals for a school of clinical medicine. There was a new dynamism in the university administration. Douglas Veale, appointed university registrar in 1930, came to Oxford armed with the experience of having been

12 J. Howarth, "Science Education in Late-Victorian Oxford: A Curious Case of Failure," *English Historical Review* 102 (1987): 334–71.
13 Paul K. Hoch and Edward J. Yoxen, "Schrödinger at Oxford: A Hypothetical National Cultural Synthesis which Failed," *Annals of Science* 44 (1989): 278–319.

private secretary to successive ministers of health. Having been party
to the discussions at the Ministry of Health concerning the development of a postgraduate medical school in Oxford, he was supportive
of the Nuffield benefactions.[14] A.D. Lindsay, the master of Balliol and
vice-chancellor between 1935 and 1938, backed efforts to increase the
strength of science and medicine.[15] Thus the academic refugees encountered an evolving situation that was in certain respects favorable but was
still rife with contradictions. Florey's relations with the Nuffield Committee were at times acrimonious,[16] as were Lindsay's relations with Lord
Nuffield.

The structure of Oxford as a collegiate university was decentralized, arising from traditional resistance to the "Germanization" of Oxford with the
rejection of centrally organized faculties. This can be illustrated by the response to academic refugees. In May 1933 a committee was established
consisting of the vice-chancellor (traditionally the head of a college – from
1932–35 the office was filled by the Reverend F.J. Lys, the provost of
Worcester College), as well as the master of Balliol (Lindsay), the president
of Magdalene (George Stuart Gordon), the newly elected warden of All
Souls (the economist W. G. S. Adams), and Farquhar Buzzard (the Regius
Professor of Medicine and a council member of the SPSL). The colleges
thus shaped the decentralized pattern of Oxford's response, and the university's role was merely reactive. In June 1933, Hebdomadal Council (one of
the governing councils of the university) expressed the hope that colleges
and departments would consider favorably the temporary accommodation
of foreign scholars as research students or teachers. An important stipulation
was that there should be "no charge on the University."[17] The pattern of
varying college initiatives was established. For example, in June 1933 the
university endorsed the proposal by All Souls that foreign scholars should
be invited to hold Chichele lectureships.[18] In October 1938 it was agreed
that the university should hold a central reference file including applications

---

14 For an overview on the modernization of the Oxford medical school, see Charles Webster, "Med-
    icine," in Brian Harrison, ed., *The History of the University of Oxford*, vol. 3: *The Twentieth Century*
    (Oxford, 1994), 317–44. On Veale, see E. Williams in *Dictionary of National Biography*. On the
    Nuffield benefactions, see Jennifer Beinart, *A History of the Nuffield Department of Anaesthetics,
    Oxford, 1937–1987* (Oxford, 1987), 22–6, and Gustav J. Fraenkel, *Hugh Cairns: First Nuffield
    Professor of Surgery, University of Oxford* (Oxford, 1991), 101–25.
15 Drusilla Scott, *A. D. Lindsay: A Biography* (Oxford, 1971), 228–37. D. Phillips, "Lindsay and the
    German Universities: An Oxford Contribution to the Postwar Reform Debate," *Oxford Review of
    Education* 6 (1980): 91–105.
16 Robert G. Macfarlane, *Howard Florey: The Making of a Great Scientist* (Oxford, 1979), 296–7.
17 UA RC/1, June 21, 1933, notice from the University Registry.
18 UA RC/1. This proposal was accepted by Hebdomadal Council on June 21, 1933.

from medical scientists.[19] (This was consulted in February 1939 by L.J. Witts, Nuffield Professor of Clinical Medicine, looking for a suitable bio-chemist or chemist.[20]) The university also acted as a channel for applications to the Rockefeller Foundation, resulting in equipment grants for physicists and chemists and a £300 Rockefeller grant to All Souls for the economist Jacob Marschak.[21]

Faced by the academic refugee question, the university administration took charge of external representation rather than any direction of the internal response. The university registrar would intercede with the Home Office at the request of a head of department. This involved a substantial amount of personal case work, which extended to looking after the family matters and personal welfare. This can be well illustrated by the registrar's efforts on behalf of Ernst Chain, when Florey informed the registrar that Chain's personal worries were having a bad effect on his academic work. In 1936 the registrar contacted the Aliens Department of the Home Office concerning a visa for Chain's cousin, and again in March 1939 for Chain's sister and mother.[22]

One of the most striking aspects of Oxford's decentralized response was the differing level of contributions by various departments and by colleges to the SPSL appeals of 1935 and 1939. All Souls, Balliol, Christ Church, Magdalen, and University Colleges took major initiatives in providing hospitality and donations to the SPSL. Table 4.1 shows varying levels of support for refugees among the colleges (although the uneven distribution of endowments has also to be taken into account). The university limited its activities to raising the block grant available for lectures by refugees to £270 in March 1939. The registrar was helpful to the SPSL in arranging for a fund-raising meeting in February 1939.[23] But rather than the hoped-for central fund, there was only a coordinating committee, which gave preference to scholars with prospects for re-migration.[24]

Although the admission of students was (and is) essentially a college matter, it should be noted that Lindsay had in July 1939 gained support for a

19 UA FA6/18. This file contains details of only a few researchers, including Erich J. Kraus, pathologist; Felix Hawrowis, biochemist; Laznitski, biochemist; Heinz Meyerhof, biochemist; Arthur Simons, neurologist; Fritz von Gutfeld, bacteriologist.
20 UA FA 6/18, letters from Witts, Feb. 7 and 16, 1939.
21 UA RC/1, letters to the Rockefeller Foundation from the University Registry dates July 31, Aug. 2 and 4, 1933. The application for Rockefeller funding for the philosopher Hans Reichenbach was refused.
22 UA RC/1, Florey to Registrar, June 17, 1936; Ryder to Aliens Dept., March 18, 1939; Florey to Registrar, April 9, 1939.
23 UA PSL/1.
24 UA PSL/2 file 1, Circular of Vice-Chancellor to Heads of Colleges, Jan. 28, 1939; Lindsay to Registrar, Oct. 14, 1939.

Table 4.1 Oxford colleges' financial support of the Society for the Protection of Science and Learning and to refugee scholars

	1935* £	1939⁺ £	Other support	Reply to suggestion that colleges contribute to central fund
			Donations to the SPSL	
All Souls	520	650 +350 (1940)	J. Marschak (1933–35) E. Cassirer (1933–35) International Student Society (£50) Refugee Scholars Fund of Hebrew University Jerusalem (£100) G. Karkov (£250×2) F. Hertz (£100×2) F. Buchardt (£400) H. Kantorowicz (£300) M. Wolff Grünhut (£300)	No
Balliol	50	1000	1 Research lecturer for 3 years £250–300 per annum	
Brasenose	—	100		
Christ Church	250	826		
[Private donations by Canons]		146		
Corpus Christi	—	110	P. Jacobsthal (£100) Cassirer (£500) Pfeiffer (£100)	Probably yes
Exeter	—	10		
Hertford	—	10		Yes
Jesus	—			

92

Donations to the SPSL

	1935* £	1939+ £	Other support	Reply to suggestion that colleges contribute to central fund
Keble	—	—	—	No
Lady Margaret Hall	—	10 from individual Fellows	+Hospitality for Leubuscher and Blochmann in established posts	Yes
Lincoln	—	20	Research fellowship for Wellesz	No
Magdalen	150	20 1000	Grants for Koeppler and Walzer Schrödinger (£562)	
Manchester	—	—	Supported F. Braun and Heinemann	
Merton College	—	10	£200 for 5 years to Pringsheim	No
New College	450	50/year		Possible
Nuffield College	—	—		
Oriel College	—	—	Support to R. Klibansky 1934–42	No
Pembroke College	—	25	£30 per annum to a German Jewish undergraduate	
Queen's College	£1.15	500	Jellinek (£150) Calvet (£50) Kuhn (£150×3)	Offers £500
St. Anne's	—	—		
St. Benet's Hall	—	—		
St. Catharine's Society	—	—		No
St. Edmund Hall	—	—		No
St. Hilda's	personal contribution by J. de Mann	—	Hospitality to Dr. Ehrlich	Referable

Table 4.1 (*cont.*)

	Donations to the SPSL			Reply to suggestion that colleges contribute to central fund
	1935* £	1939+ £	Other support	
St. Hugh's	—	10	Accommodation for woman from Charité Hospital, Berlin	No
St. John's	—	?	£250 per annum for Rothfels	Yes
St. Peter's Hall	—	—		
Somerville	—		Support for L. Labowsky and Käthe Bosse Offer to Dr. Herzog-Hauser	No
Trinity	—	25 for 3 years		Yes
University College	55	900		
Wadham	50	100 for 1 scholar		No
Worcester	£5.5	—		
Home students	—	—	Miss Neumann Miss Schulz Mrs. Jaeger	

*Includes commitments to continuing annual grants 1935–1938.
+Includes commitments to continuing annual grants 1939–1941.
— Denotes no contribution.

Sources: SPSL 129/2. PSL/2, 17, revised summary of information received in reply to Mr. Vice-Chancellor's circular to colleges on Jan. 28, 1939. PSL/3, Replies to Vice-Chancellor.

scheme whereby refugee students and Czechoslovak students could be admitted without college fees. Extended to all refugees by university decree of October 31, 1939, this helped a number of Czechoslovak and Polish scientific and medical students. Miss B. Wolf (St. Hugh's), who had been assistant at the Institute for Cancer Research at the Charité university hospital in Berlin, applied for exemption before being supported by the Nuffield Institute for Medical Research.[25]

The medical refugees were a broad spectrum, ranging from medical students to eminent elderly figures. For some, such as the Nobel Prize-winning pharmacologist Otto Loewi,[26] the neuroanatomist Benno Schlesinger,[27] the internist Heinrich Schwarz,[28] the physical chemist Kurt Wohl,[29] the pediatrician Heinrich Lehndorff, as well as for the Spanish biochemist Severo Ochoa,[30] Oxford provided a temporary refuge. The elderly medical refugees evoked the values of a general humanitarianism and a particular respect for German medical science among their sponsors. This can be illustrated by Otto Neubauer,[31] distinguished in cancer research; Stefan Jellinek, a Viennese pioneer of electropathology; and Adolf Wallenberg, a physician from Danzig with interests in comparative neurology.[32] Although the university's policy of providing temporary hospitality was well suited to elderly refugees or to those intending to re-migrate, others were keen to find career openings and to settle permanently.

The numbers of refugee medical scientists contrast to a complete absence of general practitioners and dental surgeons in practice before 1945. The wife of M. Hornik was a psychoanalyst. One exceptional case was Ilse Sachs, who was research assistant at the Nuffield Institute for one year from August 1938 and who later worked for the blood transfusion service. Another was the Spanish refugee surgeon Joseph Trueta, who had expertise in treating war wounds, and because of strictures of the British Medical Association

25 UA PSL/2 file 1. The application is dated March 7, 1940.
26 Fred Lembeck and Wolfgang Giere, *Otto Loewi: Ein Lebensbild in Dokumenten* (Berlin, 1968), 63 and 187.
27 SPSL 424/13. Benno Schlesinger had been a demonstrator for Julius Tandler in Vienna and held a Rockefeller fellowship [in 1931]. He was in Oxford with Le Gros Clark from 1939 to 1940.
28 SPSL 385/2. Heinrich Schwarz was invited to research in endocrinology in the department of physiology with a grant from the SPSL in 1939.
29 SPSL 227/5. Wohl left the department of botany for Princeton University in 1942.
30 SPSL 418/9.
31 Neubauer file, Wellcome Unit for the History of Medicine, Oxford. Bernard Schepartz, "Otto Neubauer: A Neglected Biomedical Scientist," *Transactions and Studies of the College of Physicians of Philadelphia*, ser. 5, vol. 6 (1984): 139–54. Gerlind Büsche-Schmidt, *Otto Neubauer: Leben und Werk* (Herzogenrath, 1992).
32 P. Glees, "Adolf Wallenberg, 1862–1949," *Monatsschrift Psychiatrie Neurologie* 119 (1950): 255–6, cited as offprint.

had to "direct" the professor of surgery working in mobile accident units. The neurologist Francis Schiller came after the fall of Paris with a Prague M.D., and assisted with establishing a blood bank (in the new Bodleian Library). Under Cairns, he became surgical registrar at the Radcliffe Infirmary. Renate Schulz underwent a wartime medical education in Oxford and subsequently returned as house officer to the Radcliffe Infirmary by 1948. Two dental surgeons received permission to practice: Robert Munz and Otto Pick.[33] Others, such as the dental surgeon Eva Glees, only received permission to practice in 1948, and were confronted by shockingly low standards in British dentistry and professional coldness to a female colleague. In other areas of growth such as social medicine, there were no immigrants but continental influences. Here the first professor John Ryle (an SPSL activist) was in contact with the pioneer of social medicine Henry Sigerist and had been much influenced by Ludwig Wittgenstein when he was a hospital porter at Guy's Hospital.[34]

The most interesting and distinguished grouping researched in the area of physiology, biochemistry, and pharmacology. Hermann ("Hugh") Blaschko, Edith Bülbring, Ernst Chain, Paul Glees, and Hans Krebs came to Oxford between 1935 and 1950 to fill career posts. It is worthwhile looking at the situation in generational terms. The older generation of physiologists and biochemists of Hill and Hopkins, who were the elder statesmen overseeing the immigration, were born between the 1860s and the 1880s. An intermediate generation that required technical assistance included the biochemist Peters born in 1889, Burn born in 1892, Cairns in 1896, Robert Mackintosh in 1897, and Florey in 1898. The immigrant generation that had a creative impact was born in the decade after 1900: Blaschko and Krebs in 1900, Bülbring in 1903, Chain in 1906, and Hans Epstein and Glees in 1909.

This active nucleus shows a fruitful Berlin–Oxford axis.[35] Blaschko, Chain, Bülbring, and Krebs had research experience in Berlin or under the

33 On Pick, see SPSL 372. His practice was at 25 St. John Street, Oxford. Munz practiced at 181 Woodstock Road, Oxford.

34 See also Eva Glees, "From Lessingstrasse to Oxford Road: Not a Straight or Easy Way," unpublished MS, 1988, 98. For Ryle-Sigerist contacts, see the Ryle-Sigerist collection at the Wellcome Unit for the History of Medicine, Oxford. I am indebted to Prof. Michael Shepard of the Maudsley Hospital for the point about Wittgenstein.

35 For the long-term impact of Berlin biochemistry, see H. Harris, "The City of Berlin and Some Modern Approaches to the Cancer Problem," *International Cell Biology (1980–81)*, papers presented at the Second International Congress on Cell Biology, Berlin (Berlin, 1981), 3–12, cited as reprint. Michael Engel, "Paradigmenwechsel und Exodus: Zellbiologie, Zellchemie und Biochemie in Berlin," in *Exodus von Wissenschaften aus Berlin* (Berlin, 1994), 296–341. On Blaschko, see also Nicholas Russell, "Independent Discovery in Biology: Investigating Styles of Scientific Research," *Medical History* 47 (1993): 432–41.

Berlin-trained Meyerhof. Bülbring researched under Paul Trendelenburg and then Friedemann (who later collaborated with Dale) at the Virchow Hospital,[36] Krebs with Alfred Goldscheider at the Third Medical Clinic, and then with Peter Rona at the chemical department of the Pathological Institute, before moving to Warburg's department at the Kaiser Wilhelm Institute (KWI) for Biology.[37] Chain studied at the KWI for Chemistry and completed a doctorate under Rona in enzyme chemistry, and Blaschko also attended Rona's courses before moving to the institute of Meyerhof, who regarded Rona as providing fundamental preliminary training for any aspiring biochemist.[38] Epstein completed a doctorate in 1934 in physical chemistry under Bodenstein. (The proximity of the Berlin institutes of physical chemistry to pharmacology and hygiene should be noted.) To the Berlin-oriented researchers should be added Severo Ochoa, who worked on the chemistry and physiology of muscle tissue under Meyerhof, and had researched in London on enzymes in 1931. They came to laboratories where there was a tradition of visiting postdoctoral researchers, and for their part they were prepared to learn new techniques and approaches. Thus Meyerhof had arranged for Blaschko to visit Hill's laboratory in 1929; Blaschko described his return in 1933 as "more like a homecoming." Chain took a Cambridge Ph.D. under Hopkins. Krebs continued work on the metabolism of amino acids under Hopkins, whose major interest was oxidation, leading to the discovery of the citric acid cycle. Both Blaschko and Krebs introduced Warburg manometry to Cambridge medical teaching.

Biochemistry – the discipline that had the greatest impact on Oxford – was itself marginal in Germany. In 1926, Hopkins criticized the lack of German biochemical institutes. Meyerhof and Warburg, despite their prestige as Nobel Prize winners, were figures who were marginal to the German medical community, detached in their KWIs. Indeed, Rockefeller funding played a major role in building up their resources. This marginality was all the greater for the researchers such as Blaschko, Chain, and Krebs, who all had insecure positions in Germany. Blaschko's career under Meyerhof was interrupted by sickness, Chain was an unemployed postdoctoral researcher, and Krebs was an assistant physician in the medical clinic in Freiburg. Areas

36   SPSL papers, 413/5. Obituary notices in Alison F. Brading, *Physiological Society Annual Report* (1990) and M. Ord, *Lady Margaret Hall Brown Book* (1990). Alison Brading, "Edith Bülbring F.R.S. (1903–1990)," in Lynn Bindman, Alison Brading, and Tilli Tansey, eds., *Women Physiologists: An Anniversary Celebration of Their Contributions to British Physiology* (Colchester, 1993).

37   Frederic L. Holmes (*Hans Krebs*, vol. 1: *The Formation of a Scientific Life, 1900–1933*) sees the period with Otto Warburg as more formative than the time with Peter Rona.

38   For an appreciation of Peter Rona, who died in Hungary during the war, see *Arzneimittelforschung* 10 (1960): 327.

of only slight impact included botany under the ecologists Arthur Tansley, and from 1937, T.G.B. Osborn (who gave temporary hospitality to the physical chemist Kurt Wohl), physiology (quiescent since the great era of Sherrington), and zoology under the conservative morphologist E.S. Goodrich. The non-impact is explained partly by inertia and underfunding inherent in the fragmented Oxford system and partly by the holistic ethos of the sciences, which were resisting biochemical reductionism and genetics. It should be noted that supporters of academic refugees were often those willing to support other radical causes. Thus the anatomist Wilfred Le Gros Clark (who took on Glees) and Florey joined in protests against Franco.[39] Yet such radicalism was not evident in Mackintosh, whose anesthetics unit was on Franco's side.

A number of younger academics with Jewish backgrounds (many not being refugees) had gained college and university posts, notably Isaiah Berlin as philosophy fellow at New College. In 1939, Cecil Roth was appointed to a readership in postbiblical Jewish studies. A few appointments were made of academic refugees (for example, Jacob Marschak became reader in statistics, and in 1936, F.E. Simon became reader in thermodynamics), although none was in medicine. Undercurrents of dissent were aroused on the appointment of Eduard Fraenkel as Corpus Professor of Latin. In pressing for greater assistance for refugees, G.R. Driver observed: "There is in many quarters a disinclination to put such persons [i.e. refugees] on our governing bodies or to fill our Common Rooms (already often full to overflowing) with foreigners of whom we often know personally very little."[40]

The situation in medicine was that the refugees remained on the margins of even the new subject areas that Nuffield was supporting. The Nuffield Committee for the Advancement of Medicine was asked to provide grants only if satisfied that the research could not be undertaken by any available British subject.[41] Although a number of Spanish research workers were supported (for example, the neurologist Pio del Rio-Hortega between 1937 and 1940), only in 1941 were there several grants from the Nuffield Committee for Medical Research benefiting Glees, Ludwig Guttmann, the anesthetics research team (Epstein, Mendelsohn, Weiler), the orthopedic

39 Jim Fyrth, *The Signal Was Spain: The Aid Spain Movement in Britain, 1936–39* (London, 1986), 201.
40 UA PSL/2. Letter from Godfrey Rolles Driver (later professor of semitic philology) proposing a university-wide fundraising scheme.
41 UA FA 6/1/2, Oct. 29, 1938, concerning the application by Le Gros Clark on behalf of Schlesinger.

surgeon Ernst Guttmann (a Czech), and other women, Bülbring, Renate Schöntal (a Polish refugee biochemist), and Wolff.[42] More broadly, there was mounting concern about indigenous British professionals losing job opportunities. This was voiced in the sciences by a Society of British Chemists and more broadly by newspapers such as the *Daily Express*, supporting the "little men" of the British medical profession in opposing the job-hungry aliens.

Those chairs filled with outsiders were themselves more liable to support those whom Hopkins described to Florey as of alien "race and foreign origin." Whereas Chain expected to migrate to Australia, he ended up working with an Australian – Florey – in Oxford. Despite the personality differences between Florey and Chain, both were allergic to the social conventions of English polite society. Isaac Berenblum, Polish born but with British qualifications, worked at the Dunn Institute on cancer research from 1936 until 1948, when he moved to the Weizmann Institute. The Australian professor of surgery, Cairns, gave hospitality to Guttmann at the Nuffield Institute for Medical Research (but supported with a grant from Balliol and the SPSL), and in August 1939 Trueta was sponsored by Girdlestone. Harold Burn, a student of Hopkins and Dale, came from London in 1937 with Bülbring (for whom he obtained financial support from the Nuffield Committee) and appointed Blaschko in 1943. The biochemist Rudolf Peters offered a post to Krebs, and the position was temporarily filled by Severo Ochoa as Nuffield research assistant, investigating vitamin B_1. Thus marginal disciplines benefited from the expertise of German-trained researchers able to apply chemistry to medicine.

Mackintosh, the first European professor of anesthetics, was a London clinician who was in need of technical expertise. The Oxford vaporizer – which laid the foundation of modern anesthetics – was the result of collaboration between the first Nuffield Professor of Anesthetics, Mackintosh, and the Berlin chemist Hans Epstein, with initial input from the physicist Kurt Mendelssohn during 1940, when Epstein and Mendelssohn lost their positions at the Clarendon Laboratory when it was turned over to war-related research under the physicist Lindemann.[43] Epstein had supported himself in Berlin from 1934 to 1939 manufacturing acoustic equipment, and this applied expertise proved particularly useful.[44]

This situation is paralleled in the penicillin research work, to which Chain

---

42   UA FA6/1/2, Nuffield Committee for the Advancement of Medicine.
43   Jennifer Beinart, *A History of the Nuffield Department of Anaesthetics*, 54–9.
44   SPSL 327/1 and 429/3.

contributed. It was Chain who participated in crucial experiments establishing the therapeutic value of penicillin, but difficulties with co-workers, the intrinsic complexity of such research requiring the diverse talents of a research team, and perhaps also his lack of clinical qualifications meant that having seen the promised land, others took the lead in the transition from laboratory research to therapeutic trials and then on to large-scale manufacture. Although the war gave applied medical research a new significance and improved the standing of refugees, their position was still marginal. Epstein has remained in obscurity, and Chain's frustrations at Florey's refusal either to patent penicillin or to make his post secure led to his departure for Rome after the war. While Chain exposed a lack of commercialism among academic researchers, the pharmacological researches of Blaschko and Bülbring, who laid the foundations for an understanding of catecholamines, were oriented toward basic physiology rather than commerce.

Glees falls into a different – but no less successful – class. He was a Catholic who as a medical student in Bonn had fallen in love with a Jewish student of dental surgery and medicine. They had married in London in 1936 while Glees was employed as a researcher in the Netherlands, and after much hesitation they had moved to England in July 1939, when he went to the Strangeways Laboratory in Cambridge. His academic strength was in experimental physiology. Bülbring brought his work to the attention of Le Gros Clark, who obtained a Nuffield grant for his research in Oxford from March 1940. Glees became demonstrator in the department of human anatomy, combining research into nerve regeneration (conducted in association with Ludwig Guttmann). He moved to the department of physiology in 1945. Although he gained the reputation as an outstanding teacher, he was never appointed to a college fellowship. He was the only one of these academic refugees to return to Germany – but only in 1961 to the University of Göttingen and to the Max Planck Institute for Physiology. Thereafter, he spent several years in Cambridge.[45]

For others with extensive experience of clinical practice, the laboratory was necessary for survival but restrictive. Ludwig Guttmann, previously a neurologist at Breslau, was frustrated at being confined to laboratory research. His offers to assist with the development of the Wingfield-Morris Orthopedic Hospital (another Nuffield-assisted venture in Oxford) or at the head injuries hospital at St. Hugh's were declined. Instead he was encouraged to continue with experimental research on sweating that did not

---

45 SPSL 358/3. See also Eva Glees, "From Lessingstrasse to Oxford Road. Not a Straight or Easy Way," unpublished MS, 1988.

go well.[46] In 1943 he welcomed the challenge of opening a spinal injuries unit at Stoke Mandeville, where he applied a radically different philosophy, formulated from prior German experience, to the treatment of paraplegics. Stoke Mandeville rapidly became a major therapeutic center, and the patronage of royalty made this into a pillar of the British establishment.[47] However, Eric Guttmann, a psychiatrist from Prague, was more successful in working with Cairns on head injuries.

THE CRISIS OF WAR

The outbreak of war increased the pressures on the university and refugees. There were in 1940 approximately 1,000 "aliens" in Oxford, of whom 477 were from enemy countries.[48] It is by no means straightforward to establish a complete list of medically related refugees in Oxford. A few moved to the United States, notably Loewi and Heinrich Lehndorff, a Viennese pediatrician who was supported by Balliol until obtaining an American visa in November 1939. In addition to those already mentioned, there came Paul Berkenau, who was to assist at the Warneford Psychiatric Hospital, and Robert Munz (a dental surgeon who was a friend of Chain and was perhaps the first to use penicillin to treat dental abscesses). There were also a few medical students: Cahn-Nernst, Fraenkel, the younger Jellinek, Nohl, and Renate Schulz.[49] Although medicine was underrepresented in proportion to refugee academics in other academic disciplines, it is striking that only a few of the medical staff were interned. With the arrival of evacuated London clinical medical students, and a range of new hospital and laboratory services such as the Emergency Public Health Laboratory Service located at the Dunn School, came an increased need for teaching and laboratory staff. Yet initially the refugees were either excluded from medical laboratories and hospitals or placed under severe restrictions.[50]

September 1939 until 1941 was a period of crisis because of a flood of evacuees, internments, tribunals, and police surveillance, worsened by the fear of a Nazi invasion, which reached a peak in May 1940. By 1940, in addition to the refugees from Central Europe, 20,000 evacuees arrived in Oxford, many of whom were Jews from London's East End. There was a severe shortage of accommodation, despite the efforts of a refugee com-

---

46   Fraenkel, *Hugh Cairns*, 134–5.
47   S. Goodman, *Spirit of Stoke Mandeville: The Story of Sir Ludwig Guttmann* (London, 1986), 82–109.
48   "1,000 Aliens in Oxford," *The Times*, May 25, 1940, 3.
49   Information from Eva Glees, who also mentions a Dr. Klopstock from Berlin.
50   For Hill's views on the waste of the medical expertise of the refugees, see *Parliamentary Debates* 367, no. 5 (Dec. 3, 1940), 484–9.

mittee in New Inn Hall Street and institutions such as a home for fifteen German-Jewish children at Linton Road in North Oxford. W.G. Ettinghausen (university lecturer in German), in an address to the Oxford Jewish Congregation in May 1940, noted the upheavals caused by the rapid expansion of a small Jewish community of half a dozen families and a few Jewish university students. The early 1940s saw a rise in incidents of popular anti-Semitism, and refugees were suspected of being "fifth columnists."[51] In such a hostile atmosphere, there was considerable mutual help and assistance among the refugees. Glees developed an intellectually stimulating friendship with Wallenberg. There were intellectual activities such as medical lectures (held in the department of human anatomy) because of the numbers of unemployed doctors, as well as social gatherings.[52]

The internment crisis focused attention on the problem of academic refugees, prompting the university to take responsibility for all academic refugees. Thus the very pressures that made the university demand, for a brief period, blanket internment worked in the slightly longer term for the integration of refugees within Oxford. After detention came evaluation and then release, with the registrar energetically making the case for individual scholars and their family dependents, and subsequently assisting their assimilation into British society as well as their career development. A distinction needs to be drawn between public statements and liberal opinions that became the overriding determinants of policies. Sir John Anderson, the Home Secretary and Minister of Home Security, had opposed a policy of general internment (it is interesting to note that he was partly educated at the University of Leipzig).[53] This was the line supported by Sir Alexander Maxwell, the Undersecretary of State. His private secretary, Jennifer Williams, cooperated with great efficiency and tact with the university registrar. Having connived with the registrar to defuse the tensions surrounding "alien academics" in Oxford, the Home Office introduced the "C" class for interned German and Austrian academics on August 1, 1940, so extending the Oxford and Royal Society schemes on a countrywide basis.

Initially, internment threw the medical refugees into crisis, threatening the fragile positions that had been attained. Even when not interned, they were excluded from laboratories. Given the importance of the laboratory

51   David M. Lewis, *The Jews of Oxford* (Oxford, 1992), 66, 78. Tony Kushner, *The Persistence of Prejudice: Anti-Semitism in British Society during the Second World War* (Manchester, 1989), 73–77.
52   Letter from Eva Glees, Aug. 26, 1991, describing these lectures, which included Jellinek on electrotherapy, Wallenberg on neurology, R. Freudenberg (then at Moorcroft House, Uxbridge) on insulin treatment, and Ledermann (a general practitioner from Berlin) on general practice.
53   Kushner, *Persistence of Prejudice*, 145–6. Peter and Leni Gilman, *"Collar the Lot!" How Britain Interned and Expelled its Wartime Refugees* (London, 1980).

to research workers, their exclusion on security grounds was a profound shock, and the situation was similar for those with medical qualifications, who were banned from hospitals on the grounds that they might have contact with military casualties. The rapid German advances in May 1940 generated widespread fear of an invasion. The vice-chancellor and Oxford's chief constable considered that the special security orders for coastal areas that affected Cambridge ought to be extended to Oxford. Their fears were publicized in *The Times* of May 25:

Aliens are a potential menace, and we feel they should be interned. They can be sorted out after internment if necessary. It is the general opinion of the University that the regulations covering the coastal counties should be extended to this area.[54]

The registrar was worried about "aliens – some naturalized" – having free access to laboratories, privately commenting, "In some of the science departments it would be the easiest thing in the world to blow the whole place up."[55] On May 25 the Nuffield Committee for Medical Research declared that none of the enemy aliens in its employ were engaged in work vital to the Nuffield scheme and that the committee would not protest against any general internment. The registrar reported that the committee members were "not so much worried about sabotage as about individuals. I think myself that the only action we can take is against possible sabotage, and that for the time being all *enemy* aliens might be excluded from the Departments."[56] The registrar then contacted the Home Office:

We are anxious about the aliens. Because we are a University town we have probably a much bigger percentage of them to the rest of the population than most other towns. Many of them are working in labs in some of which important government work is being carried on and are therefore particularly well qualified to sabotage them if so disposed. We are taking certain steps ourselves to protect them, but they cannot, in the nature of things, be half as effective as clearing out any suspicious characters there may be. I have consulted the Chief Constable. . . . What I really want to know is, when the comb-out of aliens is going to begin? I understand that they are going to be hauled before tribunals.[57]

With the implementation of general internment, families were divided, in one case a father had to leave his one-day-old newborn offspring. Thirty-five undergraduates were interned, and undergraduates taking their final examinations were unable to complete their papers and practicals. One student could not be released to attend an oral exam for a hoped-for first-

54 "1,000 Aliens in Oxford," *The Times*.
55 UA CQ/11/17 file 1, Registrar to H. Butler, May 13, 1940.
56 UA CQ/11/17, Registrar to Vice-Chancellor, May 25, 1940.
57 UA CQ/11/17 file 1, Registrar to Home Office, May 21, 1940.

class degree, others could not complete the practical part of examinations, and a medical student seeking to find a hospital where she could undertake midwifery training was confronted by repeated refusals. So-called "naturalized aliens" were a cause for concern as more difficult to keep under surveillance.[58] Sexual behavior aroused suspicions – a young woman chemist was suspect for having been seen in the company of Royal Air Force officers.[59]

On July 3, 1940, the Oxford and Cambridge Joint Standing Committee decided to make no representations for the release of any interned alien or to request that any restrictions on those still at liberty might be lifted. However, the registrar expressed certain doubts to the Home Office about the decision not to assist "those who were credibly reported to be harmless, and academically useful. The fact remains that we have obligations to some of them who might easily have got jobs in foreign universities or employment of that kind if we had not tempted them to stay with us."[60] At this prompt from the registrar, the situation was obligingly defused by the Home Office, wishing to secure the release of those whose work was of national importance. On July 10, 1940, the Home Office suggested that the university convene a special committee for interned alien academics, grading them for eventual release. Included were all academics living in Oxford as a "University City," whether or not they had any connections with the university or colleges.[61] Oxford thus attained a unique position by having a local committee, although a few weeks later the University of Cambridge on its own initiative established a committee for the release of interned aliens. Other committees acted on a nationwide basis: There was a Royal Society Committee for interned scientists, a committee of the British Academy for academics other than at Oxford, and a committee of university vice-chancellors and principals for those engaged in teaching and administrative work for the universities. The residue was dealt with by the SPSL.[62]

The Oxford Committee consisted of the vice-chancellor (G.S. Gordon, president of Magdalen and a specialist in English literature), the provost of

58 UA CQ/11/17 file 1, meeting of the Registrar with the Personal Secretary of Alexander Maxwell on July 11, 1940.
59 UA CQ/11/17 contains various observations on immorality. Kushner, *Persistence of Prejudice*, 109, concerning sexual fears and stereotypes.
60 UA CQ/11/17 file 1, Registrar to Williams, July 5, 1940.
61 UA CQ/11/17 file 1, Jennifer Williams to Walter Adams, July 10, 1940, and G. S. Gordon to Alexander Maxwell, July 12, 1940.
62 Home Office, *Civilian Internees of Enemy Nationality: Categories of Persons Eligible for Release from Internment* (Aug. 1940).

Oriel (William David Ross, a classicist who had extensive experience in chairing government departmental committees on working conditions), and the provost of Queen's (R.H. Hodgkin, a historian). In a manner reminiscent of the undergraduate examinations, the refugee academics were placed in three classes. Class I contained aliens engaged in work directly related to the war effort. Class II consisted of "scholars of great distinction whose contributions to the progress of knowledge are in a class apart." Class III contained other researchers, supposedly of less distinction, and six science undergraduates.[63] For the sciences, the evaluation of their work was left to the Royal Society and to the scrupulously impartial judgment of Hill and Hopkins.

The drawing up of a class list was of immense benefit (see Table 4.2). It assisted assimilation in translating the qualifications of refugees in terms familiar to Oxbridge academics, and it meant that each refugee was assessed individually. Once the list had been compiled, the vice-chancellor and registrar became proprietary, scolding the Home Office when a Class I or II or a case on humanitarian or medical grounds was not promptly released, and awarding "bonus marks" and jocularly offering an honorary degree when duly acted on. At the same time, the registrar, with a firm sense that classification was only worthwhile as long as it served the purpose of ensuring prompt release, instructed the Home Office that there was scant difference between Class II and III, so ensuring that there should be no excuses in neglecting the Class IIIs.[64] By October 1940, the registrar pointed out that a Class III might really be a Class I if the broader classification of the White Paper of August 1940 were to be applied.[65] For the refugees, the list was also beneficial as those with no formal links to the university became its responsibility. Release from internment would be followed by invitation to tea with the registrar and further assistance. Character and age were taken into account, youth being in itself a cause for suspicion. The vice-chancellor's committee commented on undergraduates and research students:

The Committee had difficulty in deciding about the possible danger of setting these young men free in general. Most of them profess, and (we believe) have a sincere desire to help this country, but the committee does not know whether

63   UA CQ/11/17, letter from the Registrar to the Home Secretary, July 22, 1940. SPSL 129/1, University of Oxford to the Home Office, July 28, 1940.
64   UA CQ/17/11 file 1, Home Office to the Registrar, Sept. 3, 1940, the Registrar to Sir Alexander Maxwell's Private Secretary, Sept. 5, 1940.
65   UA CQ/11/17 file 2, Registrar to Home Office, Oct. 1, 1940.

Table 4.2 *Vice-chancellor's committee classifications*

Name	Age	Subject
CLASS I		
Buchardt, Fritz	38	Statistics and economics
Kosterlitz, Rolf	32	Psychotherapy
Moos, Siegfried	36	Statistics and economics
Olden, Rudolf	55	Modern history
Steiner, Gustav	45	Medicine
Uhlig, Johannes		Statistics
CLASS II		
Braun, Martin	36	Classical literature
Brink, K.O.	NA	
Eisler, Robert	64	Theology
Grünhut, Max	47	Criminal law
Hornik, M.	42	Modern history
Jacoby, Felix	NA	
Levy, Arthur	56	Law
Maas, P.	59	Ancient Greek lexicography
Rothfels, H.	49	Modern history
Schulz, F.	61	Roman law
Vivante, Leone	53	Philosophy
Vogel, J.	37	Writer
Walzer, R.	40	Arabic philosophy
Wolff, M.	67	Comparative law
CLASS III		
Alexander, F.	32	Archaeology
Goldschmidt, R.H.	58	Psychology
Heinemann, F.H.	45/50	Philosophy
Jacobsthal, P.	60	Celtic archaeology
Kramm, H.H.	30	Pastor
Kripps, H.H.E.A.	30	Education
Labowsky, Norbert	64	NA
Leyden, Wolfgang von	29	Philosophy
Meinhard, H.	38	Ethnology
Minio-Palluello, L.		Medieval philosophy
Momigliano, Arnaldo	32	Ancient Greek
Pfeiffer, S.	51	Ancient Greek
Pringsheim, Fritz	57	Law
Rohatyn, S.	34	Law
Steindl, J.		Economics
Waismann, Fredrich	44	Philosophy
Wellesz, E.	54	Byzantine and ancient music
Zuntz, Gunther	38	New Testament research
UNCLASSIFIED		
Cassirer, E.		Philosophy

Sources: SPSL 129/1 University of Oxford; UA CQ/11/17 file 1

the authorities can satisfactorily weed out those whose allegiance might revert if things went really badly. It does feel however that men with good honors degrees in science would, in fact, be of great use scientifically, especially if some plan for using them systematically under discreet supervision could be worked out.[66]

Again this shows how the refugee was valued for superior technical expertise. On September 28, 1940, the university was informed of the Home Office's decision to treat alien undergraduates as English ones, allowing continuation of studies in science and medicine.[67]

There was much lobbying by the dependents and colleagues of individual academics accompanied by more general criticisms. On July 1 the registrar informed the Home Office: "I am being a good deal harassed about our interned aliens, who, to judge from the accounts given by their friends must be a remarkable set of people."[68] W.H. Walsh of Merton College argued that the committee has been "extremely narrow and cautious in its interpretation" by not regarding university teaching as work of

national importance. . . . One would have thought that a learned body, with liberal traditions, would not have confined utility to immediate utility for the war-effort, but would have seen that it was in a proper sense, useful too that the pursuit of knowledge should be continued in spite of the present conditions by those who had the opportunity; and would have striven to give the most generous interpretation of the government regulations.[69]

R.G. Collingwood, the philosopher, protested against the irony that scholars who came here for freedom should be interned.[70] Sisam of Oxford University Press reflected:

I suppose it is a muddle and not intentional cruelty. But our stronghold in the United States was the academic world, which was in arms against the Nazi treatment of scholars and very active politically. A few well known scholars who go under (literally or metaphorically) will be worth a whole Ministry of Information to the German propaganda there.[71]

---

66 UA CQ/17/11 file 1.
67 UA CQ/11/17 file 2, Home Office to the Registrar, Sept. 28, 1940.
68 UA CQ/17/11 file 1, Registrar to Williams, July 1 1940.
69 UA CQ/11/17, W. H. Walsh to the University Registrar, Aug. 8, 1940.
70 UA CQ/11/17 file 1, Collingwood to Vice-Chancellor.
71 UA CQ/11/17 file 1, Sisam to the Registrar, July 18, 1940.

The vice-chancellor complained to the Home Office of slowness and clum-
siness in responding to requests for release.

Having drawn up its list, the university registrar put great energy into
ensuring that the Home Office complied with its recommendations.
When the application for the release of Gustav Steiner was turned down
in August 1940, the registrar was irritated by the imprecision of the refusal. There had been a failure to grasp that Steiner did not come into
contact with any patients, let alone those from the armed forces, that he
did not need to hold a medical qualification for research work, and that
in any case Steiner (a neurologist) was a medical graduate of Vienna.
Steiner was duly allowed to resume work at the Radcliffe infirmary.[72]
The registrar secured permits for other refugees to resume work in the
infirmary. Mackintosh secured these for his research group, pointing out
that the research was relevant to the ventilation of submarines, and there
was only contact with unconscious patients. It took less than a week to
obtain a permit from the Aliens War Service Department for Grita
Weiler (who had Polish nationality and a Berlin M.D.) to do anesthetics research, and for Epstein (who was not interned).[73] The case for allowing Renate Schulz to be able to resume her medical studies at the
Radcliffe Infirmary was vigorously pursued.[74] Family dependents were
helped: An apprenticeship as an electrical technician was found for the
son and a friend of the son of the historian Hans Rothfels. The registrar
went to great lengths to remove restrictions regarding the curfew and
travel on others, helped with lodgings and troublesome tenants, and
gave advice on career prospects, combining efficiency, tact, and friend-
liness.[75]

The war then broke down personal and academic barriers. The length
of time in internment was about three months (see Table 4.3). Compared
with the humanities, relatively few doctors and scientists were interned.
Among the medically qualified not interned were Ludwig Guttmann,
Glees, and Munz. The war also provided a stimulus for the large-scale
production of penicillin and anesthetics and for building up the department

---

72 UA CQ/11/17 file 1, Registrar to Home Office, Aug. 23, 1940, and Steiner to the Registrar,
    Oct. 17, 1940, on permission having been granted.
73 UA CQ/11/17 file 2, Mackintosh to Registrar, Oct. 4, 1940, concerning Weiler; Registrar to
    Mackintosh, Oct. 8, 1940; permit from Aliens War Service Dept., Oct. 10, 1940; Mackintosh to
    Registrar concerning Epstein, Oct. 22, 1940.
74 UA CQ/11/17 file 2, Registrar to Home Office, Oct. 7, 1940, and letter of thanks from Fritz
    Schulz to the Registrar, Oct. 16, 1940.
75 UA CQ/11/17 files 1 and 2, for numerous instances of assistance by Veale.

Table 4.3 *Interned Oxford academics*

Name	Reviewing committee	Subject	Date of internment	Free on/ before
Alexander, F	HO	Archaeology	7/22/40	10/3/40
Borkenau, P	RS	Medicine	7/20/40	—
Braun, M	HO	Classics	8/9/40	10/3/40
Brink, K.O	HO		7/22/40	10/22/40
Burchardt, F	HO	Economics/statistics	7/22/40	—
Cahn-Nernst, C.H.W	HO	Medicine	8/1/40	10/3/40
Cantoni, G	RS		7/20/40	—
Carsten, F.M.L.		History	—	—
Cassirer, E	HO	Philosophy	—	—
Eisler, R	HO	Theology	8/9/40	9/2/40 (on medical grounds)
*Ellinger, L.P	HO	Chemistry	7/22/40	10/29/40
Forchheimer, K		Economics		10/8/40
Goldschmidt, R.W	HO	Psychology	8/9/40	refused, released 4/3/41
*Gruenfeld, G	HO	Chemistry	7/22/40	—
Gruenhut, M	HO	Criminology	7/22/40	10/12/40
Hammelmann, H.A	SPSL		8/29/40	—
Heinemann, F.H	HO	Philosophy	8/1/40	10/3/40
Hornik, M	HO	History	7/22/40	10/7/40
Jacobsthal, P	HO	Archaeology	7/22/40	10/3/40
Jacoby, F	HO		8/9/40	10/3/40
Jellinek, S	RS	Medicine	7/20/40	10/3/40
Kosterlitz, R	HO	Psychology	7/22/40	—
Kramm, H.H	HO	Theology [pastor]	7/22/40	—
Kripps, H.H.E.A	HO		7/22/40	10/3/40
Labowsky, N	HO		8/1/40	10/3/40
Levy, A	HO	Law	8/9/40	free
Levy, H.L	HO		9/2/40	free
von Leyden, W	HO	Philosophy	8/1/40	11/22/40
Maas, P	HO	Classics	7/22/40	8/29/40
Mars, H	SPSL		8/9/40	—
Meinhard, H	HO	Ethnology	7/22/40	10/3/40
Minio-Palluello, L	HO	Philosophy	7/22/40	—
+Miré		Industrial law	6/25/40	—
Momigliano, A	HO	Ancient history	8/1/40	11/9/40
Moos, S	HO	Economics	7/22/40	10/3/40
*Mueller, G	HO	Chemistry	7/22/40	—
Munk, Miss I	RS	Chemistry	8/9/40	—
Nohl, H.C	HO	Medicine	8/1/40	refused
*Nussbaum, H.M.K.	HO	Agriculture	7/22/40	—
Olden, R	HO	Law	7/22/40	10/3/40

Table 4.3 (*cont.*)

Name	Reviewing committee	Subject	Date of internment	Free on/ before
*Paneth, H.R	HO	Chemistry	7/22/40	—
Pfeiffer, R	HO	Classics	7/22/40	11/3/40
Prag, A	RS	Mathematics	7/20/40	—
Pringsheim, F	HO	Law	7/22/40	refused 10/26/40 referred 12/2/40
Rohatyn, S	HO	Law	7/22/40	10/11/40 (on medical grounds)
Rothfels, H	HO	History	7/22/40	10/3/40
*Schmidt, G.M.W.	HO	Chemistry	7/22/40	—
Schulz, F	HO	Law	7/22/40	by 10/14/40
*Schulz, Miss R	HO	Medicine	8/1/40	free
Steindl, J	HO	Economics	7/22/40	10/18/40
Steiner, G	HO	Medicine	7/22/40	10/3/40
Stern, H.W.	UB		8/29/40	—
Stern, W.B.	HO		8/29/40	10/31/40
Uhlig, J	HO	Statistics	7/22/40	refused 10/23/40 granted 1/4/41
Vivanti, L	HO	Philosophy	8/1/40	11/15/40 (on medical grounds)
Vogel, J	HO	Literature	7/22/40	10/29/40
Waissmann	HO	Philosophy	7/22/40	10/3/40
Walzer, R	HO	Arabic	7/22/40	10/3/40
Weinstock, S	HO		7/22/40	10/18/40
Wellesz, E	HO	Music	7/22/40	10/14/40
Wolff, M	HO	Law	7/22/40	—
Zuntz, G	HO	Theology	7/22/40	11/1/40

Notes: HO = Home Office. UB = Universities Board. SPSL = Society for the Protection of Science and Learning. RS = Royal Society.
* = Undergraduate. Note that humanities undergraduates have not been included.
+ = Ruskin College.
Sources: UA CQ/11/17. File 2, 1 Oct. 1940 to 31 Dec. 43

of pharmacology. Among the outstanding wartime research groups was the collaboration of anatomists, physiologists, zoologists, and surgeons who applied their research to nerve injuries and skin grafting. Ernst Guttmann (a Prague M.D.) worked in the department of zoology with J.Z. Young on peripheral nerve injuries, as did Guttmann and Glees. This work also led to developments that laid the foundations of modern immunology by Peter Medawar.[76]

Whereas the 1930s and 40s were a period of frustration for German-trained medical scientists at Oxford, the 1950s were an era of acceptance at a time of scientific expansion. Notions of utility gave way to the building up of basic science. Krebs, for example, moved away from nutrition-oriented research, toward problems in basic biochemistry. From 1951 Bülbring worked on smooth muscle research, developing the legacy of Hill and Meyerhof. The appointment of Krebs in 1954 initiated concerted efforts to introduce molecular biology to Oxford. Krebs's success as a scientific empire-builder challenged traditional values by giving research priority over teaching. Nikolaas Tinbergen came to zoology (not as a refugee but as a victim of the German occupation of Holland and as an exponent of ethnological research as developed by Konrad Lorenz). Schrödinger's frustrations can be contrasted with Michael Polanyi's intellectually creative period in Oxford, when he absorbed the ideological values concerning teleology and freedom in science from the cytologist J.R. Baker and the ecologist Tansley.

For the biochemists, a straightforward transfer of German academic approaches and professional structures was not viable. There needed to be a positive response by refugees to the British situation, which was itself undergoing rapid transformation. Blaschko fused methods learned from Meyerhof with Cambridge biochemistry and the physiology of Barcroft and Hopkins. Chain benefited from a Cambridge Ph.D. obtained under Hopkins, and Hopkins's laboratory was also fruitful for the maturing of Krebs's research on metabolic pathways. Bülbring initially was interested in pediatrics, but her collaboration with Burn set her on a pharmacological career. Krebs extended the range of Hopkins's nutritional research. Guttmann was fortunate in that his talents were appreciated by the Medical Research Council, and he developed an ability to interact with British clinicians on a broader social front.

Hopkins was farsighted in his hospitality to German-trained biochemists, and like Hill he applied the values of tolerance and intellectual pluralism so as to create a fruitful haven for German-trained biochemists. His expecta-

76 Fraenkel, *Hugh Cairns*, 139.

tion was that expertise in areas such as enzyme chemistry would contribute
to solving nutritional problems rather than contributing to chemotherapy.
Yet at the time, even the scientific community did not understand the
potential of this type of work and of particular researchers. In 1935 Krebs
wrote of Chain: "More of a musician than a scientist and would do better
in music than in chemistry. Rates C minus."[77] But Krebs's letter announc-
ing the citric acid cycle was rejected by *Nature* in 1937. There was a lack
of understanding of the potential of biochemistry concerning the development of molecular biology, studies of metabolism, and, above all, of
chemotherapy. There were similar barriers to clinical medicine. Balliol reduced the grant to Guttmann in 1938 because of his poor prospects for
permanent employment in Britain.

Oxford continued to inject distinction into its medical faculties by drawing on its Commonwealth contacts, facilitated by Rhodes scholarships. As
Charles Webster, in his contribution to the official history of the university,
observes: "Many distinguished European and Jewish refugees found their
way to Oxford but few ended up in chairs in the medical school." Assimilation into wider university life was remarkably slow. Krebs was the first
to achieve a college fellowship on appointment to a chair in 1954. Bülbring
only became a college fellow in 1960 when appointed to a personal chair,
and Blaschko in 1964. Glees, although praised as "a live wire in both teaching and research," never attained a fellowship despite extensive college
tutorial work but achieved professorial rank in Germany.[78] Thus, despite
considerable professional distinction, Oxford colleges were tardy in assimilation, and despite later honors all the erstwhile refugees retained the aura
of marginality. When Krebs came, he adopted the stance of a reformer,
pressing for equal advantages for departmental teaching staff. Although non-
collegiate lecturers became entitled to college fellowships, university research staff remained without any such entitlement. The parallel may be
drawn with those dependent on SPSL finance and the development of
outside-funded contract research. Although Oxford had rejected the
German-style institute, academic refugees confronted the university with
the problem of how to assimilate research staff. The academic refugees thus
represented the convergence of two antithetical traditions.

For these immigrants, Britain was the incarnation of a liberal society, and
indeed Hopkins and Hill fulfilled such expectations. Symptomatic of the
rise in status was a shift to conservatism of Chain, who married into the

77 SPSL 366/6.
78 OU CQ/11/17 file 3, exchange of letters between the Registrar and Liddell, Nov. 11 and 12,
    1946.

Beloff family, and of Krebs, who developed sociobiological solutions to social problems such as youth delinquency. Blaschko, who married a Quaker, remained true to enlightened progressive views. Ilse Sachs married Arthur Cooke, a physicist (and future warden of New College). Patterns of assimilation of the medical students trained in Oxford are more complex as they pursued careers elsewhere or outside the university. During the war there emerged a second generation – of sons and daughters of refugees who qualified in medicine in Oxford. Among these were Gus Fraenkel (a pupil of Cairns) and Renate Schulz. Three out of four Glees children embarked on medical careers (and another is a leading authority on the political history of the emigration). John Krebs is a highly respected authority on animal behavior in Oxford. This second generation, equipped with British degrees and acculturated at a relatively young age, have been successful, although hardly identifiable as a social group.

This account has examined the variation of individual experiences, while identifying expertise in physiology and biochemistry as the most sought after qualifications of those medical scientists who came to Oxford. Yet in tracing individual paths and unraveling complex chains of personal and academic relations, which took particular individuals on tortuous routes to Oxford, certain generalities should not be lost from sight.

First, there was no concerted university response to the Nazi persecution and dismissal of academics. Plans for a central university assistance fund in 1939 collapsed. There was no coordinated strategy either at a humanitarian level or to select the best potential researchers and teachers to strengthen areas of weakness in the basic medical sciences or in clinical medicine. Just as the British government devolved the admission of refugee scientists to the scientific community, so despite the efforts of the SPSL, Oxford left the matter of places for displaced researchers to the initiative of individual academics, colleges, and departments. Greater numbers might have been given hospitality and career appointments, if there had been a greater will to implement a coordinated plan for the rescue of dismissed academics. However, the SPSL enjoyed considerable support from certain well-placed individual British academics, and its policy of creating informal contacts and meetings was the most appropriate in the circumstances.

Although each academic's career has unique features, the impact of refugee doctors and scientists was less that of direct transfer and more that of a creative response and constructive synthesis with those academic disciplines and medical specialties open to innovation. The experience of emigration allowed certain scientists who came to Oxford a high degree of self-fulfillment in their research and personal lives. Yet invisible barriers preventing full assimilation and the gaining of status and influence within Oxford University and the broader academic community remained. Ironically, the most academically and professionally successful figure of the "Oxford group" (albeit a latecomer) – Hans Krebs – sought to recreate the social forms of a German professor, emphasizing research as a major priority and thereby challenging teaching-oriented British systems of science education and career structures. His outspoken and highly critical agenda of reform only had very partial success outside his department, although within his institute he did much to improve the conditions of highly talented researchers. His synthesis was a distinctive hybrid, as for so many other of the immigrants who amalgamated innovative features of British and German cultures. However successful in their research, medical scientists were unable to transcend fully their mentality of isolation as research workers, and to become assimilated into the cultural, social, and intellectual structures of the receiving society.

PART TWO

Psychology, Psychoanalysis, Pedagogy

5

Emigré Psychologists after 1933:
The Cultural Coding of Scientific and
Professional Practices

MITCHELL G. ASH

Examining the changes – or resistance to change – in the theorizing, research, and professional practices of German-speaking émigré psychologists
after 1933 presents an important opportunity to learn about the impact of
culturally conditioned scientific and professional styles in this discipline.
Recent studies of historical and contemporary scientific practices have sen-
sitized us to their rootedness in more local and situational as well as national
cultural contexts.[1] In psychology, too, conceptions of both scientific and
professional subject matter and practices differed by culture, although the
differences were often gradual rather than absolute, and there were local
variations within each national style.

In German-speaking Europe, both limited opportunities for new disciplines in the established system of higher education and the knowledge-
interests of experimenting psychologists themselves made it opportune for
them to compete for professorships in philosophy, which in turn influenced
their research priorities toward philosophically relevant topics in human
cognition. In the 1920s, philosophically oriented experimental psychology
participated fully in the struggle of competing world-views characteristic of
that time; it also lived in uneasy balance with varied attempts to transform
the field into a science-based profession, and to expand its subject matter
and methodological options accordingly. In the Nazi period, due mainly to
demand for psychological assistance in officer-selection for the Wehrmacht,

---

1 Jonathan Harwood, "National Styles in Science: Genetics in Germany and the United States between the World Wars," *Isis* 78 (1987): 390–414; Harwood, *Styles of Scientific Thought: The German
Genetics Community, 1900–1933* (Chicago, 1993); Jane Maienschein, "Epistemic Styles in German
and American Embryology," *Science in Context* 4 (1991): 407–27; Nathan Reingold, "The Peculiarities of the Americans, or Are There National Styles in the Sciences?" *Science in Context* 4 (1991):
347–66.

a synthesis occurred based on a predominance of personality theory and diagnostics that would last into the 1960s.[2]

Before this had happened, however, Nazi anti-Semitism and political pressure had forced the removal or resignation and emigration of seven full professors and fifteen associate professors who had specialized in psychology, including the heads of four of the five leading psychological institutes in German-speaking universities.[3] The impact of Nazism in this field thus corresponds to the pattern that Klaus Fischer has suggested for émigré scientists in physics. Although émigrés made up only 14.6 percent of the membership of the German Society for Psychology – slightly lower than Fischer's figure of 15.4 percent for all academics – the toll was far higher in the upper ranks of the discipline.[4] Five full professors – one-third of all scholars of that rank in the field in the German Reich – were removed by the Nazi civil service law. These included William Stern (Hamburg), Max Wertheimer (Frankfurt/Main), David Katz (one of only two professors dismissed in Rostock), and Wilhelm Peters (Jena). All emigrated within a year. The fifth, Otto Selz, professor at the commercial academy in Mannheim, remained in Germany until 1939, then emigrated to Amsterdam, from where he was deported to Auschwitz and murdered.

Wolfgang Köhler, a non-Jew who headed the Psychological Institute at the University of Berlin, was one of the few German professors who publicly protested against the Nazis' dismissals. After trying for two years to preserve a semblance of autonomy against persistent attacks by Nazi students and denunciations by careerist colleagues, he left Berlin in 1935 for a position at Swarthmore College.[5] After 1938, the director and associate director of the Vienna Psychological Institute, Karl and Charlotte Bühler, and many of their students, joined the exodus. Adding up the considerable number of émigrés who worked outside the university system or who had

---

2 For overviews, see Mitchell G. Ash, "Psychology in Twentieth-Century Germany: Science and Profession," in Geoffrey Cocks and Konrad H. Jarausch, eds., *German Professions, 1800–1950* (New York, 1990), 289–307; Ulfried Geuter, *The Professionalization of Psychology in Nazi Germany*, trans. Richard Holmes (Cambridge, 1992).

3 For the following, see Mitchell G. Ash, "Disziplinstruktur und Wissenschaftstransfer – deutschsprachige Psychologen in der Emigration," *Berichte zur Wissenschaftsgeschichte* 7 (1984): 208–9; Geuter, *Professionalization*, 52ff.

4 Klaus Fischer, "Die Emigration von Wissenschaftlern nach 1933: Möglichkeiten und Grenzen einer Bilanzierung," *Vierteljahresschrift für Zeitgeschichte* 39 (1991): 535–49; Fischer, "Die Emigration deutschsprachiger Physiker nach 1933: Strukturen und Wirkungen," in Herbert A. Strauss et al., eds., *Die Emigration der Wissenschaften nach 1933* (Munich, 1991), 28–9.

5 Mary Henle, "One Man against the Nazis – Wolfgang Köhler," *American Psychologist* 33 (1978): 939–44; Mitchell G. Ash, "Ein Institut und eine Zeitschrift: Zur Geschichte des Psychologischen Instituts der Universität Berlin und der Zeitschrift *Psychologische Forschung* vor und nach 1933," in Carl-Friedrich Graumann, ed., *Psychologie im Nationalsozialismus* (Berlin and Heidelberg, 1985), 113–37.

recently completed their training yields a total of 120 émigré psychologists. Of these, 80 went to the United States, 12 to Great Britain, and 11 to Palestine; the others scattered to Turkey and various Latin American countries.[6]

In the United States, where two-thirds of the émigrés eventually went, a growing university network offered greater opportunities for institutional independence in psychology, but at the cost of implicit and at times explicit demands – willingly met – that academic psychologists present their work as both quantitative and socially relevant science. Efforts in this direction first peaked during World War I, when the mass IQ testing of soldiers brought the discipline to public awareness.[7] In the 1920s, the emergence of new funding sources such as the Laura Spellman Rockefeller Memorial intensified efforts in the field of child development, with the aim of transforming education.[8] Despite considerable conflict between academic and applied psychologists, by the mid-1920s the transformation of the field into a science-based, highly specialized profession was far further advanced in America than in German-speaking Europe.

German-speaking psychologists were no strangers to demands for quantification and social relevance; the differences appeared in the purposes, the referents, and the preferred styles of quantification. Kurt Danziger has distinguished three differences between the German or Austrian and American scenes that are important for understanding changes in émigrés' research and professional practices and their reception after 1933.[9]

1. A growing preference in America for "group data" – studies addressing variation *among* or across individuals rather than the behavior or cognition *of* individuals. This trend began in intelligence testing and educational psychology, and was oriented to the needs of education administrators for

6   The preceding data come from a biographical list of émigré psychologists published in preliminary form, with criteria of selection, in Ulfried Geuter, ed., *Daten zur Geschichte der Psychologie* (Göttingen, 1986), 1: 207–26, and since updated from the files of the Society for the Protection of Science and Learning, Bodleian Library, Oxford.

7   Franz Samelson, " 'Putting Psychology on the Map': Ideology and Intelligence Testing," in Allen Buss, ed., *Psychology in Social Context* (New York, 1979), 103–68; Richard von Mayrhauser, "The Practical Language of American Intellect," *History of the Human Sciences* 4 (1991): 371–93; Joanne Brown, *The Definition of a Profession: The Authority of Metaphor in the History of Intelligence Testing, 1890–1920* (Princeton, N.J., 1992).

8   Franz Samelson, "Organizing for the Kingdom of Behavior: Academic Battles and Organizational Policies in the Twenties," *Journal of the History of the Behavioral Sciences* 21 (1985): 33–47; Elizabeth Lomax, "The Laura Spellman Rockefeller Memorial: Some of its Contributions to Early Research on Child Development," *Journal of the History of the Behavioral Sciences* 13 (1977): 283–93.

9   Kurt Danziger, "Social Context and Investigative Practice in Early Twentieth-Century Psychology," in Mitchell G. Ash and William R. Woodward, eds., *Psychology in Twentieth-Century Thought and Society* (Cambridge, 1987), 13–34; Danziger, *Constructing the Subject: Historical Origins of Psychological Research* (Cambridge, 1990).

classification instruments, but soon spread to basic research in learning and cognition. German-speaking psychologists employed quantification, but tended far more – in keeping with the traditional ideal of *Bildung* as personal self-cultivation – to emphasize processes *within* or the characteristic personality structures *of* individuals, rather than differences *among* individuals.

2. A shift in the relation of experimenter and subject, from a situation of more nearly equal status and potentially exchangeable roles, as had originally prevailed in German research, to one in which the experimenter was clearly in control and the "subjects" would more accurately be called "objects" responding to variables manipulated by the experimenter. Concomitant with this was a growing emphasis in America on the parceling out of "independent" and "dependent" variables and the construction of quantifiable functional interactions between them over holistic phenomenological investigation. The counterpart to this tendency in clinical research was the treatment of individuals as collections of independently variable measurable traits. Corresponding changes occurred to some extent in Germany and Austria as well; but older styles of working based on the self-selection of an educated elite rather than the training of expert professionals, and holistic assumptions also derived from German cultural tradition, persisted.

3. A technocratic orientation, foundational to both of these features, that was far more widespread and less ambivalent in America than in Germany and was by no means confined to applied psychologists. Even Clark Hull's 1936 presidential address to the American Psychological Association, in which he set out a hypothetical-deductive model of learning theory with the hope of placing psychology on a scientific footing comparable with that of classical physics, included the hope that such work would eventually encompass moral behavior; in an earlier letter to a Rockefeller Foundation official, he stated confidently that such a science would help to build "a more rational society."[10] In German-speaking Europe, too, the displacement of a discourse oriented toward the world-view or identity needs of an educated elite by that of administrative, instrumental reason began in the 1920s and accelerated in the 1930s. But both the objects and the style of that discourse differed from those of American testing and learning theory.

These émigré psychologists' stories show that the categories of adaptation or assimilation often employed in earlier studies of the "intellectual migra-

---

10   Clark L. Hull to Warren A. Weaver, March 3, 1934. Rockefeller Archive Center, North Tarry-
     town, New York, RG 3, series 915, box 4, folder 37; Hull, "Mind, Mechanism and Adaptive
     Behavior," *Psychological Review* 44 (1937): 1–32.

tion" are too simple. Emigré psychologists did not only submit to a new cultural order, turning themselves and their work inside out. They also mobilized biographical, institutional, and conceptual resources from both their past and their American circumstances to create new practices. In doing so, they emphasized their disagreements with some of the core assumptions of American psychologists. Theirs was a case of what I would like to call acculturation by opposition; for it was precisely because they differed from the mainstream that they were noticed and had an impact.

Relevant for understanding the reception of the émigrés is the fact that American psychology is not a monolithic entity, but a collection of specialties that emerged at different times. The shift from cognition to learning theory as the predominant field of basic research began in the 1920s, paralleling the growth of child studies; the emergence of personality and social psychology as important specialties came in the 1930s; the growth of clinical psychology followed in the 1940s and 1950s. This sequence has determined the three examples to be considered here. Each comes from one of the institutes or theory groups that were decimated by Nazism, and each relates in turn to developments in one specialty within American psychology.

First, Gestalt psychology is presented as an example of clashing styles in basic research in experimental psychology. Second, Berlin psychologist Kurt Lewin, a close associate of the Gestalt theorists in Berlin, who became the founder of group dynamics in America, is considered as a leading representative of practice-oriented basic and applied research in social psychology. Finally, Hedda Bolgar, a student of Vienna professor Charlotte Bühler's, who became a clinician, is discussed as a case of the conversion of practice-oriented basic research into a tool of professional practice in the then-emerging field of clinical psychology. The psychologists in all three examples had successful careers. As will be clear, however, in all three cases differences in the cultural coding of their practices, and thus difficulties in the transplantation of research or professional styles across cultures, remained.

GESTALT PSYCHOLOGY: A CLASH OF RESEARCH STYLES

Briefly and broadly characterized, the Gestalt psychologists' goal was not to discover covering laws that could account for the variance in different subjects' perceptions under given conditions, but to search for what Max Wertheimer, the founder of Gestalt theory, often called the "essence" of phenomena.[11] By this he meant the order believed to inhere in phenomena as experienced under particular stimulus conditions, not correlational or other contingent functional relationships between independent and dependent variables. With its emphasis on inherent order and meaning (*Sinn*), Gestalt theory and experimentation expressed an aesthetic concept of science fundamentally opposed to technological metaphors of mind drawn from classical mechanics. Sometimes Wertheimer spoke of "good" phenomena, those that most clearly and immediately exemplify the structure of experience in a given situation. The challenge was to construct experimental situations in such a way that "good" phenomena could happen. The most famous examples are the so-called *phi* phenomena – apparent motion without a moving object, the visual basis of motion pictures – and the so-called "Gestalt laws" thought to govern the spontaneous (self-)organization of objects in the perceptual field.

Although Wertheimer first presented his Gestalt laws in the form of demonstrations using simple geometric figures, he emphasized that quantitative research, usually employing threshold measurements, would be needed to determine, for example, whether proximity or similarity of objects to one another was more important in perceptual grouping. Experiments in the Berlin and Frankfurt psychological institutes used such standard measurement techniques, and often employed parametric design as well – systematic variation of stimulus parameters in order to confirm or disprove particular explanations of the phenomena in question. The issue was not one of qualitative versus quantitative research, but rather the referent of quantification. Sought were events *within* individuals, not the differences *among* or across individuals that were becoming the norm in American psychology in the 1920s.

During visits to the United States before their emigration, the Gestalt theorists became well known for their critique of behaviorism. From the first, that critique focused primarily on the presupposition underlying the behaviorists' research practices. Köhler made the point, for example, that both sensation-based cognitive psychology and behaviorism assumed the existence of atomic units (sensations or reflexes) and combined them ad-

11   For further background, see Mitchell G. Ash, "Gestalt Psychology: Origins in Germany and Reception in the United States," in Claude Buxton, ed., *Points of View in the Modern History of Psychology* (Orlando, Fla., 1985), 295–34; Ash, *Gestalt Psychology in German Culture, 1890–1967: Holism and the Quest for Objectivity* (New York, 1995).

ditively without considering dynamic interactions among them, or even observing whether the pieces are actually present in experience or behavior. Analysis is needed in science, Köhler emphasized, but it is important to choose appropriate, natural units from which to begin.[12] The initial reception of Gestalt theory in the United States was ambivalent. Psychologists' responses ranged from sympathetic skepticism to the hostility reflected in such titles as "The Phantom of the Gestalt." At the practical level, pedagogues were unsure how the new approach could help them in their work. The Gestalt theorists thus missed a connection with the growing research empire in child development then being constructed with Rockefeller Foundation support. Nonetheless, their critique of behaviorism encountered enough sympathy to win an endowed research professorship for Kurt Koffka at Smith College in 1927.[13]

After the Nazis forced the permanent emigration of the remaining founders of Gestalt theory and many of their students to the United States, changes occurred in the school's presentation, methodology, and institutional setting. Most significant for this topic was one subtle change in research practice – a shift to "Americanized" methods that occurred in Wolfgang Köhler's psychophysiology. In Berlin, Köhler had begun to investigate phenomena such as successive comparison and recall patterns, which he thought would yield significant clues about the brain events underlying perception. At Swarthmore College in the late 1930s, working in a laboratory of his own design, he began to use newly developed EEG (electroencephalograph) equipment to try to discover such brain events directly.[14]

Köhler pursued this program by taking up the so-called "figural aftereffects" initially examined by James J. Gibson.[15] Gibson had found, for example, that a curved line appears less curved after a few minutes' steady inspection; when it is removed and a straight line shown in the same place, the new line seems curved in the opposite direction. To explain such displacements, Köhler hypothesized that when direct current flows through brain cells, these become resistant to the flow, which is then deflected elsewhere. He had already postulated such "satiation" effects two decades earlier to explain sudden changes in the perception of ambiguous figures –

---

12 Wolfgang Köhler, *Gestalt Psychology* (New York, 1929).
13 For details, see Michael M. Sokal, "The Gestalt Psychologists in Behaviorist America," *American Historical Review* 89 (1984): 1240–63; Ash, "Gestalt Psychology."
14 Wolfgang Köhler, *Dynamics in Psychology* (New York, 1933).
15 James J. Gibson, "Adaptation, Aftereffect and Contrast in the Perception of Curved Lines," *Journal of Experimental Psychology* 16 (1993): 1–31.

the "Gestalt switches" later made famous by Thomas Kuhn.[16] His early work on figural aftereffects with Hans Wallach, himself an émigré psychologist and former student of Köhler's, used the systematic phenomenological approach they had employed in work on other topics in Berlin to test the accuracy of Gibson's interpretations. In keeping with the traditional mode of experimentation in Germany, experimenter and subject often reversed roles, as Köhler or Wallach acted both as tester and testee. The use of measurement was quite crude in this exploratory study. Statistical assessment of results was absent, and individual differences were acknowledged only in passing.[17]

By the late 1940s and early 1950s, Köhler and his co-workers, mainly American M.A. degree candidates and postdoctoral fellows, had proceeded to exact measurements of direct currents in the cortexes of cats and humans.[18] In his reports of the results, Köhler continued and extended the criticism he had addressed to behaviorism in general in the 1920s, taking psychologists to task not only for making assumptions that were inadequate to psychological facts but also for failing to notice that the instruments they conventionally used were heavily dependent on theory. Because investigators presupposed what he called the "conduction hypothesis" – that nervous transmission always proceeds in short, linear bursts with no interactions among the transmission lines – they expected "all valuable information" on electrical patterns in the cortex to come from "waves of limited duration." They therefore worked with capacity-coupled amplifiers constructed for the study of rapidly oscillating currents and kept the stimulation time short. This makes it "difficult for certain other facts to announce their presence in the records" – the slow, steady currents spreading continuously through the cortex that Köhler believed to be the correlates of figural aftereffects and form perception in general.[19] Although Köhler foregrounded his opposition to the basic assumptions of the physiologists he was addressing, in

16 Wolfgang Köhler, *Die physischen Gestalten in Ruhe und im stationärem Zustand: Eine naturphilosophische Untersuchung*, 2d ed. (Erlangen, 1924), 206ff.
17 Wolfgang Köhler and Hans Wallach, "Figural Aftereffects: An Investigation of Visual Processes," *Proceedings of the American Philosophical Society* 88 (1944): 269–357.
18 Wolfgang Köhler and David A. Emery, "Figural Aftereffects in the Third Dimension of Visual Space," *American Journal of Psychology* 60 (1947): 159–201; Köhler and Richard Held, "The Cortical Correlate of Pattern Vision," *Science* 110 (1949): 414–19; Köhler, Held, and Daniel N. O'Connell, "An Investigation of Cortical Currents," *Proceedings of the American Philosophical Society* 96 (1952): 290–330; Köhler and O'Connell, "Currents of the Visual Cortex in the Cat," *Journal of Cellular and Comparative Physiology* 49 (1957): suppl. 2:1–43.
19 Köhler, Held, and O'Connell, "An Investigation of Cortical Currents," 293. This criticism parallels current analyses of the role of instruments in science, e.g., Timothy Lenoir, "Models and Instruments in the Development of Electrophysiology, 1845–1912," *Historical Studies in the Physical Sciences* 17 (1986): 1–54.

such remarks he subtly signaled acculturation as well by adapting to the apparatus-driven research style of the community in which he was working.

Köhler later wrote that physiological psychology was "primarily an American enterprise," and that "probably all European psychologists who came to this country learned from their American colleagues to be much stricter about experimental proof than they had been before."[20] Both statements need to be taken with a grain of salt. Work in physiological psychology using EEG apparatus occurred in Germany and in Austria as well in this period.[21] As for "experimental proof" in America, Köhler had been just as strict in Germany. What was actually wanted was a different style of experimentation. Köhler had claimed long before that such direct psychophysiological investigations were both possible in principle and of fundamental importance.[22] In the United States he had the technology to carry them out, and he used it.

Taking that step was problematic in two respects. First, to make his empirical tests work, Köhler had to assume a geometric correspondence of perceptual forms and underlying brain events – just the opposite of the functional isomorphism he had originally wanted to show.[23] Second, he exposed himself to refutation on his own terms – or rather, those he had adopted from the Americans. Köhler's demonstration of direct cortical currents in cats and humans appeared to support his attribution of figural aftereffects to "satiation" processes in the cortex. Karl Lashley, Roger Sperry, and others, however, showed that inserting insulating mica strips into the cortexes of monkeys to block current flow did not prevent them from perceiving forms.[24] For physiological psychologists this ended the matter. Köhler's response and his suggestions for further experiments were generally ignored.[25] Until very recently, research in neuropsychology continued to be dominated by studies of single cortical cells or cell groups – atomism incarnate.

20 Wolfgang Köhler, "The Scientists from Europe and Their New Environment" (1953), in Mary Henle, ed., *The Selected Papers of Wolfgang Köhler* (New York, 1971), 423, 428.
21 See, e.g., Hubert Rohracher, *Die Arbeitsweise des Gehirns und die psychischen Vorgänge* (Leipzig, 1939); Rohracher, *Die elektrischen Vorgänge im menschlichen Gehirn* (Leipzig, 1941).
22 Wolfgang Köhler, *Die physischen Gestalten*, 193 n. 1.
23 Köhler and Emery, "Figural Aftereffects."
24 Karl S. Lashley, K. L. Chow, and Josephine Semmes, "An Examination of the Electric Field Theory of Cerebral Integration," *Psychological Review* 58 (1951): 123–36; Roger W. Sperry and N. Miner, "Pattern Perception following Insertion of Mica Plates into the Visual Cortex," *Journal of Comparative and Physiological Psychology* 48 (1955): 463–9.
25 Wolfgang Köhler, "Unsolved Problems in the Field of Figural Aftereffects," *Psychological Record* 15 (1965): 63–83; Mary Henle, "The Influence of Gestalt Psychology in America," in Robert B. Rieber and Kurt Salzinger, eds., *Psychology: Theoretical and Historical Perspectives* (New York, 1980), 177–90.

A further example of the impact of research style on the integration of Gestalt theory into American psychology brings us closer to the preference for parceling out "factors" or variables and the statistical assessment of results mentioned previously as characteristic of American psychology. In the late 1940s and early 1950s, attaching themselves to the growing popularity of psychoanalytic concepts, experimenters took what they called a "new look" at cognition, studying the effects of unconscious dynamic factors such as mental set or attitudes on perception. In 1951, Abraham S. Luchins, formerly Max Wertheimer's assistant at the New School, took the "new lookers" to task for pitting such theoretically derived "factors" against one another, rather than treating perception as a unified process. In response to this, Jerome Bruner, a leading proponent of the "new look" who considered himself basically sympathetic to the Gestalt viewpoint, wrote, "I for one feel severely hampered by the injunction not to separate perceptual, cognitive and motivational variables. How shall I do my experiments?"[26]

This incident suggests that the ambivalent reception of Gestalt theory in American psychology was not due solely to the predominance of neobehavioristic learning theory over perception and cognition in the 1930s and 1940s, as has been contended in the past.[27] Even when cognition returned to the forefront of basic research in the 1950s and 1960s, tensions remained because of fundamental differences in research style. The Gestalt theorists comprehended perception as a unitary whole process, and tried to develop physiological models to explain its dynamics. Such efforts were not easily compatible with their American counterparts' attempts to construct quantitative functional relationships between (hypothetical) parts, dimensions, or aspects of experience and discover statistical models, or covering laws that would account for the variance in individual subjects' responses. Given the practical origins of American investigators' allegiance to statistical confirmation in the needs of school administrators and others for classification instruments, there appears to be a direct connection in the case of Gestalt theory between developing methodological priorities within a discipline – linked in turn to societal demands on its practitioners – and the reception accorded to émigrés' ideas and methods.

26 Jerome Bruner, "One Kind of Perception: A Reply to Professor Luchins," *Psychological Review* 58 (1951): 308, in response to Abraham S. Luchins, "An Evaluation of Some Current Criticism of Gestalt Psychological Work on Perception," *Psychological Review* 58 (1951): 69–95.
27 Jean M. Mandler and George Mandler, "The Diaspora of Experimental Psychology: The Gestaltists and Others," in Donald Fleming and Bernard Bailyn, eds., *The Intellectual Migration: Europe and America, 1930–1960* (Cambridge, Mass., 1969), 371–419.

THE LEWIN GROUP:
FROM THE GROUP AS DATUM TO ACTION RESEARCH

Like the Gestalt psychologists, Kurt Lewin accepted the double identity of philosopher and experimenting psychologist. But an early work entitled *The Socialization of the Taylor System*, written just after the abortive German revolution of 1918–19 and published in 1920 in a series edited by independent Marxist thinker Karl Korsch, reveals an underlying practical aim of even his academic research – to humanize the factory system with the aid of psychological expertise.[28] Lewin and his Berlin students acted on this intention in research on the psychology of will and affect. The topics chosen included the "satiation" effect of repetitive tasks, memory for completed and uncompleted tasks, the effect of success and failure on children's and workers' level of aspiration, and the dynamics of anger. Two central and still appealing features of this work were the attempt to study ordinary life situations in a laboratory setting, and the careful attention paid to the interaction of experimenter and subject – to the experiment itself as a social situation.[29]

Lewin criticized American-style statistical methods in a leading American journal as early as 1931, saying they yielded only statements such as, "eight-year-olds in New York tend to behave this way, while six-year-olds in California act like this." Instead of this approach, he tried to recreate ideal-typical situations, embodiments of human-environment interactions in the laboratory, a procedure analogous in his view to the thought experiments about motion in an ideal, frictionless medium from which Galileo derived the law of free fall.[30] That law is stated in numbers rather than words, and Lewin's Berlin group had no objection to quantitative arguments. In his student Blyuma Zeigarnik's classic study of the retention of uncompleted tasks, for example, the fact that such tasks are remembered far longer than completed ones was shown quantitatively.[31] Different from American- or Anglo-Saxon-style "group data" was the form of inference, and the ultimate aim to which it was subordinated. For Lewin, recreating dynamic interactions in the laboratory and making quantitative inferences about some of

28 Kurt Lewin, *Die Sozialisierung des Taylorsystems: Eine grundsätzliche Untersuchung zur Arbeits- und Berufspsychologie*, Praktischer Sozialismus, no. 4 (Berlin-Fichtenau, 1920).
29 See Joseph De Rivera, *Field Theory as Human Science: Contributions of Lewin's Berlin Group* (New York, 1976); Danziger, *Constructing the Subject*, 135ff.
30 Kurt Lewin, "The Conflict between Aristotelian and Galileian Modes of Thought in Contemporary Psychology," *Journal of General Psychology* 5 (1931): 141–77.
31 Blyuma Zeigarnik, "Über das Behalten erledigter und unerledigter Handlungen," *Psychologische Forschung* 9 (1927): 1–85.

the effects of those interactions were necessary preliminaries to the formal representation and measurement of the (psychological) field forces at work in such interactions.

However, Lewin became known in the United States before 1933 not as theoretician, nor even as an experimental psychologist of action and emotion, but as a specialist in child development with an approach alternative to that of behaviorism. Lewin's first positions in America after 1933 brought him into the research empire in child development that had been created with Rockefeller funding since 1925, and thus put him squarely at the interface between basic and applied research. Central to his subsequent development was the position arranged for him by Rockefeller Foundation official Lawrence K. Frank at the Iowa Child Welfare Research Station in 1935.[32] The station's official task was to investigate and assure the development of normal children. Although the station was primarily oriented to basic research, its director in the 1930s, George Stoddard, emphasized the possibility of improving children's development by altering their living conditions with "projects that are engineering in type."[33] He thus expressed a commitment to social change via basic research that had long been propounded by the Progressive movement. It was in this setting that Lewin and the small but devoted following he assembled around him – including émigré psychologist Tamara Dembo, who had been his student in Berlin, and several younger Americans – created the research on "authoritarian" and "democratic" leadership in children's play groups that established his reputation in America.

In their initial report, Lewin and Ronald Lippitt already employed a vocabulary that was only then becoming fashionable in America by speaking of "operational" definitions of the behavioral styles to be investigated. In the "authoritarian" play group, both the task – making theatrical masks – and its execution were defined by the leader at every stage, one step at a time; the leader remained aloof from the group, intervening only to criticize. In the "democratic" group, the leader acted as a member of the group, facilitating decisions on how and with what materials to proceed, providing technical advice only when asked, and only in the form of alternatives from which the group chose.[34]

32 For further details, see Mitchell G. Ash, "Cultural Context and Scientific Change in Psychology: Kurt Lewin in Iowa," *American Psychologist* 47 (1992): 198–207.
33 George Stoddard, "The Second Decade: A Review of the Activities of the Iowa Child Welfare Research Station, 1928–1938," *University of Iowa Studies in Child Welfare* 15 (1938): 17–18.
34 Kurt Lewin and Ronald Lippitt, "An Experimental Approach to the Study of Autocracy and Democracy: A Preliminary Note," *Sociometry* 1 (1938): 292–300. For a more complete listing of

The furthest-reaching change by far was the idea of experimenting with groups as such at all. The stated methodological aim of the experiments with groups was to get away from studying group-individual relationships and construct experimental situations "where group life can proceed freely," in order to consider "the total group behavior, its structure and development."[35] This is analogous to the holistic research style Lewin had created before his emigration. The purpose was to transfer that ideal-typical method from human–environment interactions in individuals to group behavior. The implicit assumption was that in both kinds of subject matter a procedure that retained the essential structural relations of everyday life situations would yield a more believable experimental picture than the manipulation of isolated independent and dependent variables. Thus a dimension of continuity from the Berlin years is evident. But the dimension of change revealed by the contemporary ideological resonance of the categories chosen could hardly be overlooked, even though Lewin denied that these ideal types were intended to correspond to any historical reality.

By 1931 Lewin had already recognized the significance of the "social atmosphere" of a school for education, and of "ideology" – meaning shared norms and values – for the psychology of reward and punishment.[36] The experimental style of his Berlin group was characterized from the beginning by attention to the interaction of experimenter and subject. Before 1933, however, the preferred social unit in Lewinian experiments was usually a dyad – a group consisting of two rather than more people. Only in Iowa did Lewin begin to work experimentally with larger groups as units. Thus it appears that a fundamental change in at least one significant aspect of Lewin's research style was a result of his emigration.

A further dimension of change becomes clear in the Lewin group's studies of frustration and regression.[37] On one level these studies continued the Berlin research program in the field of action and emotion, and combined it with developmental issues. The concept of regression itself was familiar to Lewin from his reading of Freud and Adler before 1933. But when the

group characteristics, including those of the so-called "laissez-faire" group studied later, see Ronald Lippitt and Robert K. White, "The 'Social Climate' of Children's Groups," in Roger G. Barker, J. S. Kounin, and Harold F. Wright, eds., *Child Behavior and Development: A Course of Representative Studies* (New York, 1943), 487.

35 Lewin and Lippitt, "An Experimental Approach to the Study of Autocracy and Democracy," 292.
36 Kurt Lewin, "Sachlichkeit und Zwang in der Erziehung zur Realität" (1931), in Franz E. Weinert and Horst Gundlach, eds., *Kurt Lewin-Werkausgabe*, vol. 6: *Psychologie der Entwicklung und Erziehung* (Bern, 1982), 215–24; Lewin, "The Psychological Situation in Reward and Punishment" (1931), reprinted in *A Dynamic Theory of Personality* (New York, 1935), 127.
37 Summarized in Roger G. Barker, Tamara Dembo, and Kurt Lewin, "Frustration and Regression," in Barker, Kounin, and Wright, eds., *Child Behavior and Development*, 441–58.

Lewin group in Iowa began to investigate the topic systematically, changes in the culture of experimentation became noticeable. Thus the text speaks not of the psychology of action and affect, but of behavior theory. More important than such terminological adaptations was the instrument employed as a sort of diagnostic ruler to establish and measure regression. Lewin's assistant, Roger Barker, who had learned the use of intelligence testing and related measurement techniques at Stanford, constructed a two-dimensional coordinate system, in which the children's mental ages were correlated with the results of a seven-point "constructivity scale" that had been created for this study. The scale consisted of ratings of observed play units according to their richness and originality. If the "constructiveness" ratings for play in test situations were not as high as those for children of the same mental age in free play, then one spoke of regression.[38] Thus in these studies, just the sort of statistical inference Lewin had criticized only a few years before became the chief support for the reliability and validity of the results. The quantitative argument was confined to a single section of the study, which was framed by other sections giving a carefully developed phenomenology of the behavior to be measured. Nonetheless, it appears clear that in this case not only the general research style but also the methods and even the argumentation reflect a complex mobilization of conceptual and methodological resources developed in Germany and in the United States.

Lewin and his co-workers quickly transferred the model of theory and experimentation first developed for the study of children's play groups to studies of leadership and conflict resolution in adults. The most interesting aspect of this work in this context is the optimism that Lewin expressed in studies with Alex Bavelas on "Training for Democratic Leadership."[39] The very idea that it is possible not only to select people – in this case youth group leaders – for democratic leadership by their behavior or personality characteristics, however determined, but to make such leaders even out of people who had not already been recognized as such, correspond well with the hopes of the liberal, socially activist wing of American psychology at that time. This is true as well for Lewin's "action research" studies of conflict resolution in the workplace – an American resurrection of the program he had advocated in his 1920 essay on the "socialization" of Taylorism.

It was here that Lewin ran up against a limit defined by his own allegiance

38 Barker, Dembo, and Lewin, "Frustration and Regression," 452–3; see also Roger G. Barker, "Settings of a Professional Lifetime," *Personality and Social Psychology* 37 (1979): 2137–57.
39 Alex Bavelas and Kurt Lewin, "Training in Democratic Leadership," *Journal of Abnormal Psychology* 37 (1942): 115–19.

to the values of his host culture. In a 1946 essay "Frontiers in Group Dynamics," published two years after he had left Iowa and had founded the Research Center for Group Dynamics at MIT, he responded to the claim that his approach focused too narrowly on small groups and paid insufficient attention to social and historical context. Mobilizing conceptual resources from his Berlin period, he invoked an analogy from physics by calling contextual factors "boundary conditions" or "frames of reference." He acknowledged that these had to be specified, just as physicists specify the parameters within which their equations hold, if the aim of "integrating the totality of the factors that determine group life" were to be achieved.[40] Thus he noted the influence of cultural factors on job performance in a study of conflict resolution at the Harwood Manufacturing Corporation. In this case, southern rural women received pay so much higher than their previous living standard "that they did not care to make more money even for a relatively small additional effort." He also noted the potential for conflict between the goals of training for democratic leadership and the "values of the larger cultural setting," which justified his suggestion of creating "cultural islands" during change.[41] Ultimately, however, societal and cultural "boundary conditions" retained the secondary role in Lewin's theory and research that they had already acquired for him in Germany.

In other contexts, Lewin was fully aware of the need to change such conditions in certain circumstances. Commenting on race relations in America, for example, he acknowledged that work in small groups alone would not bring fundamental change unless international political conditions supported it: "Intergroup conditions in this country will be formed to a large degree by events on the international scene, especially by the fate of the colonial peoples."[42] Unfortunately, he never found a way to integrate such intuitive insights systematically into his theorizing or his action research. Instead, what might be called a liberal technocratic perspective remained paramount. He continually referred to group work as "social engineering" or "social management"; and the provision of technical advice to managers was the often-stated purpose of the work he envisioned under the heading of group dynamics. As Lewin presented his work to new au-

---

40 Kurt Lewin, "Frontiers in Group Dynamics" (1946), in Dorwin Cartwright, ed., *Field Theory in Social Science: Selected Theoretical Papers* (New York, 1951), 193; see also Lewin, "Psychological Ecology" (1943), in *Field Theory in Social Sciences*, 185–6.

41 Lewin, "Frontiers in Group Dynamics," 215, 231–2; on the Harwood Manufacturing study, see Alfred J. Marrow, *The Practical Theorist: The Life and Work of Kurt Lewin* (New York, 1969), chap. 14.

42 Kurt Lewin, "Action Research and Minority Problems" (1946), in Lewin, *Resolving Social Conflicts: Selected Papers on Group Dynamics [1935–1946]* (New York, 1948), 215.

diences, the original goal of his German research – the humanization of work itself – may have lost the central position it had once had. What had started out as acculturation by opposition at the level of research practice in the work on "group atmospheres," became something closer to assimilation in social practice.

THE VIENNA SCHOOL:
FROM PRACTICE-ORIENTED BASIC RESEARCH TO
CLINICAL PRACTICE

Considering émigrés from the Vienna Psychological Institute affords an opportunity to examine transformations in the matrix extending from practice-oriented basic research to professional practice. There are three good reasons for paying attention to the Vienna school in this context. First, all but one of the Austrian émigrés came from Vienna. Second, Austrians made up 40 percent of émigré psychologists. Third, they comprised a still higher proportion (50 percent) of those who took up clinical and other practical careers after their emigration. The share of Austrians in practical work rises to 65 percent of those who emigrated at age 30 or younger.[43]

Austrians were so prominent among émigrés who became professionals because the Vienna Psychological Institute, along with those in Hamburg and Jena, was at the forefront of the transition to practice-oriented basic research in German-speaking psychology.[44] The institute was founded in 1922 in part because the leaders of the Social Democratic Party's school reform program hoped for scientific support for their child-centered approach to education. The most important institute department for the case discussed here was that of child and youth psychology, led by Charlotte Bühler and her associates Hildegard Hetzer and Lotte Schenck-Danzinger. In rooms located at the city's child adoption center (*Kinderübernahmestelle*), the department's researchers, most of whom were women, created so-called *Kleinkindertests* – performance measures for assessing the behavioral development of infants.[45]

43 Mitchell G. Ash, "Österreichische Psychologen in der Emigration: Fragestellungen und Überblick," in F. Stadler, ed., *Vertriebene Vernunft*, vol. 2: *Emigration und Exil österreichischer Wissenschaft* (Vienna and Munich, 1988), 256–7.

44 Mitchell G. Ash, "Politics and Psychology in Interwar Vienna: The Vienna Psychological Institute, 1922–1942," in Ash and Woodward, eds., *Psychology in Twentieth-Century Thought and Society*, 144–65; G. Benetka, *Zur Geschichte der Institutionalisierung der Psychologie in Österreich* (Vienna, 1990).

45 Hildegard Hetzer and Käthe Wolf, "Baby-Tests," *Zeitschrift für Psychologie* 107 (1928): 62–104; Charlotte Bühler and Hildegard Hetzer, *Kleinkindertests* (Leipzig, 1932); Hetzer, "Kinder- und jugendpsychologische Forschung im Wiener Psychologischen Institut von 1922 bis 1938," *Zeit-*

Three points about the department's work are important in this context. First, the methods used in these tests combined qualitative observation of behavioral patterns with statistical assessment. Second, however, the primary referent of quantification was not differences *among* individual children, but those *between the same child's performance earlier and later in development*. But this developmental focus also presupposed age-group norms that could not be derived without comparing children with one another. Third, and most significant, the tests were research and diagnostic instruments simultaneously. The tests and their associated studies, together with research on school-age children and youth based in part on the systematic interpretation of diaries, were components of Charlotte Bühler's attempt to construct a comprehensive biopsychological account of what she called "the course of human life" – an ancestor of what is now called life-span development psychology.[46] They also supported the construction of developmental norms that would be useful to institutions like the adoption center. The similarity of this project to the aims of the program funded by the Rockefeller Foundation in child development organized in America at this time was not coincidental. As a Rockefeller fellow in 1924, Bühler had acquired some of her techniques – particularly the combination of behavioral observation and statistical assessment – from Yale child psychologist Arnold Gesell; and Rockefeller funding had supported many of the Vienna institute's doctoral students.[47]

After the fall of the Social Democratic government in Vienna and the installation of an authoritarian regime in 1934, the women in the department of child and youth psychology continued working more or less as before, only without the ideological umbrella of reformist socialism. Despite nostalgic accounts to the contrary,[48] many émigré psychologists from Austria were products more of this 1930s milieu than of "Red Vienna." Particularly the younger ones among them were willing and able to engage in applications-oriented basic or in straightforward applied research, and had acquired some of the diagnostic tools that helped prepare them for work in clinical and applied fields in the United States.

schrift für Entwicklungspsychologie und Pädagogische Psychologie 14 (1982): 175–224; Lotte Schenck-Danzinger, "Zur Geschichte der Kinderpsychologie: Das Wiener Psychologische Institut," *Zeitschrift für Entwicklungspsychologie und Pädagogische Psychologie* 16 (1984): 85–101.

46 Paul Lazarsfeld et al., *Jugend und Beruf: Kritik und Material* (Jena, 1931); Charlotte Bühler, *Der menschliche Lebenslauf als psychologisches Problem* (Leipzig, 1933).

47 Charlotte Bühler file, Rockefeller Foundation Archives, LSRM box 57, folder 51; Lomax, "The Laura Spellman Rockefeller Memorial."

48 See, e.g., Sheldon Gardner and Gwendolyn Stevens, *Red Vienna and the Golden Age of Psychology, 1918–1938* (New York, 1992).

How did the practices they brought with them compare or clash with the statistically based style of personality testing and assessment that was just then becoming entrenched in America? The case of Hedda Bolgar, who completed her doctorate in 1934 under Charlotte Bühler's direction, is a first step toward answering that question.[49] Even before the German invasion of Austria, Bolgar had written to various clinics in the United States to inquire about improving her mastery of diagnostics, and had received an offer from the Michael Reese Clinic in Chicago. At Reese she encountered an unusually effective constellation of psychiatrists and psychologists cooperating under the leadership of Samuel Beck.

After the war, she became chief psychologist at the Chicago Mental Hygiene Clinic, which made possible contracts to clinical training programs at three universities. It was in this setting that she and a former Vienna colleague, Liselotte Fischer, brought out an adult version of a diagnostic instrument they and Charlotte Bühler had created in the 1930s for use in child development studies. The instrument was called the "World Test," because it was based on observing children at play in an object-filled environment of their own construction, rather than on paper-and-pencil tests or play with single toys. The immediate antecedents of the test were psychoanalytic play therapy techniques created by Melanie Klein and others. In the Vienna institute, the aim had been to adapt it for use with normal children.[50]

Important here are the culturally formed, holistic concepts of personality and of testing instantiated in the test. "Personality is a Gestalt and therefore essentially oversummative," Bolgar and Fischer wrote.[51] The most effective diagnostic instrument is therefore not a pencil-and-paper test designed to determine the amount of particular traits subjects have, but "one which elicits the most significant sample reactions to as accurate a sample environment as can be produced in an experimental situation. The freer the experimental situation, the more spontaneous and therefore more significant the reactions." The word "significant" is not used here to mean the statistical values of test results across individuals, but to mean the value of reactions from a person for the assessment of that person. Bolgar and Fischer

---

49 The following information comes from Hedda Bolgar interview with author, Los Angeles, Jan. 14, 1984.
50 Hedda Bolgar and Liselotte K. Fischer, "Personality Projection in the World Test," *American Journal of Orthopsychiatry* 17 (1947): 117–28. A certain irony, and a source of lingering resentment on Bolgar's part, is that her route to successful acculturation was blocked at first by her own teacher, Charlotte Bühler, who had already published a saleable version of the test (Charlotte Bühler and George Kelly, *The World Test: A Measure of Emotional Disturbance* [New York, 1941]).
51 Bolgar and Fischer, "Personality Projection," 117.

openly disparaged the administrative aims of their emerging field – "the mere labeling with a psychiatric tag" – then becoming widespread in clinical psychology.[52]

Their approach to measurement corresponds to their overall position. They defined a "normal" performance as one "observed in not less than 50 percent of all cases" – hardly a sophisticated scoring technique even by then-current standards. The composite picture of such a "normal" performance was no more than an ideal type extrapolated from their protocols; if it was quantitatively derived, they did not say clearly how. Completely missing was any attempt to single out particular normal or abnormal "traits" and determine their frequency independently of testees' overall behavior. A reading of the sample protocol they provided makes it quite clear that the clinical interpretation of single individuals' behavioral patterns was far more important to Bolgar and Fischer than labeling them as normal or deviant from a statistically derived group pattern.[53]

In this case, as in those of Wolfgang Köhler and Kurt Lewin, opposition to the predominant style of working in a given specialty did not lead to career rejection. Hedda Bolgar became director of the clinical training program at the University of Chicago in 1950. It was then that she became more intensively involved with psychoanalysis. After psychoanalyst Franz Alexander brought her to Mount Sinai Hospital to head the department of clinical psychology in the late 1950s, she helped organize the California School for Professional Psychology, an independent training institute. In 1974 she became the director of the Wright Institute, one of the most important psychotherapeutic training centers on the West Coast.

Bolgar's case illustrates how the mobilization of resources acquired in Europe in interaction with contemporary societal trends in America made possible a significant career in research-based professional practice, especially for younger émigrés. Important to this career was the conversion of implicit research into explicit diagnostic instruments. But precisely that process points to a certain tension in research styles. Further research is needed to determine whether that tension was entirely a clash of national cultures, or is better understood as a culturally colored variation on the controversy over clinical versus statistical prediction that marked the disciplinary demarcation of clinical psychology from other specialties in the 1950s.

52 Bolgar and Fischer, "Personality Projection."
53 Bolgar and Fischer, "Personality Projection," 124ff.

CONCLUSION

In all three of the cases examined here, émigré psychologists remained remarkably true to the culturally coded modes of working they had developed
in Europe, even as they sought and found niches in America. Common to
all of these approaches were holistic assumptions and opposition to concepts
of scientific procedure based on different assumptions that were widely
shared in American psychology. The reception of each approach abounded
in ironies.

In his work in psychology, Wolfgang Köhler made a limited effort to
adapt to local preferences in that specialty, but even that effort made it
possible in the end for the Americans to refute him on their terms. One
way out of such a situation would have been to carve out niches where
Americans could have been systematically trained in the Gestalt way of
knowing. After they left Germany, the founders of Gestalt theory all obtained positions where they could do excellent research but could not train
Ph.D.s. Köhler remained at Swarthmore until his retirement in 1955. Outstanding students came to study for B.A. and M.A. degrees as well as do
postdoctoral research with him; his colleagues David Krech, Richard
Crutchfield, and Edwin Newman were influenced by his ideas; and Köhler
himself was treated with respect, becoming in 1959 the only foreign-born
scientist to be elected president of the American Psychological Association.
But the lack of American students put the Gestalt viewpoint at a decided
competitive disadvantage compared with the neobehaviorist research institutions headed by Clark Hull and Kenneth Spence at Yale and Iowa, respectively, in the 1940s and 1950s, or the many centers for cognition
research in the 1950s and 1960s. In a recent essay, Mary Henle remarks
with some irony that contemporary cognitive scientists, by taking up issues
the Gestalt theorists had once raised, are supplying "the manpower" they
had lacked in the past.[54]

Kurt Lewin not only adapted to American psychology in the 1930s and
1940s, he helped to reshape it by opening up new problems, such as the
behavior of groups, to experimental research. Although he shared the technocratic dreams of Americans who wanted to change people and their social
relationships for the better, the way he tried to do this – experimenting
with groups as wholes and employing action research alongside laboratory
studies – put him at odds with mainstream preferences and conventions.

---

54 Mary Henle, "Rediscovering Gestalt Psychology," in Sigmund Koch and David E. Leary, eds., *A
    Century of Psychology as Science* (New York, 1985).

He circumvented that obstacle by utilizing foundation funding to found new research institutions, such as the Center for Group Dynamics at MIT, by creating informal organizations such as the "Topology Group," and by helping to found and lead the Society for the Psychological Study of Social Issues. When he died suddenly in 1947, at the age of 57, he was at the height of his career and influence.

By the late 1950s, according to his student Dorwin Cartwright, the limits to the impact of Lewin's mode of working had become clear. Neobehaviorist learning theory still dominated research on behavior that could be subjected to statistical scaling, while Lewin's approach and various Americanized variants of psychoanalysis were dominant in social psychology and personality research, where concepts and methods were necessarily less numerically precise in order to be effective.[55] Even in experimental social psychology, the concept of science on which Lewin had based his work was either ignored or met with complete incomprehension. His experiments with groups were admired as effective manipulations, and Lewin himself was elevated to iconic status as the founder of the specialty, but some of his most prominent students rejected his model of procedure. Instead they reconstructed what they took to be Lewinian research on the basis of by-then standard American experimental methodology, which prescribed the parceling out of independent and dependent variables and thus presupposed the very elementarism he had criticized. Other students and former co-workers, however, tried to continue his research style, and thus contributed to the development of ecological psychology.[56]

For Hedda Bolgar, as for many other émigrés, particularly the women among them, clinical or practical work was necessary for survival at a time when academic employment was scarce. Austrian psychologists in particular had the experience and motivation necessary to adapt by this means. The rapid growth of clinical psychology and other practice-oriented research areas after 1945, then, gave these émigrés further professional opportunities, and in many cases also chances for academic careers – a development that did not take this form in German-speaking Europe until twenty years later.[57] Bolgar participated in this development by converting research tools

55 Dorwin Cartwright, "Lewinian Theory as a Contemporary Systematic Framework," in Sigmund Koch, ed., *Psychology: A Study of a Science*, vol. 4: *General Systematic Formulations* (New York, 1959), 7–91.

56 Kurt Danziger, "The Project of an Experimental Social Psychology: Historical Perspectives," *Science in Context* 5 (1992): 309–28; Roger G. Barker, *Ecological Psychology: Concepts and Methods for Studying the Environment of Human Behavior* (Stanford, Calif., 1968).

57 On the growth of clinical psychology in the United States, see Albert R. Gilgen, *American Psychology since World War II: A Profile of the Discipline* (Westport, Conn., 1982); chap. 9.

into diagnostic instruments, yet she did so in a manner opposed to the predominant statistical mode of testing. Ultimately, linking up with psychoanalysis became her road to success, as it was for many American clinicians. Sander Gilman argues that the psychoanalysis Jewish émigrés brought to America seemed attractive because it was based on a biomedical model of medical practice.[58] On this interpretation, although Bolgar came from the humanistic milieu of the Vienna institute, she eventually attached herself to a different scientific culture.

As these case studies show, acculturation was not simply a process of submission to the discursive norms and scientific or professional practices that prevailed in a host culture. Rather, the émigrés mobilized biographical, conceptual, and methodological resources and reconstructed them to do a job, often opposing rather than passively accepting prevailing research and professional styles. In doing so, they did not fundamentally change American psychology but substantially enriched it.

58 Sander Gilman, "Constructing the Image of the Appropriate Therapist: The Struggle of Psychiatry with Psychoanalysis," in Edward Timm and Naomi Segal, eds., *Freud in Exile: Psychoanalysis and its Vicissitudes* (New Haven, Conn., 1988).

6

Psychoanalytic Science:
From Oedipus to Culture

EDITH KURZWEIL*

In 1944, in "Psychoanalysis and Sociology," Heinz Hartmann, who would be the leading psychoanalyst for years to come, stated that many problems belonging to the social sciences must be examined with the help of psychoanalysis.[1] By 1950, he argued for the creation of a common conceptual language for the social sciences, in order to define sociological problems in terms of their psychological meaning and, vice versa, to formulate psychological ones in direct relation to the social structure.[2] The following year, at a meeting of the Psychoanalytic Section of the American Psychiatric Association, Talcott Parsons, the leading American sociologist, stated that the influence of psychoanalysis had "deepened and enriched the understanding of human motivation and had become pervasive in the social sciences."[3]

Only fifteen years before, Rudolph Loewenstein, who would become Hartmann's co-author of the most central concepts in so-called American ego psychology, which would come to dominate psychoanalysis worldwide, had taken what we would consider the most standard "biological" approach, which he had based squarely on the Oedipus complex.[4] How did Loewenstein get from his classification of the four phases in the development of male sexuality that "normally constitute the genital automatism" – desire, erection, ejaculation, orgasm – to his "pertinent propositions for

* A version of this chapter with the same title has already appeared in *Psychoanalytic Review* 79, no. 3 (1992).

1 Heinz Hartmann, "Psychoanalysis and Sociology" (1944), in *Essays on Ego Psychology: Selected Problems in Psychoanalytic Theory* (New York, 1964), 19.
2 Hartmann, "The Application of Psychoanalytic Concepts to Social Science" (1950), in *Essays on Ego Psychology*, 90.
3 Talcott Parsons, "The Superego and the Theory of Social Systems," in *Social Structure and Personality* (New York, 1964), 17; this article was reprinted from *Psychiatry* 15, no. 1 (1952).
4 M. Cénar and Rudolph Loewenstein, "Mechanisme des inhibitions de la puissance sexuelle chez l'homme," *L'Evolution Psychiatrique* 3, no. 5 (1936): 5–25.

interdisciplinary cooperation?"[5] How come that already by 1949 he was
accepting and defining "instinctual drive not [as] identical with the one
used in animal psychology, but [as] a construct particularly designed to
describe the phenomena of conflict in man which psychoanalysis studies?[6]
Simply put, what had led him to broaden the notion of "biology?"

Loewenstein's metamorphosis, I believe, developed in the context of
what my sociological colleagues would call his life experience – that is, in
the adaptation to his intellectual environment, which in turn was being
altered by the increasing acceptance of psychoanalysis by medicine. Hartmann, on the other hand, had already addressed this issue before he left
Vienna and soon spoke of "the subject's relation with and adaptation to
reality" as a necessary indicator of mental health. In his theory, Hartmann
explained that adaptation was emotional *and* biological. (For Loewenstein,
who was rescued late, spoke no English, and had to conduct psychoanalyses
to support himself and his family, "listening," I was told, took on a new
dimension.[7]) And along with the other psychoanalysts forced to leave Europe and thus the cradle of their discipline, Loewenstein and Hartmann
began to evolve psychoanalysis from a new existential situation – from their
responses to American reality and to their exodus. Since they were in the
habit of explaining their personal experiences psychoanalytically, these were
bound to permeate their theories.[8]

These experiences included (1) the shock of being delegitimated as psychoanalysts and as human beings; (2) becoming victims of a virulent, racially
based anti-Semitism; (3) being helped to escape on the strength (mostly) of
being physicians, who could get jobs in hospitals; (4) being penniless; (5)
having to learn English – the tool of their trade; (6) having to penetrate a
struggling profession; (7) being ignorant of American society and politics;
and (8) being expected to provide the intellectual tools to help defeat Hitler.
In the process, they furthered their professional acceptance by stressing what
they had learned in close proximity to Freud, by adapting to their host
country as quickly as possible, and by pursuing the "scientific" aspects of
psychoanalysis as they thought Freud might have done.

5 Cénar and Loewenstein, 5.
6 Cénar and Loewenstein, 6. He quotes Heinz Hartmann, Ernst Kris, and Rudolph Loewenstein,
   "Notes on the Theory of Aggression," in *The Psychoanalytic Study of the Child* (New York, 1949),
   vols. 3–4.
7 Reminiscence by Hedda Bolgar. Loewenstein told her that he was forced to take on patients while
   his English was still extremely deficient. So he learned by listening, by waiting with interpretations.
8 In an interview with David James Fischer (*Society* 28 [March/April 1991]: 68) shortly before his
   death, Bruno Bettelheim recalls that Freud told him, "Heinz has to put on his glasses which change
   all clinical experience into adaptation." However, Hartmann did not develop this concept into a
   central theory until after his exodus.

The émigrés recognized, by means of introspection and observation, that just like biological organisms, only the most adaptive (though not all of these) had been able to survive. As psychoanalysts they were in a unique position to penetrate the psychic mechanisms of differential adaptation, which would then foster professional acceptance. In fact, the émigrés felt themselves propelled toward exploring the deepest, intrapsychic structures of the personality, and their connections to biology, in line with scientific criteria as well as with their own (changing) links to culture – links that they kept investigating in line with their moves from Vienna and Berlin to Paris and New York, and with those of colleagues who had gone to London.

THE REALITIES OF LOSING A HOMELAND

Unlike most other German and Austrian (and later on Czech, French, and Hungarian) middle-class and professional Jews, psychoanalysts belonged to a closely knit international association and thus were in a position to ask for and receive the sort of personal assistance from abroad most of their countrymen tended to lack. In addition, the more enlightened of their American colleagues appreciated the émigrés' theoretical sophistication and experience in treating patients and in training psychoanalytic candidates. So, aside from the human concerns, the leading Americans, such as Lawrence Kubie and Bertram Lewin, were aware of the professional advantages they might reap by collaborating with the émigrés. In that sense, their former proximity to Freud was useful; and it would be even more so when, soon after his death, reminiscences would be invoked also to clarify theoretical points.[9] However, friendship and the customary American human instinct to save people suffering from political repression or natural disasters came together in the efforts to rescue these colleagues.

Thus on March 19, 1938, in his capacity as chairman of the Emergency Committee on Relief and Immigration of the American Psychoanalytic Association, Lawrence Kubie wrote a letter to all members, with a solicitation form:

Detailed and trustworthy information is now available on the situation in Austria, both from Dr. Ruth Brunswick (who telephoned from Paris immediately on arriving there from Austria early this morning) and from the State Department in Washington, where various officials were interviewed by the chairman of this committee yesterday. Some official advice from the State Department is worth heeding.

---

9   In 1940, an issue of *Psychoanalytic Quarterly* (vol. 9, no. 2) was dedicated to reminiscences about the influences of Freud, mostly by those who had known him – both émigrés and Americans.

The information from Austria indicates the seriousness of the local situation in Vienna, – with carefully organized confiscation of property, minute searching of private homes, etc. Apparently, however, this is done with official formality and not with mob violence. No physical violence has been suffered by our friends to date, although they have been searched, minutely questioned, and some properties and money at the *Verlag* [publishing house] have been confiscated. Through diplomatic channels efforts are being continued to win a special permission for Professor Freud to leave. These efforts are being conducted largely through Dr. Ernest Jones, who is still in Vienna.

In the course of his visit to the State Department, Kubie apparently learned that the government wanted to help but advised caution: "No amount of haste will enable anyone to escape [legally or illegally] on whom the new regime has already centered its resentments." And because "no legal traveling permits are being issued anyhow, . . . there are certain advantages in delay, such as avoiding the destruction and confiscation of valuable papers, [and] physical violence to refugees en route." Kubie went on to detail the reasons why State Department officials suggested that affidavits and moneys be transmitted through them. He continued:

It is extremely difficult for anyone in the State Department to indicate a definite amount of money as the basic amount required to guarantee a year's support for an immigrant. They recognize that people coming in with fine medical and psychiatric reputations, with specialized skills, which can be put to immediate use, can expect in a short time to be earning at least a part of their own living. For such people they demand less in the way of a guarantee than for those whose future economic security is less certain. The only approximation which I could get was that for a family of three or four, who could not be expected to earn any material sum of money within a year, they would want a guarantee of about $5,000.

In a follow-up letter of March 31, 1938, Kubie reported that "the situation in Vienna looks, if anything, more distressing than before." He noted that very few Austrian Jews had been able to leave, and that all those who would leave were allowed to take with them no more than twenty schillings ($4). He went on to say that affidavits had been secured for a large number of psychoanalytic colleagues in Austria, but that much more money would be needed "for food, shelter, and traveling expenses for those who get across the border . . . [as well as] living expenses during the first months of their arrival."

Four weeks later, the "psychoanalysts who desire to emigrate to the U.S.A." would receive a three-and-a-half page, closely typed "bulletin of information," advising them of the legal regulations surrounding the practice of psychoanalysis in America, which, essentially, was "defined as the practice of medicine" – in whatever state the question had been raised. This

meant that psychoanalysts had to "secure licenses for the practice of medicine before practicing psychoanalysis"; that they had to consider the fact
that in many states noncitizens were barred; that they had to pass an English
proficiency exam; that because of overcrowding (on the East Coast), newcomers would have to endure "a certain amount of isolation and loneli-
ness," but that they would receive advice and financial support. The rules
of the American Psychoanalytic Association about the training of candidates
(in accepted institutes) were outlined. And "well-trained laymen" would
be given the status of "honorary guests" in local psychoanalytic societies.
Information about procuring visas and travel money, and a questionnaire
that would enable the Americans to assess potential émigrés, were appended.
(The minutes of the New York Psychoanalytic Association during the second half of 1938 repeatedly mention Kubie's admonition – backed by Sandor Radó – to be cautious, and to heed the advice of their contacts in the
State Department not to make waves, and to be patient.)

I have supplied these details to demonstrate that the American psychoanalysts were inordinately intent on aiding their colleagues (Kubie, along
with Bertram Lewin as treasurer and Betty Warburg as secretary, carried
on a formidable amount of work while continuing to practice psychoanalysis) and that the émigrés who had been distinguished individuals had been
reduced to helpless, dependent beggars. They had to adapt, to rely on hand-
outs until they passed their medical boards and their English exams.

Moreover, the psychoanalyst's Emergency Committee was affiliated with
the National Coordinating Committee for the Resettlement of Foreign
Physicians, which itself did not have unanimous backing by the profession.
In fact, doctors around the country soon feared for their livelihoods, so that
in all but New York, New Jersey, Connecticut, Massachusetts, Maryland,
and Ohio, exclusionary laws had already been passed, and it was feared that
some of these states might succumb to pressure as well. From Kubie's
"Memorandum on the Problem of Refugee Physicians" we learn that his
pressure led him to urge émigré physicians not to "remain in our eastern
seaboard states."[10]

By November 22, 1937, twenty-nine individuals had arrived (two neu-
ropsychiatrists, three lay analysts, two medical students, and twenty-two
physicians), who had been "members of one of the recognized European
[psychoanalytic] societies." Apparently to avoid further legal restrictions,
and while urging the newcomers to take jobs elsewhere, Kubie argued also

10 See, especially, the files of Paul Federn (Library of Congress, Washington, D.C.), the files of the
    Emergency Relief Committee at the library of the Payne Whitney clinic in New York, among
    others.

that it was essential for them to spend some time in New York at first. There they could find friends, take the medical boards most promptly and enjoy reciprocity, join tutoring groups, and "for many who have been tragically disturbed by the uprooting and the enforced transplantation of their lives, immediate further migration becomes psychologically and emotionally impossible, arousing great anxiety and depression and endangering the ultimate happy adjustment to this new environment."

Clearly, Kubie's psychoanalytic explanation for the émigrés' preference for New York also was an attack on the many arguments in medical journals that American medicine could not absorb all these doctors without causing unemployment to native physicians. Nevertheless, Kubie and his committee actively tried to find them jobs. Among others, they sent Rudolf Eckstein, "a partially analyzed psychologist," to teach at the Crouch School in New Hampshire; they found a medical internship for Dr. Margaret Hitschmann at the New England Hospital; and they filled a position in the School of Social Work at Chapel Hill.[11]

These pressures must have daunted all but the strongest among the émigrés who had just escaped Hitler. To survive, they continuously had to adapt. Inevitably, these pressures must have influenced their thinking, must have led them to confuse personal, familial, and societal issues, and to explore these on the most abstract psychoanalytic levels. Those theoretically inclined as well as "adaptable," such as Hartmann, Ernst Kris, and Loewenstein, soon found that the existing theoretical paradigms were not entirely adequate.

We know that when the first émigrés arrived in America, the medicalization of psychoanalysis not only had been enacted legally but had become a fact of life; that therefore the émigré analysts interacted with physicians, mostly with psychiatrists, and thus were leaning ever more heavily on scientific language. We also know that during that time, psychoanalysis increasingly penetrated American culture. And we learn from the records of Kubie's committee that thanks to its work, proportionately fewer physicians fell victim to Hitler's destruction of the Jews, that proportionately greater numbers received visas before the American quota was exhausted. Is it possible, I now wonder, that the theory about "the guilt of the survivors" toward those who perished in the death camps was triggered not only by the overall guilt of having remained alive, while so many millions of Jews had been systematically exterminated, but by the fact that special efforts had

11   Letter of May 18, 1939, to Dr. Warburg, concerning two openings in Chapel Hill for a "psychiatrically trained man" to teach normal psychology and behavior study to first year students of social work as well as abnormal and clinical study to more advanced students.

been made to save physicians? Their early rescue had contributed to the exhaustion of the quota and thus to what amounted to "preferential treatment." This is particularly clear from the extensive correspondence of, for instance, Paul Federn, whose family could not get to America for that reason. (I am not arguing that the notion of guilt is to be discarded but that the psychoanalysts were the only ones to turn it into a theory.)

To give a summary of the political and cultural atmosphere the émigrés were dropped into, and to surmise how they might have come to terms with the new situation, is nearly impossible. But a letter from Kubie to Edward Glover dated November 2, 1939, might give us some clues:

> The psychological situation here with regard to the war is full of paradoxes. You can hardly find a man in any walk or stratum of life who does not feel at least that it is to our interest for the democratic allies to win; and in most cases they will go as far as to say that it is vital to us. Instead of deducing from that the conclusion which seems to me to be unavoidable, namely, that in that case it is both indecent to stay out and to our interest to go in at once, they rationalize our inactivity by an endless series of excuses, – the allied blunders since the war (shutting their eyes to our own), the suspect position of the Chamberlain government with regard to possible Nazi-Fascist leanings; the fascistic developments in France (or their suspicions of them); the three thousand miles of intervening ocean; etc. etc. Around every dinner table the fight wages; with the majority somewhat uncomfortably silent, – and the main battle coming between some articulate proponent of our neutrality, and some equally articulate proponent of intervention.

If Kubie, whose close relatives were not endangered, felt this way, how must the traumatized émigrés have taken to, and judged, the indifference of most of the citizens in their new country?

ADAPTATION AS A THEORETICAL APPROACH

Hartmann stated after arriving in America, and after a scant two-year stay in Paris, that "adaptation to social structure and cooperation is essential to humanity."[12] He proceeded to explore the relevant mechanisms of such "adaptation" by focusing on intrapsychic conflict and the resulting integration and coordination of contradictory drives, along with Freud's postulates in *The Ego and the Id* (1923). Still, his theoretical opponent Karen Horney and her followers would soon be more successful in explaining matters of culture and wartime morale to the broader public.[13] They increasingly relied

---

12 Heinz Hartmann, *Ego Psychology and the Problem of Adaptation* (1939; English translation: New York, 1958), 31.
13 Edith Kurzweil, "Les psychanalystes new-yorkais de 1933 à 1943," *Revue internationale de l'histoire de la psychanalyse* 5 (1992): 243–58.

on Freud's sociological observations rather than on the more technical ones, and these dovetailed with some findings the anthropologist Margaret Mead was calling "preconscious."[14]

Within the New York Psychoanalytic Institute, theoretical issues, which ostensibly were about the training of candidates but which had enormous significance for the future of the theory and the movement, were already brewing in 1939. Karen Horney (followed by Harry Stack Sullivan, Clara Thompson, and William V. Silverberg) was opposed, primarily, to Kubie's, Radó's, Fritz Wittels's, and Bertram Lewin's clinical "orthodoxy," and accused them of being domineering. Horney's major themes of dissent were (1) that it is often more productive to address a patient's present in order to understand his/her past rather than begin with getting insight into this past, and (2) that the thrust of what was taught to psychoanalytic candidates was culture-bound rather than universal. Her opponents maintained that she was teaching her own views and that candidates in training were not being introduced to the classical Freudian concepts they considered crucial to psychoanalysis.[15] Again, we have Kubie's assessment in a letter to Glover from November 22, 1939:

I think I hinted to you that this [new] curriculum was the fruit of a pretty violent struggle, in the course of which I was quite unwillingly erupted into the presidency of the [New York Psychoanalytic] Society and into the midst of a rather unpleasant scrap. The situation which lay behind it was briefly that we were developing four cliques not only among the Society members, but among the students: a group of students who were under exclusive Horney influence, – another group under exclusive Radó influence, – another group under Kardiner's influence, – and a group that had a more general classical training. Each group was more or less hermetically sealed from the other, and you can imagine how much confusion, lopsided and inadequate training, and mutual distrust and hostility all of this generated.

This curriculum was designed in order to insure some kind of reasonable orderliness in the sequence of the students' studies, – and to make it certain that every student would have to be exposed to all possible influences.

14 See "Discussion of Dr. Mead," March 8, 1942, in Dora and Heinz Hartmann papers, Library of Congress, Washington, D.C.: "If Dr. Mead's presentation was so particularly interesting to us, it is not only so because of the 'objectivity' of the method. Equally important is the fact, that in the choice of the material, in her ideas about what is relevant and what not, and in the few interpretations she gave, Dr. Mead relies upon psychological ideas that agree with the experiences and concepts of at least the analysts among us. There is no approach wholly [acceptable] to our theoretical concepts and it is preferable to state explicitly the concepts she relies upon, rather than using them preconsciously. 'Common sense' questions and answers, although some people like them better, at least in this field, as being allegedly less prejudicial than a theoretical fundament, are as a matter of fact far more dangerous to the objectivity of our findings; they cannot as easily be controlled as the explicit use of theoretical actions can."

15 Edith Kurzweil, "Les psychanalystes new-yorkais de 1933 à 1943."

As we know, America entered World War II half a year after Horney's resignation in May 1, 1941. By then, she had attained visibility, mostly through her books, *The Neurotic Personality of Our Time* (1937) and *New Ways in Psychoanalysis* (1939). Basically, she did not trace neuroses to biological drives but emphasized life circumstances and the role of childhood affection. Her opponents did too, but she denounced their "theoretical paths . . . [as leading] into blind alleys . . . [and as] a rank growth of abstruse theory and a shadow terminology."[16]

The difference between the "classical" analysts and Horney's followers became clear also in statements of how psychoanalysis might best help the war effort. In 1943, Horney's Committee on the War Effort issued bulletins on, for instance, the "Dynamics of Group Panic" and the "Understanding of Individual Panic." And Horney stated:

We must vigorously reject the idea that panic is inevitable . . . the high morale of the English after Dunkirk, was to a great extent, the reaction to catastrophe. Imminent danger and fear brought people together and led to an increased mutual respect and the realization that they needed each other. . . . Therefore in our long-term planning for emotional stability, we must foster and facilitate the whole idea of inter-relationship in home life, school life, business life, social life, community life. . . . The enemy tries every device to make people feel *helpless!* We must use every device to make people feel *helpful!*[17]

At about the same time, during a discussion about the state of the Emergency Service Fund at a meeting of the New York Psychoanalytic Society, Horney's opponents decided, for instance, to extend the functions of this committee (even though emigrants no longer were arriving) in order to assist "the men now in the armed forces . . . [upon their] return to civilian life." They also supplied psychoanalyses of Hitler[18] and other studies predicting behavior under conditions of war.[19]

On July 5, 1944, a meeting was called to find out "how the New York Psychoanalytic Society, as a body, can assist in the war effort." Essentially, they discussed means of applying clinical knowledge to "interview returnees and those otherwise involved (wives, sons, and daughters of soldiers in the armed services)." They further referred to the clinics they already had established, and to the importance of "keeping records of such work, in case

16   Karen Horney, *The Neurotic Personality of Our Time* (New York, 1937), 20–1.
17   Karen Horney, *American Journal of Psychoanalysis*, Committee on War Effort, 1943, Bulletin no. 3.
18   Walter Langer, *The Mind of Hitler* (New York, 1972). At the time, this was a classified report and thus not published.
19   See, e.g., Kurt Eissler, "The Efficient Soldier," in Warner Muensterberger and Sidney Axelrad, eds., *The Psychoanalytic Study of Society* (New York, 1960), 39–97; see also Kurt Lewin's various studies of stress and of leadership in groups.

of lawsuits." In any event, once more "war work" was conceptualized as clinical intervention – a repeat of what had happened at the time of World War I, when psychoanalysts had begun to deal with war neuroses. Hence we are able to note that the focus on generalizing from one-on-one therapy among the émigrés – all of whom belonged to the American Psychoanalytic Association, and most of whom were physicians – *did* represent a close continuation of Freud's earlier practices. (Whether or not this was useful is a moot point.) This central concern was furthered by, and itself furthered, the need to extend Hartmann, Kris, and Loewenstein's ego psychology. And it did establish many research projects in hospitals, child guidance clinics, and other institutions that were intent on using psychoanalysis. Paradoxically, as these projects took hold and their findings were incorporated into our general psychological lore, "the power of theorizing failed to equal the power of [Freud's] clinical insights," so that Hartmann had to remind his colleagues that " 'good' hypotheses aided his discoveries as well as their meaningful interrelation."[20] Such discoveries in turn were based on therapy with individual patients, on what would be grouped under the "scientific studies of children" *in statu nascendi,* and on those of "adult personality traits whose underlying mechanisms can be traced back to their roots in specific childhood experiences – dynamically and genetically – more completely than is possible through the direct analysis of children."[21]

REFOCUSING PSYCHOANALYTIC THEORY

Technically, Franz Alexander, Karen Horney, Sandor Radó, and Felix and Helene Deutsch were no longer émigrés. They had come to America before the Anschluss in 1938. But within the medical profession their foreign accents as well as their European background defined them all, and they pursued the same aims for psychoanalysis – although via increasingly separate paths. They all explored the scientific questions as well as adaptation, morale during wartime, the cure of war neuroses, ego–development, and psychosomatics. To understand the psychic mechanism that such inquiries engendered, to pinpoint where the environment "entered" the psyche, the so-called classical psychoanalysts reexamined and refined Freud's structural theory (id, ego, superego). But they also accepted the American scientific ethos and the language of medicine. Because personality structure is formed between birth and the Oedipal period (here would be their central theo-

20   Heinz Hartmann, "Mutual Influences of Ego and Id," in *Essays on Ego Psychology,* 181.
21   Quotation from Edith Jacobson, "The Child's Laughter," in Anna Freud, Heinz Hartmann, and Ernst Kris, eds., *The Psychoanalytic Study of the Child* (New York, 1947), 40.

retical advances and disagreements), they had to engage in empirical studies of the young and to understand their adult patients from the theoretical perspectives they now were exploring.

The majority of Hartmann's publications between the time he left Vienna and the end of World War II were on cultural issues. However, by looking through the Dora and Heinz Hartmann files in the Library of Congress, I found contributions for symposia, and all sorts of notes, many of them in a shorthand I could not decipher, as well as typed copies of participation at meetings – all of them indicating his parallel concern with the scientific side of psychoanalysis. For instance, on December 6, 1941 (shortly after his arrival), Hartmann spoke at a symposium on instincts, elaborating on Robert Waelder's contribution, which held that "the term instinct in psychoanalysis means something very different from what it means in other branches of science." In fact, Hartmann maintained that "instinct" was a double meaning. In addition to the genetic relation between animal instinct and human drive, there is "the relation between animal instinct and human Ego-function." On March 7, 1942, in another discussion with Waelder, he spoke of classes of instincts and of the importance of showing "by which concrete psychical means the 'biological program' of 'self-preservation' gets realized." And in an undated note, he went into the "Ego-Id differentiation" and its consequences for the understanding of instinctual drives in men.

Thus Hartmann's seminal work of 1946, which he published together with Kris and Loewenstein and which set out to integrate the many strands of research that had been undertaken during the preceding six years by all psychoanalysts, represented much of his thinking during his exodus. In any event, this paper would be accepted as the most important contribution, first, to guide further studies and then to deviate from them.[22] The authors began by describing the status psychoanalysis had attained:

Psychoanalysis has developed under social conditions rare in science. . . . The situation of the 1940s is hardly reminiscent of the period of early teamwork; large groups of psychoanalysts work in ever looser contact with each other and the diffusion of psychoanalytic concepts in psychiatry, their extension into psychosomatic medicine, social work, and various educational and psychological techniques opens up new vistas of development.[23]

Eager to bring all the modifications and reformulations of Freud's theories under one roof, these authors tried to integrate early hypotheses and later

22 Heinz Hartmann, Ernst Kris, and Rudolph Loewenstein, "Comments on the Formation of Psychic Structure," in Anna Freud, Heinz Hartmann, Ernst Kris, eds., *The Psychoanalytic Study of the Child* (New Haven, Conn., 1946), 2:11–38.
23 Hartmann, Kris, and Loewenstein, "Comments on the Formation of Psychic Structure," 11.

shifts and emphases and to address "problems of ego development and superego formation."[24] And they expected to clarify psychoanalytic terms
from a structural perspective by separating them from and subordinating
them to questions of libidinal development. They also maintained that the
concepts of id, ego, and superego were already *in incubo* in some of the
formulations of the 1890s – which indirectly would "delegitimate" theoretical foci on the simpler "topographic" distinctions such as conscious and
unconscious. By demonstrating that recently accumulated empirical data *did*
fit into Freud's "three centers of psychic functioning (characterized by their
developmental level, their amount of energy, and their interdependence at
a given time)," they further justified their claims.[25] Their relation to Freudian orthodoxy was to be the subject of many subsequent controversies. But
Freud himself had not been clear. In *Beyond the Pleasure Principle* (1920), he
had concluded that "the ego is the true reservoir of the libido," but two
years later he reversed himself and "recognized the id as the great reservoir
of the libido." According to Strachey, Freud had envisaged two processes:
(1) Original object cathexes go out from the id to the ego indirectly; (2)
the whole libido goes from id to ego and reaches objects only indirectly.[26]
In any event, Hartmann, Kris, and Loewenstein chose to read Freud in the
following way:

   1. They stayed away from biological correlation and from Freud's parallels between the psychic and the central nervous systems because Freud
had once said that he preferred using psychological terminology until an
adequate physiological vocabulary would be available.[27]

   2. They considered the use of metaphoric language as nonscientific
because "metaphor infringes on meaning and anthropomorphizes the structural concepts."

   3. They decided to "replace the word 'ego' in Freud's text by the word
'self' " because Freud had used the term ambiguously, sometimes referring
to the whole person, sometimes to his psychic organization.

   4. Instead of speaking of superego approval and disapproval, they con-

24   Ibid., 13.
25   Ibid., 14.
26   Sigmund Freud, *The Ego and the Id and Other Works* (1923), *Standard Edition of the Complete Psy-
     chological Works of Sigmund Freud*, vol. 19 (1961; reprint: London, 1981): 63–6. In a superficial way,
     objects are people and object relations are interpersonal relationships – although these concepts
     refer to unconsciously "internalized" meanings and potential interpretations inducing the subject
     to behave in a certain way.
27   Hartmann, Kris, and Loewenstein, "Comments on the Formation of Psychic Structure," 15. The
     English translation of "Jenseits des Lustprinzips" into "Beyond the Pleasure Principle," it has been
     argued, fails to render Freud's meaning correctly, and yet is taken at face value. The crucial word
     here is "jenseits," which could be translated as "on the other side of" but could also imply "on
     the other side of life."

centrated on degrees of tension between psychic mechanisms. Such an approach was to lead toward a developmental model of ego control. Child studies had yielded much empirical information on the effects of toilet training – of stimuli influencing conflicts between elimination and retention, the child's attempts to control, and the mother's requests – and they expected to systematize these data. Because Freud's own metaphors had led them to understand the part anthropomorphism plays in introspective thinking, the authors said they would use his structural concepts and would separate them from the drives.[28]

5. They held that the defense mechanisms controlling instinctual drives take root toward the end of the first year; and they found that by then the child's lasting object relations (to mother) were in place. In this "newfound security," they noted, anxiety was taking on new shapes.[29]

6. After establishing that defenses were central, they concentrated on specific ego defenses – to cope with id impulses, the outer world, and later with the superego. Now repression was thought to demarcate sharply the boundaries between id and ego.[30] (This was why in the 1950s and 1960s American candidates would be taught that the analytic focus *must* be on defense mechanisms.)

7. They described the "replacement" of the pleasure principle by the reality principle as a learning process that transforms libidinal energy into aim-inhibited libidinal energy. And this process, they noted, enriched the child's inner world.[31]

8. Summarizing Freud's ideas on superego formation during the Oedipal period, the authors wanted to explain how early (and rigid) moral conduct becomes differentiated. Hence they distinguished the child's identification with the idealized parent (his perception was altering along with maturation) from the psychic energy that gets sublimated and used in idealization and from the internalized aggressive attitudes, which were found to be the energy behind superego demands.

9. Unlike Freud, who thought that personality development was more or less complete at this point, Hartmann, Kris, and Loewenstein expected existing psychological structures to be modified by development itself. (This supported Piaget's theory of children's moral development – from moral "absolutism" to differentiation – via a gradual adjustment of superego functions during latency.)

---

28 Hartmann, Kris, and Loewenstein, "Comments on the Formation of Psychic Structure," 17–21.
29 Ibid., 27.
30 Ibid., 28–30.
31 Ibid., 30.

10. As adolescents look for support outside the family, the authors continued, they may choose a new set of ideals. In this process, the condition that had accompanied superego formation in the first place – rebellion – was said to be reactivated. And this situation was found to trigger changes in identification.

11. But the superego, the authors now declared, also takes its clues from cultural forces, which impinge on its functions. And they maintained that when social values change rapidly and new ones do not replace them, or when "new ideals of conduct do not supplement the older structure of the superego," individuals become compliant.[32]

In conclusion, Hartmann, Kris, and Loewenstein stated that they had relied on data based on the reconstruction of life histories in psychoanalytic observation, the study of regressive phenomena in neuroses and psychoses, observation of children, and on historical and anthropological knowledge. Now they urged that these hypotheses be tested in studies focusing on, for instance, the communication between the child and the mother in the preverbal stage, on reactions of mother and child to toilet training. Their findings not only would explain the earliest processes of differentiation but would be useful in "retrospective investigation" – that is, in the psychoanalysis of adults.[33]

The best of these studies, all of them adapting the scientific language we expect doctors to use, were published in their new annual, *The Psychoanalytic Study of the Child*. However, the theoretical thrust no longer would be derived from American data alone but would feature studies by such London counterparts as Anna Freud on "The Psychoanalytic Study of Infantile Feeding Disturbances," Dorothy Burlingham on "Twins" (a former focus of Hartmann's research), and Willie Hoffer on "Diaries of Adolescent Schizophrenics (Hebephrenics)." All of them had come from Vienna. And in 1946, contributions by émigré "Americans" included Edith Jacobson on "The Child's Laughter," Berta Bornstein on "Hysterical Twilight State in an Eight-Year-Old Child," René Spitz on "Anaclitic Depression," and Jenny Waelder Hall on "The Analysis of a Case of Night Terror."

FURTHER "SCIENTIFIC DIRECTIONS"

In 1947, David M. Levy, who had sent a questionnaire to candidates at the time of Horney's defection from the New York Psychoanalytic Institute

---

32   Ibid., 34–5. They also noted that conformity arises in adolescence and stated that questions of mass psychology and fascism are rooted at this juncture. But they did not explain how they got from observations of specific adolescence to social phenomena.
33   Ibid., 36.

and who soon thereafter had left (together with Abram Kardiner, Sandór Radó, and George Daniels) to form the Center for Psychoanalytic Training at Columbia University, wrote a little book on *New Fields of Psychiatry*, demonstrating their enormous expansion – along with the influence of the émigrés. Child guidance, which Levy stated had been non-existent until after the Institute of Juvenile Research, starting in 1920, followed the ideas of Adolph Meyer, Alfred Binet, and Freud. Since then, a "specific" psychiatric approach had spread. Terms such as "maternal overprotection" and "maternal rejection" had become accepted – for children who are examined "socially, psychologically, psychiatrically, and medically" – in several hundred child-guidance clinics around the country.[34] Levy summarized accumulated knowledge that could predict recidivism, which could then be used by lawyers in defense of criminals and against them by parole boards. And he outlined the many collaborations with social work, with educational, industrial, and military psychiatry – most of it initiated by émigré psychoanalysts or their students – and especially by the military occupying defeated Germany. In this context, a typed memo in the Hartmann files is of interest. For Hartmann refers to

the preliminary conference called by the Conference on Germany after the War, and held on April 29 and 30, 1944, [which] struggled through to an agreement as to the need for a fairly fundamental change in the character structure of the German people. The present typical structure, based upon a *status* concept (superiority – subordination), was found to exhibit a peculiarly dangerous dualism of dominance – subordination, on the one hand, and individualism – romanticism, on the other. We are asking the educational panel to help us determine what specific things can be done in German education to change this character structure into one more compatible with the sound ends of an orderly society.

And he goes on to prepare specific questions the participants ought to be ready to answer – about education in general, pre-school environment, and adult education. Clearly, neither Hartmann nor his colleagues saw a rift between cultural/societal and theoretical/clinical issues. Instead, they considered the hundreds of so-called scientific investigations into the functions of the ego as relevant to *all* of psychoanalysis.

Among such studies was Edith Buxbaum's "The Role of a Second Language in the Formation of Ego and Superego." She found that two English-speaking boys of German background lost their conspicuous accent during their analysis, even though Buxbaum herself had a heavy accent. By rejecting the influences of American culture, they had expected to win their fathers' approval – a defense against unconscious castration fears. Like Rich-

---

34   David M. Levi, *New Fields of Psychiatry* (New York, 1947), 32.

ard Sterba, she postulated a "pathological accent" as similar in etiology to slips of the tongue, stuttering, or the misuse of words, and she argued that these may be employed as "additional defense mechanism[s], reinforcing repression, and also as a means of weakening the strength of the superego."[35] René Spitz, in both the first and second volumes of *The Psychoanalytic Study of the Child*, reported on the treatment of severely disturbed children at a foundling home. He examined the consequences of deprivation of maternal care, maternal stimulation, and maternal love, and of severe isolation; and he demonstrated the psychosomatic damage these conditions tended to inflict – seriously impaired resistance to disease, a high rate of mortality, and eating disorders. Thus this study dovetailed with Anna Freud's on "Infantile Feeding Disturbances," which arise as byproducts of early feeding habits and the mother's notions of what constitutes an adequate feeding regime.[36] Anna Freud related these disturbances to the interference by the mother during specific phases – the oral, oral-sadistic, or anal, or the fantasies of the phallic phase – and to the correlative loss of pleasure in eating. In the same volume, Anna Maenchen commented on the fact that unlike Anna Freud and Dorothy Burlingham in England, psychoanalysts in America had little opportunity to observe the impact of the war on the developing superego, although young boys often were affected by its ideological aspects, and by the absence of their fathers – which also contributed to the fact that they did not develop strong superegos.[37]

I could quote other studies, but what distinguishes them all is the ironclad adherence to Freud's structural model of 1923 and its scientific ethos. For roughly twenty years, such longitudinal studies as Margaret Mahler's on individuation and separation, René Spitz's on infants, and Robert Bok's on adolescents were continued – alongside the more culturally (and literarily) oriented studies. Franz Alexander's psychosomatic institute in Chicago, although not precisely in the mainstream, kept attracting medical talent as well. All of these endeavors in turn encouraged more investigations by many native-born Americans, who had become psychoanalysts. Some, such as Charles Fischer, cooperated with psychiatrists and neurophysiologists in dream studies at, for instance, Mount Sinai Hospital in New York. Many other investigations were being supported by the National Institute of Mental Health, and by other agencies trying to find out more about child de-

35 Edith Buxbaum, "The Role of a Second Language in the Formation of Ego and Superego," *Psychoanalytic Quarterly* 18 (1949): 279–89.
36 Hartmann, Kris, and Loewenstein, *Psychoanalytic Study of the Child*, 119–32.
37 Anna Maenchen, "A Case of Superego Disintegration," in Freud; Hartmann, and Kris, *Psychoanalytic Study of the Child*, 257–62.

velopment in order to ensure healthy growth, or to prevent crime and delinquency. Clearly, questions of individual adaptation (to institutions, environment, changing conditions) remained as central as the rational, scientific approach to clinical studies, which had to be maintained in order to receive funding.

In fact, the model of "ego-psychology" remained central until the late 1960s, when so-called self-psychology became popular. Heinz Kohut, its proponent, was also an émigré from Vienna, although he was younger and had studied in the United States, where he became a member of the Chicago Institute for Psychoanalysis. The other major psychoanalytic theorist to change the central thrust is Otto Kernberg, who left Vienna as a child, became a psychoanalyst in Chile, and introduced his version of object-relations theory (an amalgam of the ideas of Edith Jacobson, Melanie Klein, and Angel Garma) to the Americans. All in all, I have demonstrated that the émigré psychoanalysts were responsible for a new direction in psychiatry and that they spread psychoanalytic ideas to the entire culture – to practices of child rearing, social work, and general medicine. Ultimately, the émigrés influenced the general thrust of the social sciences, the study of literature, and the prevalent beliefs about the roots of the psyche.

7

The Impact of Emigration on German Pedagogy

HEINZ-ELMAR TENORTH AND KLAUS HORN

I

Of all the academic disciplines, pedagogy is the one least familiar to emigration researchers in Germany and elsewhere. Although studies and discussions devoted to education specialists working on a practical level are by no means unknown, the subject has gained neither widespread currency nor a reputation as a scholarly discipline.[1] Despite the lack of such a reputation – even to this day – pedagogy in Germany has grown continuously and taken on a much more prominent role over the course of the twentieth century. Historically, the teaching of pedagogy as a theoretical subject began outside the universities in teacher training seminars in the early nineteenth century, and from there spread to colleges of education and similar institutions in the twentieth century. Since the period 1900 to 1920, it has been taught in an applied form at specialized institutions of higher education or *Fachhochschulen* – for example, in the training of social workers and vocational teachers.

With its development, pedagogy has contributed significantly to the German academic and professional scene as the basis for a large number of teaching and educational professions and as a discipline in its own right. Therefore, when studying the emigration of German scientists and scholars, we ignore pedagogy at our own peril. By looking at it, we can show the impact of emigration in a specific case – namely, on a discipline that had not yet gained a firm academic footing by 1933. Beyond this specific case, we can also observe the consequences of emigration for the social sciences and the humanities more generally.

In this chapter, we trace specific features associated with the history of German pedagogy set against the background of scientists and scholars compelled to emigrate by the Nazis beginning in 1933. At the same time, we

---

1 Since 1988, this project has been sponsored by the Deutsche Forschungsgemeinschaft as part of its research program on the emigration of German scientists after 1933.

156

raise a number of general questions for emigration research. The forced emigration of education scholars did not simply change the face of a single discipline. In a sense, it was responsible for shaping the structure of the group of disciplines concerned with educational issues. The history of education scholars' emigration is therefore significant not only for what it tells us about the subject proper but also because it sheds light on the history of the humanities and social sciences in Germany, before and during the Nazi era.

From our vantage point, it is difficult to assess whether or not the perspectives raised and methodological problems posed are unique to pedagogy. It is our impression, however, that in legal studies, for example, the links between the discipline and the profession raise similar analytical problems, and changes in patterns of reflection attributable to emigration are likely to present similar difficulties. In other words, all disciplines not confined to academic organizations but associated with clearly defined social systems and real-world professions require methods of historical analysis different from those applicable to subjects whose roles within the scholarly universe are sufficiently apparent and whose application problems have been separated from actual scientific work.[2]

In what follows, we explain and verify the central theses presented in this introduction. First we describe the particularities of German pedagogy as an academic subject before 1933. Then we examine the significance of emigration and re-migration by considering people and social structures, as well as the knowledge base of the discipline.

II

Since the early twentieth century, German pedagogy has shared the status of an academic discipline with other contemporary sciences.[3] By academic discipline, we mean a "community of discourse" on a clearly defined and agreed-on "theme," one employing a research methodology specific to the

2 Fortunately enough, comparative research on German professions has produced some very useful material of late; see the volumes by Geoffrey Cocks and Konrad H. Jarausch, eds., *German Professions, 1800–1950* (New York, 1990); Charles E. McClelland, *The German Experience of Professionalization: Modern Learned Professions and their Organizations from the early Nineteenth Century to the Hitler Era* (Cambridge, 1991); Hans Siegrist, ed., *Bürgerliche Berufe* (Göttingen, 1988); and others, recently discussed by Peter Lundgreen in "Akademiker und 'Professionen' in Deutschland," *Historische Zeitschrift* 254 (1992): 657–70.
3 See Rudolf Stichweh, *Zur Entstehung des modernen Systems wissenschaftlicher Disziplinen: Physik in Deutschland 1740–1890* (Frankfurt/Main, 1984), esp. 7ff, for the sociological significance of the term "discipline" as defined here; Werner Flach, *Thesen zum Begriff der Wissenschaftstheorie* (Bonn, 1979), discusses the methodological and not socially determined significance of communication within a discipline.

problems it examines. But the community of Germans communicating about education displays certain distinctive theoretical and social peculiarities that give it a special place within the context of twentieth-century disciplines.

Although pedagogy became established as a subject in its own right within the German academic system around the turn of the century, it was and remains divided, both in institutional and cognitive terms. In the universities, prominently represented by Theodor Litt, Herman Nohl, and Jonas Cohn (who was later forced to emigrate), it existed first and foremost as a philosophical and normative discipline – in sharp contrast to the empirical and psychological educational research also carried out at universities (for example, by Ernst Meumann or Aloys Fischer). Scientific pedagogy was also taught and practiced outside the universities, in teacher training institutes and in the training of social workers and economics teachers. But in these locations it had more of a practical than a strictly scientific bias, was more likely to be dogmatic rather than critical and detached, and in some cases covered only the didactics of a subject.[4]

The somewhat diffuse manifestations of pedagogy reflect the discipline's social and theoretical identity, for its status was and remains rather uncertain. In interdisciplinary, institutional, and political terms, it lacked the recognition of more traditional subjects, and in its theoretical endeavors pedagogy seldom showed itself capable of presenting a genuine potential for distinct knowledge or of employing a research methodology that set it apart from other disciplines. Consequently, crisis and sharp internal debate have been a constant feature of pedagogy since the 1920s. Up to the present, moreover, it lacks a single coherent means of communication. German-language journals in the field have traditionally provided a platform for a very broad spectrum of authors, and continue to do so.[5] Whereas over half the contributors to the *Zeitschrift für Pädagogik*, the discipline's flagship journal, come from the ranks of educational scholars at universities, only about a quarter of the articles in journals on the margins of the discipline – for example, about adult education – are written by scholars affiliated with universities.[6]

The natural sciences have carved out a distinctive place for themselves

4   A survey of the history of the subject is presented in Peter Zedler and Eckard König, eds., *Rekonstruktion pädagogischer Wissenschaftsgeschichte* (Weinheim, 1989); for the specific history of economics education see Uwe Pleiss, *Wirtschaftslehrerbildung und Wirtschaftspädagogik* (Göttingen, 1973).
5   Observations by a committed outsider are particularly instructive here, as in Siegfried Bernfeld, *Sisyphos oder die Grenzen der Erziehung* (Vienna, 1925; reprinted Frankfurt/Main, 1967).
6   These data follow unpublished findings of Jürgen Baumert, formerly at the Max-Planck-Institut for educational research in Berlin.

largely because of specialized research. And psychology too has gradually developed as a discipline chiefly recognized for its unique research. In contrast, pedagogy has competed unsuccessfully with the other cultural sciences and humanities throughout the twentieth century and has failed to achieve an autonomous theoretical status. It also remains entwined in the web of educational practice and its attendant ideological and professional controversies. Ultimately, its status depends on the political forces seeking to rule either within and/or through the educational system.

Educational knowledge in Germany and the dynamics of its genesis, dissemination, and use throughout the twentieth century therefore encompass a broad range of topics and have employed various dominant standards of assessment. As a result, numerous trends and schools in pedagogy as well as the groups and camps in the pedagogical profession have emerged and have become established as reflections of political and/or religious milieus and philosophical orientations.

The difficulties of a historical analysis of pedagogy are two-fold. On the one hand, no study of the emigration of scientists and scholars would be complete if it failed to consider the different periods – before 1933, after 1933, and the postwar period. On the other hand, such a study must also take account of the specific historical forms of communication on educational issues, as manifested in the sources and methodology employed for their treatment. We would be painting a distorted picture were we merely to accept the standard criteria of a science, from today's viewpoint as well as in retrospect, and fix our attention solely on the pursuit of pedagogy at universities. Therefore, an analysis of emigration in this scholarly field and the individuals it affected raises all the difficulties that are typical of the discipline itself. In the history of the subject during the twentieth century, the émigrés represent only one segment of this multifaceted discipline, a segment that is by no means homogeneous or clearly defined in terms of temporal, social, institutional, or cognitive dimensions. Looking at the biographical data of individuals and analyzing the stock of disciplinary knowledge amplifies these difficulties and the distinctive peculiarities of the subject all the more.

III

Let us first examine the problems of establishing the number of émigrés. In scientific educational research it has been widely assumed that the number of émigrés from the discipline was rather small. Hardly more than twenty, if one counts only the academic establishment; a few more, but still less

than one hundred, if the practical pedagogues are included.[7] Apart from the
source used, the figure depends on how the discipline is defined. We employ a definition of the discipline as above all a community of discourse.
We then further subdivide that community according to zones representing
the focal points of this communication, allocated, for example, to institutions, fields of work, or to schools of thought. In this way, it is possible to
distinguish between the discipline's "core area," represented by education
scholars at universities, and "marginal" zones, as well as to identify the links
between them and internal structures.[8] Similarly, we have defined the number of émigrés first of all by looking at communication and communicators
in pedagogy before and after 1933 as reflected in the recognized specialist
literature, and then proceeded to divide them into various constituent
groups. Our initial results show that even taking a random sample of journals,[9] the number of émigrés among pedagogy writers prior to 1933 is
considerably greater than has generally been assumed. At the present stage
of our analysis, the number of émigrés already adds up to 227. In other
words, emigration affected about 8 percent of a total of some 2,800 authors
whom we have identified as having contributed to the scholarly communication in education during the period between 1926 and 1933.[10]

This finding is remarkable for several reasons. First, in constructing our
sample of journals, we not only included publications such as *Neue Blätter
für den Sozialismus* and *Zeitschrift für psychoanalytische Pädagogik*, whose contributors had been greatly affected by this process because of the latter's
political orientation. We also looked at others such as *Die Erziehung* – the
voice of the prevailing contemporary orthodoxy – and *Das Bayerische Bil-
dungswesen* – in order to avoid a one-sided concentration on Prussia. Not

7   The first strategy and the identification of about 20 émigrés was the choice of a working group in
    Siegen (Peter Menck et al.), also supported by the Deutsche Forschungsgemeinschaft program on
    the emigration of academics; on this strategy, see Georg Wierichs, "Wissen von Erziehung –
    inhaltsanalytisch untersucht," in Klaus-Peter Horn and Lothar Wigger, eds., *Systematiken und Klas-
    sifikationen in der Erziehungswissenschaft* (Weinheim, 1994). The second strategy is presented in
    Hildegard Feidel-Mertz, ed., *Schulen im Exil: Die verdrängte Pädagogik nach 1933* (Reinbeck, 1983);
    this list is much longer, consisting of about 74 émigrés.
8   In this grouping we have followed Nicholas C. Mullins, *Theories and Theory Groups in Contemporary
    American Sociology* (New York, 1973); we use the term "pedagogical establishment" to denote those
    persons who work in the education system but are free from the compulsion to teach and have
    the opportunity to ponder, research, write, and reflect. For the term, see Niklas Luhmann and
    Karl-Eberhard Schorr, *Reflexionsprobleme im Erziehungssystem* (Stuttgart, 1979), esp. 338ff.
9   Klaus-Peter Horn and Ludger Helm, "Zwischen Ist und Könnte: Probleme wissenschaftshisto-
    rischer Bilanzierung am Exempel der Emigration," in Dietrich Hoffmann and Helmut Heid, eds.,
    Bilanzierung erziehungswissenschaftlicher Theorieentwicklung (Weinheim, 1991), 209–37.
10 Whereas the overall number of authors is finite, there may well be a need to make additions to
    the group of émigrés, since our classification was based entirely on information from the *International
    Biographical Dictionary of Central European Emigrés, 1933–1945* (Munich and New York, 1980–83).

Table 7.1 *Authors who emigrated after 1933 compared with all authors of selected pedagogy journals, 1926–32*

	Authors (total)	Later émigrés (total/%)	Publications (total/%)
All journals	613[a]	27[a]/4.4	82/7.2
Bayerisches Bildungswesen	192	–	–
Die Erziehung	222	16/7.2	26/61
Internationale Zeitschrift für Erziehung	74	3/4.1	3/3.8
Internationale Zeitschrift für Individualpsychologie[b]	20	1/5.0	17/40.5
Zeitschrift für psychoanalytische Pädagogik	117	9/7.7	36/12.9

[a]Not the number of different journals since authors in two different journals have been counted twice.
[b]This journal reflects Adler's ideas of psychoanalysis. Only those authors who wrote contributions for the *Heilpädagogik* (pedagogy of healing) section are considered, so that not all individual psychologists will be regarded as educators.

unexpectedly, the number of émigrés among the contributors to the various journals differs considerably (see Table 7.1). The percentages range from 7.7 among the psychoanalytical authors to nearly zero among contributors to regional journals and those oriented toward teaching. With respect to theoretical orientation, once again, the largest numbers of émigrés are to be found among psychoanalytical authors; in terms of political orientation, socialists and communists are most strongly represented. Most profoundly affected were of course Jewish scholars of education, regardless of their theoretical or political stance.

Supplementing the standard picture previously presented, our analysis also reveals that the most respected journals in the field, such as *Die Erziehung*, a bourgeois journal devoted to the humanities, had 7.2 percent émigrés before 1933. We included among its authors those who were not counted according to standard criteria – for example, professor status – such as Hans Weil or Walter Feilchenfeld. Communication on education before 1933 was thus more open than the accepted view suggests, and emigration did not just duplicate the splits that existed prior to 1933. The Nazis were the ones who created the one-sided view of a *Katheiderpädagogik* (the academic core of the discipline) that was concentrated in the universities. That view did not reflect existing realities, nor was it the sole factor of communication in German pedagogy. Pedagogy before 1933 was not only open in a communicative sense but also saw itself as a discipline primarily concerned with teaching and with narrower topics, rather than socially defined by considerations of nation or race. The case of the Jewish humanities expert Elisabeth Blochmann, a member of the "Nohl" school close to *Die Erziehung*, who, finding herself in exile, reacted with total incomprehension, is a classic confirmation of this thesis.[11]

Thinking in historiographic and systematic terms, our method of using communication as the identifying factor for the area covered by the discipline not only serves to show the historic face of the subject until 1933 more clearly; it also does justice to the émigrés.[12] In contrast to studies covering only certain groups, it seems to us that our method produces representative and historically appropriate results for the discipline as such. For it is now possible to uncover the extent to which emigration affected the subject as a whole and trace the different impact it made on the "core" and "marginal" areas.

The various definitions of the discipline and the different sources used not only make their impact felt when it comes to determining the proportion of remigrants among the émigrés; they also shed light on the structure of the discipline as a decisive factor influencing emigration and re-migration as such.[13] But even here it is possible to recognize the significance of various fields of activity and subdisciplines.[14]

Table 7.2 shows the available findings from existing studies. These reveal not only the total number of émigrés and remigrants but also major differences in the findings that are still cited to this day.

It is quite clear from three of the four studies that those who did not return form the largest group. This is indeed so in the applied field of pedagogy, although not among the émigrés from the academic core of the discipline, as Table 7.2, column IV shows. Here, surprising as it may seem, re-migrants are in the majority. But column IV also shows that

---

11 This emerges very clearly from her correspondence with Martin Heidegger; see Joachim W. Storck, ed., *Martin Heidegger, Elisabeth Blochmann: Briefwechsel, 1918–1969* (Marbach/Neckar, 1990).

12 It goes without saying that this method of identifying a group of émigrés is not without its problems. One of these is how to treat authors who only turned their attention to scientific pedagogy once they had left Germany (e.g., Karl Mannheim). The random sample of journals is also a matter requiring discussion. Another unsolved question is the difference between the published lists of émigrés (e.g., in the *International Biographical Dictionary*) and the information available; an exhaustive survey is only likely to be possible for certain subgroups.

13 For a more extensive treatment of this issue, see Klaus-Peter Horn and Heinz-Elmar Tenorth, "Remigration in der Erziehungswissenschaft," *Exilforschung* 9 (1991): 171–95.

14 Our sources were the information given by Feidel-Mertz, *Schulen im Exil*, 232ff, the records on specific subjects in the *International Biographical Dictionary*, and data from our own research project covering mainly the "core" area of pedagogy (the Frankfurter Korpus). We did not, however, include Katharina Petersen and Karl Linke in our calculations, since they returned to Germany before 1939.

Table 7.2 *Emigrés and re-migrants among education scholars: categorized as returnees and nonreturnees after 1945 in various studies and sources*[a]

	I Feidel-Mertz		II "Education"[b]		III "Social work"[b]		IV Frankfurter Korpus	
Total émigrés	74	%	115	%	117	%	50	%
Basis of calculation[c]	69	100	112	100	113	100	44	100
a) Returnees	22	31.9	28	25.0	9	8.0	19	47.5
b) Partial returnees	7	10.1	10	8.9	13	11.5	9	15.0
c) Nonreturnees	40	58.0	74	66.1	91	80.5	16	37.5

[a]"Returnees" are academics who returned to Germany permanently after 1945, some with institutional backing. "Partial returnees" are émigrés who returned to Germany for a longer period but then went back to their adopted country. "Nonreturnees" are those who chose not to re-migrate. Although they might have published articles in Germany, they often no longer had any personal contacts.
[b]These terms are from the register of the *International Biographical Dictionary of Central European Emigrés, 1933–1945* (Munich and New York, 1980–83).
[c]Total number of émigrés minus the number who were imprisoned following German occupation of their countries of exile and put to death in concentration camps.

the number of émigrés from the academic core area of the discipline – the zone that enjoyed public prestige and a solid reputation prior to 1933 – is greater than the figure of slightly less than the 20 generally cited. The specific difficulties of emigration and re-migration studies concerning this discipline are also apparent. Different definitions of the discipline lead to different figures, and thus to different percentages or numbers of re-migrants. In the studies considered, these vary between 9 percent, based on figures from the *International Biographical Dictionary* for re-migrants in the field of "social work," and 47.5 percent, considering the inner circle of academics among the émigrés. The figures established by Feidel-Mertz on the one hand and the *International Biographical Dictionary* on the other for the applied side of the discipline do not differ greatly and are probably based on an identical definition of the category or educational practice.

Is it possible to provide a systematic explanation of the differences based on historical reasons and not just the definition of the discipline? We believe that one explanatory factor is to be sought in the difference between the first and second generations of émigrés.[15] Whereas in Fei-

15 The studies and sources give different proportions of first and second generation émigrés. For the distinction, see Horst Möller, *Exodus der Kultur: Schriftsteller, Wissenschaftler und Künstler in der*

del-Mertz and the Frankfurter Korpus of pedagogy the share of émigrés of the first generation (born before 1905) totals over 85 percent, the *International Biographical Dictionary* figures suggest a much more even balance, with the proportion of first generation émigrés much lower (59.1 and 63.2 percent, respectively). The conclusion is that the number of re-migrants varies with the proportion of the two generations of émigrés in a discipline.

This is not only because the émigrés of the second generation (born after 1904) were less likely to return to their country of origin. It is also that the first generation mainly includes people from the academy – that is, the core of the discipline. This finding may also reflect problems beyond the range of a single discipline. "Humanists" (*Geisteswissenschaftler*), particularly in the the field of education in its German variant, seem to have been confronted with greater problems abroad than natural scientists because of their distinctive way of thinking. For this reason, it may be that they felt more inclined to find their way back to Germany. The biography of Richard Hönigswald, professor of philosophy and pedagogy in Breslau and Munich until 1933, is an example. He was unable to speak and write English nor to accommodate himself to another type of scientific thinking in the United States. Therefore his work in exile was produced exclusively for the German context, and he remained unpublished and unnoticed in American pedagogical circles.

It should also be pointed out that among those whom the *International Biographical Dictionary* regarded as "social workers," we find the smallest proportion of returnees compared with the other sources. There were more, however, who returned for brief periods rather then resettling permanently. It seems that there was a general tendency to reestablish contacts with Germany after 1945, while at the same time rejecting the idea of returning altogether. The best example of this is the prominent role that Walter Friedlaender played as a writer and teacher in reestablishing social work in Germany after 1945, although he never returned permanently from his American exile.

The various sources thus give widely differing figures for the number of re-migrants, and only taken together do they show the significance for a discipline that was broken down into numerous subfields. This illustrates that it is not possible to speak about pedagogy without looking at the subject's inner structure. In the scale of emigration and re-migration after 1933

Emigration nach 1933 (Munich, 1984); for greater detail, see Horn and Tenorth, "Remigration in der Erziehungswissenschaft," esp. 179ff.

there are major differences between education specialists attached to the established academic milieu, notably at universities and in teacher training, and those engaged directly in educational practice.[16]

Taken together, the re-migration – 63 returnees, 25 partial returnees, 206 nonreturnees – confirm this not only for those involved in projects of the so-called *Reformpädagogik* (progressive education movement), who were still in close contact with academic life, but also for other segments – above all, those engaged in social work.[17] Social work is an area that besides being a clearly defined field of activity prior to 1933 and greatly affected by emigration, was also involved in re-migration in its own particular way. Averages for re-migration across the whole discipline, however, conceal these distinctions. Aggregate figures are also influenced by the low indicators for the group of people included under the heading "social work." The figures given indicate that statements on high or low figures of returnees are not only selective and dependent on the source used, but also vary with the actual segment concerned. Among certain groups of these émigrés, the re-migration quota is just as high or even higher than the values given by Möller (1984) for emigration in general – 31.9 percent for practical education workers and 47.5 percent for academics (see Table 7.2, columns I and IV). As a result, one should not generalize findings about re-migration too quickly or overinterpret the figures for subgroups of pedagogy.[18]

IV

The impact of emigration was not restricted to individuals, but extended to the thematic structure of communication in the discipline. In a second stage, therefore, we looked at the changes on this level and asked more specifically what differences can be found in the topics covered by communication about education in 1926 and 1955. Following our definition of a discipline as a community of discourse centered on certain topics and

16   For 1933 figures, see Heinz-Elmar Tenorth, "Deutsche Erziehungswissenschaft, 1930–1945: Aspekte ihres Strukturwandels," *Zeitschrift für Pädagogik* 32 (1986): 299–321.

17   The figures have been adjusted to allow for duplication among the sources, although they overlap only to a small extent. The totals before adjustment are 78 returnees, 39 partial returnees, and 221 nonreturnees.

18   This is all the more so considering that the studies used here on the remigration of educational scientists are likely to be incomplete in themselves. Feidel-Mertz claims to have a record – so far unpublished – with more than 1,000 names of pedagogical-political émigrés; see Feidel-Mertz, "Reformpädagogik auf dem Prüfstand: Zur Funktion der Schul – und Heimgründungen emigrierter Pädagogen," in Manfred Briegel and Wolfgang Frühwald, eds., *Die Erfahrung der Fremde: Kolloquium des Schwerpunktprogramms "Exilforschung" der Deutschen Forschungsgemeinschaft* (Weinheim, 1991), 206.

methods, we used pedagogy journals of the period from 1926 to 1955 as a database.[19] In this way, we avoided the problem of looking at the discipline entirely on the basis of a preselected circle of people. Taking a representative spectrum of communication on educational issues at a given time as carried on in journals makes it possible to confirm or reject assumptions about the people and cognitive contents constituting the discipline. This is why we have conducted our analyses of the scholarly content of the discipline in such a way as to allow an examination of the most prominent theses on the significance of emigration.

The basis for our consideration is a selection of pedagogy journals that may be regarded as representative and constituting a good indicator of communication about the topics in question. Because the large number of pedagogy journals renders an exhaustive survey impossible, we have used contemporary sources in which journals were already specialized and classified by disciplines and subdisciplines.[20] The selection seeks to take account of the distinctions already obtaining at that time and among the current subdisciplines of pedagogy, as well as the treatment of educational issues in adjacent disciplines (that is, in youth studies, which had not yet become a field in its own right, and in educational psychology, which must be regarded as intermediate to the reference subjects).[21]

We were also careful to apply our survey not only to prevalent orthodoxies but to consider the entire political and ideological range of communication. This led us to select the range shown in Table 7.3. A comparative examination of the topics and analyses presented in the selected journals reveals finely structured patterns of communication. The change in topics and their frequencies allow specific conclusions to be drawn about the significance of emigration. Our analysis of developments in the stock of knowledge was based on classification and quantification on the one hand, and hermeneutic-interpretative case studies devoted to specific topics on the other.[22]

19 On the significance and function of periodicals in the modern academic system, see, e.g., Stichweh, *Zur Entstehung des modernen Systems wissenschaftlicher Disziplinen*, 394ff. Apart from journals, we also looked at the teaching of scientific pedagogy on the basis of lists of lectures at German universities.
20 Sperlings's newspaper and journal address directory is one such source. *Sperlings Zeitschriften und Zeitungsadressbuch: Handbuch der deutschen Presse* (Leipzig, 1914–45). The total number of all journals in this source devoted to "Erziehungs – und Unterrichtswesen," "Wohlfahrtspflege und Fürsorgewesen" as well as "Volksbildungswesen" ranged from 427 in 1928, to 473 in 1931, to 294 in 1939.
21 On the process of discipline formation in the twentieth century, see the discussion of recent research in Heinz-Elmar Tenorth, "Disziplinierung ohne Disziplinbildung: Pädagogisches Denken im Kontext von Jugendforschung und pädagogischer Diagnostik," *Sozialwissenschaftliche Literaturrundschau* 5 (1992): 56–66.
22 In the quantifying analyses, the titles of all contributions in the sample of journals and, additionally, of the scientific pedagogy contributions written by émigrés for the émigré press are coded according

Table 7.3 *Structure of sample of journals used for the analysis of topics in pedagogy*

	1926–32	1933–44	1945–55	Total
General science of education	11	16	8	35
Education system	8	9	7	24
Adult education, "Volksbildung"	4	4	3	11
Remedial education	5	4	2	11
Social work	4	4	4	12
Education, psychology Juvenile studies	2	2	1	5
Total	34	39	25	98

At present, we can only show a small sample of the large number of results. Accordingly, we restrict ourselves to giving certain findings and data indicating the trend of change and some of its features. We then use an example of a qualitative analysis as a way of revealing the theoretical significance of emigration.

As was to be expected, the quantitative findings show a change in topics before and after 1933. The replacement of authors and restructuring of the journal market was accompanied by a shift in the frequency and the degree of attention to all of the topics included in our classification system. But these changes also betray a fine structure associated with emigration, and can be interpreted with respect to its impact on pedagogy.

Comparing the percentages of topics on educational issues by (future) émigrés and non-émigrés from the mid-1920s reveals that the émigrés were more likely to deal with educational issues related to politics and the state, society and community, culture and the arts than other topics. Education scholars who later remained in Germany, however, were preoccupied first and foremost with issues of education and *Bildung* (cultivation or education in the highest sense), defined in the context of organizations and professions – for example, *Volksbildung* (mass education) and issues of adult education, schools, job training, and social work. It seems that those education scholars who later emigrated tended to look beyond the organized education system to society as such and were less willing to narrow their outlook to existing constraints of the state and the pedagogical profession. This finding is borne

to a classification system and processed for statistical analyses. For details, see Klaus-Peter Horn, Heinz-Elmar Tenorth, and Ludger Helm, "Zur Klassifikation des Wissens der Erziehungswissenschaft im 20. Jahrhundert," in Horn and Wigger, *Systematiken und Klassifikationen in der Erziehungswissenschaft*.

out not only in the frequency of topics but also in the ways the topics were linked together by the authors. Future émigrés gave far less attention to the public or state and professional control aspects of the education system than did those who remained in Germany. This topical openness also reflected the fact that the majority of émigrés occupied a position on the margins of the discipline. Whereas the *Kathederpädagogen* did not see national educational questions as their sole theme – although it was the main one – teacher trainers (particularly in parts of the Reich with social democratic governments), social workers, and adult educators were highly receptive to engaging larger societal issues and the whole variety of educational tasks. It may be regarded as a well-founded hypothesis that as a result of emigration, pedagogy lost the close contacts it once had with social movements.

Of the numerous qualitative studies we undertook on educational knowledge at the time, we restrict ourselves here to taking a closer look at the concept of weltanschauung.[23] This had been one of the key categories in German social philosophy and educational debates since the 1890s. The theme arose when the modernization of German society undermined all clearly formulated, traditional, ideological, and normative orientations. And it became central to the field of education because after 1890, public education and *Bildung* were discovered as the central medium for reestablishing the certainties that were no longer to be found in society at large.[24] In other words, education was to create the unity that was nowhere to be found in the fragmentation of social camps and political parties up to 1933; and weltanschauung was the topical focus that allowed the articulation and discussion of unity and standard formulas in pedagogy and society.

We have based our analysis on articles that appeared in journals published during the Weimar Republic and after 1933. The historical material available allows a comparison between the arguments of (future) émigrés and the thinking of non-émigrés. We have selected a total of seventy-one articles spanning the years 1926 to 1944.

It is significant that the treatment of weltanschauung as a topic was discussed most in the crisis-ridden years from 1930 to 1933. Immediately after 1933, scholars lost interest in it. Not until 1939, and then again in 1941–

---

23 Other studies, e.g., were based on the concept of "organic way of thinking," "race," "young generation" and "politicization"; see Klaus-Peter Horn and Heinz-Elmar Tenorth, " 'Politisierung,' 'Jung Generation,' 'Organische Denkweise': Zum Selbstverständnis der pädagogischen Reformbewegung im Spiegel einiger ihrer Zeitschriften," in K. Hoffmann, ed., *Peter Petersen und die Reformpädagogik* (Hagen; 1991), 57–80, with results similar to those discussed here.
24 The context is examined in Heinz-Elmar Tenorth, "Kulturphilosopie als Weltanschauungswissenschaft: Zur Theoretisierung des Denkens über Erziehung," in Rüdiger von Bruch, Friedrich W. Graf, and Gangolf Hübinger, eds., *Kultur und Kulturwissenschaften um 1900: Krise der Moderne und Glaube an die Wissenschaft* (Stuttgart, 1989), 133–54.

42, did it again account for over 40 percent of the articles dealing with the connection between society and education. It might also be expected that among the world-views discussed since 1930, there would be a clear shift from liberal and left-wing outlooks to those of a Germanic, national(-socialist), and racist nature. In turn, differences exist between the topical links drawn by émigrés and those by non-émigrés, with the émigrés again showing a wider range.[25]

We also compared the ways of thinking and arguments of émigrés and non-émigrés in an analysis based on the qualitative method – that is, the classical, hermeneutic approach as it is traditionally used in the history of ideas. This analysis not only corroborates our expectations but also creates certain problems. The assumption of a consistent difference throughout between the educational knowledge contributed by émigrés and that stemming from non-émigrés is ultimately untenable.

A detailed analysis of the relevant texts on weltanschauung shows that the clear differences presumed to exist regarding theme and frequency between émigrés and non-émigrés disappear as soon as one looks at arguments and their form. The émigrés adhered to the way of thinking and to the style of argument usually employed by all writers on education and *Bildung* issues in Germany.[26] The articles examined in this connection cover all areas and subdisciplines of education, and also extend to the full range of political orientations from left to right. The most frequent subjects discussed throughout the period, apart from weltanschauung in the context of school, were general issues regarding the significance of weltanschauung for societal and/or political questions. Our authors comprised representatives of the pedagogical establishment, the core area of the discipline, as well as teachers and other practicing educators and outsiders, especially theologians. As was to be expected, no émigrés are to be found after 1933, whereas – rather surprisingly – authors who might be regarded as belonging to various religious denominations continue to appear, although only until 1936. Our basic assumption about multidisciplinary participation as it reflects educational issues is thus borne out.

The following findings are among the most astonishing results of an analysis of arguments. We certainly did not expect to find the results laid out in such clear relief.

25 For this purpose we used the GRADAP (Graph Definition and Analysis Package) to identify all word links, ie., common topics, in a set of data.
26 Studies carried out using a quantitative content analysis by our colleagues Peter Menck and Georg Wierichs (Siegen) have produced results in which, like our own, the arguments employed by émigrés and non-émigrés (in the case of Menck and Wierich: arguments on education) differ little from each other.

1. There appears to be no knowledge or mode of argument that is exclusive to émigrés. The difference in distribution that we took for granted, mainly along the emigration/non-emigration line, was not confirmed, not even in the structure of the arguments employed by authors. To reduce the matter to its simplest terms, a comparison within and among the groups of authors reveals identical, similar, or at least related topics and forms of argument among and outside the émigré pedagogues. The differences within the non-émigré and émigré groups of authors, respectively, are at the same time at least as pronounced as those between these groups in many respects.

2. Predominant is a difference that plays a significant role in German pedagogy to this day – namely, that between pedagogues engaged in teaching and those who take a more detached, distanced point of view – that is, between practically and theoretically orientated pedagogues.[27] In concrete terms this means that the most prominent distinction in pedagogues' arguments on weltanschauung tends to be found between the "practical" debate on specific educational tasks and a "theoretical" pattern of argumentation geared to research and analysis. Faced with the multiplicity of world-views, pedagogues – whether émigrés or non-émigrés – asked on the one hand "What can be done at school or in social work?" and on the other whether the school has any task to fulfill in this respect – that is, whether the weltanschauung in question – for example, national socialism or socialism – is legitimate? Or, in the face of scientific results, does it turn out to be nothing more than an ideology?

3. The analysis of the arguments employed thus points first and foremost to the continuity of pedagogical thought in the modern age, and only after that to the breaks and upheavals forced by the twentieth century. Our results point to a continuity of prolonged duration, since modern pedagogical thinking keeps its mark on the structure of educational discourse both before and after 1933, even – it would seem – under National Socialism. It is, in other words, detachable from ideological differences and resistant to the consequences that supposedly result from Nazism. In short, pedagogical discourse – social and temporal differences notwithstanding – remains embedded in the duality of "engagement" versus "detachment," "practical reflection" versus "theory." In this respect, the émigrés do not greatly differ from other German education scholars before and after 1933.

---

27   See Jürgen Baumert and Peter Martin Roeder, "Forschungsproduktivität und ihre institutionellen Bedingungen – Alltag erziehungswissenschaftlicher Forschung," *Zeitschrift für Pädagogik* 36 (1990): 15–27.

V

Our conclusion raises problems for anyone seeking to trace the development of pedagogy in Germany from 1926 to 1956 and to identify the significance of emigration in this context. Certainly, unmistakable ideological differences exist between the émigrés and the non-émigrés, reflected in the choice of topics as well as the commitment to social camps and their particular educational concerns. But these differences are not reflected in the characteristic style and status, or in the theoretical form of pedagogical argumentation. These factors of pedagogical knowledge are much more likely to reveal differences among education scholars as such than they are to uncover distinctions between émigrés and non-émigrés.

Therefore, what significance, apart from altered biographies, can be attached to the thesis of "loss" suffered by the discipline as a result of this emigration? What would seem to be crucial here are the social, rather than the theoretical, consequences. The findings available to us – on various topics and on authors engaged in pedagogical discussion after 1945 – reveal most clearly that educational debate turned inward and lost the breadth of its points of reference that it had displayed prior to 1933, not the least through the theorists who were forced to emigrate. A university teacher such as Oswald Kroh, who was one of the editors of *Die Erziehung* until the end of World War II and who was hardly the model of a scholar opposed to National Socialism, became firmly reestablished as a psychologist after 1945. Among the émigrés was a cosmopolitan psychoanalyst, the socialist pedagogue Siegfried Bernfeld. At least until 1933, he was feared as a provocative contributor to pedagogical discourse from the outside; he took refuge during his émigré years in the history of psychoanalysis, and did not want to return to Germany after the war. As a result, his work fell into obscurity in that country until the late 1960s.

It seems to us, therefore, that the major implication of emigration for pedagogy in Germany is that it was thrown back onto itself, restricted in engagement to discussions of policy in the public education system and of philosophical method. "Detached" research moved to other disciplines, and the "engaged work" with social issues and the connections to social movements that the émigrés had displayed returned only at a later stage. Although our investigation thus far provides strong evidence in favor of such conclusions, we are still in the process of studying the precise circumstances of the shifts in the social and theoretical composition of the subject after 1945.

PART THREE

Social Sciences

8

Dismissal and Emigration of German-Speaking Economists after 1933

CLAUS-DIETER KROHN

The history of the institutional development of modern economics as a discipline and its intellectual history has yet to be fully investigated. What we do know comes mostly from outsiders to the "brotherhood," who have to a great extent limited their explorations of the past to the question of how knowledge was promoted by key figures in the field. The fact that the "sciences" – as defined by Thomas Kuhn – also represent complex social processes of change, defined by a variety of factors within science and outside it, has remained unnoticed. The topic of dismissal and emigration" of economists from Nazi Germany, the turning points in their lives and careers, as well as the problems of acculturation in their adopted countries, however, can hardly be illustrated by an approach that focuses on the history of economic analysis, with its interest in the linear accumulation of knowledge.

An initial glance at the list of émigré economists reveals several peculiarities. Many of the emigrants came from the same universities. In my study on the New School for Social Research, which, in its rescue programs in the years 1933 through 1940, granted asylum to a great number of expelled scientists, I have pointed out that this institution sheltered, above all, scholars from the so-called "Kiel School" and from the University of Heidelberg.[1] A systematic survey of the dismissals from German universities (see Table 8.1) now shows that the number of ousted scholars who later emigrated was generally the highest in the departments of economics at those two centers and at the University of Frankfurt.

It is worth noting that the University of Frankfurt had by far the largest staff in the field of economics, as is revealed by a national survey. Originally founded by Jewish merchants shortly before the outbreak of World War I,

---

1 Claus-Dieter Krohn, *Intellectuals in Exile: Refugee Scholars and the New School for Social Research* (Amherst, Mass., 1993), 13ff.

Table 8.1 *Scholars dismissed from German universities*

University	Staff (1932–33)[a]	Dismissals after 1933	percent	no. emigrated
Frankfurt	33	13	40	9
Heidelberg	11	7	63	5
Kiel	10	5	50	2

These figures are in striking contrast with those of other institutions of higher education, for example:

Berlin	21	5	24	4
Freiburg	11	1	9	—
Hamburg	12	4	33	3
Cologne	20	4	20	1
Munich	13	—	—	—
Tübingen	11	—	—	—

[a]Figures are for the winter semester.

the university was intended above all to support research in the modern social sciences – a broad aim that included the fight against the spread of anti-Semitism in German society.[2] Unlike the two other modern city-run universities in Cologne and Hamburg, it had already begun its work in 1914. At that time, the structural problems caused by World War I opened up an infinite field of activity to social sciences. Yet, whereas the universities of Cologne and Hamburg, both founded in 1919, would continue to be guided for a long time to come by the comparatively narrow traditions of their institutional predecessors – a commercial college and a so-called Co-lonial Institute (*Kolonialinstitut*), respectively – Frankfurt developed into a center for critical, interdisciplinary, modern social science.

In the 1920s in Kiel, Bernhard Harms, the director of the Institute of World Economy and Maritime Traffic, succeeded in engaging a number of younger scientists, among them Adolph Lowe, Gerhard Colm, Hans Neisser (all with Jewish backgrounds), and, later on, Fritz Burchardt and Alfred Kähler, whose research was directed less toward theory than practice. At the beginning of the Weimar Republic, many of them worked in the different administrative offices of demobilization, where they became in-

2   Bertram Schefold, *Wirtschafts- und Sozialwissenschaftler in Frankfurt am Main* (Marburg, 1989); Notker Hammerstein, *Die Johann-Wolfgang-Goethe Universität Frankfurt am Main: Von der Stiftungsuniversität zur staatlichen Hochschule*, vol. 1: *1914–1950* (Neuwied, 1989).

timately familiar with the immense problems of postwar reconstruction. This experience was to have a significant influence on their research in different fields of macroeconomic planning.

In Heidelberg, the liberal spirit of the two Weber brothers, Max and Alfred, and of Emil Lederer, a disciple of Eugen von Böhm-Bawerk, finally triumphed. Unlike almost everyone else in Germany, Lederer turned socialist and taught economics in the classical tradition – that is, as a comprehensive social theory. The largest group of those academic recruits who tried to combine the aura of the traditional university with progressive aims gathered there. In later years, Lederer's student Jacob Marschak argued that the provocative intellectual climate in Heidelberg, especially through the influence exerted by the circle around Stefan George with its romanticizing elitism, had been such a strain on the nerves of the younger critical intellectuals that under the slogan "We need the eighteenth century!" they tried to continue the tradition of the Enlightenment. This approach included the Anglo-Saxon classicism of Adam Smith, who considered economics and social analysis a uniform, rationally determined process.[3]

Compared with that, the picture conveyed by the other universities listed in Table 8.1, with their much lower numbers of dismissals, shows the extent to which the milieu of the academic mandarins, which had come down from the *Kaiserreich*, remained intact during the Weimar Republic. Even after 1918, at the universities of Munich and Tübingen, for instance, offering a chair to a Jew or a scholar on the political left – the second reason for dismissal stated in the civil service law of 1933 – was unthinkable. In Freiburg, the dismissals affected only Robert Liefmann, an outsider to both the scientific community and the university who was merely an honorary professor. A patriotic Protestant of Jewish origin, he chose not to emigrate; in 1940, in the course of a brutal lightning operation aimed at expelling the Jews of Baden, he was transported to the French concentration camp at Gurs, where he died a miserable death only a few weeks later.

The Friedrich Wilhelm University in Berlin considered itself the flagship university for the sciences in the German Reich. If we take the quota of dismissals as an indicator of creative and innovative research approaches developed during the 1920s, then its leading position in economics cannot have been overwhelming. A closer look shows this self-assessment to be even less tenable. Of the five people dismissed, two were full professors (Lederer and Ignaz Jastrow) and three were honorary professors or associate

---

3 Jacob Marschak to Hans Speier, April 14, 1977. Speier papers, State University of New York at Albany.

professors without civil service status (Julius Hirsch, Charlotte Leubuscher, and Alfred Manes). Strictly speaking, the two full professors should not be counted among this group of seven, for it was only in the winter semester of 1931–32 that Lederer had been called to Berlin by the Prussian Minister of Education, despite fierce opposition from the faculty. And Jastrow was at the time of his dismissal already a seventy–nine-year-old emeritus professor. Except for him, all of the dismissed scholars emigrated. If one considers the age structure of the group of full professors, it becomes evident that Lederer, being fifty-one years old, was a rank outsider. With the exception of one more professor in his late fifties (Ludwig Bernhard), all of the others were over sixty-five.

The department of *Staatswissenschaften* at the University of Berlin represented a gerontocratic body of notables such as could hardly be found at any other university. Insulated against the influence of new forces, they cultivated the tradition of the so-called Historical School of Economics. This line of thought represented a specifically German social and intellectual tradition. It emerged in the nineteenth century in opposition to the universal approach of classical Anglo-Saxon economics, and tried to prove that there are no general supranational economic laws. In the course of the "national upheaval" initiated by National Socialism, this school had hoped for another intellectual revival. This is documented by the embarrassing publications through which Werner Sombart or Friedrich von Gottl-Ottlilienfeld, for example, tried to ingratiate themselves after 1933.[4]

The importance of the universities of Frankfurt, Heidelberg, and Kiel, which were to become the centers of dismissals and emigration in the field of social sciences, is underscored by the further numbers of émigré economists who did not come from the university milieu. The number of economists from other fields of research who took their doctor's degree at the universities of Frankfurt and Heidelberg during the 1920s and who subsequently had to leave Germany is by far larger than that of economists who took their degree at other universities (see Table 8.2). Comparing the respective frequencies of doctorates earned at these universities with those earned before 1918 confirms that many of the traditional universities did not welcome Jewish and socialist students even during the Weimar Republic. The universities of Munich and Leipzig exemplify this pattern. Whereas before 1918, eight of those who subsequently emigrated received their doctorates from Munich and three of them received their degrees from

---

4   Friedrich von Gottl-Ottlilienfeld, *Volk, Staat, Wirtschaft und Recht* (Berlin, 1936); Werner Sombart, *Deutscher Sozialismus* (Berlin, 1934).

Table 8.2 *Doctoral degrees of the economists in exile*

	1910	1918–33
Berlin	5	10
Bonn	1	3
Breslau	2	4
Cologne	—	4
Erlangen	1	1
Frankfurt	—	14
Freiburg	6	6
Giessen	—	1
Göttingen	3	2
Greifswald	—	—
Halle	—	—
Hamburg	—	1
Heidelberg	3	16
Jena	—	3
Kiel	1	6
Königsberg	—	—
Leipzig	3	—
Marburg	1	1
Munich	8	4
Münster	—	—
Rostock	—	—
Tübingen	—	2
Würzburg	1	2
Vienna	12	30
other	8	8
took their degrees in exile	—	7
not known	—	9
total	55	134

Leipzig, during the interwar period only four and none, respectively, did so.

The situation in Austria offers a remarkable contrast to that in Germany. It seems that the University of Vienna had monopolized academic training in economics. In comparison with the forty-two émigrés who received their doctorate from the university, only one was awarded a degree from another Austrian university (Innsbruck). Furthermore, the large number of doctorates conferred by the University of Vienna during the 1920s is striking. As will be shown subsequently, many of these young economists were to become representatives of the so-called neoclassical "Austrian School." In some cases, they did not emigrate for political or "racial" reasons but because they never had a chance to start an academic career at the small number of universities in Austria.

The rate of dismissals from the universities of Frankfurt, Heidelberg, and Kiel is even more significant if it is seen in relation to the average size of the German universities. According to my findings, a total of 57 economists were discharged from the universities after 1933. Given a total number of 241 economists, this is equivalent to a dismissal quota of 24 percent. This figure corresponds exactly to that yielded by the surveys carried out by the Rockefeller Foundation in its function as a relief agency and as the biggest financial supporter of international efforts for the rescue of scientists expelled from Germany. Including the personnel of colleges of technology and commercial colleges, the foundation calculated a staff in economics of 390 people, of whom 93 were dismissed.[5]

The Rockefeller Foundation survey is of great significance because it also includes all assistant lecturers and other part-time personnel on the basis of detailed information that would be impossible to reconstruct today. These people can be ignored, however, because in most cases they were denied a renewal of their lectureships simply because it was an avowed objective of the National Socialists to reduce academic training altogether. Yet this did not put an end to their careers, for they could continue working as economists in government and the private sector.

We now know that 169 economists from German universities, colleges, research institutions, and from the government were dismissed after 1933 (see Table 8.3: 169 Germans, 45 Austrians, and 5 economists from Prague = 219). It has already been suggested that this figure is not identical with the number of émigré economists. For example, of the 57 persons dismissed from German universities, 33 emigrated, which corresponds to an emigration quota of 60 percent. This figure confirms previous surveys on the emigration of scientists; it can therefore be considered a reliable average value.[6]

This sample's high emigration rate of about 85 percent (169:144) compared with the 60 percent of the university staff owes itself to the fact that economists from different intermediary research institutes are included. These were mostly institutions of the labor movement, which employed researchers such as Fritz Naphtali, Adolf Sturmthal, Jürgen Kuczynski, and others, as well as the staff members of the Institute of Social Research in

---

5 "Changes in Teaching Corps in Economics in German Higher Institutions, 1932 to 1936," manuscript, Rockefeller Foundation Archive, RG 2, 141/1050.
6 Cf. *List of Displaced German Scholars* (London, 1936).

Table 8.3 *Emigration profile of economists dismissed after 1933*

No. dismissed (169 in Germany, 45 in Austria, 5 in Prague)		
from universities and colleges		145
from the administration		23
from other research agencies		51
	total	219
No. who emigrated		
from Germany		144
from Austria		40
other (e.g., German University at Prague)		5
	total	189
No. of non-emigrants		
from Germany		25
from Austria		5
	total	30
No. of emigrants from the second generation		
Germany and Austria combined		94
No. who were dismissed and who emigrated	total	313

Frankfurt, who were employed by the private sector, among them Henryk Grossmann, Kurt Mandelbaum, and Friedrich Pollock. Also included were scientific consultants and journalists, such as Melchior Palyi, Carl Landauer, or Gustav Stolper.

The high degree of emigration is to be seen in connection with another peculiarity. Among the émigré professional economists was a remarkably large group of Russians, who as young Mensheviks had fled to Germany after the October Revolution. They not only shared a political profile, but they were also highly qualified younger people who gave critical impetus to the field of mathematical analysis and statistics in particular. We shall disregard a second group to which belonged, for example, Boris Brutzkus and Naum Jasny, who had worked in Germany in the field of rural economy in the 1920s. It is interesting to note that many of these young Russian socialists, among them Paul Baran, Georg Garvy (Bronstein), Nathan Leites, Jacob Marschak, Mark Mitnitzky, and Wladimir Woytinski, came together in the Berlin seminar of the ultra-reactionary mathematician Ladislaus von

Bortkiewicz in order to finish their previous studies before going to either Heidelberg or Kiel, where they then studied economics. Bortkiewicz was also a Russian by birth (born in St. Petersburg in 1868), but he had been working in Germany since the 1890s and had come to Berlin in 1901.

It is not quite clear why the Russians in particular were so strongly interested in mathematical economics and why they were to be so successful in that field; it probably constituted the only form of apparently neutral scientific work open to politically committed economists in Czarist Russia. We need only mention Marschak, who had already acted as intellectual leader of econometrics in Germany, a role that was to be strengthened when he went to the United States and became director of the Cowles Commission for Research in Economics, or Wassily Leontief, who was to receive the Nobel Prize in 1973 for his input-output analysis, which he had begun to work on in Germany and which he completed in the United States. Leontief, however, does not belong to the group of émigrés from Germany because he had already gone to Harvard by way of China in the late 1920s. Wladimir Woytinski had already left a strong impression on the internationally renowned dean of Russian economics, Mikhail Tugan-Baranowski, as a result of a theory of consumption he had developed as a young unknown student and before he disappeared into lengthy Siberian banishment after the revolution of 1905. In Berlin during the 1920s, he then became internationally known for his work, *Die Welt in Zahlen* (*The World in Numbers*, 10 vols.), part of which was translated into several foreign languages. After 1933, he was to work for many years in the U.S. Bureau of Statistics in Washington, D.C., and as research director at the Johns Hopkins University in Baltimore.

As Jews, Russians, and socialists, these people never had a chance of being offered a chair at a German university, despite the fact that most of them were naturalized German citizens. Marschak's becoming a *Privatdozent* (private lecturer) in Heidelberg in 1930 marked, if anything, the end of his academic career. The majority of the Russians worked at the research institutes of the Social Democratic Party (SPD) or of the German Federation of Trade Unions (ADGB). Some also worked at the Institute of World Economy in Kiel, which in 1926 had started to conduct a comprehensive inquiry into the structure of the German economy, commissioned by the Reichstag, that was later published in sixty volumes.

The age structure of the group reveals that the decision to emigrate was essentially dependent on the age of the individual concerned, and that the largest group of emigrants was between twenty-four and thirty-three years

Table 8.4 *Age range of economists in exile*

Year of birth	before 1880	1880–89	1890–99	1900–09	1910–12	Total
No. dismissed	27	54	46	81	11	219
Did not emigrate	12	9	5	4	0	30
Emigrated	15	45	41	77	11	189
Percentage emigrated	56	83	91	95	100	86

old, an age at which the greatest intellectual mobility and flexibility can be assumed (see Table 8.4).

Given this age structure of the economists in exile who surged into the job markets of the countries of refuge during the Depression, and considering that emigrants working in other disciplines probably showed the same age structure, it is quite understandable that the spontaneously formed and effectively working aid committees for scientists, especially the Academic Assistance Council in Great Britain and the Emergency Committee in Aid of Displaced German/Foreign Scholars in the United States as well as the financially strong Rockefeller Foundation, refused to support the younger generation so as not to deprive native colleagues of opportunities in the profession. Usually only outstanding scientists of the mid-range age group – that is, between thirty and sixty – received grants.[7] In those cases, the organizations mentioned previously undertook to supplement the scholar's salary for a fixed period, if a university were prepared to employ the emigrant and held out the prospect of giving him tenure at a later date.

For émigré scientists and scholars from almost all disciplines, the United States offered the best prospects (see Table 8.5). Thus an overwhelming number of the economists fled to the United States either directly or via third countries.

It is striking that countries that were very important to the wider intellectual emigration from Germany – such as France, for example – were only of minor importance to the economists. That the latter were on the other hand obviously speedily integrated in the United States in particular is also shown by the following summary of the émigré movement.

The approximate balance between those who chose the United States as

7   Stephen Duggan and Betty Drury, *The Rescue of Science and Learning: The Story of the Emergency Committee in Aid of Displaced Foreign Scholars* (New York, 1948), 186.

Table 8.5 *Countries of refuge chosen by economists*

United States	
Direct	57
Via third country	59
Total	116
Great Britain	
Direct	18
Via third country	7
Total	25
Palestine	6
Turkey	6
Switzerland	5
Latin America	5
Australia/New Zealand	3
France	3
Canada	2
Netherlands	2
Other countries	16
Total	48
All countries	189

the country where they first sought refuge and those who only arrived there by a roundabout route may be interpreted as a further indicator of the degree to which the flight of economists to another country functioned as a retarding factor in their careers (see Table 8.6). Domestic labor legislation and the hermetic nature of the academic system often hindered the immigration of scientists into most of the European countries. With regard to Great Britain, however, the picture has to be somewhat modified. Whereas there too a general law against the employment of emigrants existed, the British scientific community, which also created the Academic Assistance Council (largely due to the initiative of William Beveridge, the president of the London School of Economics), imposed a kind of self-taxation aimed at financing additional jobs for German colleagues. This initiative shows that exceptions were possible if the local scholarly community was committed. Thus many emigrants continued their academic careers, although sometimes only in related disciplines. It is questionable whether this is to be considered a lull in their career, or whether in these cases the emigrants were compelled to undergo new learning processes and changes in fixed patterns of thought. Some of the successful scholars

Table 8.6 *Mobility course*

Emigrants with one country of refuge	104
Emigrants with two countries of refuge	59
Emigrants with three or more countries of refuge	26
Total	189

concerned soon transfigured this "ubiquitous pressure" into a great intellectual gain.[8]

Against this background, their original training in Germany was relevant to the academic prospects of the economists in exile. Since it was unusual for younger scientists to receive help from the aid committees, the breadth of their competence was decisive to their future success in exile. Here again, the University of Heidelberg occupies an exceptional position, since it seems to have provided such a comprehensive education. Two of Lederer's students, Nathan Leites and Svend Riemer, serve as examples. They had written doctoral theses on monetary problems and on the dynamics of the business cycle, respectively, two of the central issues of the contemporary scholarly debate. After stopovers in other European countries, they both became distinguished scholars in the United States, Leites in political science and Riemer in sociology.

The highly developed capacity for universalization exhibited by some German economists is further demonstrated by the fact that a remarkably large number of emigrants came from the superior ranks of the Reich and Prussian bureaucracies, and that their academic careers only began after their flight, as exemplified by the following three biographies:

Julius Hirsch. Before 1933 – Ministry of Economics. After 1933 – University of Copenhagen

Nathan Otto. Ministry of Finance, Princeton University

Hans Staudinger. Prussian Ministry of Commerce, New School for Social Research

As bureaucrats, these people would hardly have been offered professorships, which would have allowed them to obtain the much desired non-quota visa for the United States. But all of them had taught either at the

---

8 Hans Speier, "The Social Conditions of the Intellectual Exile," *Social Research* 4 (1937): 316.

Commercial College or at the German Academy for the Study of Politics (*Deutsche Hochschule für Politik*), an institution of great importance to the culture of the Weimar Republic, and both located in Berlin. This combination of theory and professional practice was in fact the reason they were attractive to America in the era of the New Deal. Their multidimensional professional competence and the experiences of the expelled scientists from Kiel and Heidelberg, who had worked in the administrative offices of demobilization from 1918 onward, was a decisive factor in their smooth integration into the economics profession in the United States. At the same time, it sheds light on a number of the leading elites of the Weimar Republic. The legacy of World War I, with its sociostructural changes, required a new class of decision-makers who were open to new theoretical approaches and also willing to put them into practice in the context of a democratic society. Their scientific research – especially on the theory of growth, budgetary planning, and monetary theory, against the background of the German hyperinflation – was to constitute their lasting achievement in the United States.

Thus far, only the quantitative dimensions of the economists' expulsion have been presented; the qualitative aspects of this group's exodus must now be assessed. It is evident that the emigration was not a movement of individuals, but instead often depended on connections. While still living in Germany or Austria, most of the emigrants had already belonged to certain networks, such as the Kiel School or the somewhat more heterogeneous intellectual milieu of Heidelberg.

Frankfurt, Heidelberg, and Kiel, the centers of expulsion as determined by the quantitative analysis, may legitimately be considered to form such a shared network too because of the numerous interconnections. It is worth noting that these connections remained intact in exile. Thus the following personality features were decisive for success in the chosen country of refuge: individual qualification confirmed by publications, readiness to remain mobile, and integration into one or more networks. These in turn required agents and intermediaries who established contacts through personal acquaintance with colleagues or institutions in the potential countries of refuge.

Two of these networks may serve to illustrate how the transfer into the United States was carried out. At the same time, they represent differences in theoretical main currents and in institutional integration. The first of these networks was formed by the group of emigrants who came from Frankfurt, Heidelberg, and Kiel. I have already mentioned that many of them had met before while working in the administration for demobilization after 1918. They also shared an insight into the need for macroeconomic planning in order to control the serious structural changes caused by World War I.

Their great achievements from before emigration lay in research on the macroeconomic effects of unrestrained technological change on unemployment, for which the industrial rationalization that had started in the 1920s formed the empirical background. In their research they followed classical Anglo-Saxon traditions. They had revived the analysis of David Ricardo and Karl Marx concerning the disproportionate development of the modern industrial system caused by dynamic changes through technological innovations. Because of that emphasis on the structural conditions of the economic process, these German economists were dubbed the "new classicists" or "postclassicists" in contrast to the neoclassicists whose arguments were demand-oriented and based on the theory of marginal utility. After the onset of the Great Depression in 1929, they developed different concepts for a so-called "active economic policy" aimed at overcoming mass unemployment by stimulating countercyclical public demand as well as by planning measures to coordinate the technological growth process and to eliminate its inherent tendency to disconnect production, employment, and prices. These recommendations not only anticipated main elements of the later Keynesian model, they also went far beyond it because they took the technological structure as a given. The daily political commitment of the group was once more intensified in 1930 – although in vain – with the foundation of the *Neue Blätter für den Sozialismus* (New Socialist Newsletter), whose aim was to divert the middle classes from their growing preference for National Socialism.

The second network existed in Austria, and comprised the neoclassical market theorists. With fifteen scholars, they formed the strongest homogeneous group among the forty émigré economists from Austria compared with the other relatively closed circle of the Austro-Marxists (ten scholars). The neoclassicists had hardly been able to gain influence in Germany, because of the power of the Historical School of Economics.

The few adherents the School had in Germany during the 1920s, especially in Freiburg, belonged to a younger generation of scholars who were still searching for orientation. They developed their position mainly in opposition to the "war socialism" of World War I, which they saw as comprising everything that had been discussed after 1918 in relation to macroeconomic control. It was not only because of the predominance of the Historical School that the center of neoclassicism was located at the periphery of the German-speaking territory, but also – and not least – to

the sociopolitical backwardness of Austria. Even at the end of the nineteenth
century, the dual monarchy was still a developing country from the industrial point of view. Thus the neoclassicism emerging at that time, with its
methodological individualism, also had the function of a social appeal to
the bourgeoisie to activate their own forces and economically to hold their
own as a class against the powerful military and civil service state.

In opposition to the theory of objective costs, which had been developed
by English classical theorists since Adam Smith and in which the value of
goods was expressed in terms of labor, the neoclassicists formulated the
theory of subjective utility as a standard for price formation in the exchange
of goods. This constitutes their great achievement. Whereas the classical
theorists had been marcroeconomists who were production-oriented in
their argumentation and dealt with long-term trends of the emerging industrial state, the neoclassical theorists have to be considered microecono-
mists who examined the subjective preferences of individuals in the market.
Their approach, which was based on the theory of demand, shifted the
subject of analysis away from the process of production toward exchange
relations.

This social background – that is, its marginalization at the periphery and
the need to oppose both the authoritarian state and the Historical School –
also explains the specific dogmatism of German-language neoclassicism,
which became even more aggressive in the 1920s, when social democracy
and socialist theory also gained influence. One of neoclassicism's most important exponents, Friedrich A. Hayek, was one of the spiritual fathers of
Thatcherism in Great Britain in the 1980s – a latter-day illustration of the
nature of this group.

The problems of structural change discussed by the German economists
– problems that are still of interest today – seemed irrelevant to the neoclassical market theorists, since they were convinced of the self-control and
the self-healing forces of the market. Thus they attributed, for instance, the
high level of unemployment during the worldwide depression simply to
the high wage settlements achieved by union monopolies. This is an indication of the ideological narrowness of the Austrians. Their battle against
interventionist distortions of the market was directed exclusively against
labor organizations, whereas the concentration of capital was not addressed.
In contrast, it should be mentioned that the hardly less orthodox Chicago
School around Milton Friedman was at least sufficiently objective to consider both sides.

The Historical School could certainly be considered another network,
but it can be ignored here because with its focus on the national peculiarities

of economic development, its ideological association with National Socialism was in no way handicapped. Few of its exponents were forced to emigrate, with the exception of Franz Gutmann and Kurt Singer, who both went into exile as absolute loners. Gutmann emigrated to the United States as late as 1939, at the age of sixty, and Singer, who had gone to Japan as a visiting professor in 1931, went to Australia after the "Anti-Comintern Pact" between Berlin and Tokyo.

In addition to the differences in their theoretical positions, the two networks – the Austrian neoclassicists and the new classicists from Germany – were characterized by different social and institutional ties, which were to lead to different patterns of emigration after 1933. German scholars who were Jewish and/or socialist were among the first to be expelled from the universities or to be deprived of their livelihood because of the ban on and persecution of the labor movement. The Austrians, on the other hand, left more or less voluntarily during the crisis years of 1933 through 1938 – that is, before the Anschluss. This gave them the opportunity to establish solid contacts abroad, especially in the United States. But their emigration often occurred for professional reasons. In Vienna, they had lived as private scholars, and rarely had a chance to pursue an academic career because of the small number of permanent positions at Austrian universities. They earned their living as young entrepreneurs, lawyers, or assistants in the Austrian Institute of Economic Research, a private foundation of the Viennese Chamber of Commerce. The group's scientific work was pursued in Ludwig Mises's famous seminar. Although the intellectual head of the neoclassicists in the 1920s, Mises himself was only an unemployed honorary professor at the University of Vienna, and had a full-time job as secretary of the local chamber of commerce.

Austrians had just as little chance of obtaining a university position in the German Reich in the interwar years. In 1927 Mises, for example, had been recommended by several economists of the University of Göttingen for a vacant chair in the faculty of economics because of his qualifications as a theorist and extensive practical experience. However, the majority of the faculty rejected him precisely for those reasons. Instead, they appointed a representative of the doctrine of economic stages – the typical field of activity of the Historical School – whose star would become ascendant under National Socialism.

The professional and sociological profile of the Austrians was to be of crucial importance for their future emigration. From the middle of the 1920s onward, they had the opportunity to satisfy their scientific ambitions as young scholars by going to the United States on two-year Rockefeller

Foundation scholarships. This foundation, which had been promoting medical research since the beginning of the twentieth century, had, in view of the worldwide unresolved economic and social problems caused by World War I, developed an extensive program in the social sciences. In this context, it had tried to call on the creative young economists of Europe, or rather of the German-speaking regions, as well. Before 1933, German new classical theorists were awarded research funds. The Institute of World Economy at Kiel, for example, was considered a mecca for economic research by the Rockefeller Foundation, and thus received tens of thousands of dollars in grant money. Younger Americans were also sent there on study visits. Among other important German centers supported by the Rockefeller Foundation were the University of Heidelberg, where several of Lederer's assistants were supported, and the German Academy for the Study of Politics in Berlin.

In contrast, the Austrians accepted offers of scholarships in the United States before 1933. Most of them – such as Hayek, Gottfried Haberler, Fritz Machlup, Oskar Morgenstern, and Gerhard Tintner, to mention just a few – went to the United States for periods of two years in the late 1920s. Thus they were able to establish a network of close contacts, which later helped them receive appointments as full professors at American universities in the 1930s, even before the National Socialists marched into Austria. In fact, the last scholarship holders, such as Machlup and Morgenstern, deliberately used their stay in the United States after 1933 to look for employment there, anticipating the deterioration of the political situation in Europe. They returned to Vienna only to settle their personal affairs.

Although the Germans did not have this chance, a different opportunity presented itself after their flight – to gain immediate and considerable influence in the rescue operations organized by the scientific community. This applies, for example, to Lowe from Kiel and Frankfurt, and to Marschak. Because of their reputations as an economic researcher and a mathematical economist, respectively, they had, on the recommendation of Lionel Robbins from the London School of Economics and Redvers Opie from Oxford, received temporary jobs at the universities of Manchester and Oxford as early as the summer of 1933. They soon became the most important informants of the Academic Assistance Council (AAC). For lack of detailed information of its own, the AAC regularly sent compilations of petitions for assistance to Lowe and Marschak and a few other representatives of the discipline, asking them to accept an academic ranking.

It is interesting to see how they dealt with this privilege, being themselves in socially and psychologically unique positions. In contrast to other consultants, they did not support only theoretical or political sympathizers. Lowe especially enjoyed a reputation as an uncommonly conciliatory scientist and a good teacher. He succeeded in making a deep impression on the organization of the AAC, when he pointed out at the beginning that he considered the assessments requested by the AAC as too vague and too generalized. Instead, he suggested differentiated selection criteria of his own, which were then adopted. These included the question whether someone had already been in the business for some time, whether he was a novice to the science, whether he was within the German line of thought or represented rather the Western type of science, and so forth. Hayek, who had left Vienna in 1932 to take a position at the London School of Economics, reacted altogether differently when he too was consulted. He curtly pointed out that he could only say something about first-class economists since he usually did not notice the others.[9]

Lederer played a comparable role in the United States. In 1933, Alvin Johnson, the director of the New School for Social Research, saw the chance to gather together the intellectual potential that had been driven from Germany in a newly founded university. One of Johnson's good acquaintances was Lederer, who at the outbreak of National Socialist terror after the Reichstag fire had gone abroad on a lecture tour from which he did not return. He was designated the first dean, and made suggestions for the recruitment of the faculty. This gigantic project was made possible by the New Deal.

The winning over of the core group of the new classicists for the New School can be called programmatic. This school had been founded after World War I by progressive Americans, among them the economist Thorstein Veblen, the historian Charles Beard, and the philosopher John Dewey, on the model of the German *Volkshochschule* – that is, an institution for adult education. Johnson, through his activities as editor of the *Encyclopaedia of the Social Sciences* – modeled on the German *Handwörterbuch der Staatswissenschaften*, a work he had taken up in the late 1920s – knew more about the academic situation in Germany and the whole of Europe than almost any other American because a great number of European scientists had been called on for cooperation. In addition to Lederer, Johnson requested help from Gerhard Colm and others from the core group of the German new classicists. Being a committed adherent of the New Deal, Johnson tried to gather together those émigré scholars whom he hoped would release im-

9   Cf. Correspondence of Adolph Lowe with the Academic Assistance Council, Dec. 3, 1934; correspondence of Friedrich A. Hayek with the Academic Assistance Council, Jan. 21, 1934. Society for the Protection of Science and Learning Archive, Bodleian Library, Oxford.

portant new impulses into the general atmosphere of change created by the new American economic program. Thus the "University in Exile" (the future Graduate Faculty of the New School), founded as early as fall 1933, soon developed not only into the most important outpost of the New Deal brain trust but also into a unique center of the critical social sciences now expelled from Germany. By 1945, more than 170 emigrants had taught there, either temporarily or permanently.

The scientists of the New School defended the Roosevelt program with numerous publications, research projects, and expert opinions. The conflict was soon to affect all of the economists in the Western industrial states when the British economist John Maynard Keynes presented a model in his famous book, *General Theory of Employment, Interest and Money*, published in 1936, aimed at overcoming the world depression with the help of governmental fiscal policy, through deficit spending and increasing demand.[10] In the liberal capitalist countries of the English-speaking world, such a debate on state intervention was something new. In Germany, however, it had a long tradition. It was only at the end of the 1920s that economics had been freed from the authoritarian encrustations of the Historical School and reformulated for an up-to-date economic policy by the new classicists. This is exemplified by Colm's major work, *Volkswirtschaftliche Theorie der Staatsausgaben* (Economic Theory of Government Expenditures), published in 1927.[11] This was a trailblazing book because its author was the first to inquire into governmental spending policy. There always had been studies on government revenues in modern economics, studies that dealt above all with the undisturbed collection of taxes for the payment of government expenditures. Colm, however, developed a theory in which the state was assigned a crucial control function in the economic process, based on its spending policy.

After the outbreak of World War II, the economists of the New School also took on the role of important contacts for the administration in Washington, which expected to get the information needed for a future European and international postwar order from the former experts for demobilization now gathered at that school. Colm had been called into the budget office as early as 1938, and from there he soon rose to a position on the staff of presidential advisers. Furthermore, with the help of either the Rockefeller Foundation or the Emergency Committee, the New School placed many of the German economists with research institutions that had the status of

10 John Maynard Keynes, *The General Theory of Employment, Interest, and Money* (London, 1936).
11 Gerhard Colm, *Volkswirtschaftliche Theorie der Staatsausgaben: Ein Beitrag zur Finanztheorie* (Tübingen, 1927).

quasi-governmental institutions, such as the National Bureau of Economic Research. Experts in public finance, insurance economists, planning theorists – in short, representatives of academic disciplines that had not existed in the United States until then – cooperated in the development of new models on general accounting or in the organization of the new American social security system.

The new classicists' major contribution to American scholarship was made in the field of financial theory and theories of growth. Today this kind of research would be termed structural analysis and indicative financial planning. It comprised, for example, the analysis of the correlation of dynamic technological change, population increase, and increases in public expenditures. The interest in surveys such as these was characterized not only by economic motives and concerns about fiscal policy but also by eminently sociological issues. With increasing industrialization and a growing population, the demands made on the public authorities also became heavier, and if they were not met this could result in a deterioration of loyalty to the political system, such as the expelled scientists had witnessed only recently in Germany. Therefore they stressed a fact still neglected at that time – that social expenditures in the broadest sense were higher in richer countries with fewer objective needs than in poorer countries.[12]

Whereas the new classicists came to the United States as committed New Dealers, the Austrian neoclassicists were just as vehemently opposed to the New Deal. To a large extent, they received chairs at East Coast universities, then intellectually on the defensive. They were qualified not only because of their scientific orthodoxy but also because some of them were not of Jewish origin. For in those years, Jews had no chance of getting a job at Ivy League universities. A man like Arnold Wolfers, who had been among the reform economists of the German Academy for the Study of Politics and who had belonged to the group of religious socialists, was regularly employed by Yale University in 1933 only because he had denied both his Jewish origin and his intellectual socialization. He therefore broke off all contact with his former comrades after his emigration. Whereas both Joseph A. Schumpeter and Haberler were called to Harvard in 1936, and Morgenstern to Princeton in 1938, someone like Machlup, being of Jewish origin, at first had to tolerate a post in the backwoods at the University of Buffalo.

Whereas the Germans saw part of what they had fought for in vain in

---

12 Gerhard Colm, "Theory of Public Expenditures," *Annals of the American Academy of Political and Social Science* 183 (1936): 6; Colm, "The Ideal Tax System," *Social Research* 1 (1934): 319.

Germany take shape in the New Deal, and whereas the leftist spectrum of the intellectual emigration therefore venerated Roosevelt as a guiding figure, the Austrian market theorists reacted quite differently. In unison, the president and his staff of advisers were accused of phrase-mongering, and Roosevelt was even put on the same level with Hitler. In 1932 Schumpeter, who out of a sense of indignation at the fact that he had lost a position in Berlin to Lederer, accepted the Harvard position, but soon felt that he had jumped out of the frying pan into the fire. After Roosevelt's electoral victory, he made no secret of the fact that under these circumstances he should have stayed in Germany. Manifesting little political farsightedness, he also made no distinction between Hitler and the preceding Social Democratic cabinets of the 1920s. Following the surrender of the Weimar Republic to the National Socialists, he presented the following analysis to the Rockefeller Foundation: "I know something of the governments which preceded Hitler's and I can only say that I am quite prepared to forgive him much by virtue of comparison."[13] Similarly, Mises considered "Roosevelt's policy . . . no less dangerous and corruptive than Hitler's." Judgments about Keynes were much the same. Although the German economists felt themselves confirmed by Keynes's work, the Austrians considered it nothing but "inflation propaganda." Such verdicts may still be seen within the framework of controversies that conformed to the scientific debate. Denunciations such as Hayek's, "The man is becoming more and more a public menace," however, went beyond such limits.[14]

Spurred on by generous two-year scholarships from the Rockefeller Foundation and by the prospect of an academic career, many of the Austrians overestimated their own capacities when coming to the United States, which they considered an intellectual desert. When advised by Hayek "to educate the gentlemen in America a little bit," the Rockefeller fellow Machlup answered from New York: "The lack of education and the incapacity to argue logically are simply outrageous. In comparison to Columbia, academic work in Berlin under the direction of Schmoller must have been highly theoretical." Considering that people who "have for years been dealing with economics have not the faintest idea of the essential things," he was seized by a deep gratitude for having studied in Vienna.[15]

Equally presumptuous were the scholars' verdicts concerning their in-

---

13 Joseph A. Schumpeter to Rockefeller Foundation, May 2, 1933, Rockefeller Foundation Archive, RG 2, 717/91/725.
14 Friedrich A. Hayek to Fritz Machlup, March 19, 1934. Machlup papers, Hoover Institution, Stanford University, box 164.
15 Fritz Machlup to Friedrich A. Hayek, Oct. 26, 1934. Machlup papers, Hoover Institution, Stanford University, box 164.

tegration in the United States. Accordingly, Machlup attributed his employment at the University of Buffalo in 1935 to his commitment as a teacher of economics. His appointment "on merits" differentiated him, so he thought, from the "emergency professors" at the New School expelled from Germany. There, according to Machlup, a university with forty students had been established especially for the group around Lederer.[16] A "leftist business," the neoclassicists used that institution only to forward applications for help they had received from desperate European colleagues. Only in very few cases did the Austrians, Machlup and Schumpeter in particular, actually help. Among those they did help was Adolf Weber's student Georg Halm from Würzburg, who was meant to be transferred to Erlangen because his wife was of Jewish origin and for whom they found a place at Tufts College near Boston in 1937, where he taught for the next thirty years. In contrast, during the precarious months after the defeat of France in 1940 and in the course of its second big rescue operation of endangered European scientists, the New School offered generous help to its theoretical opponents, such as Hayek or Wilhelm Roepke in Geneva. Roepke gratefully accepted the invitation, only to deal with it dilatorily until he knew for certain whether he could stay in Europe.

Obviously these arrogant critiques of New Deal America reflect the aggressive bunker mentality that had characterized the Austrian school from the start. But there was more to it than that. Already at the end of the 1920s, when nobody thought about emigration, the then private lecturers Andreas Predöhl and Morgenstern, from Kiel and Vienna, respectively, exchanged letters concerning their professional expectations, including the prospects they might have in the United States. "I could see myself," wrote Predöhl, "leading the life of a great banker or industrial leader in America. Under no circumstances that of a university teacher. Better to spend all one's life as a private lecturer at the smallest German university." Morgenstern, who had just returned from a lecture tour to Paris, answered no less plainly: "You can see again and again what a ridiculous country this America is . . . I wonder what a smarter American feels like when coming to Paris for the first time???"[17] Later on, however, after living in the United States, Morgenstern was to revise his opinion, whereas Predöhl did not have to face this existential moment. Instead he made a career for himself under the Nazis as director of the Institute of World Economy at Kiel.

---

16 Fritz Machlup to Georg Halm, Aug. 29, 1935. Machlup papers, Hoover Institution, Stanford University, box 164.
17 Correspondence between Andreas Predöhl and Oskar Morgenstern, March 19 and May 1, 1928. Morgenstern papers, William R. Perkins Library, Duke University.

Such passions concerning the American scientific community were also manifested by Roepke, Moritz Julius Bonn, and others – exclusively free-enterprise economists, who considered themselves the avant-garde of civil society. They represent the traditional patterns of self-identification of the German bourgeoisie, which, in contrast to the middle classes of Western Europe or the United States, had never fought for the right to participate in politics. It had claimed for itself a form of elitist "culture" that, so it believed, distinguished itself from Western "civilization." This intellectual disposition seems also to have been a characteristic of neoclassical market theory in its German version; its attacks on the United States as the model country of free market forces cannot be interpreted otherwise. This again explains the deductive narrowness some of them manifested well into their late years – a narrowness that could hardly differentiate between the budgetary traditions in Germany and Austria and modern concepts of regulation that had been developed from an insight into the limited range of the laws of the market. These economists could not or would not take note of the liberal impulse that was the basis for both the New Deal and Keynes's theory.

Only gradually did some of these economists modify their perceptions and old theoretical conceptions; otherwise, the great impact of the Austrian neoclassicists would be inconceivable. These scholars considered the approaches to macroeconomic planning of the New Dealers a productive challenge. This is probably best exemplified by game theory, developed by Morgenstern and the mathematician John von Neumann. It aims at establishing a model that comprises the different manifestations of human social behavior so as to find answers to the questions raised by monopolies and other deviations from the doctrine of the market. In opposition to the model of individual utility presented by the neoclassicists, game theory tries to prove, for example, that a great variety of interests and irrational motivations determine human decisions and actions. Within this theory, man was no longer regarded simply as a *homo oeconomicus* oriented toward material maximization but rather as a social being who has to consider the motives and actions of the other "players" in uncertain markets.[18] Mises, Hayek, and Haberler, however, remained rooted in orthodoxy, as is illustrated by Hayek's *The Road to Serfdom*, published in 1944, or by Mises's *Omnipotent Government: The Rise of the Total State and Total War*, published the same year.

18   Oskar Morgenstern and John von Neumann, *Theory of Games and Economic Behavior* (Princeton, N.J., 1944).

In contrast to the German new classicists, these economists hardly ever made an effort to reflect on the experiences they had had in their new social surroundings in the United States. At the New School, such considerations often formed the subject of interdisciplinary debates. The discussions focused on the learning process of emigration and the possibilities of overcoming the Teutonisms that German scientists had perhaps brought along in their theoretical baggage.

Looking back on the emigration of the German-speaking economists, one realizes that much has already been buried. Both the years of the New Deal and the short phase of John F. Kennedy's presidency constitute singular deviations from the liberal market-oriented sociopolitical development in the United States. Once they had ended, the pendulum of public consciousness again swung back to conventional traditions of thought. Accordingly, the neoclassicists always found success, whereas the new classicists met with the same fate as the other New Dealers. They became marginalized. Their message was carried on, however, by a small group of outsiders. In spite of these quite disparate later developments, the following is true for both groups. The scientists embedded in these two networks were remarkably successful in their professional and personal careers in the countries of refuge, not only measured against the starting conditions of their expulsion but also compared with normal career trajectories. In retrospect, these émigré economists could quite plausibly consider themselves "emigration profiteers" too.[19]

---

19 Adolph Lowe, "Die Hoffnung auf kleine Katastrophen," in Mathias Greffrath, *Die Zerstörung einer Zukunft: Gespräche mit emigrierten Sozialwissenschaftlern* (Reinbek, 1979), 145.

9

Emigration of Social Scientists' Schools from Austria

CHRISTIAN FLECK*

INTRODUCTION

As indicated by the title of this book, "Forced Migration and Scientific Change," I shall not discuss the normal case of scientific change – what the internal view would refer to as "cognitive progress" – but scientific change at the social as well as institutional levels. The discussion focuses on three aspects. First, I will concentrate on the forms of scientific systems that existed in the different German-speaking countries before their governments drove many scientists into exile; in this case, the analysis will look at the changes that science and scientific systems underwent in the wake of this "output" of émigrés, and thus assess the situation in terms of social and/or cognitive "losses." A second approach will focus on the cohort of émigrés and investigate the changes that individuals, scientific schools, or – if evidence for this can be furnished – whole disciplines underwent during the process of emigration. Generally, the level of aggregation of such an analysis will be relatively low – that is, close to the individual. A third course – practically inverse to the first approach – will focus on the changes disciplines and scientific systems experienced in those countries that assimilated larger numbers of émigrés. An analysis of the "input" will be conducted under the heading of "gains."[1] These complementary cost-benefit accounts will start from a relatively high level of aggregation – that is, they will analyze changes in

---

* I am grateful to the participants of "Wissenschaftswandel durch Emigration" at the Wissenschafts-kolleg in Berlin for their valuable comments and criticism of an earlier version of this chapter. And I hope that despite the limited scope of this essay, I have been able to clarify some of the misunderstandings. I wish to thank Reinhard Müller for his helpful comments and Ursula Stachl-Peier for the translation. Part of the research presented here was supported by a grant from "Förderung der wissenschaftlichen Forschung" in Vienna (P 8831–SOZ).

1 See Alan Bloom, *The Closing of the American Mind* (New York, 1987) for a different view.

scientific communities, scientific cultures, and possibly also scientific styles.[2]

In addition to the methodological problems that such an attempt to "measure" scientific change presents, several conceptual difficulties arise. For instance, the usual presumption is that the scientific disciplines developed independently in the different nation-states or language communities, and were sufficiently separate by the time the forced migrations started to warrant the conclusion that the forced exile of a segment of the scientific community and its subsequent integration into different scientific cultures were causally linked to the scientific changes that their new home countries underwent at the time. Conversely, if we presume that a general diffusion of cognitive styles and disciplinary contents had occurred before emigration, then the "losses" and "gains" might equally well be attributable to this factor. However, in the current state of research we seem to be justified in assuming that despite limited diffusion in some isolated cases, national scientific cultures (or those within a language community) developed relatively autonomously on the whole during the interwar period. In any event, the following discussion, in which I will consider the first two of the possible variants previously outlined, will assume such wide-ranging independence.

In this connection, two further qualifications are called for. First, my observations will be restricted to a geographically delimited segment of the German-speaking scientific community. Since developments in Austria display a number of specific characteristics – which I will discuss in detail subsequently – I believe that a separate analysis of this partial section of the larger German-speaking scientific community is justified.[3] Second, I will limit my discussion to the social sciences. Although I am more interested in and conversant with sociology and social research, I will include in the analysis other fields that are closely associated with sociology, given the rather fuzzy borders between different social scientific disciplines at the time. I am in fact anticipating one of the results of my considerations when I note at this point that virtually all of the scientists who ended up working as sociologists in exile had held different positions during their longer or shorter careers in Austria. The lack of disciplinary differentiation, coupled with the non-existence of a sociological profession in Austria, re-

2   For details on scientific culture, see Wolf Lepenies, *Die drei Kulturen: Soziologie zwischen Literatur und Wissenschaft* (Munich, 1985); on the concept of scientific communities, see Diana Crane, *Invisible Colleges: Diffusion of Knowledge in Scientific Communities* (Chicago, 1972); on scientific styles, see Johan Galtung, "Structure, Culture, and Intellectual Style: An Essay Comparing Saxonic, Teutonic, Gallic, and Nipponic Approaches," *Social Science Information* 20 (1981): 817–56.
3   Cf. Christian Fleck, *Rund um Marienthal: Von den Anfängen der Soziologie in Österreich bis zu ihrer Vertreibung* (Vienna, 1990).

quire that we ignore the familiar boundaries between the disciplines as we know them today.

EMIGRATION FROM AUSTRIA AND ITS CAUSES

One specific characteristic of the Austrian situation should be emphasized from the start. During the period in which the German Reich was under National Socialist rule, Austria in fact experienced two dictatorial regimes: the authoritarian *Ständestaat* after 1933, which has on occasion been referred to as "Austro-fascism" – a label it does not really deserve since it lacked the totalitarian character of the National Socialist regime, for reasons that cannot be discussed here – and Nazi rule after 1938.[4] However, this should not be construed to mean that the *Ständestaat* fostered anti-Nazi attitudes – as is at times maintained by some – and erred only because of the methods it employed.[5]

A comparison of the effects that the two dictatorial regimes had on the scientific community highlights the difference between them. In general, one can say that the *Ständestaat* did not persecute individual scientists as long as they did not take a public stance against the regime, but even in such cases there were exceptions.[6] Indeed, the *Ständestaat* exemplifies a rather sloppy type of dictatorship.

Hence if we first focus our analysis on the personal aspects, we find in Austria during this period two phases of emigration that differ both in respect to their structure and the numbers involved. The years between 1933-34 and 1937 were primarily years of creeping emigration, while sudden and immediate exile was to be the typical pattern of emigration after the Anschluss.[7] A more detailed analysis reveals that although there were some

4   Cf. Emmerich Talos and Wolfgang Neugebauer, eds., *Austrofaschismus: Beiträge über Politik, Ökonomie und Kultur 1934–1938*, 2d ed. (Vienna, 1984); Gerhard Botz, *Krisenzonen einer Demokratie: Gewalt, Streik und Konfliktunterdrückung in Österreich* (Frankfurt/Main, 1987).

5   Gert-Klaus Kindermann, *Hitlers Niederlage in Österreich: Bewaffneter NS-Putsch, Kanzlermord und Österreichs Abwehrkampf 1934* (Hamburg, 1984).

6   Max Adler, who was not only a Social Democratic city councilor and a member of the Bundesrat (the upper house of the Austrian parliament), but was also well known for his radical social democratic views, which he expressed in numerous public appearances, was never really attacked by the regime, and was allowed to continue his lectures as long as he did not use "suspect socialist" titles. His later reserve and reluctance to speak out in public is also evident in the leading role he played during the voluntary dissolution of the Vienna Sociological Society – we do not know anything about his motives. In contrast, the "Verein Ernst Mach," the popular organization of the neo-positivistic Viennese Circle, headed by Moritz Schlick, was forbidden by the authorities after the February battles in 1934; see Friedrich Stadler, *Vom Positivismus zur "Wissenschaftlichen Weltauffassung am Beispiel der Wirkungsgeschichte von Ernst Mach in Österreich* (Vienna, 1982).

7   Emigration "in anticipation of things to come" could be the title of a further possible approach that would extend the analysis to the years before 1933.

dismissals during the early period of the *Ständestaat*, political persecution, arrest, and expatriation remained exceptional occurrences, and were directed mainly against social democrats, revolutionary socialists, and communists, few of whom were at the time working as scientists at universities, and practically none as social scientists. After the new employment regulations of 1933, it was primarily Nazi supporters who were banished at first from the universities.

Again, it was not as if the *Ständestaat* were taking a resolute stand against the Nazis. It was that the self-assertive and brusque manner of many Nazi teachers had irritated the regime.[8] The *Ständestaat* acted outwardly like a constitutional state, founded on the rule of law – it enacted laws, enforced decrees, and even granted those it had disciplined the right of appeal.

Around 1934, the great majority of émigrés were therefore National Socialists who moved to the Reich. These emigrations must not be seen as just a normal stage in the teachers' careers, involving appointment to new positions in a neighboring country where German was also spoken.[9] In a countermove, several Austrian nationals (for example, Friedrich Hertz and Franz Borkenau) were later to return to their native country after the National Socialists had seized power. For them, Austria was to prove the first stop on their way into exile, just as it was for several German scientists (for example, Dietrich Hildebrand) who first fled to Austria to escape Nazi persecution. This type of emigration might be labeled "escape to a familiar environment."

Among those banished from the universities after 1933 were two very prominent figures who were associated with the social sciences. Sigmund Freud and Heinrich Gomperz were barred from lecturing when a new statutory retirement age came into force. Again, these measures were directed primarily against the Nazi members of the staff. Gomperz emigrated to California, while Freud stayed in Vienna until after the Anschluss.[10] In his case, the new measure was virtually ineffective since he was no longer lecturing at the university by that time.[11]

Among the émigrés who left Austria for political reasons during the first

8 The tenured staff were obliged to swear a new oath of allegiance, which some Nazis refused to do, resulting in their dismissal.
9 Adolf Günther, Friedrich Keiter, and Hans Bobek, e.g., left for political reasons.
10 Gomperz went to the University of South California in Los Angeles, where he died in 1942. See Herbert A. Strauss and Werner Röder, eds., *International Biographical Dictionary of Central European Emigrés, 1933–1945* (Munich and New York, 1980–83).
11 Ernest Jones, *The Life and Work of Sigmund Freud* (New York, 1953/1955/1957) does not mention this; it might have prompted Freud to remark that "we will put up with a lot from Austrian fascism since it will hardly treat us as harshly as its German cousin." Sigmund Freud, *Briefe, 1873–1939* (Frankfurt/Main, 1968), 434 (our translation).

few years of the *Ständestaat* were Paul F. Lazarsfeld and Otto Neurath, both of whom happened to be abroad during the clashes in February 1934 and subsequently decided it was preferable not to return home. A few communist activists, such as Leo Stern, Hugo Huppert, and Rudolf Schlesinger, might be counted among the peripheral proponents of the social sciences. All in all, only a few social scientists left Austria during the regime of the *Ständestaat*. Of all the social scientists who emigrated after 1933, only about one-fifth fled the country before 1938. However, the social scientists who emigrated after 1936, when the July agreement between Austria and Germany foreshadowed future events and intimated that the Austrian dictatorial regime would not be able to survive for much longer,[12] should probably be included among the émigrés who escaped from Nazi terror. One exception is Marie Jahoda, who was arrested in 1936 for working for the social revolutionary underground organization and became the only social scientist to serve a long prison sentence before she was forced to leave the country.[13]

More serious than the personal losses during this time were the social and cultural changes that the regime imposed. After 1933–34, left-wing and liberal intellectuals were deeply distressed, albeit for different reasons. The defeat of the social democratic labor movement had left both old and young social democrats shattered, and had shaken their deep-seated optimism. The grotesque notion of the *Vaterländische Front* – that Austria was the better German state because it was Catholic – irritated liberal democrats and assimilated Jews alike. The fragile network of scientific communication, which was largely founded on personal contacts, collapsed; the ruin of individual careers after the Anschluss really only completed the destruction of Austria's scientific culture. Thus a paradoxical picture of Austria emerges. The *Ständestaat*, which was quite moderate in comparison with the Nazi regime, drove only a small minority of social scientists into exile, yet it wreaked havoc on Austria's cultural and scientific systems. Since the social sciences rely on everyday language, common sense views, and shared assumptions of the members of society for the development of their scientific discourse – all of which sets them apart from the natural sciences – they require an intellectual climate and a mentality that is hopeful and positive. It appears that there is a necessary prerequisite for social science research – that social scientists feel there is at least some prospect that their findings might be applied in future scientific discourse or planning. Widespread

---

12   Cf. Bruce F. Pauley, *Hitler and the Forgotten Nazis: A History of Austrian National Socialism* (Chapel Hill, N.C., 1981).

13   For more details, see my introduction to Marie Jahoda, *Arbeitslose bei der Arbeit: Die Nachfolge-untersuchung zu "Marienthal" aus dem Jahr 1938* (Frankfurt/Main, 1989).

pessimism and growing despair with social and political developments are the worst imaginable conditions for social science research. Social scientists unfortunately lacked the optimism that was still found in left-wing political circles after 1934; the latter were confident that their victory was only a matter of time, and that the authoritarian *Ständestaat* would soon be overthrown.[14]

Alongside the destruction of the cultural environment came the economic ruin of the country. Austerity budgets led to redundancies and pay cuts. The weakened private sector – which even in the past had been reluctant to invest in innovative technologies and R&D and hence, in the face of the economic decline, was even less prepared to subsidize social science research – felt unable to make up for the shortfall.[15] The ban on the labor movement eventually cut the last two sources of funding: the Chamber of Labor (*Arbeiterkammer*) and the Vienna city government, both of which had helped pay for scientific research during the democratic phase of the First Republic.

EMIGRE AUSTRIAN SOCIAL SCIENTISTS: NUMBERS AND COMPOSITION

Before I turn to the cognitive aspects of scientific change, I will present some quantitative data. Some caution as to the validity of the following data needs to be exercised, however, because they reflect the current state of research on emigration from Austria.

Scholarship in Austria has largely ignored the emigration of its scientists and scientific culture in the 1930s.[16] If exile, emigration, and expulsion were addressed at all, it was done mainly by contemporary historians; an early exception had little impact.[17] William I. Johnston deserves credit for including accounts of the later careers of some of the scientists and scholars

---

14 The title of a historical survey already indicates this: Walter Wisshaupt, *Wir kommen wieder: Eine Geschichte der Revolutionären Sozialisten Österreichs, 1934–1938* (Vienna, 1967).

15 One of the reasons why the *Wirtschaftspsychologische Forschungsstelle*, which should have financed itself, failed, was that it received few commissions from the private sector. See " 'Ich habe die Welt nicht verändert': Gespräch mit Marie Jahoda," in Matthias Greffrath, ed., *Die Zerstörung einer Zukunft: Gespräche mit emigrierten Sozialwissenschaftlern* (Reinbek, 1978).

16 See Norbert Grass, ed., *Österreichische Rechts-und Staatswissenschaften der Gegenwart in Selbstdarstellungen* (Innsbruck, 1952ff.); August M. Knoll, "Soziologie in Österreich seit 1918: Ein bibliographischer Bericht," in Akademische Arbeitsgemeinschaft, ed., *Die Wiener Universität, Geschichte, Sendung und Zukunft* (Vienna, 1952), 133–7; August M. Knoll, "Austria," in Joseph Roucek, ed., *Contemporary Sociology* (New York, 1958), 807–23; Franz Nemschak, *Zum 25jährigen Bestand des Österreichischen Institutes für Wirtschaftsforschung* (Vienna, 1952); Ferdinand Westphalen, *Sociology and Economics in Austria: A Report on Postwar Developments* (Washington, D.C., 1953).

17 *Österreicher im Exil 1934 bis 1945* (Vienna, 1977). In 1958, Gerald Stourzh and Friedrich A. Hayek compiled a mimeographed list of Austrian scientists in the United States, including scholars who were not émigrés of the Nazi period.

he surveyed in his (albeit incomplete and at times misleading) overview of Austrian intellectual history until 1938.[18] The problem of science emigration was occasionally addressed in studies of individual authors, schools, or disciplines.[19] Just as the history of Austrian science between the turn of the century and the dictatorial regimes was at first investigated almost exclusively abroad, it was again West European and American writers who first focused attention on Austrian émigré scientists, although they usually did so not in separate studies but as part of wider surveys of emigration from German-speaking countries.[20] It was not until the late 1980s that Austrian

18 William I. Johnston, *The Austrian Mind: An Intellectual and Social History, 1848–1938* (Berkeley, Calif., 1972).
19 For information on the "Wiener Kreis," see Viktor Kraft, *Der Wiener Kreis: Die Ursprünge des Neopositivismus: Ein Kapitel der jüngsten Philosophiegeschichte*, 2d. enlarged ed. (Vienna, 1960) and Stadler, *Vom Positivismus zur "Wissenschaftlichen Weltauffassung."* Surveys of the history of psychoanalysis devote relatively more space to the emigrations: Jones, *The Life and Work of Sigmund Freud*; Wolfgang Huber, *Psychoanalyse in Österreich seit 1933* (Vienna, 1977); Wolfgang Huber, ed., *Beiträge zur Geschichte der Psychoanalyse in Österreich* (Vienna, 1978). Other "schools" were paid attention to only in the recent past. For Austro-Marxism, see Ernst Glaser, *Im Umfeld des Austromarxismus: Ein Beitrag zur Geistesgeschichte des österreichischen Sozialismus* (Vienna, 1981). For the Bühler School, see Charlotte Bühler, "Die Wiener Psychologische Schule in der Emigration," *Psychologische Rundschau* 16 (1965): 187–96; Achim Eschbach, ed., *Bühler-Studien* (Frankfurt/Main, 1984); Lotte Schenck-Danzinger, "Erinnerungen an Karl und Charlotte Bühler – die Bedeutung der Wiener Schule der Psychologie für die Pädagogik," in Erik Adam, ed., *Die österreichische Reformpädagogik, 1918–1938* (Vienna, 1981), 225–35; Lotte Schenk-Danzinger, "Zur Geschichte der Kinderpsychologie: Das Wiener Institut," *Zeitschrift für Entwicklungspsychologie und Pädagogische Psychologie* 16 (1984): 85–101; Mitchell G. Ash, "Psychology and Politics in Interwar Vienna: The Vienna Psychological Institute, 1922–1942," in Mitchell G. Ash and William R. Woodward, eds., *Psychology in Twentieth-Century Thought and Society* (Cambridge, 1987), 143–64; Gerhard Benetka, *Zur Geschichte der Institutionalisierung der Psychologie in Österreich: Die Errichtung des Wiener Psychologischen Instituts* (Vienna, 1990). On individual psychology, see Erik Adam, ed., *Die österreichische Reformpädagogik, 1918–1938* (Vienna, 1981). On economics, see Franz Baltzarek, "Ludwig von Mises und die österreichische Wirtschaftspolitik der Zwischenkriegszeit," *Wirtschaftspolitische Blätter*, no. 4 (1981): 127–39; Stephan Böhm, "Austrian Economics – Geschichte und philosophische Wurzeln," *Wirtschaftspolitische Blätter*, no. 2 (1981): 119–29; Stephan Böhm, "The Austrian Tradition: Schumpeter and Mises," in Klaus Hennings and Warren J. Samuels, eds., *Neoclassical Economic Theory* (Boston, 1990), 201–41; Alois Brusatti, "Die Entwicklung der Wirtschaftswissenschaften und Wirtschaftsgeschichte," in *Die Habsburgermonarchie, 1848–1918*, vol. 1: *Die wirtschaftliche Entwicklung*, ed. Alois Brusatti (Vienna, 1973), 605–24; Alexander Hörtlehner, "Ludwig von Mises und die österreichische Handelskammerorganisation," in *Wirtschaftspolitische Blätter*, no. 4 (1981): 140–9; Eduard März, "Grosse Denker der Nationalökonomie der Zwischenkriegszeit," in Norbert Leser, ed., *Das geistige Leben Wiens in der Zwischenkriegszeit* (Vienna, 1981), 86–97; Eduard März, *Joseph Alois Schumpeter – Forscher, Lehrer und Politiker* (Vienna, 1983); Werner Neudeck, "Die Entwicklung der Wirtschaftswissenschaften in Österreich 1918 bis 1938," in *Geistiges Leben im Österreich der Ersten Republik* (Vienna, 1986), 220–30. For more extensive discussion of the neglect of the emigration in the case of sociology, see Fleck, *Rund um Marienthal*, 9–34
20 Johnston, *The Austrian Mind*; Allan Janik and Stephan Toulmin, *Wittgenstein's Vienna* (New York, 1973); Carl E. Schorske, *Fin-de-siècle Vienna: Politics and Culture* (New York, 1980); and the anthologies to which Austrians contributed, including Wolf Lepenies, ed., *Geschichte der Soziologie: Studien zur kognitiven, sozialen und historischen Identität einer Disziplin* (Frankfurt/Main, 1981); M. Rainer Lepsius, ed., *Soziologie in Deutschland und Österreich, 1918–1945* (Opladen, 1981); Ivar Oxaal et al., eds., *Jews, Antisemitism and Culture in Vienna* (London, 1987). The authors of the two Austrian overviews were, typically, former emigrants: Albert Fuchs, *Geistige Strömungen in Österreich, 1867–*

social scientists also began to look at the issue. In 1987, these investigations culminated in a conference entitled "Vertriebene Vernunft" (exiled reason) and in two volumes of collected essays that bear the same title.[21] Austrian studies on the topic of science emigration thus far are of four different kinds: (1) studies that survey the history of disciplines, mainly concentrating on the history of ideas and dealing with émigré scientists in varying degrees of detail[22]; (2) studies of individual schools that include the issue of emigration in their analyses[23]; (3) studies of individual scientists and scholars that, not surprisingly, include the most detailed accounts of time spent in exile[24]; (4) reprints or new editions that have (once again) made

1918 (1949; Vienna, 1984); Hilde Spiel, *Glanz und Untergang: Wien 1866 bis 1938* (Vienna, 1987). See Martin Jay, *The Dialectical Imagination: A History of the Frankfurt School and the Institute of Social Research, 1923–1950* (Boston, 1973); Rolf Wiggershaus, *Die Frankfurter Schule: Geschichte, theoretische Entwicklung, politische Bedeutung* (Munich, 1986); Claus-Dieter Krohn, *Wissenschaft im Exil: Deutsche Sozial- und Wirtschaftswissenshchaftler in den USA und die New School for Social Research* (Frankfurt/Main, 1987); Gerhard Hirschfeld, " 'The defense of learning and science . . . ': Der Academic Assistance Council in Grossbritannien und die wissenschaftliche Emigration aus Nazi-Deutschland," *Exilforschung: Ein internationales Jahrbuch* 6 (1988): 28–43; Ilja Srubar, ed., *Exil, Wissenschaft, Identität: Die Emigration deutscher Sozialwissenschaftler, 1933–1945* (Frankfurt/Main, 1988); Mitchell G. Ash, "Central European Emigré Psychologists and Psychoanalysts in the United Kingdom," in Julius Carlebach et al., eds., *Second Chance: Two Centuries of German-Speaking Jews in the United Kingdom* (Tübingen, 1991), 101–20.

21 Friedrich Stadler, ed., *Vertriebene Vernunft*, vol. 1: *Emigration und Exil österreichischer Wissenschaft, 1930–1940* (Vienna, 1987); Stadler, ed., *Kontinuität und Bruch, 1938–1945–1955: Beiträge zur österreichischen Kultur und Wissenschaftsgeschichte* (Vienna, 1988); Stadler, ed., *Vertriebene Vernunft*, vol. 2: *Emigration und Exil österreichischer Wissenschaft, 1930–1940* (Vienna, 1988).

22 Josef Langer, ed., *Geschichte der österreichischen Soziologie, Konstituierung, Entwicklung und europäische Bezüge* (Vienna, 1988); Rudolf Haller, *Studien zur Österreichischen Philosophie* (Amsterdam, 1986); Haller, "Zur Historiographie der österreichischen Philosophie," in *Von Bolzano zu Wittgenstein: Zur Tradition der österreichischen Philosophie* (Vienna, 1986), 41–53; Josef Ehmer and Albert Müller, "Sozialgeschichte in Österreich: Traditionen, Entwicklungsstränge und Innovationspotential," in Jürgen Kocka, ed., *Sozialgeschichte im internationalen Überblick: Ergebnisse und Tendenzen der Forschung* (Darmstadt, 1989), 109–40; Wilhelm Brauneder, ed., *Juristen in Österreich, 1200–1980* (Vienna, 1987). For details about Austrian university-based psychological trends, see also Ulf Geuter, *Die Professionalisierung der deutschen Psychologie im Nationalsozialismus* (Frankfurt/Main, 1984); Ulf Geuter, ed., *Daten zur Geschichte der deutschen Psychologie* (Göttingen, 1986–87); Mitchell G. Ash and Ulf Geuter, eds., *Geschichte der deutschen Psychologie im 20 Jahrhundert* (Opladen, 1985). The same situation applies in the case of the émigré economists. Only a general overview of their histories is contained in Claus-Dieter Krohn, "Die Emigration der österreichischen Schule der Nationalökonomie in die USA," in Friedrich Stadler, ed., *Vertriebene Vernunft*, 2:402–25; Karl Müller, "Die Idealwelten der österreichischen Ökonomen," in Stadler, eds., *Vertriebene Vernunft*, 1:238–75; Karl Müller "Die nationalökonomische Emigration: Versuch einer Verlustbilanz," in Stadler, ed., *Vertriebene Vernunft*, 2:374–86. Stephan Böhm, "Austrian Economics – Geschichte und philosophische Wurzeln" and Böhm, "The Austrian Tradition: Schumpeter and Mises" contain little historiographical information.

23 Hans-Joachim Dahms, ed., *Philosophie, Wissenschaft, Aufklärung: Beiträge zur Geschichte und Wirkung des Wiener Kreises* (Berlin, 1985); Johannes Reichmayr, *Spurensuche in der Geschichte der Psychoanalyse* (Frankfurt/Main, 1990).

24 For information on Schumpeter, see Eduard März, *Joseph Alois Schumpeter – Forscher, Lehrer und Politiker*; on Wilhelm Reich, see Wilhelm Burian, *Psychoanalyse and Marxismus: Eine intellektuelle Biographie Wilhelm Reichs* (Frankfurt/Main, 1972) and Karl Fallend, *Wilhelm Reich in Wien: Psychoanalyse und Politik* (Vienna, 1988); on Rudolf Eckstein, see D. Oberläuter, *Rudolf Eckstein –*

accessible the work of some émigré scientists, or work that was first published in exile.[25] Virtually no collective biographies (prosopographies) have been published that take the fate of particularly hard-hit disciplines as their point of departure to investigate the lives and careers of their émigré members. This can probably be explained by the fact that virtually no so-called "basic research" has been conducted in Austria or on the conditions that obtained in Austria.[26] Although research to date has concentrated mainly on monographs about individual émigrés, the lives and careers of only a few social scientists have so far been described; not even the most important and influential figures have as yet been fully researched, which makes comparative studies very difficult. Apart from autobiographies,[27] virtually no studies have dealt with the problem of acculturation of individual émigrés in their host countries; even biographies are marred by the same shortcoming, which is obviously attributable to the lack of research grants for study visits. Even the question of what impact the emigrations had on the development of science in Austria and on various disciplines after 1933–34 has so far not been studied systematically.[28] Thus Austrian research on forced

Leben und Werk: Kontinuität und Wandel in der Lebensgeschichte eines Psychoanalytikers (Vienna, 1985). On Edger Zilsel, see J. Dvorak, *Edgar Zilsel und die Einheit der Erkenntnis* (Vienna, 1981); on Paul Lazarsfeld, see Paul Neurath, "Paul Lazarsfeld und die Institutionalisierung empirischer Sozialforschung: Ausfuhr und Wiedereinfuhr einer Wiener Institution," in Ilja Srubar, ed., *Exil, Wissenschaft, Identität*, 67–105; Wolfgang R. Langenbucher, ed., *Paul F. Lazarsfeld: Die Wiener Tradition der empirischen Sozial- und Kommunikationsforschung* (Munich, 1990); on Otto Neurath, see Friedrich Stadler, *Vom Positivismus zur "Wissenschaftlichen Weltauffassung,"* on Marie Jahoda, see Christian Fleck, "Marie Jahoda," in Friedrich Stadler, ed., *Vertriebene Vernunft*, 2:345–59; on Felix Kaufmann, see H. G. Zilian, *Klarheit und Methode: Felix Kaufmanns Wissenschaftstheorie* (Amsterdam, 1990); on Alfred Schütz, see Helmut R. Wagner *Alfred Schütz: An Intellectual Biography* (Chicago, 1983); Elisabeth List and Ilja Srubar, eds., *Alfred Schütz: Neue Beiträge zur Rezeption seines Werkes* (Amsterdam, 1988); on Hans Kelsen, see Rudolf A. Métall, *Hans Kelsen: Leben und Werk* (Vienna, 1969), as well as a number of unpublished Ph.D. theses not cited here.

25 See, e.g., individual volumes of the "Klassische Studien" series edited by Karl Acham and published by Böhlau Verlag (Vienna), the "Wiener Kreis – Schriften zum logischen Empirismus" series published by Suhrkamp Verlag (Frankfurt/Main), and work in the field of economics, especially by the Viennese School, published by Philosophia Verlag (Munich). Most, but not all, volumes contain in their introductions references to the careers and lives of their authors in exile. For two examples showing very different approaches, see Hans Kelsen, *Vergeltung und Kausalität*, reprinted with an introduction by Ernst Topitsch (1941; reprinted: Vienna, 1982) and Richard von Mises, *Kleines Lehrbuch des Positivismus: Einführung in die empiristische Wissenschaftsauffassung*, ed. Friedrich Stadler (1939; reprinted: Frankfurt/Main, 1990).

26 Helmut Müssener, *Exil in Schweden: Politische und kulturelle Emigration nach 1933* (Munich, 1974).

27 Not all the autobiographies and self-portraits, as well as transcripts of radio interviews, most of which were published in Germany, are listed here because they cannot be considered results of research on science emigration, even though they are valuable sources of information. On this issue, see Alfons Söllner, "Deutsch-jüdische Identitätsprobleme: Drei Lebensgeschichten intellektueller Emigranten," *Exilforschung: Ein internatonales Jahrbuch* 3 (1985): 349–58.

28 Initial attempts in Friedrich Stadler, ed., *Kontinuität und Bruch, 1938–1945–1955*; Gernot Heiss et al., eds., *Willfährige Wissenschaft: Die Universität Wien, 1938–1945* (Vienna, 1989); Christian Fleck,

migration in the social sciences has not yet advanced much beyond descriptions of the lives and careers of individual scientists and global surveys of the losses suffered by individual disciplines.

Quantitative data have been based almost exclusively on the information contained in the *International Biographical Dictionary of Central European Emigrés* – not only in Austria, I should add. Roughly one-tenth of the scientists included in this handbook are Austrian social scientists.[29] The following tables are based on a more comprehensive data base, which also permits a comparison between scientists who emigrated and those who remained in Austria (see Table 9.1).[30]

The 71 percent rate of emigration for social scientists as a whole suggests that not all who refused to emigrate were included. Further evidence for this assumption comes from the lower rates of emigration obtained for those groups for which virtually complete data on the numbers of émigrés and non-émigrés were available. For instance, 54 percent (n=140) of Austrian sociologists emigrated, or 57 percent (n=114) if the cohort of those born in the 1920s is not included. Since they had not been able to complete grammar school before 1938 they cannot really be considered emigrating scientists (see Figures 9.1 and 9.2). I should like to stress once more that the figures quoted here present only an approximate indication of the real numbers of Austrian émigrés. More detailed findings have so far been obtained only for partial populations.

A collective biographical evaluation of a group of forty-six sociologists and scholars closely associated with sociology (the criterion applied was whether the selected scientists were listed in dictionaries of sociology, or whether they had produced publications that could be said to be essentially sociological, even though the authors might perhaps not belong to the discipline of sociology per se) produces some interesting results, especially

"Soziologie in Österreich nach 1945," in Christoph Cobet, ed., *Einführung in Fragen an die Soziologie in Deutschland nach Hitler, 1945–1950* (Frankfurt/Main, 1988), 123–47; Kurt R. Fischer and Franz M. Wimmer, eds., *Der geistige Anschluss: Philosophie und Politik an der Universität Wien, 1930–1950* (Vienna, 1993).

29 See Christian Fleck, "Vertrieben und Vergessen: Ein Überblick über die aus Österreich emigrierten Soziologen," in Langer, 257–78, where the total number of émigré Austrian social scientists is given as 293, a figure which is based on the Strauss-Röder handbook.

30 A register of names at the Archiv für die Geschichte der Soziologie in Österreich (AGSÖ), Graz, is currently being compiled by Reinhard Müller. This allowed us to make only rough evaluations. Currently, the database includes entries from various relevant encyclopedias and handbooks (Strauss-Röder handbook, *Soziologenlexikon, Bibliographia Judaica Österreichische Juristen, Neue österreichische Biographie, Österreichisches Biographisches Lexikon, Kürschners Gelehrtenlexikon, Wer ist's?*), lecture schedules from Austrian Universities and research data collected in university archives, surveys, and from personal communications.

Table 9.1 *Emigré Austrian social scientists by discipline*[31]

Discipline[a]	Number	No. of émigrés (%)	Difference[b]
Sociology	140	53.6	+41
Economics	70	69.5	+1
Psychology	46	84.8	+5
Psychoanalysis	66	89.4	+13
Political Science	30	86.6	−3
Law	25	40.0	−8
Contemporary history	27	81.5	−11
Social philosophy	30	73.3	+1
Other disciplines	155	72.2	+82
Total	589	70.6 (n=414)	+121

[a]Scientists were assigned to the disciplines they belonged to for the longest period of time, or just before they emigrated.
[b]Absolute percentages compared with the data in Christian Fleck, "Soziologie in Österreich nach 1945," in Christoph Cobet, ed., *Einführung in Fragen an die Soziologie in Deutschland nach Hitler, 1945–1950* (Frankfurt/Main, 1988), 123–47.

when set against parallel findings for German émigrés. The average age at the time of emigration was just thirty-two years. Fifteen percent of émigrés had not yet obtained degrees (children are not included in these statistics).[32] Seventy percent had completed a Ph.D., but only seven of the émigrés included in this analysis had been appointed to a lectureship before they emigrated: Johann Mokre, Johannes Messner, Erich Voegelin, and Otto Neurath (who had been dismissed from his position at the University of Heidelberg when he participated in the Munich soviet republic in 1919). Three held the post of full professor: Josef Dobretsberger, Walther Schiff, and Friedrich Hertz. Hertz had been relieved of his post at the University of Halle in 1934, and returned to Austria. At the top of the list of countries that absorbed émigrés are the United States (66 percent), followed by Great Britain (17 percent). The remaining eight émigrés sought refuge in Palestine (four), Switzerland (two), the Soviet Union, and Turkey (one each).[33]

31 The column "Difference" refers to an earlier survey of the Strauss-Röder handbook. The differences resulted from, on the one hand, the different classification that was employed and, on the other, the more comprehensive database that was available.
32 That is, people who were born in Austria, yet left before completing school. They include Lotte Lazarsfeld-Bailyn, Fred Hirsch, Edith Kurzweil, Suzanne Keller, Fred Massarik, and Kai T. Erikson.
33 We did not always include the country to which the émigrés went first, but the country where they were in 1945.

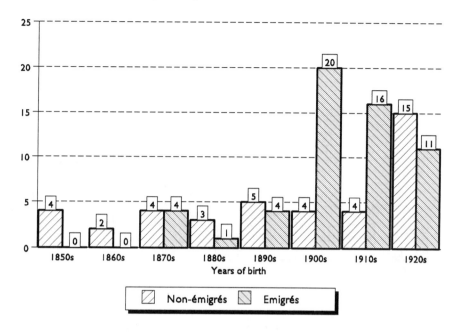

Figure 9.1 Austrian sociologists: émigrés and non-émigrés (by year of birth).
Source: AGSÖ Personendatei (see fn 30 in this chapter).

Although they might not always have been immediately successful, the majority of émigrés were able to establish themselves permanently in the countries to which they fled. Thirty obtained tenured positions as professors, on average after thirteen years and at forty-one years of age. If those six émigrés who returned to the German-speaking area after the defeat of the Nazi regime to resume their old positions or acquire new posts are included – their median age was a few years older than the émigrés who did not return – we arrive at a "success rate" of 78 percent. However, the number of returnees – this applies not only to our sample but generally to the situation in Austria – is negligible, and much lower than for Germany. According to estimates, about one-third of German social scientists returned to East or West Germany (only those physically fit enough to do so are included in these data). In the Austrian case, it was mainly the proponents of the specific brand of Catholicism that the *Ständestaat* had fostered who returned home after 1945: Dobretsberger, Mokre, Wilhelm Koppers, and Robert Heine-Geldern. Members of the left and Jews were not welcome and, as in previous decades, were excluded from the universities. Only a

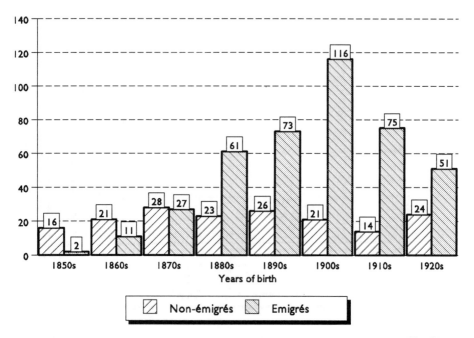

Figure 9.2 Austrian social scientists: émigrés and non-émigrés (by year of birth). *Source*: AGSÖ Personendatei (see fn 30 in this chapter).

small minority ever tried to return to Austria, and none of those who did return was offered a professorship.[34]

The topic "forced migration and scientific change" is not limited to emigration that was prompted by the advent of the National Socialist regime, so we need to mention at least two further waves of emigration that are usually ignored by those overviews centering on the impact of the Nazi regime. A reminder that social scientists left Austria even prior to 1933 for reasons other than what might be labeled academic mobility also indicates the circumstances that triggered the subsequent waves of emigration, and it might also throw light on some of the further causes, besides the fear of Nazi terror. Finally, if we look at the postwar years, we will also see that

---

34 It was not until the late 1960s that émigrés stood a realistic chance of establishing themselves within the scientific system, which meant that for the majority of them it was really too late. Examples include Kurt Blaukopf and Paul Neurath from our sample; Kurt W. Rothschild, Karl R. Stadler, Walter Simon, Eduard März and Josef Steindl were at least appointed (honorary) professors, although late in life. See Fleck, "Vertrieben und Vergessen," and Fleck, "Emigration und intellektuelle 'Ausdünnung' der Nachkriegssozialdemokratie," in Rudolf Ardelt and Hans Hautmann, eds., *Arbeiterschaft und Nationalsozialismus: In memoriam Karl R. Stadler* (Vienna, 1990), 669–89.

the emigration of scientists did not stop with the end of the war and the destruction of the Nazi system.

Indeed, postwar Austria proved quite unique in the way it rid itself of its Nazi past. The reunion with the Reich it had reverently celebrated seven years previously was equally loudly deplored after the war was over and decried as domination by a foreign power, as a yoke that had finally been cast off. For the scientific community, this mimicry of the collective mentality had immediate institutional consequences, which the scope of this essay does not permit us to develop in detail.[35] Suffice it to say that nationals of the German Reich who had been appointed to university posts after 1938 in the *Ostmark* automatically lost their positions, and that a few Austrian Nazis likewise fell afoul of denazification commissions. However, they were not without jobs for long, as they quickly managed to exploit their networks of personal contacts.

The rotation of jobs that the denazification process triggered brought several prominent scientists to Germany's western zones of occupation; among them were Arnold Gehlen, Günther Ipsen, Otto Brunner, Franz Ronneberger, Hans Bobek, Werner Conze, and also two eminent natural scientists who were later to receive the Nobel Prize: Konrad Lorenz and Karl Frisch. Not only those who proved useful to America's military research were transferred across the Atlantic; even some arts scholars and social scientists, for example, Ludwig Bertalanffy and Peter R. Hofstätter, went overseas.[36] The young "émigrés," the type exemplified by Peter L. Berger or Paul Feyerabend, come closest to our image of migrants in search for work, yet they really belong to a different chapter in the history of Austrian scientific exports. More closely linked to our period of investigation are the emigrations at the beginning of the Cold War, when Austrian communists were forced to leave the country and took refuge in the former GDR. Among them were Leo Stern and Walter Hollitscher.

SCHOOLS OF SOCIAL SCIENCE IN THE INTERWAR
PERIOD AND THEIR DISINTEGRATION BECAUSE
OF FORCED MIGRATION

The discussion thus far might have created the false impression that emigration has to do exclusively with the expulsion of individuals. In the fol-

---

35 See Fleck, "Vertrieben und Vergessen."

36 Tom Bower, *The Paperclip Conspiracy: The Hunt for Nazi Scientists* (New York, 1988). For Austrian examples, see *Grenzfeste Deutscher Wissenschaft: Über Faschismus und Vergangenheitsbewältigung an der Universität Graz* (Vienna, 1985), 43.

lowing, I will show that enforced migrations also affected the collective body of scientists to a great extent.

The interwar social science scene is famous as a period of prolific literary production. Among the sociological highlights that were first published at the time are: Max Adler's *Lehrbuch der materialistischen Geschichtsauffassung* (1930), which may be considered an introduction to Marxist sociology; Otto Neurath's *Empirische Soziologie* (1931), Alfred Schütz's *Sinnhafter Aufbau* (1932), and Felix Kaufmann's *Methodenlehre* (1936), all philosophical discussions – with different emphases – of issues pertaining to the social sciences; Edgar Zilsel's *Geniestudie* (1926) and Ernst Grünwald's *Wissenssoziologie* (1934), which mark different stages in the gradual dissociation of the sociology of knowledge from the philosophical history of ideas; and empirical studies by Hildegard Hetzer (1929), Paul F. Lazarsfeld (1931), Käthe Leichter (1932), and Marie Jahoda and Hans Zeisel (1933).[37] The other social science disciplines were equally productive. Examples are the third generation of the Viennese proponents of the theory of marginal utility, or the psychologists of the Bühler circle, and the disciples of Freud, Adler, and Kelsen. Within a span of just ten years, all published important works. These publications underscore Rene König's judgment that sociology reached a short peak before 1933, and was brought to an abrupt end when the National Socialists seized power; his assessment of the Weimar Republic is equally valid for Austria.[38]

When one reads Austrian or foreign histories of science in Austria, one might gain the impression – which can be shown to be false – that this prolific output in the interwar period was largely due to the productivity of the country's academics, and that the originators were mainly university lecturers.[39] When we scan the names of the lecturers who taught at Austrian universities in 1938, however, a huge discrepancy becomes obvious. Few familiar names will be found; those authors whose works continue to be

37   Max Adler, *Lehrbuch der materialistischen Geschichtsauffassung: Soziologie des Marxismus* (Berlin, 1930); Otto Neurath, *Empirische Soziologie: Der wissenschaftliche Gehalt der Geschichte und Nationalökonomie* (Vienna, 1931); Alfred Schütz, *Der sinnhafte Aufbau der sozialen Welt: Einführung in die verstehende Soziologie* (Vienna, 1932); Felix Kaufmann, *Methoden der Sozialwissenschaften* (Vienna, 1936); Edgar Zilsel, *Die Entstehung des Geniebegriffs: Ein Beitrag zur Ideengeschichte der Antike und des Frühkapitalismus* (Tübingen, 1926); Ernst Grünwald, *Das Problem der Soziologie des Wissens: Versuch einer kritischen Darstellung der wissenssoziologischen Theorie*, ed. Walther Eckstein (Vienna, 1934); Hildegard Hetzer, *Kindheit und Armut* (Leipzig, 1929); Paul F. Lazarsfeld, ed., *Jugend und Beruf: Kritik und Material* (Jena, 1931); Marie Jahoda and Hans Zeisl, *Die Arbeitslosen von Marienthal: Ein soziographischer Versuch über die Wirkung langdauernder Arbeitslosigkeit* (Leipzig, 1933); Käthe Leichter, *So leben wir . . . 1,320 Industriearbeiterinnen berichten über ihr Leben* (Vienna, 1932).
38   René König, *Soziologie in Deutschland: Begründer, Verfechter, Verächter* (Munich, 1987), 388–440.
39   See Johnston, *The Austrian Mind*, and Dirk Käsler, *Die frühe deutsche Soziologie 1909 bis 1934 und ihre Entstehungsmilieus* (Opladen, 1984).

quoted or even discussed in detail rarely figure, and the names of the majority of holders of university posts go unrecognized (for sociology, see Table 9.2).[40]

The question thus arises whether and to what extent this prolific literary output was linked to the degree of institutionalization that the social sciences experienced. A definition of institutionalization – which at first glance might perhaps appear rather unorthodox – could be as follows: A discipline is institutionalizing when it can be studied by coming generations of students. The study of a discipline again presupposes three things: examples that can be followed, comprehension of the rules that have to be observed when new knowledge is to be generated, and opportunity for practice. It presumes the existence of a social and organizational base that permits the teaching of novices. Ideas and theories alone do not make history; at best they may survive difficult times like messages in a bottle. Theoretical constructs and conceptions of research programs require their public dissemination, organizational skills on the part of their proponents, and promotion by external sponsors in order to take effect.

This implies that at least two preconditions have to be satisfied: that sufficient human resources are available so that the roles of researcher, teacher, and student can be adequately filled; and that appropriate social networks are established to make possible the communication and exchange of ideas. The development of the social sciences during the First Austrian Republic stagnated at all those levels that were institutionally relevant. The loss of two German-speaking universities after the breakup of the Habsburg empire (in Prague and the smaller university in Chernovtsy) shrank the academic market; few new chairs were established before 1930, many of them to be lost following major cut-backs in the early 1930s.[41] The ratio of lecturers to professors, which is central to a successful academic career, had steadily worsened since the turn of the century.[42] A further factor that added to the plight of the social sciences was that the old faculties of law and state theory, which might have provided a fitting base for the nascent social sciences, were increasingly dominated by National Socialists and their fellow travelers.

At this point, the concept of "schools" can serve as an organizing frame-

40 In the other disciplines the situation was not quite as drastic, yet it was not significantly better either. The three holders of economics chairs at the University of Vienna were Othmar Spann, the undistinguished scholar Ferdinand Degenfeld-Schonburg, and Hans Mayer.
41 In 1913, Austrian universities had a total of 363 chairs, in 1932 – 426, and in 1936 – 315.
42 In 1899, the ratio of lecturers to professors in the law and political science faculties was 1:6; in 1932, it had dropped to 0:9. See Christian Fleck, "Rückkehr unerwünscht: Der Weg der österreichischen Sozialforschung ins Exil," in Stadler, *Vertriebene Vernunft*, 1:186–7.

Table 9.2 *Sociologists and "part-time" sociologists at Austrian universities prior to 1938*

Status	Lecturers in sociology		"Part-time" sociologists	
	before 1918	1918–38	before 1918	1918–38
Full professorships	0 0	O. Spann (1921 Vienna Univ) A. Günther (1923 Innsbruck)	L. Gumplowicz (Admin. Theory) E. Ehrlich (Roman Law) J. Schumpeter (Economics) F. Wieser (Economics)	H. Kelsen (State theory) J. Dobretsberger (Economics) F. Wieser (Economics)
Tenured professorships	0	W. Heinrich (1923 WH Vienna) J. Sauter (1935 Vienna Univ) *E. Voegelin (1935 Vienna Univ)	H. Kelsen (Constitutional Law)	
Private lecturers, professors, but not holding a chair	0	M. Adler (1921 Vienna Univ) J. Baxa (1932 Vienna Univ) *K. Radakovic (1934 Graz Univ)		L. Mises (Economics) Ch. Bühler (Psychology)
Private lecturers	0	W. Andreae (1925 Vienna Univ) H. Riehl (1928 Graz Univ) H. Roeder (1933 Vienna Univ) *A. M. Knoll (1934 Vienna Univ)	W. Jerusalem (Philosophy) L. M. Harmann (History)	F. Kaufmann (Philos. of Law)

Note: The category "Lecturers in sociology" includes all lecturers who submitted their habilitation theses in "sociology" or *Gesellschaftslehre* (social theory), plus holders of chairs of sociology or social theory – always in addition to further major subjects. The year of appointment or submission of the habilitation thesis and the name of the university is given in brackets. "Part-time" sociologists refers to scientists whose publications made a contribution to sociology (this is not a complete list). Their main disciplines are given in parentheses.
*Academics who held further professorships in addition to the chairs of sociology or social theory.

work (see Table 9.3). There is a considerable body of evidence that suggests that the development of the social sciences in Austria was carried
out above all by schools or school-type groupings. Nearly all of the social
scientists whose names we are still familiar with either belonged to such a
school or were associated with one. Of all the social science schools, the
following groupings were arguably the most productive: schools that successfully stepped beyond the narrow confines of their discipline, such as
the economists around Ludwig von Mises, the legal scholars around Hans
Kelsen, and the psychologists around Charlotte and Karl Bühler.[43] Mainly
for the purpose of comparison, I will include two further groups in this
analysis. One is the group around Othmar Spann, who claimed they were
different than the main current of contemporary sociology because of
their "universalistic" approach, as they preferred to call it. The few university posts there were in sociology were occupied by members of the
Spann School. The second group, centered at the University of Innsbruck, is comparable to the Spann group in its impact on contemporary
science, even though its members were treated with less respect than the
former group at the time.[44] If we want to paint a relatively complete picture of the state of the social sciences during the interwar period,
however, we need to include two further groupings, which were politically oriented but organized along school-type lines: Social Catholics and
Austro-Marxists.[45]

Speaking of schools will only make sense if I can show that their internal
cohesion was stronger than possible personal links between different
schools. Table 9.4 shows that only a small minority were members of more
than one school; the members of the Kelsen School, whose interests included the social sciences, were most often active in other environments as
well. The type of multiple membership that we see, with scholars belonging
to both a scientific school and a Social Catholic or Austro-Marxist grouping,
suggests that this is a prototypical double allegiance to both a scientific
school as well as a politico-ideological environment.

---

43 The other two schools of psychology active at the time, the Adlerians and Freudians, are not
    included in these data, just as the Vienna Circle has been excluded. Psychoanalysis devel-
    oped independently and quickly acquired an international reputation. The Adlerians and the
    members of the Vienna Circle – at least those whose work was important for the social sci-
    ences – also belonged to other groupings and schools, yet are here only classified as belonging to
    these.
44 See the review by Leopold von Wiese, "Adolf Günthers Alpenwerk," in *Kölner Vierteljahreshefte
    für Soziologie* 8 (1929–30): 420–7.
45 For details, see Fleck, *Rund um Marienthal*, 75–118.

Table 9.3 *Schools of social science during the interwar period*[a]

Name	Social Catholics	Spann	Innsbruck Social Research Institute	Mises	Kelsen	Bühler	Austro-Marxists
Type	milieu	school	school	school	school	school	milieu
Duration	before 1938 and after 1945	1919–38 and after 1945	1925–33	1920–38	1918–30	1922–38	before 1934
Size	10–100	10–30	10–20	8–30	11	10–20	12–50
Age variance	17	7	—	7	16	10	15
Non-emigrants	18	11	—	4	4	3	5
Emigrants	15	1	1	8	7	7	22
E-rate	45	8	—	66	64	70	81
Relevant public	Catholics	political elite	German nation	academic	academic	academic	proletariat
Sponsors	church, political circles	industry and commerce, political circles	local elite, NdW[b]	Chamber of Commerce, Rockefeller Foundation	—	Vienna, Rockefeller Foundation	Chamber of Labor, trade unions
Approach	persuasive	persuasive	popular, educational	argumentative	argumentative	argumentative	argumentative

[a]"Non-emigrants," "emigrants," and "rate of emigrants" (E-rate) are calculated on the basis of the AGSÖ register; the other data (group sizes and age variance) are based on my own work; for the computation of age variance, only the core values (i.e., smaller numbers of quoted group sizes) were included.

[b]Notgemeinschaft deutscher Wissenschaft.

Table 9.4 *Multiple memberships (X) in several schools of social science during the interwar period*

Name	Social Catholics	Spann	Mises	Kelsen	Bühler	Austro-Marxist
Dobretsberger	X		X			
Jahoda					X	X
Kaufmann			X	X		
Knoll	X	X		X		
Lazersfeld					X	X
Sauter		X		X		
Vöegelin		X	X	X		
Winter	X			X		

CHANGE THROUGH EMIGRATION

We may at this point conclude our analysis of the different types of schools and turn to the issue of how these groupings fared in exile. How many members of the schools decided to emigrate? How successful were they in establishing themselves abroad? To what extent did the schools succeed in preserving their social cohesion or at least in maintaining an intensive intellectual exchange? And what changes did exile impose on their programs?

High rates of emigration can be noted for the schools of von Mises, Bühler, Kelsen, and the Austro-Marxist groupings (see Table 9.3), which incidentally were the schools that had developed the most comprehensive theoretical base. From the fact that over two-thirds of their members were driven into exile, we may infer that those few members who did stay in Austria were unable to save their schools from disintegration. Even after the war, these schools stood little chance of revival unless they received some fresh ideas from returning émigrés. As already noted, it was mainly members of the Catholic camp who returned after 1945. We should mention that the few emigrants who returned came back to Austria with a more open mind and less provincial narrow-mindedness. Johannes Messner may be cited as an example in this connection. He had become acquainted with and came to appreciate the British welfare state during exile and integrated this experience into his Catholic-oriented social theory.[46]

---

46   One may compare Messner's *Die berufsständische Ordnung* (Innsbruck, 1936) with, e.g., his *Das Naturrecht* (Innsbruck, 1950).

The most common country of exile was the United States (though Jahoda, Hertz, Schlesinger, and Messner spent the war years in Britain). Only the Austro-Marxist émigrés headed for other countries as well (Great Britain and Sweden), which appears to have accelerated the break up of their associations. For the social sciences as a whole, we can say that the events of the two dictatorships destroyed completely the scientific culture, scientific discourse, and all scientific schools, with the exception of the universalistic school of Othmar Spann, which dominated the social sciences in postwar Austria until the 1970s.

In the Second Austrian Republic, the parties, governments, and universities did not make any effort to reconstruct the destroyed scientific system. Plans made by some émigrés (for example, by the Austrian University League in America and by Friedrich Hertz) were disregarded.[47] Meanwhile, the majority of the well-known émigré social scientists established themselves in the academic systems of the more hospitable Western countries.

Attempts by the various schools to establish themselves in a host country met with different degrees of success. The success story of the Vienna School of Economics is well documented, whereas the Kelsen School seems to have been less successful.[48] Hans Kelsen went to California after brief stays in Geneva and Prague, followed by William Ebenstein, a former lawyer and later one of the prominent figures in international politics. Felix Kaufmann, Erich Hula, and Ernst Karl Winter were appointed to posts at the New School for Social Research in New York (the last temporarily). Erich Voegelin received his first full-time position at Louisiana State University; Johann Mokre also ended up in provincial America, whereas Dobretsberger led a rather secluded existence, first in Turkey and later in Egypt. The former students of the Bühlers were, as is well known, more successful than their teachers. Else Frenkel and Egon Brunswik soon began successful careers at the University of California at Berkeley. Paul Lazarsfeld, who began as a social psychologist, became a sociologist in the United States; he used his position at the Bureau of Applied Social Research at Columbia University to help numerous émigrés with short-term or longer-term financial sources (for example, Herbert Menzel, Hans Zeisel, Herta Herzog, Paul Neurath, Peter M. Blau, and also some German scholars such

---

47 For an analysis of the proposal of the Austrian University League, see Fleck, Rückkehr unerwünscht; for Hertz's attempt, see some of his unpublished papers in the Hertz file in the archive of the "Society for the Protection of Science and Learning (SPSL)" at the Bodleian Library, Department of Western Manuscripts, Oxford.
48 Claus-Dieter Krohn, *Wissenschaft im Exil.*

as Siegfried Kracauer and Theodor W. Adorno).[49] Many of the later émigrés had spent some time in the United States before 1933, as visiting or exchange professors or as Rockefeller Fellows. Yet the sense of familiarity with the host country that such visits engendered was often quite deceptive, as the fate experienced by the Bühlers clearly demonstrates.[50]

In this connection, we must not forget to mention the large number of young émigrés who at the time they left Austria were, at best, university graduates, and carved out brilliant careers for themselves in exile. A good indicator for the success of the younger Austrian émigrés is, for example, the list of the contributors to the *International Encyclopedia of the Social Sciences*. The following social scientists with Austrian origins joined the editorial advisory board of this publication: Paul F. Lazarsfeld, Geraldo Reichel-Dolmatoff, Bert F. Hoselitz, Heinz Eulau, and Erik H. Erikson. A much longer list could be cited from the directory of contributors. This success was not restricted to the United States. Also in England we can find a great number of prominent social scientists from Austria.

One should not overlook the fact that surely an equal number of Austrian social scientists had considerable difficulties in exile. In part these were due to war-related complications. This was so in the case of the only recently rediscovered Austrian social historian Lucie Varga, who worked with Lucien Febvre and published important essays in the *Annales* that helped to spread some of the ideas of Bronislaw Malinowski; she died in France during the German occupation.[51] Better known is the tragic fate of the social theorist and philosopher of science Edgar Zilsel, who could not establish himself in the United States and took his own life there in 1944.[52] While success can be reported and summarized relatively easily, this is not so for the opposite, as these cases show. Difficulties following the flight from Austria can only be analyzed individually and require further detailed studies.[53]

49 David E. Morrison, "Paul Lazarsfeld: The Monography of an Institutional Innovator," Ph.D. diss., University of Leicester, 1976.

50 See Lewis Coser, *Refugee Scholars in America: Their Impact and Their Experiences* (New Haven, Conn., 1984): Ash, "Psychology and Politics in Interwar Vienna"; and Charlotte Bühler's autobiographical paper, in Ludwig J. Pongratz et al., eds., *Psychologie in Selbstdarstellungen* (Bern, 1972), 9–42.

51 See Lucie Varga's introduction to her *Zeitwende: Mentalitätshistorische Studien, 1936–1939*, ed. Peter Schöttler (Frankfurt/Main, 1991).

52 For a detailed discussion of the Zilsel case, see Christian Fleck, "Marxistische Kausalanalyse und funktionale Wissenschaftssoziologie: Ein Fall unterbliebenen Wissenschaftstransfers," *Yearbook 1992 of the Institut Wiener Kreis* (Dodrecht, 1992); and two forthcoming publications from Hans-Joachim Dahms about Zilsel and the Frankfurt School (in the yearbook cited previously published by Suhrkamp Verlag in 1993).

53 Biographical studies about two such émigrés are being conducted by two of my collaborators – Dietmar Paier on Else Frenkel-Brunswik and Reinhard Müller on Gustav Ichheiser. Both studies were   published in 1994. For Ichheiser, see Floyd Rudmin et al., eds., "Gustav Ichheiser in the

The question of whether the schools were able to continue their inter-school exchanges defies an easy answer. More sources of information, especially letters, need to be tapped before we can attempt a definitive answer. For these reasons, I can only hazard a guess. It seems that the large majority of Austrian social scientists never liked to look back, with the exception of a few Austro-Marxists, especially those who had emigrated to Britain and Sweden. A useful indicator of when the émigrés finally turned against Austria is the point in time at which they started to use a foreign language in their private correspondence. The few sources that I have had the opportunity to use indicate that Austrian scientists quickly adapted to their new environments.

This might be attributable to several causes. First, most of the émigrés were used to moving around the regions of the Habsburg monarchy. Only a few of them were old established citizens of Vienna (there is no need to mention other Austrian towns because none of the émigrés came from outside Vienna). In addition to their early experience of migration and attendant cultural adaptation, the younger generation of émigrés (see Figures 9.1 and 9.2) had the further advantage that they came mainly from cosmopolitan, intellectually oriented, and socially aware backgrounds.

The Austrians generally lack the kind of rigid adherence to native traditions that some German emigrants showed in relation to German idealism. Even in the 1920s and before, Austrian social scientists had been much closer to the English-speaking world than their German counterparts.[54] Theodor Gomperz, for example, translated and edited the *Collected Works* of John Stuart Mill, Wilhelm Jerusalem translated William James and worked hard to popularize pragmatism, and Johann Mokre translated parts of Bertrand Russell and Alfred Whitehead's *Principia Mathematica* into German. The Viennese School of Economics had been influenced by the classical English school of economics since the days of Carl Menger (contrary to their German counterparts of the Historical School), and the Viennese neopositivists followed in the footsteps of British empiricism. Given this cosmopolitan outlook of the Austrian émigrés, which was widespread among the left at the time, we may assume that they were eager to establish new networks of social and work relations. Their cooperation on various publications (for example, the *International Encyclopedia of Unified Science* of the neopositivists, many years of cooperation between Lazarsfeld and Rob-

---

History of Social Psychology: An Early Phenomenology of Social Attribution," *British Journal of Social Psychology* 26 (1987): 165–80.

54   Applying Galtung's typology of scientific styles, one would have to say that the Austrian style of pursuing science shows closer proximity to Anglo-Saxon than to Teutonic traditions.

ert K. Merton, and the cooperation between Else Frenkel, Daniel Levinson, and Nevitt Sanford in the authoritarian personality study) confirms this view, as do their attempts to join in the scientific debate (which, however, were not always entirely successful, as is attested to by the correspondence between Alfred Schütz and Talcott Parsons, and by Felix Kaufmann's efforts to cooperate with John Dewey).[55] The Austrians did not display the kind of idiosyncratic isolation that was a feature, for example, of the members of the Frankfurt School.

The theoretical programs of the different schools underwent different degrees of modification. In general, we may say that the process of acculturation brought with it a stronger tendency toward specialization. Interdisciplinary or multidisciplinary approaches were abandoned in favor of greater specialization, which often meant that the social scientists were forced to choose between different scientific styles and fields that they had pursued equally intensively before. Lazarsfeld, for instance, had to renounce his sociographic aspirations, just as he gave up his interest in social psychology. The economist Adolf Sturmthal became an expert on industrial relations, Hans Zeisel became a sociologist of law, and Bert F. Hoselitz began to concentrate his research efforts on economic and cultural developments. Greater specialization and professionalism also put an end to more practice-oriented political approaches. No longer were suggestions for research topics and the practical application of results almost inevitable by-products of the process of fitting them into an ideological framework. This trend toward greater specialization hit the sociologists particularly hard. Yet it would be misleading to attribute the blame solely to forced migration, since the same tendency can be observed among the other sociologists working in the 1930s. Still, the consequences were not all negative. Alfred Schütz, for example, greatly influenced the development of phenomenological sociology and ethnomethodology.

In the case of the psychologists of the Bühler School and the legal scholars around Kelsen, a different phenomenon emerged during the acculturation process. Since there was little demand for their legal expertise – many were specialists in constitutional law or administrative law – the legal scholars had to effect a more radical reorientation than all the other émigrés. International law, international relations, and political science became their new fields of action, in which some achieved international fame, including William Ebenstein, Heinz Eulau, and of course Kelsen himself. Less drastic were

---

55   See Anton Amann, "Alfred Schütz und Talcott Parsons: Zur scheinbaren Folgenlosigkeit eines Briefwechsels," in Stadler, *Vertriebene Vernunft*, 2:332–44, and H. G. Zilian, *Klarheit und Methode.*

the changes demanded of the psychologists; above all, they had to familiarize themselves with psychoanalysis, which few of them had used before other than privately.[56] Yet even the Bühlers' disciples tended to specialize, which had serious consequences for the social psychological orientation that the school had begun to develop in the 1930s. Ludwig von Mises clung to the position he had elaborated in Vienna with a degree of tenacity that almost verges on stubbornness. Other economists, as we know, were more open to new influences or developed theories of great influence inside the academic discourse. A great deal of contemporary economics is dependent on works of "Austrians," which, as is well known, is a label within economics.

A detailed analysis of the works of the individual scientists may require that we slightly revise this general view. One point we must bear in mind is that for many scientists, migration opened up opportunities they would not have had in Austria. Even if we imagine, for the sake of argument, that the *Ständestaat* and the Nazi regime had not happened, there would not have been the same number of positions for them to fill, let alone the same advantageous climate, given the discrimination prevalent in Austria, as the scientists found in their host countries. In Austria, only a handful of sociologists taught at universities between 1945 and the 1970s; this compares very unfavorably with the more than two dozen professors of sociology who launched successful careers in the United States before the 1950s.

No more than an overview can be offered here. Because schools were chosen as units of analysis, the limitations on the statements that can be made at this level of aggregation must be taken into account. Nonetheless, some tentative conclusions can be ventured. Austrian science and scholarship have yet to recover from the loss that resulted from the exile of so many social scientists.[57] A surprisingly large number of these émigré social scientists had successful careers in the countries where they settled, perhaps, among other reasons, because they had already had experience with regional mobility in Austria, and because they grew up in an intellectual culture that was not exclusively oriented to academic career aspirations, as was the case with comparable groups in Germany. In other words, émigré Austrians were more adaptable. The émigrés' contribution to what is generally called

56   Edith Kurzweil, *Freud und die Freudianer* (Stuttgart, 1993); Mitchell G. Ash, "Central European Emigré Psychologists and Psychoanalyists in the United Kingdom," in *Second Chance: Two Centuries of German-Speaking Jews in the United Kingdom*; Bruno Bettelheim, "Kulturtransfer von Österreich nach Amerika, illustriert am Beispiel der Psychoanalyse," in Stadler, *Vertriebene Vernunft*, 2:216–20, presents convincing arguments that psychoanalysis underwent significant changes even in the United States.

57   Cf. Helga Nowotny and Christian Fleck, "A Marginal Discipline in the Making: Austrian Sociology in a European Context," in Brigitta Nedelmann and Piotr Sztompka, eds., *European Sociology at the Turn of the Twentieth Century* (Berlin, forthcoming).

the progress of science, however, should not be rated too highly. None of the significant intellectual innovations of the second half of the twentieth century can be said to have been brought in the luggage of Austrian émigrés, as some have asserted.[58] But the émigrés certainly did contribute more to the normal scientific development of their disciplines than their colleagues who remained behind.

Thus there is good reason to claim that forced migration led to scientific change in Austrian science and scholarship, but it will not be possible to show an equivalent gain for the systems of science in the countries of settlement. It would be very surprising if one could prove that a small group of young, lower-status immigrants had produced fundamental change in social science disciplines with hundreds or even thousands of members. One reason for this non-causation of scientific change through emigration is the difference in sheer size between the natural and the social sciences and their subdisciplines in these years.[59] The niche-existence of Austrian economics and the rediscovery of ethnomethodology – "the specialty that came in from the cold," as Nicholas Mullins calls it – may serve as examples in support of this thesis.[60] The analysis of individual cases, which could not be undertaken in this context, will naturally modify this picture, since the shape of people's thinking generally changed as a result of the altered circumstances that emigration brought with it.

58 For the celebration of the Austrian spirit, see Johnston, *The Austrian Mind*, and the various exhibitions on the topic of fin-de-siècle Vienna.
59 The investigation of Klaus Fischer on the natural sciences demonstrates this thesis; see Fischer, "Die Emigration deutschsprachiger Physiker nach 1933: Strukturen und Wirkungen" and "Wissenschaftsemigration und Molekulargenetik: Soziale und kognitive Interferenzen im Entstehungsprozess einer neuen Disziplin" – both in Herbert A. Strauss et al., eds., *Die Emigration der Wissenschaften nach 1933: Disziplingeschichtliche Studien* (Munich, 1991), 25–72, 105–35.
60 Nicholas C. Mullins, *Theories and Theory Groups in Contemporary American Sociology* (New York, 1973).

10

The Vienna Circle in the United States and Empirical Research Methods in Sociology

JENNIFER PLATT AND PAUL K. HOCH[*]

It is well known that most of the logical positivists of the Vienna Circle emigrated to America in the 1930s or 1940s, and there became academically prominent and intellectually influential. The general trend of American sociology between 1930 and 1960 is typically seen as positivistic, and it is common to connect these two points and to suggest that developments in sociology were influenced or caused by the migration of the Vienna Circle and the dominance of their ideas.[1] The nature of the proposed connection varies, and some scholars, such as Christopher G.A. Bryant, see the influence as only minor.[2] These ideas, however, are not normally grounded in any systematic, detailed research of the actual connections and influence of empirical sociology. This chapter aims, in contrast, to look more closely at what actually happened. In doing so, it will inevitably raise some general methodological questions with regard to tracing influence.

Who should be counted as a member of the Vienna Circle? Some scholars have included thinkers such as Ludwig Wittgenstein and Karl Popper, who were in Vienna at the same time and who had contacts with members of the Circle, although they were not actually members. We have excluded them from this study. Another potential group is those who were never based in Vienna but who kept in close touch with the Circle and regarded

[*] The authors wish to acknowledge the British Academy and the Economic and Social Research Council (grant R000234322) for their support of the research for this chapter. They would also like to thank the University of Chicago Library's Department of Special Collections, Columbia University's Rare Book and Manuscript Library, the University of Washington Library's Manuscript and University Archives Division, and the University of Minnesota Library's Archival Section for their assistance.

[1] See, e.g., Gideon Sjoberg et al., "The Case Study Approach in Social Research," in Joe R. Feagin, Anthony M. Orum, and Gideon Sjoberg, eds., *A Case for the Case Study* (Chapel Hill, N.C., 1991), 30; Robert W. Friedrichs, *A Sociology of Sociology* (New York, 1970), 94; Peter Halfpenny, *Positivism and Sociology* (London, 1982), 46–61.

[2] Christopher G. A. Bryant, *Positivism in Sociological Theory and Research* (London, 1985), 144–5.

themselves as part of the same movement. The people around Hans Reichenbach and the Society for Scientific Philosophy in Berlin, for example,
make one such group, and pragmatically will be counted as belonging to
the Circle. Reports indicate, however, that Felix Kaufmann, who attended
meetings of the Circle, did not regard himself as a member because his
intellectual position differed, and thus he will be treated as marginal.[3] We
have excluded visitors and close contacts from the United States or Britain
such as philosophers Alfred Ayer, Albert E. Blumberg, Charles W. Morris,
Ernest Nagel, or Willard van Orman Quine. Although they attended Circle
meetings and associated themselves with it, they were clearly based in other
countries and in other intellectual environments.

Our criteria for inclusion as core members of the Vienna Circle are thus
both intellectual and social. Those whom we regard as most relevant for
practical purposes are those who eventually migrated to America, especially
those who wrote general works on the philosophy of science or social
science. The key individuals are Gustav Bergmann, Rudolf Carnap, Herbert
Feigl, Philipp Frank, Kurt Gödel, Carl G. Hempel, Otto Neurath, and
Reichenbach.[4] The difficulty of drawing clear boundaries between those
who should and should not be included already highlights issues surrounding the nature of diffusion processes, which we will discuss in more detail
subsequently.

The great majority of the members of the Vienna Circle had intellectual
backgrounds in physics or mathematics, with their philosophy originating,
and in some cases continuing, as a side interest rather than a disciplinary
base. In Vienna at the time, this breadth of interest was not as unusual as it
may now seem. Although originally trained as an applied physicist and
economist, Otto Neurath was the only one who thought of himself as a
sociologist. Probably none of the others had specific interests in the social
sciences while in Vienna, despite the general awareness of psychoanalysis
common to Viennese intellectuals at the time. Their distinctive concerns,
however, focused on ideas of potentially general applicability, about the
conditions for making meaningful statements, and about scientific method
generally. From the Circle's earliest days, at least a few social scientists knew
something of its ideas and were interested in them, even if they took them
in "by osmosis."[5] Most of them were economists and psychologists, which

3 Rudolf Carnap, "Intellectual Autobiography," in Paul A. Schilpp, ed., *The Philosophy of Rudolf Carnap* (La Salle, Ill., 1963), 20.
4 Interview with Leonard Linsky, March 1990; the notes for all of the interviews used in this chapter are in Jennifer Platt's possession.
5 Marie Jahoda, "The Emergence of Social Psychology in Vienna," *British Journal of Social Psychology* 22 (1983): 345.

probably has as much to do with the strengths of contemporary Viennese social science as it does with particular intellectual affinities. Many students from all of the faculties at the University of Vienna attended Rudolf Carnap's introductory lectures on philosophy, in which he analyzed the exact meanings of expressions and made connections with the psychologists Charlotte and Karl Bühler's psychological analysis of language.[6]

After emigrating to the United States, more of the Circle's members became professional philosophers. Although they received a warm welcome in the United States, many American philosophers were hostile to their views.[7] Indeed, their reception was perhaps warmer outside philosophy. The welcome came from a subgroup of philosophers, some of whom, such as Morris, Nagel, and Quine, had already visited them in Vienna, natural scientists (such as Percy W. Bridgman) who had already developed an interest in philosophical matters compatible with theirs, and some social scientists.[8]

Before the Vienna Circle emigrated, philosophy of science scarcely existed as a distinct specialty in the United States. Morris Cohen and his student Ernest Nagel were its main representatives, although the pragmatists John Dewey, William James, and Charles S. Peirce had all published relevant work. A number of books about scientific method and related topics were already in circulation, but most of them had been written by scientists as a sideline. Among the books commonly referred to in the sociological literature, although not specifically about social science, are those by C. West Churchman (an American operations researcher with a strong interest in methodology), Karl Pearson (a British statistician and eugenicist), Henri Poincaré (a French mathematician and physicist), Arthur Ritchie (a British biochemist), Frederic W. Westaway (a scientist and, possibly, school teacher), and Abraham Wolf (a British professor of logic and scientific method).[9]

Once in the United States, Bergmann, Feigl, and Hempel all became involved to varying extents with the social sciences and their philosophy,

6   Hans Zeisel, "L'école viennoise des recherches de motivation," *Revue francaise de sociologie* 9 (1968): 5.
7   Interview with Carl G. Hempel, July 1989. Morris R. Cohen, *A Dreamer's Journey* (Glencoe, Ill., 1949), 194.
8   It is interesting that the views of the Circle were not generally well received among philosophers – mainly neo-Kantian "metaphysicians" – in German-speaking countries. Laurence D. Smith, *Behaviorism and Logical Positivism* (Stanford, Calif., 1987), 47; Viktor Kraft, *The Vienna Circle* (New York, 1969), 53.
9   C. West Churchman, *Elements of Logic and Formal Science* (Philadelphia, 1940); Karl Pearson, *The Grammar of Science* (London, 1937); Henri Poincaré, *Science and Hypothesis* (London, 1905); Arthur D. Ritchie, *Scientific Method* (New York, 1923); Frederic W. Westaway, *Scientific Method* (London, 1924); Abraham Wolf, *Essentials of Scientific Method* (London, 1925).

as did Nagel who, although of American origin, had visited the circle in Vienna and who had developed extremely close personal and intellectual ties with its members. The additional social and behavioral scientists, including but not confined to those who were themselves of Viennese origin (such as Egon Brunswik, Paul Lazarsfeld, and Oskar Morgenstern), became actively involved in the intellectual concerns and discussions that continued to link the group, even though they no longer all lived in the same town or met regularly. Perhaps more important, however, is that a number of social scientists actively welcomed the Circle's ideas because they were compatible with their own. John B. Watson, the originator of behaviorism, was no longer active in academic life, but behaviorism was still a significant movement in psychology, with admirers in sociology; physicist Percy W. Bridgman's operationism was also widely influential.[10] These intellectual tendencies, combined with a more general support for the idea of being "scientific," constituted the context in the social sciences that made the Circle's ideas welcome. Feigl later remarked that "The closest allies our movement acquired in the United States were undoubtedly the operationalists, the pragmatists and the behaviorists."[11]

Despite the sometimes misleading accounts given in thumbnail sketches of the history of the period,[12] the Vienna Circle and these American movements appear to have originated entirely independently of each other, although the Mach and Russell/Whitehead connection made some contribution to the origins of each. Watson's *Psychology from the Standpoint of a Behaviorist* was published in 1919, Bridgman's *The Logic of Modern Physics* in 1927, and George A. Lundberg's *Social Research* in 1929.[13] The Circle's manifesto appeared only in 1929, and when Feigl visited the United States in 1930–31, he met Watson and Bridgman and discovered sympathetic thinkers whose work was not familiar to most members of the Circle and who did not know of the Circle's work. Laurence D. Smith's important book on the relation between behaviorism and logical positivism shows convincingly that the leading American psychologists Edward Tolman, Clark Hull, and B. F. Skinner, who have been assumed to have been

---

10   As Maila L. Walter points out, however, what it meant to Bridgman was very different from what it meant to his supposed disciples in sociology and psychology, and he was not happy with what others made of his original ideas. Walter, *Science and Cultural Crisis* (Stanford, Calif., 1990), 164–89.

11   Herbert Feigl, "The *Wienerkreis* in America," in Donald Fleming and Bernard Bailyn, eds., *The Intellectual Migration* (Cambridge, Mass., 1969), 643, 661.

12   See, e.g., Mark Blaug, *The Methodology of Economics* (Cambridge, 1980), 11.

13   John B. Watson, *Psychology from the Standpoint of a Behaviorist*, 2d ed. (Philadelphia, 1924); Percy W. Bridgman, *The Logic of Modern Physics* (New York, 1928); George A. Lundberg, *Social Research: A Study in Methods of Gathering Data* (New York, 1929).

228   *Jennifer Platt and Paul K. Hoch*

strongly influenced by the Circle, had all developed the ideas that most resembled theirs independently.[14] Home-grown American movements were already underway, specifically in the social sciences as well as in philosophy, which both sides saw as in some sense related or sympathetic. This enables us to dismiss the ideas that the Vienna Circle was entirely responsible for subsequent developments, although that does not imply that they played no role in them; rather, it complicates the question of influence.[15]

For there to have been influence, the ideas of the Vienna Circle must have made a difference to what sociologists thought and did. It is of course a precondition of such influence that sociologists must have come across their ideas and had the opportunity to become familiar with them, whether or not the ideas came with the label "Vienna Circle." For ideas to make a difference, they must be – or be perceived as – novel, and must be used. Circle ideas were not totally novel, however, and this makes it harder to tell whether or not others have been influenced by them. When related ideas from other sources were also current, similarities or compatibilities between the bodies of work could stem from other sources.[16] There can be similarities without influence – and there can also be influence without close similarity, in which the influencing ideas are connected with others to make a new synthesis, or the use is based on imperfect understanding of what the original thinkers had in mind. What is required is direct evidence that those potentially influenced were acquainted with the work in question and drew on it, and that this actually made a difference to what they did. In this case, there are two levels at which a difference could be made, that of abstract discussion and that of research practice. It cannot be taken for granted that practice follows from precept, and some attention will be given to each.

Before we consider the evidence about influence in sociology, there is another problem that has to be mentioned. The ideas of the Vienna Circle were not a fixed entity, crystallized in their 1929 manifesto and remaining

14 Smith, *Behaviorism and Logical Positivism.*
15 In 1916, Charles A. Ellwood attributed an "objectivism" in sociology, which has obvious features in common with the later "positivism," to the influence of Durkheim. In this he probably erred (see Jennifer Platt, "The U.S. Reception of Durkheim's *The Rules of Sociological Method*," *Sociological Perspectives* [1995]), but it indicates how a different version of historical influence could be constructed. Ellwood, "Objectivism in Sociology," *American Journal of Sociology* 22 (1916): 289–305.
16 Cf. the mistake of assuming that Max Weber's *verstehen* (understanding) influenced the emergence of participant observation, and the apparently Keynesian economic policies stemming from other theoretical sources. Jennifer Platt, "Weber's *verstehen* and the History of Qualitative Research," *British Journal of Sociology* 36 (1985): 448–66; Walter S. Salant, "The Spread of Keynesian Doctrines and Practices in the United States," in Peter A. Hall, ed., *The Political Power of Economic Ideas* (Princeton, N.J., 1989).

static thereafter. Not only were the implications of their original distinctive positions further developed, but their thinking also moved on. Feigl, indeed, said that most of their early doctrines had changed as a result of internal as well as external criticism.[17] It is arguable that they were more influential outside technical philosophy at a later stage, when they had established themselves in the United States and published more in English and on the social sciences. But by that point their ideas had become less distinctive and had indeed evolved in response to their new intellectual context and its influences. However, some key initial themes in their work were as follows. They were committed to the idea of the unity of all sciences, in whatever field, including the social sciences. They were committed to physicalism, as part of the perceived need for an intersubjective observation language. Their criterion of meaning was an empiricist one – "verifiability" – and they were strongly opposed to the alternatives, which they saw as "metaphysical." They stressed the distinction between analytic and synthetic propositions, and saw only synthetic (empirical) propositions as adding to knowledge of reality. However, their own work emphasized formal logical analysis and the language of propositions, so they were concerned with the logical analysis of scientific statements. They saw the appropriate model of theorizing and explanation as a deductive one.

We turn now to consider the evidence about their influence on sociology. The first places to find it should be those in which people are most likely to make general statements about scientific method: textbooks and monographs on method. Every textbook on sociological research methods published in the United States between 1930 and 1960 has been examined for references to works by members of the Vienna Circle.[18] From this it is clear that direct citation of the works of members of the Circle was minimal, and most of it occurs relatively late in the period. The first reference found that has any connection with the Circle is in 1949,[19] and that is only to the book by Kaufmann, which is listed as supplementary reading. It is not surprising that the first more serious and central reference should be in Marie Jahoda et al.'s textbook from 1951,[20] since Jahoda herself was a refugee from Vienna who had moved in related groups. Other works of technical philosophy are also little cited. Where relevant topics are raised, it is American

17 Feigl, 221.
18 The year 1930 was selected as the starting point because although it was possible to have been influenced by them earlier, it is the approximate date at which the permanent emigration started and their publications began to appear in English.
19 Pauline V. Young, *Scientific Social Surveys and Research* (New York, 1949).
20 Marie Jahoda et al., *Research Methods in Social Relations* (New York, 1951).

and British writers who are much more often cited, and the works that are more often drawn on are those of a relatively elementary or popularizing nature, such as Cohen and Nagel,[21] or relate explicitly to issues in the social sciences, such as those by Lundberg.

Where textbooks discuss scientific method generally, they rarely present its definition as controversial or outline the positions of rival schools of thought. This means that if they are taking a stand in relation to these, it may need to be inferred. Sometimes, however, the ideas used and the authors cited are drawn quite eclectically from different schools, or the issues are discussed in such a broad and superficial way that no position in relations to the questions disputed is implied.[22] Sociological methods textbooks are at the very least highly selective in the questions of technical interest to philosophers to which they refer. We cannot, for instance, recall any reference to the meaningfulness of synthetic a priori propositions, although statements about the place and relative value of induction and deduction are fairly common. In addition, the statements about scientific method that are made often have a rather emptily pious character, performing a Sunday ritual to be dispatched before continuing with life's daily practical business; there is not necessarily a close correspondence between the general principles declared and the concrete methods recommended. Even, for instance, the well-respected textbook by William J. Goode and Paul K. Hatt,[23] which starts with several chapters on issues of scientific method, rapidly moves on to concentrate on techniques related to surveys, with little attention to their relation to experimentation advocated earlier or to the validity of their operational definitions. The main focus of most textbooks is on methods of data-collection and statistics. Of the few more monographic treatments of relevant issues, those not by Lundberg are often actively hostile to scientism.[24]

Ideally, one would wish to approach the issue of the influence of philosophical ideas on research methods by looking at the research that was carried out at different periods and the methods that it used. There is, however, a practical difficulty in doing this and making the connection with confidence. Most reports of empirical research do not make statements of philosophical positions; they report what was done and draw empirical conclusions. Most statements of philosophical positions are made in books

---

21 Morris R. Cohen and Ernest Nagel, *An Introduction to Logic and Scientific Method* (London, 1934).
22 See, e.g., Young, *Scientific Social Surveys and Research.*
23 William J. Goode and Paul K. Hatt, *Methods in Social Research* (New York, 1952).
24 See, e.g., Charles A. Ellwood, *Method in Sociology* (Chapel Hill, N.C., 1933); Robert M. MacIver, *Social Causation* (New York, 1942); Florian Znaniecki, *The Method of Sociology* (New York, 1934).

and articles to which the general issues they raise are central. Intellectual specialization within disciplines is such that relatively few people both write on such general issues and carry out empirical research. This means that there are rather few cases in which we both know the general ideas someone held and can inspect the research he did. Such cases are well worth looking at, and we shall look closely in particular at the one of Lundberg, who did do both and was actively interested in the Circle.

It is more practical, if less precise, to get a general picture by looking relatively impressionistically at changes at the level of the whole discipline; this is also more appropriate if the influence has been transmitted indirectly and without conscious affiliation. The major change in American sociological research methods over the relevant period was the emergence of the modern survey, and the replacement of the prewar "case study method" by the newly rationalized conception of participant observation.[25] Can either of these be connected with the direct influence of the Circle's ideas? It seems highly implausible to suggest this for the survey; Jean M. Converse's historical account makes it clear that a whole range of different influences, many of them non-academic, converged to produce the eventual synthesis.[26] The key role played in developments by Lazarsfeld may well mean, however, that there was some indirect influence. (It should not be assumed that an emphasis on quantification has any significance here. Not only was there a long-standing American tradition of quantification in the census and other government research that was quite without philosophical inspiration, but also, as Hans Zeisel points out,[27] when you are doing market research as Lazarsfeld did, you certainly will not earn your fee unless you can refer to the numbers of customers.) Participant observation might seem a much less plausible candidate for influence – but some of its early practitioners from the 1940s thought of it as direct rather than indirect observation, and wrote of it in quite a behavioristic spirit[28]; indeed, Chris Argyris wrote of William F. Whyte's *Streetcorner Society* as based on a position following that of "Bridgman and other positivists."[29] However, it rapidly developed very different meanings in the methodological literature, and was taken over by those who emphasized the virtues of subjectivity rather than objectivity. Similarly, there is a direct connection between Charles W. Morris, a close

25 Jennifer Platt, " 'Case Study' in American Methodological Thought," *Current Sociology* 40, no. 1 (1992): 17–48.
26 Jean M. Converse, *Survey Research in the United States* (Berkeley and Los Angeles, 1987), 258.
27 Interview with Hans Zeisel, March 1990.
28 Jennifer Platt, "The Development of the 'participant observation' Method in Sociology," *Journal of the History of the Behavioral Sciences* 19 (1983): 379–93.
29 Chris Argyris, *An Introduction to Field Theory and Interaction Theory* (New Haven, Conn., 1952), 41.

philosophical associate of the Circle, and the symbolic interactionist theoretical position, which has been seen as closely associated with participant
observation, since Morris was strongly interested in the work of his Chicago
colleague G.H. Mead and wrote the introduction to a posthumous volume
of his work. The connection rested intellectually on their shared interests
in the role of symbols, formal aspects of language, and "social behaviorism."
Subsequent empirical sociologists have, however, taken up the aspects of
these shared concerns that lead away from the themes of the Circle, and
formal sociology and symbolic interactionism are usually seen as hostile to
"positivism."[30] Another American tradition, less written about as a distinct
category in texts on method, is that of laboratory research on small groups,
which was quite important in the 1950s.[31] This, however, is so obviously
related to long-standing traditions in psychology that it would be redundant
to account for it by relating it to philosophy.

The foregoing account is reasonably accurate as far as it goes, but it
follows most sociological discussions of methods in being too narrowly
limited to modes of data collection. It would be more promising to look
for influence from the Vienna Circle in phases where its ideas are more
directly relevant: theory construction, research design, the theoretical concepts that are admitted, and their operationalization. These, however, do
not lend themselves so easily to confident generalization, not least because
sociologists have not developed a consensual set of categories with which
to describe their practice. Yet more impressionistically, however, we may
suggest these changes: a greater self-consciousness about method, and a felt
obligation to describe it when reporting research; a growing commitment
to the idea of being "scientific," and an increasing tendency to associate
this with the idea of testing hypotheses rather than merely of being "objective"; an increasing recognition of the weakness of induction as a program, and acceptance of a hypothetico-deductive strategy. Some Circle
influences could well be imputed here, although the ideas are so general
that they could also have come from other directions (for example, from

30 It has been suggested that the use by the small and less prominent "Iowa School" of sociologists
committed to symbolic interactionist theory of "positivistic" methods was due in part to Gustav Bergmann's presence. This suggestion is questionable, since one of Bergmann's close associates claims that an intellectual enmity existed between him and Manfred Kuhn, the head of this
group. (Interview with Laird Addis, May 1993.) Frank Kohout, a member of the Iowa sociology
department at the time, adds that Bergmann was so skeptical of the scientific credentials of sociology
that he deterred sociology students from taking his course by telling them that however well
they did on it they would not receive a grade higher than a B. (Interview with Frank Kohout,
May 1993.)
31 Nicholas C. Mullins, *Theories and Theory Groups in Contemporary American Sociology* (New York,
1973).

Popper). None of these changes, though, necessarily affects the actual conduct of research, as distinct from the way in which it is reported; it is, for instance, notorious that the hypotheses "tested" have often been invented after inspection of the data. It would be interesting to explore the suggestion that the practice of research has changed less than its presentation.

Interviews with sixty-one leading figures with methodological interests, whose careers span the period, are available to shed further light on the subject. (The interviews were not directed toward learning about the Vienna Circle, but were open-ended explorations of the subjects' methodological careers and influences, undertaken in support of Platt's general work on the history of research methods.) Most of the books and people spontaneously mentioned in them are much more specifically sociological or social scientific. The only interviewees who spontaneously stressed anything to do with the Vienna Circle as an influence were Bernard Phillips and John T. Doby, the authors of two leading methods textbooks,[32] Lyle Shannon, and Robert Ellis. As a graduate student at Washington State in 1952–53, Phillips was taught philosophy of science by Wesley Salmon, one of Reichenbach's students. This, however, was for him only one contributory strand in a general pattern of "positivistic" influence in which the *American Soldier* research, Talcott Parsons, social psychology, and statistics courses were also important. Doby did his graduate work at Wisconsin, chosen because he liked what he saw as its rigorous and empirical – rather than philosophical – style. The methodologist/statistician T.C. McCormick was his mentor. He described the Vienna Circle as favorites of his, and said, "I think their way of putting the emphasis on hypothesis construction and theory construction interested me more, because for the most part the emphasis had been on testing without regard to the origin of the idea." Shannon was a graduate student under Lundberg and Stuart C. Dodd at the University of Washington, and has remained very much a disciple of Lundberg, whom he described as setting people onto the "logical positivism approach: operational definition of your variables, extending theory on the basis of research, basing research on testable theories." When asked to say a bit more about what logical positivism meant to him, he replied, "You create definitions of variables based on what you can observe, not saying this is the ultimate reality, just this is what you can observe." Although clearly in a broad sense compatible with the Vienna Circle's ideas, this is

---

32 Bernard S. Phillips, *Social Research: Strategy and Tactics* (New York, 1966); John T. Doby, *Introduction to Social Research* (Harrisburg, Pa., 1954). Interviews with Bernard Phillips (April 1984), John Doby (March 1991), Lyle Shannon (May 1993), and Robert Ellis (March 1991).

hardly a position distinctively associated with them, and owes at least as much to operationism as understood among sociologists. Ellis came into sociology from psychology, and took a course in 1952 at Yale from Hempel, whose ideas he associated with the tradition of experimental psychology rather than sociology as he found it in his early years in the discipline. James Davis, an important survey practitioner and writer on methods, remembered reading Kaufmann's *Methodology of the Social Sciences* as a graduate student at Harvard in the early 1950s, but said that to him being scientific then meant being objective, and that "German epistemology" was much less prevalent at that time. Thus the interviews, both in what they do and in what they do not say, confirm the picture of rather little real influence from the Circle.

An effort has been made to obtain copies of the reading lists used in relevant courses in order to see how extensively Vienna Circle works were drawn on; such lists are not often saved, so only material from the universities of Minnesota, Washington, Chicago, and Emory has been found. It is interesting to note that at Minnesota in the 1940s and 1950s, where F. Stuart Chapin had an established "scientific" position, Chapin and Neal Gross introduced students to "a rigid methodology based on the dictums of logical empiricism,"[33] and Feigl was in the philosophy department, the reading lists available for graduate research methods courses still do not mention the Circle. There is, however, an indication that students were allowed to take some of Feigl's courses on the philosophy of the social sciences; an exchange of memos agrees that they should be allowed credit for doing so.[34] At the University of Washington, if anywhere, with Lundberg heading the department, one might expect the Circle to be prominent. A lengthy general reading list from the late 1940s for graduate students on theory and methods does include Cohen and Nagel, Feigl and Mary Brodbeck's reader, and also articles by Feigl and Bergmann and Spence on topics related to psychology and by Reichenbach on probability in the social sciences; versions from the 1950s have only general articles on the philosophy of science from the *International Encyclopedia of Unified Science*. An undergraduate methods course cites only Lundberg and Pauline V. Young. At the University of Chicago, the nearest that Park's reading list for a 1932 course on methods of social research gets to the Vienna Circle is Bridgman's *Logic of Modern Physics*; otherwise, it is Pearson, Ritchie, and Dewey where the Circle might have appeared, even though some works in German are

---

33   Hans L. Zetterberg, *On Theory and Verification in Sociology* (New York, 1965), vii.
34   University of Minnesota, Dept. of Sociology, correspondence, 1948. University of Minnesota Library, AH 26.1, folder 19.

cited.[35] A little later, Burgess's lists for methods of sociological research from around 1939 to 1942 refer only to Cohen, Nagel, Pearson, Poincaré, and Lundberg.[36] The Chicago M.A. in 1959–60 did not have the Circle's works on the reading list for its compulsory courses, although the course on social theory and social research had an introductory section on "principles of theorizing" that came quite near (Cohen, Nagel, Kaufmann, Zetterberg). The Emory course "Logic of Research" in 1962 included Feigl and Brodbeck's *Readings*, as well as books by Kaufmann and Popper, along with works on sociology and on statistics. In all these courses, the overwhelming bulk of the references are not surprisingly to specifically sociological and practical sources. Even in the departments perhaps most likely to emphasize their ideas, the work of the Vienna Circle is not very prominent, and when it does appear, it is usually in versions written well after the migration and adapted to the American intellectual setting and social-scientific interests. This does not imply that it was not significant, but it does suggest that the message received by most people will have been heavily mediated.

It is helpful to our understanding of the matter to look more closely at some particular cases where there does seem to have been a strong influence from Vienna Circle ideas. The most striking instance available is that of Paul Lazarsfeld at Columbia. He refers to some of the Circle's works, and in particular acknowledges a vital influence on ideas at the center of his interests from Hempel and Oppenheim's work on typology.[37] Hempel and Nagel were in close contact with each other, with Nagel playing an important role in introducing Hempel to New York philosophical circles,[38] and Lazarsfeld kept in touch with both. For many years at Columbia he taught a joint seminar with Nagel on "The Logic of Social Inquiry"; the substantive field and the issue it gave rise to changed each year, but it always brought philosophical ideas together with social scientific work and used many Vienna Circle references.[39] The famous analysis by Nagel of the logic of functionalism probably arose from this partnership, as did a section on social-scientific explanation in Nagel's *The Structure of Science*[40]; that book acknowledges discussions with Lazarsfeld. (Hempel too wrote on functional

35 Philip M. Hauser papers, box 23, folder 7. Dept. of Special Collections, University of Chicago Library.
36 Ernest W. Burgess papers, box 30, folder 6. Dept. of Special Collections, University of Chicago Library.
37 Carl G. Hempel and Paul Oppenheim, *Der Typusbegriff im Lichte der neuen Logik* (Leiden, 1936).
38 Interview with Carl G. Hempel, 1989.
39 Ernest Nagel papers, box 20. Rare Book and Manuscript Library, Columbia University Library.
40 Ernest Nagel, "A Formalization of Functionalism," in Nicholas J. Demerath and Richard A. Peterson, eds., *System, Change and Conflict* (New York, 1967), 77–94, and Nagel, *The Structure of Science* (London, 1961), 509–20.

explanation, in a symposium on sociological theory.[41]) Lazarsfeld was of course himself also an émigré from Vienna and had moved to some extent in the same environment as members of the Circle, although he said that some writers about the Viennese milieu had exaggerated the extent to which different intellectual groups overlapped, and described his own circle as "socialist empiricists."[42] However, Bergmann was a good friend of his, and he was even involved in a discussion group there in the 1920s with some Circle members. Zeisel says that this group was an interdisciplinary one that discussed actual research rather than philosophy.[43] Its members were drawn from three main groups: socialists, economists around Ludwig von Mises, and the Vienna Circle. He reports that the Circle's new ideas were "fairly generally accepted as gospel." Lazarsfeld also had contacts with Neurath, with whom his associate and then wife Marie Jahoda worked. Probably as important as these contacts is what they reflect, which is that through his whole career he had an extremely strong interest in questions of method, at the level of logic as well as of practical detail. However, it would be highly misleading to describe him as a logical positivist, even though in the 1930s he expressed great interest in the "interrelations between logical empiricism and social research."[44] Moreover, he criticized Hempel and other philosophers of science for not paying sufficient attention to what actually happens in the social sciences: "Philosophers of science are not interested in and do not know what the work-a-day empirical research man does."[45] Clearly, he made use of philosophical ideas, but that use does not fit the model of simple direct influence; not only does he seem also to have influenced the philosophers, but the ideas he used were selected for their relevance to his own concerns and were not necessarily those most central to them.

An interesting case to contrast with that of Lazarsfeld at Columbia is Samuel Stouffer, at Chicago and then Harvard. Stouffer was generally recognized as both a leading empirical researcher and an important writer on method. He had ample opportunity to gain exposure to Vienna Circle influence. At Chicago, in the philosophy department, it was Morris, an early and crucial contact of the Circle, who was instrumental in getting Carnap

41   Carl G. Hempel, "The Logic of Functional Analysis," in Llewellyn Gross, ed., *Symposium on Sociological Theory* (New York, 1959), 271–307.
42   "Reminiscences of Paul F. Lazarsfeld," 52. Columbia University, Oral History collection, recorded 1961.
43   Interview with Hans Zeisel, 1990.
44   Louis Wirth papers, box 6, folder 9. Dept. of Special Collections, University of Chicago Library.
45   Paul F. Lazarsfeld, "Philosophy of Science and Empirical Social Research," in Ernest Nagel et al., eds., *Logic, Methodology, and Philosophy of Science* (Stanford, Calif., 1962), 470.

(who got a grant to bring Hempel and Olaf Helmer from the Berlin group to work with him in 1937–38) an appointment in 1936. The *International Encyclopedia of Unified Science* was organized from there, with Neurath visiting for meetings, and it was published by the University of Chicago Press. There was a faculty discussion group on the logic of science, in which Morris and Carnap and a number of natural and social scientists took part, but the sociologist involved was Louis Wirth, not Stouffer.[46] Wirth worked on the sociology of knowledge and science, and it was probably also relevant that he (unlike Stouffer) was a native speaker of German. He nearly wrote a monograph on the sociology of knowledge for the *Encyclopedia*. Wirth arranged for Lazarsfeld to give a talk in 1937 to the sociology department's Society for Social Research, entitled "What can social research expect from logical empiricism?"[47] and Stouffer worked closely with Lazarsfeld over many years.[48] Hempel reported that Carnap's interests were very technical, which may have accounted for his lack of contact with social scientists.[49] Lazarsfeld described asking Carnap why he did not have more such contact, to which Carnap's reply was that he did not know what he could discuss with them.[50] Stouffer had always been a quantitative sociologist, and certainly had the mathematical skills to cope with logical symbolism. However, although he did valuable methodological work, he did not have Lazarsfeld's more philosophical and generalizing interests – which could obviously be regarded as a product of milieu as much as of personality – and so stayed closer to empirical data and statistical techniques. Despite the potential opportunities, Stouffer's work at Chicago showed no trace of Circle influence.

Stouffer was at Chicago before the war, and after his involvement in famous wartime research in the army moved to Harvard. A Unity of Science congress (whose participants included Parsons from sociology) had been held at Harvard in 1939, supporters and sympathizers of the Circle such as Bridgman, Quine, Alfred North Whitehead (philosophy), and S.S. Stevens (psychology) were already on the faculty before the war, and B.F. Skinner arrived in 1948. Of Circle members, Frank and von Mises also joined the Harvard faculty, and although Frank remained a physicist, he played an active organizational role in general discussions of the philosophy of science

46 Unity of Science Movement papers. Department of Special Collections, University of Chicago Library.
47 Louis Wirth papers, box 6, folder 9. Department of Special Collections, University of Chicago Library.
48 Jennifer Platt, "Stouffer and Lazarsfeld: Patterns of Influence," *Knowledge and Society* 6 (1986): 99–117.
49 Interview with Carl G. Hempel, 1989.
50 Louis Wirth papers.

that included some social scientists.[51] The department Stouffer moved to, social relations, was an interdisciplinary one with many interesting contacts, but it did not include philosophers; its more general interests were theoretical rather than methodological. He played an important role in setting up and supervising its empirical research facilities, led the team that wrote up his wartime work as *The American Soldier,* and did new research of his own that applied and developed further the survey methods used during the war.[52] He continued to publish on research method rather than methodology in ways that typically arose fairly directly from concrete research experience. Although he certainly showed sensitivity to questions of logic, he dealt with them more as a statistician than as a philosopher. One may suspect, although we have no specific evidence on this, that what contact he had with the ideas of the Vienna Circle was mediated by Lazarsfeld, who also shared his more empirical interests; certainly there continues to be no direct trace of Circle ideas in his work.

The one prominent figure not himself of Viennese origin who clearly was directly familiar with the work of the Vienna Circle, and drew on it in his sociological writings, is George Lundberg. Since Lundberg's career spans the period from 1926, the date of his earliest publication, to his retirement in 1961, it offers an interesting case study in the influence of Vienna Circle ideas on someone who was undoubtedly familiar with and approved them. Lundberg has written his own intellectual history in some autobiographical fragments. He describes how in the first half of the 1920s there was "a pronounced swing toward empiricism" and a natural science approach, which was supported by members of the departments at Wisconsin and Minnesota where he did graduate work.[53] He reports the special influence of sociologists Stuart Chapin, Luther L. Bernard, Manuel C. Elmer, and Karl Pearson's *Grammar of Science;* these convinced him that the future of sociology was scientific. He was also a little later strongly influenced by the "sociometry" of Jacob Levy Moreno, not least because of its promise as a "technique for objectifying large areas hitherto regarded as 'too subjective' for scientific handling."[54] Lundberg does not mention the Vi-

51 Philipp G. Frank, ed., *The Validation of Scientific Theories* (New York, 1954).
52 Samuel A. Stouffer et al., *The American Soldier* (Princeton, N.J., 1949–50).
53 Otto N. Larsen, "Lundberg's Encounter with Sociology and Vice Versa," in Alfred De Grazia et al., *The Behavioral Sciences: Essays in Honor of George A. Lundberg* (Great Barrington, Mass., 1968), 1–22.
54 Jacob Levy Moreno (1892–1974) spent most of his early life in Vienna; he moved to the United States in 1925. (However, his training was in medicine and psychiatry and he was not connected to the Vienna Circle.) "Sociometry" is a technique for eliciting preferences or relationships from each member of small groups and summarizing these quantitatively and graphically to plot group structure.

enna Circle (or any German-language sources) as influences at this period, and it appears that at least his broad ideas about being scientific were established before the 1930s, when he came into contact with their thinking. His early empirical work uses crude quantification of publicly available data, addressed to current political issues.[55] (For example, whether expenditure in political campaigns affects election results, studied by correlating campaign expenditure with fluctuations in party vote.) He criticizes other commentators on these issues for not having used systematic data, and advocates a more scientific approach.

In an article as early as 1936, however, Lundberg refers approvingly to the "Vienna neopositivist school," and cites Carnap and an article by Nagel in *Erkenntnis*, the Circle's journal.[56] He corresponded with several members of the Circle, and made numerous attempts to get one or another of them onto the faculty at Washington.[57] In later books and articles, he refers regularly to them and to the Unified Science movement and to their publications, as well as to more popular and sociological works on related subjects. The context in which these references are made is that of general discussions of scientific method, sociological methodology, and the desirability of sociology being scientific in the same sense as the natural sciences. However, it is interesting too that even he makes only one fleeting reference to any work connected with the Circle in the 1942 edition of his methods textbook,[58] recommending for further study the discussion of classification by Victor Lenzen in an article in the *International Encyclopedia of Unified Science*. For general ideas about scientific method, he cites instead Pearson and Dewey, or refers the reader to his own *Foundations of Sociology*.[59] Thus, once again, the philosophers are segregated from the more practical issues of research method, even in a textbook with chapters on scientific method. It is interesting to note the somewhat different impression that is given by his private letters, where he admits that "Carnapp [sic] and Kaufman [sic] . . . leave me a good deal in doubt as to what they are doing part of the time, though, I must admit, I have not made any thorough study of either."[60] Despite this, in his case too there is some evidence that whatever

55 George A. Lundberg, "The Newspaper and Public Opinion," *Social Forces* 4 (1926): 709–15; "Campaign Expenditures and Election Results," *Social Forces* 6 (1928): 452–7; and "The Contents of Radio Programs," *Social Forces* 7 (1929): 58–68.
56 George A. Lundberg, "Thoughtways of Contemporary Sociology," *American Sociological Review* 1 (1936): 703–23.
57 George A. Lundberg papers, University of Washington Libraries, Manuscripts and University Archives Division.
58 Lundberg, *Social Research*, 112.
59 George A. Lundberg, *Foundations of Sociology* (New York, 1939).
60 Lundberg to Arthur F. Bentley, Dec. 4, 1944. Lundberg papers, box 3, folder 8.

influence was present did not all flow in one direction. Hempel wrote to him: "I have read many of your earlier publications with great interest and benefit, and I have made reference to some of your ideas in a little monograph on the principles of concept formation in empirical science."[61]

Lundberg played a prominent role in American sociology as an apostle of scientific method, and was indeed chiefly known for that. In order to characterize American sociology, however, we must note that his prominence was particularly as a controversialist; his views were regularly attacked by prominent opponents such as Herbert Blumer and Robert MacIver. Although he was mainly known for his role in these debates, Lundberg also carried out some of his own research, and at the University of Washington (after 1945) was responsible for the establishment of a "Public Opinion Laboratory" that carried out a range of studies. Little notice seems to have been taken of this work even at the time; it was of a markedly atheoretical character, and had no significant methodological innovations, although his papers sometimes seemed as concerned, for example, to demonstrate the possibility of quantification as to throw light on the substantive topic. In striking contrast to Lazarsfeld, Lundberg's work on methods was programmatic and philosophical and did not lead to any interesting developments in his own empirical research.[62]

In a retrospective article written much later, Lundberg says that there has been an increasing influence of natural science on the social sciences, and that "supported on the theoretical side by Peirce, James, and Dewey it resulted in the behavioristic development in psychology and sociology, which established itself during the second decade of the present century," and was later strengthened by the Unity of Science movement.[63] It seems plausible to accept his own account, and to interpret this history as one showing a direction of development that was reinforced and refined, rather than caused, by the work of the Vienna Circle. Even Lundberg was concerned with issues that could often be defined in terms of specifically social scientific ideas such as behaviorism, and most of the influences contributing

61 Carl G. Hempel to Lundberg, July 17, 1952. Lundberg papers, box 6, folder 21.
62 In part, this may be attributed to the fact that he had planned division of labor with his colleague Stuart C. Dodd. Lundberg would be the evangelist; Dodd would do the empirical work. ("Dimensions of Lundberg's Society as Foundations for Dodd's Sociology," Stuart C. Dodd papers, box 1, folder 2. University of Washington Libraries, Manuscripts and University Archives Division.) Dodd developed a system that was intended to be modeled on the procedures of the natural sciences, but he was very much a self-made intellectual and left the philosophical issues to Lundberg. No references to the Vienna Circle appear in the index of his magnum opus.
63 George A. Lundberg, "The Growth of Scientific Method," *American Journal of Sociology* 50 (1945): 502–3.

to push him in the direction he took were at first quite independent of the Circle.

There is an easily explicable pattern in the sequence of Vienna Circle publications that goes some way to account for the nature and timing of their influence. First, there were hardly any publications in English before the early 1930s. At that stage, their ideas reached the English-speaking public primarily through congresses in Europe and individual visitors, and the center of activity was undoubtedly the German-speaking world. Then there are some early English publications of a rather introductory nature, explaining to new audiences the position they had developed and its implications, or sometimes translating into English works already published in German.[64] By the late 1930s and early 1940s, original work of a technical nature by Circle members was being published first in English; in the same period, several publications appeared on topics having to do with the social sciences – mostly psychology and history – and it may be inferred that this had something to do with the interests they found in their new context.[65] By the early 1950s, a sufficient body of work had been established for collections of readings to be published and for collections and textbooks to appear.[66] By this later stage, however, a number of the original émigrés (Neurath, Edgar Zilsel, Kaufmann) had died, and those who were successfully established in American academic life had created networks of connections and students, which made the distinction between those who had and had not been members of the original Circle relatively unimportant. This was further eroded by the modifications made to many of the Circle's original intellectual positions, as difficulties in them were pointed out and as the discussion moved on. Few Americans read work written in German, and few sociologists would read relatively technical philosophy.[67] It is therefore to be expected that the major direct impact would come when there was an English-language book literature addressed to a nonspecialist academic public. By the time this stage had been reached the ideas were

64 See, e.g., Herbert Feigl and Albert E. Blumberg, "Logical Positivism, A New Movement in European Philosophy," *Journal of Philosophy* 28 (1931): 280–96.
65 Carl G. Hempel, "The Logical Analysis of Psychology" (1935), in Herbert Feigl and Wilfrid Sellers, eds., *Readings in Philosophical Analysis* (New York, 1949); Hempel, "The Function of General Laws in History," *Journal of Philosophy* 39 (1942): 35–48; Gustav Bergmann, "On Some Methodological Problems of Psychology," *Philosophy of Science* 7 (1940): 205–19; Edgar Zilsel, "Physics and the Problem of Historico-Sociological Laws," *Philosophy of Science* 8 (1941): 567–79.
66 See, e.g., Herbert Feigl and May Brodbeck, eds., *Readings in the Philosophy of Science* (New York, 1953).
67 On the limited knowledge of German among American sociologists in the 1930s, see Platt, "Weber's *verstehen*."

somewhat diluted, and so a distinctive impact was less likely and is bound to be harder to trace. However, that does not mean that there may not have been more indirect influence, mediated by the methodological and empirical work of such writers as Lazarsfeld and Lundberg as well as close associates such as Nagel.

Perhaps one of the reasons contributing to the relatively slight specific influence of the ideas of the Vienna Circle is the difficulty of applying some of them to a distinctively sociological subject matter. There seems to have been a more direct and meaningful relationship with psychology, and this goes beyond the historical accident of the greater importance of psychology in Vienna. Smith, while skeptical of the meaningfulness in terms of influence of many of the apparent relationships between behaviorist psychologists and logical positivism, suggests that neobehaviorist Kenneth Spence was in both camps, and that his intellectual relationship with Bergmann at Iowa was a real one, although he was a confirmed behaviorist before he met Bergmann.[68] (It is interesting to note, incidentally, that Bergmann criticizes psychologists for having adopted naive and exaggerated versions of operationism and axiomatization as parts of the "scientific" program.[69]) A natural science model works more easily with a subject that at some points is close to biology and that can relatively easily conduct laboratory experiments on some of its topics. Data on single individuals or small groups, even when not about psychophysical topics, are arguably easier to elicit in an operationist spirit than those on larger and naturally occurring social groups; the social is notoriously hard to approach in terms of physicalism. However, the plausibility of that argument is rather undermined by the enthusiasm of at least a few sociologists such as Lundberg for operationist ideas, and their relatively easy fit with the ecological/demographic tradition within sociology. Neurath of the Circle, moreover, combined its ideas with Marxism in a way that nowadays seems surprising, making the link without apparent difficulty by his conception of the implications of materialism.[70] There was, however, considerable tension between the dominant direction of Neurath's thought and the varieties of "pseudorationalism" that he began to identify in other members of the Circle. His thought, despite the importance of his social

68 Smith, *Behaviorism and Logical Positivism*, 317–18.
69 Gustav Bergmann, "Sense and Nonsense in Operationism," in Frank, *The Validation of Scientific Theories*, 53; *Philosophy of Science* (Madison, WI, 1957), 36, 87.
70 Otto Neurath, *Empiricism and Sociology*, eds. Marie Neurath and Robert S. Cohen (Dordrecht, 1973).

and organizational role, seems to have had only a minor influence on the predominantly logicist current of his colleagues' thinking.

Whatever the possibilities in principle, it is probably at least as important in practice that the enthusiasts for behaviorism and operationism were more numerous and more entrenched in American psychology than in sociology. Not only was there a qualitative versus quantitative intellectual division in sociology, established before World War II, between those who favored the "case study" and those who favored the "statistical" method, with the case study party a strong one, but the "statistical" party was at that stage still likely to draw heavily on census data and official records for ecological and demographic work rather than collect its own material by its own methods. However, it is somewhat misleading to think of the influence of the Vienna Circle as automatically indicating a heavy emphasis on quantification, even though that has become part of sociologists' stereotype of "positivism." Circle members never advocated any variety of simple number-crunching. The dominant tendencies were always toward logical and linguistic reconstruction. Neurath in particular denounced the "over mathematicization" of sociology, and thought that the exclusive reliance on unanalyzed "sense data" of behaviorism would lead to "scientific suicide."[71] Theorists were the most likely subgroup to be philosophically sophisticated, but by definition the least likely to apply their philosophical positions in empirical research. (Morris remarked in 1937 that "I doubt if Ogburn's interest is sufficiently theoretical for our purposes."[72] William F. Ogburn was a leading quantitative sociologist and proponent of "scientific" methods.) The theorists were probably also the most likely to be at ease in the German intellectual traditions and language, and so to have had early and easy access to the Circle's thought. The empirical researchers in sociology who studied abroad were more likely to be oriented to England, where Stouffer, Dodd, Mildred Parten, and Dorothy Thomas went to study at the London School of Economics or with the famous British statisticians.[73]

We conclude therefore that although the work of the Circle was very warmly received by a small but important subgroup of American sociologists, this was precisely because that subgroup was already sympathetic to

71 Otto Neurath, *Foundations of the Social Sciences* (Chicago, 1944), 12–13, 18–19, 24, 33–5.
72 Charles W. Morris to Otto Neurath, May 30, 1937. Unity of Science Movement papers, box 1, folder 16. Dept. of Special Collections, University of Chicago Library.
73 Jennifer Platt, "Anglo-American Contacts in the Developments of Research Methods before 1945," in Kevin Bales et al., eds., *The Social Survey in Historical Perspective* (Cambridge, 1992), 340–58; "Stuart Dodd: A Seminar at Brown University, Sept. 16–17, 1973," mimeograph, Stuart C. Dodd papers, University of Washington Libraries, Manuscripts and University Archives Division.

their ideas and, indeed, shared them, if they were not defined on a technical philosophical level. Especially in the initial period of the migration, however, relatively few people were directly familiar with the ideas, because they had not been expounded much in English, or been applied to issues close to social scientific practice. Those who were had personal characteristics, in terms of interest and background, that made the ideas more salient to them. Indirect familiarity, mediated via such sociologists as Lundberg and Lazarsfeld and such psychologists as Kurt Lewin and Brunswik, some of them also from Vienna or Berlin and familiar with the Circle's work before emigration, was more common.

The Unity of Science movement had some of the characteristics of a social movement, and its ideas were propagated with evangelistic fervor. Part of the evangelism consisted in recruiting potential converts to attend congresses and to write for Circle publications on topics of interest. A special effort was made to recruit representatives outside mathematics and physical science, since they were seen as necessary to the program of unifying *all* the sciences. As a result, as the archives of the movement make clear, some biologists, psychologists, and sociologists developed ties with the Circle, which did not necessarily mean that they completely shared the latter's ideas and interests. Indeed, Circle members quite often expressed doubts about the real suitability of the thinking of such recruits.[74] These ties must certainly have helped to spread knowledge of the Circle's ideas, but it would be unrealistic not to recognize that the outsiders came to them with their own agendas. American sociologists and other social scientists had their own reasons for wanting to associate themselves with the legitimacy of being scientific, and could draw on Circle work eclectically and superficially for their own purposes.

Sociological practice, however, did not necessarily have any clear link with such abstract methodological positions, of whatever tendency.[75] Here, technical philosophical arguments get translated into simple general ideas such as quantification being a good thing and introspection a bad thing, facts being different from values, or testing hypotheses being a feature of good research, and at that level the distinction between the ideas of the Circle and alternative positions may make little difference. Hans Zetterberg said in the introduction to his well-known textbook: "I am well aware that

---

74 See, e.g., Morris's comments to Neurath about a list of American names: "These men are not, of course, 'logical positivists,' but they are men of importance in the field of social sciences, and men of a disposition that will fit in with the spirit of our congresses." Charles W. Morris to Neurath, Feb. 15, 1936. Unity of Science Movement papers, box 1, folder 15. Dept. of Special Collections, University of Chicago Library.

75 Cf. Jennifer Platt, "Functionalism and the Survey," *Sociological Review* 34 (1986): 501–36.

this text does not take into account all, or even most, of the niceties elaborated by various philosophies of science. . . . However, in a text for sociology students, the details of philosophy of science are out of place, and many of the points made in works on the logic and philosophy of science have little or no relevance or consequence for sociology as it is currently practiced."[76] Other authors could well have said the same.

Thus although works by members of the Vienna Circle, and especially their students and close associates, eventually became standard references in certain contexts, it seems likely that this does not indicate that the nature of their influence was such that it made a real difference to sociological practice. It is probable that it reinforced other tendencies that already existed in American sociology, but even without such reinforcement these might have produced much the same outcome.

76   Zetterberg, ix.

11

From Public Law To Political Science?
The Emigration of German Scholars after 1933
and Their Influence on the Transformation
of a Discipline

ALFONS SÖLLNER

In this chapter, I will first sketch an outline of a topic that has as yet never been investigated in its entirety: the emigration of German political scientists (*Staats- und Politikwissenschaftler*) after the Nazis came to power. Although it may seem surprising that this topic has been neglected since several of the most prominent and interesting academic émigrés belong to this group, the reasons for this omission are easy to identify. We are dealing with a field of academic emigration in which one is from the very beginning confronted with the full complexity inherent in the application of the concept of acculturation to the history of disciplines. Even the German term *Staats- und Politikwissenschaft* represents a dubious compromise, and is a mere makeshift solution to the problem that *Staatswissenschaft*, as it existed in the Weimar Republic, can by no means be translated simply into "political science." Furthermore, there is no guarantee that it is even possible to construct a unified, clear social or institutional history of this discipline, whatever its name may be, not least because politics, which follows a logic of its own, persistently intervenes. In short, a point that applies to the most recent research, especially insofar as it is inspired by the *International Biographical Dictionary of Central European Emigrés, 1933–1945*, will probably become an even greater problem for political science – every quantitative method, no matter how refined it might be, is doomed to failure unless it is accompanied by intense qualitative analysis of the group being studied.[1]

---

1 *International Biographical Dictionary of Central European Emigrés, 1933–1945*, 3 vols. (Munich and New York, 1980–83). A survey on methods is given by Herbert A. Strauss in the introduction to his *Die Emigration der Wissenschaften nach 1933* (Munich, 1991).

246

In view of this situation, it seems advisable to practice heuristic modesty and search for a middle course between a too- demanding process of constructing theory, on the one hand, and a too-ambitious effort at quantification, on the other. The result will not be a strict and reliably documented collective biography but a quantitatively informed sketch of a group of social scientists, offering an outlook on the different dimensions of one discipline's history and their interrelations. This includes, for one thing, the delimitation of historical periods, which, if emigration is in fact to be understood as transfer of knowledge, has to comprise at least four stages: (1) the starting position before emigration; (2) the process of expulsion and migration, especially during the 1930s; (3) the integration and long-term impact in the host countries; and (4) the re-migration into or influence on the country of origin after 1945. Conceptually, we also have to distinguish between the cognitive and the social dimension; in doing this, the level of the overall discipline has to be transcended in the direction of both higher and lower levels, internally as well as externally. In the case of political scientists, it is obvious that the external aspect dominates, and constitutes an independent third dimension of a political-practical nature that will complement and modify all other dimensions.

If the emigration of political scientists is approached on the basis of such preliminary considerations, then a simple fact has to be dealt with first, a fact that represents a logical problem for our study. Political science as an independent discipline was unknown to the universities of the Weimar Republic; it was only in the course of their emigration that the émigrés themselves became "political scientists." This specific situation has to be taken into account when defining the group to be studied, and this is best done by concentrating on those persons who were on the one hand still sufficiently socialized as scholars in the Weimar Republic and who on the other, actually worked as political scientists, in a narrower sense, in the course of their emigration. This implies a limitation of the group to be analyzed according to the following criteria: People are regarded as émigré political scientists (1) who in exile, held a university position as a professional teacher or researcher in the field, and (2) who had passed at least one examination at a German-language university before emigrating.

If one sticks to these minimal criteria and applies them to the people listed in the *International Biographical Dictionary*, then one ends up with a group of sixty-four people who can be termed the first generation of émigré political scientists, as distinguished from a second generation that obtained academic degrees in the host country and is probably as extensive as the first generation. That this in fact leads to something like a generational cohort as defined by sociologists is shown by the fact that more than fifty of the sixty-four persons in our group were born between 1890 and 1915.[2]

For a closer characterization of this group, I will compile intellectual, social, and political data collected by an evaluation of the *International Biographical Dictionary*. However, the classification according to which this will be done does not follow a strictly logical model. In the first section I want to sketch the starting position of the émigrés; this outline adds color to the background of the Weimar academic scene. The next section, although sociohistorically oriented, is restricted to a kind of map and chronology of the expulsion, migration, and professional integration of this group. The third section is concerned with the émigrés' position within the discipline of political science; here, questions concerning the subject and method of their scientific production will have to be dealt with. Finally, politics will be considered to be the factor that makes the history of the émigré political scientists both interesting and complicated; a test for this is the as yet unexplored field of the émigrés' effect on postwar Germany.

THE STARTING POSITION: PUBLIC LAW AND POLITICAL SCIENCE IN THE WEIMAR REPUBLIC

That political science as a university discipline did not exist during the Weimar Republic does not mean that there were no points of intensive contact between science and politics. When looking for an analog that represented a political science of its own kind, public law presents itself. Although it was primarily part of jurisprudence, this field functioned as a point of integration for the so-called *Staatswissenschaften* (studies of public administration). Since the coming of democracy, this discipline, which was both representative and rich in tradition, had been caught in the maelstrom of politicization that challenged the legalistic tradition as a whole. Within the discipline, in what Hermann Heller called the *Krisis der Staatslehre* (crisis of public law), the normative-positivistic method was superseded by concepts from sociology and the history of ideas (*Geistesgeschichte*).[3] Accordingly, three main tendencies of Weimar public law can be distinguished

---

2   For the concept of generation, see Richard Bendix, *Von Berlin nach Berkeley: Deutsch-jüdische Identitäten* (Frankfurt/Main, 1985). A theoretically sound definition of the groups to be studied in the individual disciplines, that is, in political science, sociology, and law is urgently needed.

3   Hermann Heller, "Die Krisis der Staatslehre," *Archiv für Sozialwissenschaft und Sozialpolitik* 55 (1926).

and characterized as follows. The center was still held by juridical positivism, with Gerhard Anschütz and Richard Thoma as representatives of the prevalent liberal doctrine and Hans Kelsen as the representative of an extreme methodological position. However, this school was increasingly forced onto the defensive against the *geistesgeschichtliche* and existentialist innovations such as Rudolf Smend's integrationism and Carl Schmitt's decisionism. To this has to be added an equally strong trend toward the growing influence of sociology on public law, as advocated, for instance, by Max Weber in his sociology of *Herrschaft* (domination), in Mannheim's theory of ideology, and in Heller's *Staatslehre* (theory of the state) with nationalist leanings.[4]

Although the dispute aroused by these positions was conducted in a methodologically ambitious manner, the deeper hinge on which developments turned during the short period of the Weimar Republic was political. It was a matter of deciding on the practical interpretation of a constitution that – to use the words coined by Otto Kirchheimer – had come into the world "without decision."[5] It was a question of either its bourgeois-liberal restriction, its socialist continuation, or its authoritarian transformation. Of these alternatives, the one that finally prevailed becomes clear when the year 1933 is evoked – but not this fact alone. Results such as those compiled by Fritz Ringer on the political world-view of the "German mandarin" can easily be extended to the certainly contradictory constellation of the caste of Weimar academics. This world-view was, in a characteristic manner, ambiguous in that it was antipolitical and at the same time not apolitical, for it glorified, certainly with remarkable nuances, an authoritarian state hovering over society as the incarnation of "German" culture. It was simultaneously anti-democratic and opposed to the party system, as Kurt Sontheimer has shown not only for the extreme right. Herbert Döring has examined those Weimar university teachers who were loyal to the constitution; his results show that the representatives of the liberal center too were only *Vernunftrepublikaner* (pragmatic republicans) if not *Herzensmonarchisten* (monarchists at heart), to use expressions coined by Ernst Troeltsch. Even the political convictions of the moderate "Weimar circle" were affected by the attractiveness of the idea of a "plebiscitary leader-democracy"; sociopsychologically, this might be interpreted as a way of parrying the fear of decline. Even for left-wing specialists in public law it was difficult to transcend the hegemonic horizon of a world-view that (1) relied in the

---

4 For a survey, see Christoph, Müller and Ilse Staff, eds., *Staatslehre in der Weimarer Republik: Hermann Heller zu Ehren* (Frankfurt/Main, 1985).
5 See his *Weimar – und was dann? Entstehung und Gegenwart einer Verfassung* (Berlin, 1930).

domestic field on the formation of an elite, and (2) in foreign affairs backed the concept of the powerful state, merging these two elements in an authoritarian concept of politics.[6]

If this were the highly politicized scholarly terrain from which the émigrés had been expelled, what then were the roots that anchored the later political scientists in this terrain? The answer to this question is important because it may throw light on the degree of continuity or discontinuity between the Weimar *Staatswissenschaften* and the greatly changed conditions of emigration.

To begin with, the discipline in which the academic degree was obtained is an instructive factor. Most of the group in my sample took their doctorates in law (33), only a small number in the department of *Staatswissenschaft* (8 plus 4 who also took a law degree), and the rest in the humanities (19). A slightly different picture that still points in the same direction, however, is achieved by a cognitive assessment of the works published before emigration, which quite often reveals the characteristics of studies written to obtain a doctoral degree or the *Habilitation* (formal access to a professorship). It is clear that the results are only a rough outline of a possible trend that cannot do justice to the individual works. Nonetheless, the studies can be characterized as follows: twenty-seven can be termed juridical-legalistic, fourteen philosophical-humanistic, twelve sociological-economic, sixteen anticipate methods of political science as currently understood, and a few works inevitably combine two or more approaches.

It would not be an exaggeration to consider the spectrum of disciplines in the Weimar Republic with which we are concerned here as largely dominated by jurisprudence. Indeed it is probably correct to say that *Staatswissenschaften* in the plural designated a purely institutional identity and not a content-related or even theoretical identity. In any case, the form in which this constellation is reflected in the data can be seen as indicating that the group of later political scientists was relatively well integrated into a scientific culture that, following Thomas Kuhn, can be termed Weimar "normal science."

Almost the reverse picture emerges, however, if one looks at the actual professional roots of the émigré political scientists in the Weimar universities. Only twenty-three of them in fact held a university position, ten as tenured professors of different ranks, four as non-tenured university lectur-

6 See Fritz Ringer, *The Decline of the German Mandarins: The German Academic Community, 1890–1933* (Cambridge, Mass., 1969); Kurt Sontheimer, *Antidemokratisches Denken in der Weimarer Republik* (Munich, 1968); Herbert Döring, *Der Weimarer Kreis: Studien zum politischen Bewusstsein verfassungstreuer Hochschullehrer in der Weimarer Republik* (Meisenheim, 1975).

ers (*Privatdozenten*), nine as assistant lecturers, and six as grant recipients. On the other side, nine worked as lecturers at institutions below university level, nine worked as politicians or as state officials, and fourteen were professionals in other branches (for example, law, journalism, or the private sector). The impression of discontinuity is increased further if one inquires into political attitudes. We are probably right in assuming that the anti-democratic thinking noted by Ringer, Sontheimer, and Döring is also over-represented among the academics in law and *Staatswissenschaft*; this does not rule out a liberal and left-wing minority. If one examines the political cleavages in our group, the picture becomes a bit blurred because 26 of the émigrés show no definite political orientation. In the remaining group, however, adherents or party members of the left-wing spectrum predominate with twenty (fifteen of whom are Social Democrats), eight incline toward the liberal center (seven of these sympathize with the *Deutsche Demokratische Partei* or DDP), and ten belong to the right-wing (mostly Catholic) spectrum. Among these are a few adherents of the Austrian corporative state who emigrated quite late.

But it is not just the inconsistency in the initial constellation of our group of émigrés that makes it impossible simply to equate scholarship with the university. Rather, a frequent pattern in the history of science is that new disciplines have already taken shape in practical contexts before they are institutionalized within the university. What had happened in Germany one generation earlier in the development of sociology out of economics and social policy can also be seen, although only in a rudimentary manner, in the conceptual formation of a science of politics in the Weimar Republic. Whereas the politicizing of public law can be described as the disintegration of legal positivism, the positive pendant manifests itself in attempts to bring into being a science of politics in its own right and to institutionalize it.

The history of the German Academy for the Study of Politics in Berlin (*Deutsche Hochschule für Politik*) sheds light on this process because it embodies a characteristic intensification of these tendencies, and at the same time clearly demonstrates the difficulties inherent in the process of institutionalization. As is well known, this peculiar blending of a democratic institute of adult education (*Volkshochschule*) and a college of politics (*Fachschule*) did not attain university status during the Weimar period, despite considerable pedagogical success and its propagation of political science in its own right since its foundation. An analysis of this school in its historical context shows ambivalences similar to those characteristic of the relationship between science and politics throughout the Weimar Republic.

In relation to the history of the discipline and from the pedagogical point of view, the German Academy for the Study of Politics was highly progressive; the political world-view it propagated, however, was by no means free from anti-democratic aspirations.[7] Whereas the second tendency assumes a vividly tangible form, for instance, in the works of Adolf Grabowsky, the senior founder of the first professional journal and author of a textbook entitled *Politics*, the first tendency is represented by strictly sociologically oriented (younger) lecturers, such as Sigmund Neumann or Hans Speier.[8]

The question of assessing the continuity or discontinuity between the Weimar situation and emigration is not an easy one. However, it must to be tackled if an approach to the study of the group of political scientists based on the history of the discipline is to make sense at all. In this respect, the following quantitative comparison between the members of the German Academy for the Study of Politics and the German Association of Public Law Teachers (*Vereinigung der deutschen Staatsrechtslehrer*) may be informative, not least because it probably reveals the relation between the center and the periphery in political science. Whereas only six of the ninety-six members of this circle of established notables in German public law in 1932 became émigrés, eight (almost half of the eighteen lecturers and seminar teachers at the Berlin institute) went into exile. The comparison is the more revealing in that among these eight were not only younger and rather left-wing lecturers but also older ones, and even the liberal-conservative directors of the institute, Ernst Jäckh and Arnold Wolfers.

In sum, the majority of émigré political scientists show distinct traces of their Weimar socialization, but mostly they do not come from the conservative establishment. As far as political attitudes are concerned, there is an atypical focus on the left; extra-university jobs are as frequent as those at a university; finally, many of the political scientists who left later already took part in the formation of a modern political science before they emigrated. The potential for this kind of political science in the Weimar Republic is indicated by the fact that many of the German contributions to the *International Encyclopedia of the Social Sciences*, publication of which started in the

---

7   In recent literature there is agreement with regard to the shady anti-democratic leanings not only of the national-conservative wing, but also of the Institute's leadership, thus destroying a long-standing family legend of German political science. See Rainer Eisfeld, *Ausgebürgert und doch angebräunt: Deutsche Politikwissenschaft, 1920–1945* (Baden-Baden, 1992); and Alfons Söllner, "Gruppenbild mit Jäckh – Die 'Verwissenschaftlichung' der Deutschen Hochschule für Politik während der Weimarer Republik," in Gerhard Göhler and Bodo Zeuner, eds., *Kontinuitäten und Brüche in der deutschen Politikwissenschaft* (Baden-Baden, 1991), 41.

8   Adolf Grabowsky, *Politik* (Berlin, 1932); Sigmund Neumann, *Die deutschen Parteien: Wesen und Wandel nach dem Krieg* (Berlin, 1932); Hans Speier, *Die Angestellten vor dem Nationalsozialismus: Ein Beitrag zum Verständnis der deutschen Sozialstruktur, 1918–1933* (Frankfurt/Main, 1977).

early 1930s, were written by these émigrés; yet this fact ought not to be overrated. Most remarkable is the entry on "Political Science" written by Heller. On the one hand, it covers much of the Anglo-Saxon literature; on the other, it is practically identical with the methodological chapter in Heller's *Staatslehre*, published posthumously, which in turn is a highly ambitious summary of a thoroughly "German" theoretical tradition and which at the same time ends directly on the threshold of exile.[9] It is here, if anywhere, that we can find proof that the (underdeveloped) German history of the discipline was able "to catch up with" its (developed) American counterpart – that is, the proof of a potential that was temporarily cut off by the political situation in Germany.

PROFESSIONALIZATION WITH OBSTACLES: EXPULSION, MIGRATION, AND INTEGRATION

A first survey of the expulsion and migration of the émigré political scientists might take the shape of a chronology combined with a map. The chronological picture fits into the well-known story of political expulsion; almost half of our group emigrated as early as 1933, and the rest gradually, ending with a final wave of emigration in 1938–39, a result of both the anti-Semitic policies that led to the November progrom and the annexation of Austria. More than a third of the group migrated directly to the United States, with England figuring as the country of transit in twelve cases, France in eleven cases, Switzerland in nine cases, and several other European and non-European countries in much smaller numbers. Out of our group of sixty-four people, fifty-four finally chose to settle in the United States, five in England, and one each in Switzerland, Spain, the Netherlands, France, and Palestine.

The manifold reasons for this distribution are not under discussion here. I will merely draw attention to the two most important conditions, which were interrelated: the well-known pull-effect of the United States as the classic country of immigration, in general, and the relatively high capacity of its decentralized and large system of higher education to absorb émigrés, in particular. They made the educated middle classes' chances of being accommodated look good, and had a positive effect on the academic intelligentsia, especially since this group was usually not subject to quota regulations. While drawing attention to this positive process of "selection,"

9   Hermann Heller, "Political Science," *The Encyclopedia of the Social Sciences* (1933), 12:207; Heller, *Staatslehre* (Leiden, 1934).

however, we ought not to forget that American immigration policy had started to become increasingly restrictive as early as the 1920s. In the late 1930s, when the survival of European Jews was at stake, a massive Jewish immigration was impeded to such an extent that even the authorized quotas were not fully exhausted. Furthermore, the positive final result ought not to obscure the fact that when studied individually and in detail, the years of acclimatization of academic immigrants to the United States reveal more negative than positive experiences – the specter of "Jewish infiltration" also haunted American universities.

The raw data of migration do not tell us much unless they are linked with professional developments, in our case with the integration into academic institutions or with a successful scientific career. The evaluation shows that as early as 1933, twenty-one emigrants of the group I am concerned with were able to pursue a scientific occupation in their host country; the rest were able to do so gradually until 1943. In this, no distinction is made between country of transit and country of settlement. The institutions at which the emigrants took jobs were usually universities, colleges, and research institutes. Here, too, hardly any differences can be noticed between countries of transit and the final host countries. All in all, high mobility is characteristic of the phase of migration and the first phase of settling down, and a quite frequent change of professional positions can be observed far into the phase of establishment. On the one hand, no more than twelve émigrés show only one such change up until 1960; on the other hand, fourteen changed their occupation three times, nine four times, five six times, and one of the group even changed his job as often as eight times.

A combination of migration data with career data thus yields a quite uniform picture. Eighty-five percent of our group eventually obtained a permanent position in political science in the United States. The result allows us to focus all further reflection concerning the history of the émigrés' impact on that country. A comparative glance at England reinforces this investigative course. Of the five emigrants of our group who were able to stay in England far into the war years, only one was fully installed at an English university – namely Moritz Julius Bonn. One younger emigrant joined him after 1945, despite the fact that England was the second most important country for the admission of academic emigrants. In France, not one of our group found permanent shelter.[10] In the United States, the highest concentration of professorships is to be found at the universities on

10   See Gerhard Hirschfeld, ed., *Exil in Grossbritannien: Zur Emigration aus dem nationalsozialistischen Deutschland* (Stuttgart, 1983); and Alfons Söllner, "On Transit to America – The Emigration of German Political Scientists to Great Britain," in Werner E. Mosse, ed., *Second Chance: Two Centuries*

the east coast (Columbia University, The New School for Social Research, Harvard, Princeton, and the colleges of New York City). These are followed by a diverse group of universities and colleges in Chicago, Washington, D.C., California, and, finally, in the Midwest, in that order. The extent of this concentration should not, however, be overestimated. Besides the institutions just mentioned, there are fifty more that employed only one émigré each.

Although random constellations, which are hard to assess, probably played important roles in the migration and integration of university men, and although we have to accept the extreme vagueness and individualization of the overall process, we can nevertheless discover typical patterns of placement. One of these, which set in quite early and directly absorbed the still embryonic nucleus of Weimar political science, was the offer of a chair at Alvin Johnson's New School for Social Research, known as the "University in Exile." This center of emigration in the social sciences, probably the most important in the field, has been relatively well researched – primarily the economists and their commitment to the New Deal have been analyzed. Political scientists, including highly prominent and divergent figures such as Arnold Brecht, Leo Strauss, and Otto Kirchheimer were long-standing members of its faculty. The second well-researched center of social-scientific emigration, the Institute of Social Research at Columbia University, yields a clearer picture because, from the very beginning, it did not focus on political science, and in fact never did so. This does not mean that we are denying the status of émigrés such as Franz L. Neumann, Otto Kirchheimer, and others, but that they merely gained importance in other contexts.[11]

A second systematic channel of mediation was provided through the activities of academic relief organizations, the two most important of which were the Society for the Protection of Science and Learning, based in England, and the American Emergency Committee in Aid of Displaced German (later: "Foreign") Scholars. Analogous to what has already been said about immigration policy, a certain "selectivity" with regard to the academic transfer of knowledge has to be assumed here as well. Whereas the scarcity of financial resources, the hesitant attitude of many institutions

---

of *German-Speaking Jews in the United Kingdom* (Tübingen, 1991), 121. A study on academic emigration to France is still lacking.

11 See Claus-Dieter Krohn, *Wissenschaft im Exil: Deutsche Sozial- und Wirtschaftswissenschaftler in den USA und die New School for Social Research* (Frankfurt/Main, 1985); Peter M. Rutkoff and W. B. Scott, *New School: A History of the New School for Social Research, 1919–1970* (New York, 1986); Martin Jay, *The Dialectical Imagination: A History of the Frankfurt School and the Institute of Social Research* (London, 1973).

of higher education toward a prompt offer of permanent positions, and the simultaneous "surplus" of expelled scientists were inevitably enough to change assistance into patronage for an elite, we also have to assume that those who worked with these committees were motivated by more or less explicit interests in specific contents and forms of knowledge.

The role of the Rockefeller Foundation clearly exemplifies this complex interrelation between relief actions and science policy, since it was the most generous financier of the Emergency Committee, and this in turn was by far the most efficient institution for the transfer of émigrés into the United States. The Rockefeller Foundation was two things in one: the model of a nongovernmental organization for scientific progress in the United States, and an example illustrating that interventions on behalf of exiled scientists during the 1930s were nothing but a continuation, even an intensification, of a long-standing academic policy of promoting an elite and of utilizing a liberated potential of intelligence. This foundation also pursued far-reaching content-related aims. These included primarily the promotion of the "American" social sciences, which in a larger perspective present themselves as the scientific core of an entire culture based on the identification of political democracy, faith in science, and human progress. The international dissemination of that syndrome was to have considerable influence on the cultural history of the whole Western hemisphere after 1945.[12]

This is not meant to detract from the great services done for the German émigrés by the Emergency Committee. It excelled over other relief organizations as a result of its high efficiency and humane commitment, its farsightedness and great continuity – qualities that together with the efforts of diverse financiers, contributed to the immigration of scientists from nearly all disciplines to the United States. It is hard to say how this affected the group of political scientists, in particular; however, a comparison with the English Society for the Protection of Science and Learning is of interest, at least on one point. Whereas the latter did not even have a separate category "political science" and listed individuals belonging to this group under other disciplines, the Emergency Committee, from the very start, connected several names with this field and thus procured accommodation for them in departments of political science. This was the case with John H. Herz, Karl Loewenstein, Hans J. Morgenthau, and many others, who were thus enabled to switch from the field of public law to that of political science rather quickly. The support policy of the Rockefeller Foundation

12 J. M. H. Carson, "The Social Sciences before World War II, 1929–1938"; Carson, "The Social Sciences through the War and Postwar Period, 1939–1948," Rockefeller Foundation Archives, Tarrytown, N.Y., record group 3, series 910 SS, box 3.

reveals two things. On the one hand, those who had already been Rockefeller fellows before 1933 were quite often the ones to be promoted further. On the other hand, special attention was focused on the Deutsche Hochschule für Politik and Heidelberg's Department of Politics and State Theory (*Seminar für Politik und Staatswissenschaft*) – that is, on those institutions that came closest to the American ideal of an integrated social science.[13]

The academic establishment of this group of émigrés can only be summarized in a rather cursory manner. Although a gradual integration into the academic system is normal, the academic careers of many émigrés nevertheless show inconsistencies that are probably conditioned by emigration and therefore typical. On the one side, we have a general temporal delay of the academic career and, on the other – although only in individual cases – a remarkable late prominence. Between 1945 and 1950, forty-nine emigrants from this group of sixty-four obtained a more or less permanent position (of at least three years duration), and between 1950 and 1955, forty-six of them held such a position. High university positions were not achieved until quite late. By 1935 – five, by 1940 – seven, by 1945 – ten, and by 1950 – twelve émigrés had become full professors. However, by 1965 as many as forty-nine émigrés had achieved this status. At least two émigrés attained top positions in their professional organizations. Arnold Brecht became vice-president of the American Political Science Association in 1946. Karl W. Deutsch was elected president of the same association in the late 1960s, and in the 1970s he became president of the International Political Science Association.

The émigré political scientists' status and influence can hardly be attributed to groupings of a more social nature, as illustrated by the social economists of the New School, or to theory-guided cooperation such as was practiced at the Institute of Social Research in continuation of the Frankfurt tradition – which, as is well known, did not exactly accelerate their integration in the United States. In general, a high degree of dispersion and individualization was maintained in the establishment phase. Success and celebrity thus owed themselves to original individual contributions. The experiential and educational background specific to the émigrés. which differed clearly from that of the average American political scientist, certainly reinforced the qualifications needed for individual competition, at times with not merely original but also bizarre effects on the person's char-

---

13 Significant is the evaluation of institutions in "Social Sciences in Germany" (August 1932), Rockefeller Foundation Archives, record group 1.1, series 717 S, box 20.

acter. In the following sections, I will show that this picture is greatly modified by the specifically political activities of the émigrés; however, as long as we stick to a narrow academic criterion of success based on long-term influence – such as the foundation of a distinct "theoretical school" – our group appears to yield comparatively meager results.

EMIGRE STATUS AND IMPORTANCE IN AMERICAN POLITICAL SCIENCE

I will start this section by mentioning what I consider an important chronological correction of previous research on the political and intellectual exile from Nazi Germany. The impact of the academic émigrés was not limited to the years 1933 to 1945; rather, it did not really start until after the war. It is only by applying this larger perspective that their cognitive history gains something like the cumulative effect that constitutes a collective biography. Furthermore, it must be clear that "impact" in this case signifies a complex state of affairs that – not least owing to the previously sketched social and yet to be outlined political peculiarities of the group – can hardly be reduced to simple causal connections. Therefore I do not want to base my analysis on the laborious method of quantitative citation analysis, although it would certainly be applicable here; rather, I will attempt a more modest reduction. In order to characterize the émigrés' status within the discipline, I will identify the intradisciplinary specializations of this group on the basis of their most important publications. I will then try to correlate this with some of the trends in the discipline of political science as they manifested themselves in the 1940s and 1950s.

American political science started constituting itself as an independent discipline at the turn of the century. It showed rapid personnel and disciplinary development and followed a peculiar cultural logic. On the one hand, traditional liberalism represented the undisputed ideological horizon; on the other, the methodological orientation toward the natural sciences increasingly grew in importance. These two developmental factors, which were not always in harmony, were held together by a strongly developed cultural conviction that regarded democracy and scientism as two sides of the same coin: the political feasibility of social progress. In the Chicago School, founded by Charles Mèrriam, the trend toward a "science of politics" became predominant in the 1930s and 1940s and culminated in the so-called behavioral revolution – a quantitative and strictly empirical program that established itself as the prevalent paradigm in the 1950s and

1960s.[14] But this did not impede either the internal professional differentiation of the discipline, the pluralistic coexistence of different and even mutually exclusive theories and methods, or the field's remarkable adaptability to the cycles and crises of contemporary history. If one considers, furthermore, the enormous size of the discipline and the decentralized organization of the American university system, then one has assembled several of the quite contradictory conditions under which the émigrés exerted their influence.

It is not possible to comprehend the internal differentiation of the discipline by considering its theories and methods alone; rather, one has to examine the more or less uniform issues that developed in both research and teaching. This was the result of a survey of the discipline, organized by UNESCO (United Nations Education, Scientific, and Cultural Organization) in 1950, that clearly accepted the American political scientists' claim to leadership, although it was of international scope and was, by the way, supervised by the Austrian émigré William Ebenstein. The survey listed the following four areas as the most important ones: political theory, governmental institutions (policy), political process (politics), and international relations.[15] Now, if we classify the fifty-four immigrants to the United States from our group according to this pattern, with each of them receiving 2 points for his main fields of publication, then we get the following distribution. Of the total of 108 points, 46 go to international relations, 34 to governmental institutions, 16 to political theory, and only 12 to political process. In what way does this quantitative pattern affect the group of émigrés internally, and how does it fit into the development of the discipline when interpreted qualitatively?

First, the large share in publications in the field of international relations is remarkable. The émigrés' studies did not just cover specific relations between individual countries or traditional topics, such as international law and international organizations; they considered theoretical and methodological questions without losing their bearing on the current state of practical politics. Men such as Herz and Morgenthau, for example, became spokes-

14 Literature on the history of American political science is overabundant. I will mention only two older examples that take an affirmative and a critical position, respectively, with regard to the role of behaviorism: Bernard Crick, *The American Science of Politics* (London, 1959); Albert Somit and Joseph Tanenhaus, *The Development of American Political Science: From Burgess to Behavioralism* (Boston, 1967). More recent accounts are: David M. Ricci, *The Tragedy of Political Science: Politics, Scholarship, and Democracy* (New Haven, Conn., 1984); Raymond Seidelman and Edward J. Harpham, *Disenchanted Realists: Political Science and the American Crisis, 1884–1984* (Albany, N.Y., 1985).

15 UNESCO, Contemporary Political Science (Paris, 1950), 4.

men in the so-called "great debate" of the 1950s on the alternative of
realism versus idealism in foreign affairs. In this field, Morgenthau probably
formulated the most influential theory of the postwar era, that of "political
realism." This was superseded in the 1960s and 1970s by Deutsch's theory
of communication, which was just as influential.[16] A comparison between
these prominent men also shows that their attitudes toward behavioralism
– in the case of Morgenthau strictly negative, in that of Deutsch quite
positive – are not sufficient to explain their success. The theory of international relations was in any case a rapidly expanding field within American
political science; it was the academic parallel to the rise of the United States
to world power status after 1945. Yet the comparatively large contribution
by émigrés to this development was not restricted to brilliant individual
achievements; rather, it was part of an accumulation of theoretical competence in a group of people who knew how to make use of the experience
of emigration as a positive and decidedly international broadening of their
outlook.

By comparison, examining the field of political philosophy leads to an
interesting shift in the relation between quantitative and qualitative observations. The group of émigrés in this area is small, but it includes outstanding personalities. Its pluralism is extreme – if Arnold Brecht can be
considered an adherent of a fictive liberal center, then Herbert Marcuse and
Leo Strauss could be placed at the extreme left and at the extreme right,
respectively. Yet a visible impetus to the development of the discipline
seems to have come mainly from the conservative side. In the 1950s and
1960s, Leo Strauss, Eric Voegelin, and Hannah Arendt, among others, were
the most trenchant critics of the "behavioral revolution," and thus became
the center of a sort of theoretical counterrevolution against the ruling trend
in the discipline.[17] They could play this part because they formulated a
program of pure theory that relied on classical antiquity, Christianity, and
natural law, thus introducing pre-modern ideas into a culture that seemed

---

16   Major works are Karl W. Deutsch, *The Nerves of Government* (New York, 1963); John H. Herz,
     Political Realism and Political Idealism (Chicago, 1951); Hans J. Morgenthau, *Politics among Nations*
     (New York, 1948). As a contemporary survey, see Quincy Wright, *The Study of International
     Relations* (New York, 1955).

17   The divergent political attitudes are especially well illustrated by Arnold Brecht, *Political Theory:
     The Foundation of Twentieth-Century Thought* (Princeton, N.J., 1959); Herbert Marcuse, *One-Di-
     mensional Studies in the Ideology of Advanced Industrial Society* (Boston, 1964); Leo Strauss, *The Ancient
     and Modern* (New York, 1968). The three most influential books written by émigrés and highly
     critical of behavioralism were originally presented as Walgreen Lectures at the University of Chi-
     cago: Eric Voegelin, *The New Science of Politics* (Chicago, 1952); Leo Strauss, *Natural Right and
     History* (Chicago, 1953); Hannah Arendt, *The Human Condition* (Chicago, 1958). Cf. John G.
     Gunnell, *Between Philosophy and Politics: The Alienation of Political Theory* (Amherst, Mass., 1984);
     and Jürgen Falter, *Der "Positivismusstreit" in der amerikanischen Politikwissenschaft* (Opladen, 1982).

to be stabilized at the level of what Gunnar Myrdal calls "conservative liberalism."

Such cultural-philosophical considerations are necessary in order to understand why a few esoteric outsiders did not interrupt the liberal tradition, but managed to challenge the mainstream of the discipline as a whole. Of course, they were not immediately successful in this, but it is evident that they became the crystallizing point for a new understanding of political philosophy without which the "behavioral mood" would not have been defeated so quickly. If, for instance, it is true that the present boom of neoconservatism dates back to Leo Strauss, we are confronted with an astounding long-term émigré influence. Ironically, this occurred in part because the émigrés dodged the course of "normal science" by establishing esoteric relations between teachers and disciples – a highly political revival of the Platonic academy in the most modern country in the world.

In comparison with the fields just mentioned, the evaluation of the two remaining subdisciplines yields a fairly unstructured profile. This is probably because they constitute the bulk of American political science, uniting a large number of diverging special fields and methodological tendencies. Even the distinction between policy and politics, which has by now been canonized, between governmental institutions on the one hand and the social construction of politics on the other, proves to be of only relatively limited analytical power on closer examination.

If we stick for a moment to this distinction, however, it becomes apparent that the émigrés' achievements were in both fields of comparatively little importance. The field of politics inevitably showed (and still shows) an inclination toward domestic subjects, and it is not without reason that in Germany, politics is often translated as *Innenpolitik* (domestic politics). Only a few of the émigrés brought full competence to this task.[18] Thus it is only natural that we get the lowest scores of all in this field, for it is also here that both the quantitative and the qualitative strength of the discipline resides. American – and that means behavioralist – studies on interest groups and public opinion have been its main export article since the 1950s.

Whereas things seem to be more favorable in the field of governmental institutions, here too the interests of the discipline centered on institutions such as the Presidency, Congress, and the Supreme Court – that is, on domestic topics to which the émigrés could contribute little. This is aggravated by the fact that even the genuine competence for the new field that

18 Cf., e.g., Heinrich Rommen, *Grundrecht, Gesetz und Richter in den Vereinigten Staaten von America* (Münster, 1931); Eric Voegelin, *Über die Formen des amerikanischen Geistes* (Tübingen, 1928); and Arnold Wolfers, *Amerikanische und deutsche Löhne* (Berlin, 1930).

the emigrants had acquired during the Weimar period through the nor-mative-juridical method was of decreasing significance in American political science.[19] The contributions by émigrés, which are nevertheless notable, are characteristically located in an area that was closely related both meth-odologically and thematically to the field of international relations – in the field of comparative government. Herz, Kirchheimer, Loewenstein, Sig-mund Neumann, and Ernst Fraenkel, among others, explicitly considered themselves comparativists. Although their studies did not lead to the for-mation of schools, they were still received as outstanding individual achieve-ments.[20] Their quality depended less on the clarification of methodological or theoretical questions than on the richly documented inclusion of Euro-pean political systems. The comparative study of political systems, or of political groups and parties, was a branch of American political science that expanded for the same reason as did international politics.[21] The fact that émigrés had a significant influence on the course of development of this subdiscipline merely reinforces once again the link between the experience of emigration and scientific internationalism, which we noted previously.

To summarize, it can be said that émigrés led only a marginal existence in the central fields of research and teaching in political science. Although they remained relatively invisible as a distinct group in a field that was of gigantic dimensions by European standards, and that was furthermore un-dergoing rapid change, this does not mean that they were insignificant. Thus an evaluation of the two leading professional journals in the United States – the *American Political Science Review* and the *Political Science Quarterly* – shows a clear overrepresentation of émigrés compared with native political scientists; but the absolute numbers show that between 1930 and 1965, they published no more than about 1.5 percent of all articles. Keeping such relations in mind is probably the key to a realistic assessment of academic emigration generally.

As a group, the émigrés' status in the discipline was and remained only marginal. Wherever individual figures gained celebrity and influence, this

19 Almost all of the American contributions in the UNESCO volume are characterized by an anti-juridical affect, which can be considered almost an integral part of common sense in American political science since the 1920s.

20 The visibility of the émigrés in comparative government literature needs to be evaluated in greater detail. However, it is evident in the following works, some of which were used as textbooks at many American colleges: Gwendolin Carter and John Herz, eds., *Major Foreign Powers* (New York, 1952); Otto Kirchheimer, *Political Justice: The Use of Legal Procedures for Political Ends* (Princeton, N.J., 1961); Karl Loewenstein, *Political Power and the Governmental Process* (Chicago, 1957); Sigmund Neumann, ed., *Modern Political Parties: Approaches to Comparative Politics* (Chicago, 1956). This is also true in West Germany as we see in Ernst Fraenkel's *Deutschland und die westlichen Demokratien* (Stuttgart, 1964).

21 For a contemporary survey see R. Macridies, *The Study of Comparative Government* (Garden City, N.J., 1955).

was only because they either got caught in the center of an intellectual boom already in progress or opposed it diametrically; paradoxically, they became most visible whenever they combined both trends of the zeitgeist. This may have been the secret of the success of political philosophers such as Strauss or Voegelin, who clung to their German origins more rigidly than others, and by doing so, caused critical stagnation in the discipline as a whole. Perhaps this could also explain why it was the (narrower) spectrum of conservative émigrés and not the (broader) one of leftists and liberals who had the greater potential for founding a school. Was this a residual bonus for the "German mandarin" under the quite different conditions of American university life, especially in a discipline that paid for its modernization with considerable simplification?

PRACTICAL ORIENTATION: FIGHTING AGAINST NAZISM AND FOR DEMOCRACY

The history of the refugees from Hitler cannot be fully understood unless contemporary political history is taken into account. Racially motivated persecution cannot be separated from that which was politically motivated; the decision to emigrate was a political act even in the case of those who were not direct victims of political persecution. What devolved on émigré social scientists in accordance with their profession – namely, critical reflection on the present – became an even more urgent task in the case of political scientists. If not before, then certainly simultaneously with their departure from Germany, they had to focus their attention on European fascism in general and on National Socialism in particular. It is out of this situation that the very first émigré literature emerged, marked as it was by the shock of expulsion. This was something like a genre in its own right, in which the authors were highly affected personally and thus often adopted an imploring attitude. Its spectrum reached from pseudonymous underground writings, which were passed into Germany for diverse resistance groups, to committed essayistic and scientific works analyzing the current policies of Hitler and his adversaries. With these writings, the émigrés' claim to political practice was laid – a claim that could nonetheless only be realized in part. This marks the beginning of the theory-praxis dilemma, which was to persist throughout the period.[22]

Such engaged publications, together with more factual and objective

22 This is a point at which the political, artistic, and academic exile still presents itself as an indissoluble unity. Especially nowadays, in view of the diversification of research on exile, this common ground must not be lost.

analyses of the early period, are suited for giving our group a first political profile. Not only did they appear in characteristically large numbers – about one-third of the group published several monographs on National Socialism or on Italian Fascism, and every one of them published at least one article on the subject – they also show that the digestion of their own experiences and reflection on the political present in Germany and Europe were two sides of the same coin. This does not mean that there was a common political or even theoretical orientation in our group. Rather, the contrary was the case, as the following spectrum will show. The conservative end of the spectrum was represented by works that emerged on the threshold of emigration and not during its advanced state. Analyses such as the ones written by Gerhard Leibholz or by Erich Voegelin are clearly anti-liberal in character and even reveal sympathy for the authoritarian state. Later works by Loewenstein or Ebenstein can be read as a critique of National Socialism written in the spirit of liberalism, whereas younger authors such as Franz Borkenau or Richard Löwenthal proceeded explicitly from the Marxist theory of capitalism.[23] Once these works are brought into ideological sequence, an increasingly harsh opposition to National Socialism is revealed, which led around the end of the 1930s and especially after the escalation of World War II to a basic solidarity across all theoretical and political frontiers.

These and other analyses of National Socialism and Fascism reveal both the common adversary and the existential core of a second political socialization that the political scientists underwent in the course of emigration. It is here that the origins of their specific contributions to the history of the discipline are to be found. Their professional development shows a characteristic dynamism in the relation between theory and practice. The fortunate mediation of these two spheres represented a nearly insoluble problem for the political exile. To the academic émigrés, and especially to the political scientists among them, however, it often became an admission ticket to the professional world; for where else should the "natural" competence of the émigrés lie but in this special field, which they knew better

---

23 Significant for the first group is Gerhard Leibholz, *Die Auflösung der liberalen Demokratie in Deutschland und das autoritäre Staatsbild* (Munich, 1933), or Eric Voegelin, *Der autoritäre Staat* (Vienna, 1936); and for the second group, Karl Loewenstein, *Hitler's Germany* (New York, 1939) or William Ebenstein, *The Nazi State* (New York, 1943). The relevant essays by Richard Löwenthal appeared under the pseudonym Paul Sering in 1935 and 1936, in the *Zeitschrift für Sozialismus*, which was published in Czechoslovakian exile. That the works published by his companion Franz Borkenau are nowadays largely forgotten constitutes one of the most deplorable losses to the memory of the history of political science in Germany. In England during the 1930s, they were among the most widely read works of the political emigration. Cf. Franz Borkenau, *The Spanish Cockpit: An Eye-Witness Account of the Political and Social Conflicts of the Spanish Civil War* (London, 1937); Borkenau, *The New German Empire* (Harmondsworth, 1939).

from personal experience than any American? It may well be, of course, that the high portion of political confession was not always beneficial to the professional value of the product, but it marked the author as a committed writer and demonstrated, above all, his anti–Hitler conviction, which was considered common sense among his present or future colleagues. Yet it was exactly this genre that also produced supreme professional achievements such as the *Dual State* by Fraenkel, which he had begun while still in Germany, or Neumann's *Behemoth*, an ingenious combination of theoretical analysis, hard empiricism, and political reflection, which, in spite of its openly Marxist approach, plainly preordained a major career for its author.[24]

What held true for the debate on Fascism and National Socialism in the late 1930s and early 1940s is analogously valid for the so-called theory of totalitarianism, although this only culminated at a later date. This concept, which basically aimed at a comparison between National Socialism and Stalinism, had already been developed during the European emigration, for example, by Waldemar Gurian in Switzerland and by Borkenau in England, and was then imported in the intellectual baggage of the increasing stream of refugees into the United States, where it was perfected to a high standard of comparative political science by Sigmund Neumann. Whereas in the late 1940s it was still hardly distinguishable from the broader debate on fascism in general, in the early 1950s the term received a characteristic impetus that was already ascribable to the Cold War. It was only then that the objective of the theory of totalitariansim shifted from a comparison between to the identification of the National Socialists with Stalinist dictatorships. Individual émigrés, foremost among them Hannah Arendt, played an important part in this; yet it has to be asked to what extent the high degree of weltanschauung inherent in this theory acted equally as a motive for and as an impediment to its science-based conceptualization.[25]

Disintegrated particles of the theory of totalitarianism seem to have become part of the broad and innovative field of American research on the Soviet Union in which, during the 1950s and 1960s, émigrés like Gurian, Marcuse, and Löwenthal certainly were of great influence[26]; however, they clearly remained under the hegemony of native minds. This is by no means

24   Both Ernst Fraenkel's *Dual State* (New York and London: 1941) and Franz L. Neumann's *Behemoth: The Structure and Practice of National Socialism* (New York, 1942) became classical interpretations of Nazi Germany.

25   Cf. Waldemar Gurian, *Bolschewismus als Weltgefahr* (Lucerne, 1935); Franz Borkenau, *The Totalitarian Enemy* (London, 1940); Sigmund Neumann, *Permanent Revolution: The Total State in a World at War* (New York, 1942); Hannah Arendt, *The Origins of Totalitarianism* (New York, 1951).

26   Cf. Waldemar Gurian, *Bolshevism: An Introduction to Soviet Communism* (Notre Dame, Ind., 1952); Herbert Marcuse, *Soviet Communism: A Critical Analysis* (New York, 1958); Richard Löwenthal, *Chruschtschow und der Weltkommunismus* (Stuttgart, 1963).

surprising, considering the political explosiveness of the subject at the height of the Cold War.

Things had been much more favorable ten years earlier, when German émigrés were included in the American war effort and when the mediation between theory and practice assumed an altogether concrete and temporarily even very constructive shape. Not the simple fact as such, but the concentration and specialization of their work as scientific advisors (and not as executive officers) was a distinct specialty of the group of émigrés. A count of American governmental organizations taken in the 1940s, for example, yielded the following numbers of emigrants belonging to each staff: State Department – twelve; Office of Strategic Services – nine; Office of War Information – six; Defense Department – three; National War College – four; Office of Military Government U.S. – five; army – three; navy – two. The work done by émigrés for these institutions represents an ideal, if complex, field for an analysis of the social integration of scientific émigrés as a political process.

The example that has until now been most fully documented – the Research and Analysis Branch of the Office of Strategic Services (OSS) – makes it seem likely that there existed a constructive connection between the political ambitions of the émigrés and the practical needs of the host country. The émigrés provided their special knowledge of Germany and Europe, and in return received the acknowledgment of loyalty from the host country. "Enemy aliens," formerly eyed with suspicion, soon turned not only into "friendly enemy aliens" but almost, to use a modern and drastic term, into battle-proven patriots. This process was, however, marked by a certain paradox. Social integration was achieved in spite of the fact that from the point of view of the émigrés, their political advisory role proved a failure because their recommendations were ignored by the practitioners. Nonetheless, this or a similar give-and-take was for a notable part of the group studied the launching pad for a later academic career.[27]

The integration of German émigrés into the practice of the postwar American military government was a logical result of the war against Hitler. Although the years following 1945 are, as far as the role of the émigrés is concerned, not as well researched as the war years, a survey of our group nevertheless indicates that only a few individual prominent specialists were

---

27 I have tried to support this thesis with an "archeological" interpretation of the analyses of Germany that were written by émigrés for the Office of Strategic Services (OSS) and later on for the State Department. It was further substantiated by retrospective interviews with some of the persons involved. See Alfons Söllner, ed., *Zur Archäologie der Demokratie in Deutschland: Analysen politischer Emigranten, 1942–1949*, 2 vols. (Frankfurt/Main, 1986) and Barry M. Katz, *Foreign Intelligence: Research and Analysis in the OSS, 1942–1945* (Cambridge, Mass., 1989).

given a chance to act – for example, Brecht in the question of federalism in postwar Germany, or Loewenstein with regard to the reconstruction of the Bavarian legal system.[28] Systematic utilization of the émigrés' intelligence for the purpose of Germany's recovery, however, was never achieved. This was probably because after initially setting itself ambitious goals – for instance, in denazification or decartelization policy – the military government soon came to terms with inner-German political forces, a process that was furthered by the reorientation of American policy toward the development of capitalism and toward anti-communist containment. In a sense, the total complex of reeducation seems to be an exception. It has to be noted, however, that here too the commitment of the émigrés was less and less to assisting directly military government policies, and that they argued increasingly on their own behalf.

This slightly changed constellation of theory and practice manifests itself in a type of scientific literature that is often still under the spell of the first return to the country from which the émigrés had been expelled, and that seems to be another particularity of this group. In this kind of literature, the reconstruction of democracy in Germany is observed from an especially skeptical "émigrés' perspective" that notices continuities and restorative tendencies rather than a radically new beginning in postwar development, and at the same time combines this skepticism with recommendations for fundamental democratization.[29] Energetic, programmatic, and practical endeavors to develop an autonomous modern political science in West Germany, in which individual émigrés played a decisive role, must also be seen in this context. The description of their actual influence offers the possibility of giving for the first time a very concrete example of the mediation between politics and science. However, the factors that contributed to this mediation have also clearly become more complex. Since the field of re-migration and the émigrés' effect on postwar Germany as a whole has hardly been explored, the following considerations are purely hypothetical and serve merely as points of reference for a final perspective.

The re-migration pattern is rather clear-cut. Of our group of sixty-four, about one-third returned to West Germany and to permanent academic

---

28 See Arnold Brecht, *Federalism and Regionalism in Germany: The Division of Prussia* (New York, 1945); Karl Loewenstein, *Political Reconstruction* (New York, 1964).

29 Significant are Hannah Arendt, "The Aftermath of Nazi Rule: Report from Germany," *Commentary* 10 (1950); Franz L. Neumann, "German Democracy 1950," *International Conciliation, Carnegie Endowment for International Peace* (New York, 1950); Sigmund Neumann, "Germany: Promise and Perils," *Headline Series*, no. 52 (1950). See my article, "Zwischen totalitärer Vergangenheit und demokratischer Zukunft: Emigranten beurteilen die deutsche Entwicklung nach 1945," *Exil und Remigration: Jahrbuch für Exilforschung* 9 (1991): 146–70.

positions. A little less than one-third availed themselves of more intensive academic connections, such as visiting professorships. More than half of those who returned did so before 1950, whereas the majority of those taking up a position as visiting professors did so only after 1955. A comparison with the general quota of re-migration shows this distribution to be rather remarkable. Whereas the total number is estimated at about 26 percent, the quota of political scientists returning to their homeland is significantly higher.[30] This group more than any other contributed to the reinstatement of West German democracy, for the ideological safeguarding of which political science seemed the obvious field. However, this does not in the least imply that the foundation of the new "science of democracy" (*Demokratiewissenschaft*) was exclusively a product of reeducation, or that the émigrés were the only agents of its enforcement. On the one hand, the emigrants were by no means confronted with a tabula rasa, as is suggested by the thesis of the *Stunde Null* (zero hour). Rather, they quite soon had to deal with a situation charged with conflict – a situation that became polarized after the denazification of the universities proved a failure. On the other hand, the emigrants considered themselves representatives of the "other" – meaning, the better – Germany.

What this conflict looked like in detail and what its outcome was remain controversial. On the one hand, the most thorough study of early West German political science so far states that the émigrés took only a minor part in the institutionalization of the discipline.[31] On the other hand, it must be assumed that during the critical stage of foundation around 1950, they contributed substantially to breaking university resistance. The decisive factor in this was probably the fact that because of their close integration into the American discipline, the émigrés/rémigrés had developed thorough and definite conceptions of what the discipline's subject and especially its methods were to be, in short: What constituted its identity as an autonomous discipline? At least with respect to this question, which was decisive for the establishment of the discipline, they were able to hold their own against the law faculties, which – not without reason – feared a politically and methodologically more progressive rival and would have preferred to see a noncommittal *stadium generale* instituted instead.

How energetically the emigrants presented their ideas on this question, and how strongly they referred in this to the American model, is illustrated by the diverse programmatic writings that appeared in the context of the

---

30   See Horst Möller, *Exodus der Kultur: Schriftsteller, Wissenschaftler und Künstler in der Emigration nach 1933* (Munich, 1984), 112.

31   Cf. Arno Mohr, *Politikwissenschaft als Alternative* (Bochum, 1988), 160–2.

reopening of the Deutsche Hochschule für Politik in Berlin in 1949. These more or less openly voiced a plea for education for democracy as one of the basic objectives of the academy.[32] The departments in both Freiburg and Munich, which were founded at a later date, were based on significantly more conservative conceptions of democracy, despite the fact that the directors, Arnold Bergsträsser and Voegelin, also advocated an autonomous status for political science.[33] Further research on the émigrés' impact on West German science and culture will probably reveal that influence was increasingly absorbed and also relativized by that of local (and restorative?) forces. However, the fact remains that a modern political science could not have been established as quickly and as successfully as it was at West German universities of the postwar era without the help of the émigrés.

THE POLITICAL SCHOLAR:
A TYPE CONDITIONED BY EMIGRATION?

Perhaps the increasing interest social scientists are now showing in their own history is nothing more than the expression of loss of practical relevance in times of a *neue Unübersichtlichkeit* (Jürgen Habermas). In the case of the academic emigration after 1933, this interest is at least directed at an epoch that has not only long been neglected but that also became a direct and constituting factor in the development of West German scholarhip. What appears to be an altogether exceptional case – an involuntary and radical restructuring of the relation between scholarship and culture – nonetheless became a factor in general and long-term trends, and even accelerated them.

One of the most important and far-reaching of these trends is the internationalization of science generally. This can be seen in all disciplines, in medicine as well as in physics, in art history as well as in sociology. What is of interest with regard to the history of the émigré political scientists' influence in particular is the extent to which and the manner in which politics intervened in this process, and even more so its cultural-historical outcome. This could be described as the decided Westernization of a political culture that before had been just as decidedly

32 See, e.g., Ossip K. Flechtheim, *Politik als Wissenschaft* (Berlin, 1953); Arcadius Gurland, *Political Science in Western Germany: Thoughts and Writings, 1950–1952* (Washington, D.C., 1952); Franz L. Neumann, *Die Wissenschaft der Politik in der Demokratie* (Berlin, 1950); and Karl Loewenstein, "Über den Stand der politischen Wissenschaften in den Vereinigten Staaten," *Zeitschrift für die gesamte Staatswissenschaft* 106 (1950): 349.
33 See Arnold Bergsträsser, *Politik in Wissenschaft und Bildung: Reden und Schriften* (Freiburg, 1961); Eric Voegelin, "Was ist die politische Realität?" *Politische Vierteljahresschrift* 7 (1966): 2–54.

anti-Western. A closer analysis of this more general process of transformation represents the contribution that could be made by the study of émigré political scientists to both German and European cultural history in the twentieth century.

In a synopsis of political history, the history of his discipline, and his life history, published in 1953, Neumann argued that the social scientists who were expelled from Germany had three options: They could stick more firmly to their old identity; they could adjust themselves seamlessly to the academic system of the host country; or they could attempt a synthesis of the old and the new. According to Neumann, the émigré who chooses the third option could join the ranks of truly "political scholars," the seekers of truth, well tried by persecution, if (1) he mixes certain achievements of the German academic tradition with a specifically Anglo-Saxon professionalism, (2) he is not too wrapped up in either the one or the other, (3) he leaves behind the anti-democratic ambitions of the "German mandarin" without becoming addicted to the scientism and the belief in progress of American social science, and if (4) he faces the demands of democratic practice while adhering imperturbably to the rights of critical theorizing.[34]

Of course, Neumann's sympathies are with this type, chiefly because he represents a positive outcome of the émigrés' fate, and thus makes its normative upgrading appear to be tied to the actual requirements for professional success. However, the question arises whether or not there is also a descriptive potential inherent in Neumann's three-part model, whether or not one has in fact to write the history of the academic emigration as the emergence of a new mediation of science and politics, in which the experience of emigration itself played a decisive role. If emigration were declared a training field for cultural-historical research, the political scholar could become something like an integrating point of reference, for he represents a social type that synthesizes expulsion, migration, and integration. Moreover, insofar as he was only brought into being by the process of acculturation, the political scholar also constitutes a cognitive type that comes to rest between the two poles of the ambiguous cultural-historical constellation that he joins, and may even overcome it through a long-term learning process. The émigrés would act as agents of a contradictory, unplanned, and yet final fusion of Weimar public law and American political science. This resulted in the transformation of a single academic discipline

34 Franz L. Neumann, "The Social Sciences," in W. Rex Crawford, ed., *The Cultural Migration: The European Scholar in America* (Philadelphia, 1953).

but also contributed to changing both the form and the horizon of an entire political culture.

APPENDIX

Names of the sixty-four people who constituted the sample for quantitative evaluation. Taken into consideration were only people who actually and in a narrow sense held a teaching or research position in political science. In a few cases, for which other disciplinary allocation would be possible, a clear predominance within the discipline can be demonstrated as far as publications are concerned. However, the criteria as developed in the first section are applicable to anyone in the sample.

Arendt, Hannah	Jäckh, Ernst
Aufricht, Hans	Kaufmann, Erich
Berger, Peter L.	Kaufmann, Fritz
Bergsträsser, Arnold	Kelsen, Hans
Bonn, Moritz J.	Kirchheimer, Otto
Borkenau, Franz	Knorr, Klaus E.
Bozeman, Adda	Korsch, Karl
Brecht, Arnold	Kraus, Wolfgang
Brüning, Heinrich	Landshut, Siegfried
Deutsch, Karl W.	Leibholz, Gerhard
Dunner, Joseph	Loewenstein, Karl
Ebenstein, William	Löwenthal, Richard
Ehrmann, Henry W.	London, Kurt L.
Flechtheim, Ossip K.	Marcuse, Herbert
Fraenkel, Ernst	Meisel, James H.
Freund, Ludwig	Meyer, Ernst W.
Grabowski, Adolf	Michael, Franz H.
Gross, Leo	Morgenthau, Hans J.
Gurian, Waldemar	Morstein-Marx, Fritz
Gurland, Arcadius	Neumann, Franz L.
Hamburger, Ernst	Neumann, Robert G.
Heller, Hermann	Neumann, Siegmund
Hermens, Ferdinand A.	Newman, Karl J.
Herz, John H.	Niemeyer, Gerhart
Hexner, Ervin P.	Paechter, Heinz
Holborn, Louise W.	Possony, Stefan T.
Hula, Erich	Roetter, Friedrich

Rommen, Heinrich   Strauss, Leo
Rosen, Edgar R.   Strupp, Karl
Simons, Hans   Voegelin, Eric
Speier, Hans   Waldmann, Eric
Steiner, Kurt   Wolfers, Arnold O.

Epilogue

The Refugee Scholar in America:
The Case of Paul Tillich

KAREN J. GREENBERG

In 1953, Franz L. Neumann, a veteran of the OSS and the author of a well-acclaimed study of National Socialism, surveyed the lives of other refugees who, like himself, had fled Hitler for the United States. Tenured at Columbia, Neumann identified three categories among his colleagues in exile, distinguished refugees, aptly labeled by Laura Fermi "illustrious immigrants."[1] In the first category, Neumann placed those individuals who clung desperately to their pasts, refusing to enter the New World. In the second category, he placed those who bid adieu to their old ways of thinking and embraced, often without a backward glance, the culture of their new home. In the third category, the "most rewarding" and "most difficult," Neumann placed those individuals who wove together strands of the "new experience" with those of the "old tradition."[2]

Neumann's viewpoint, that of an émigré who had succeeded admirably within the academic establishment, lent credence to his analysis. In the nearly forty years since he penned his essay "The Social Sciences," little if any revision has been visited upon his delineations. Instead, students of the migration – led by H. Stuart Hughes and Lewis Coser – have welcomed his categories as a means of understanding the lives and works not only of refugee social scientists but of the intellectual migration in general.[3]

Despite the many constructive avenues of inquiry for which Neumann's categories can take credit, there are a number of problematic aspects to his

1 Laura Fermi, *Illustrious Immigrants: The Intellectual Migration from Europe, 1930–1941* (Chicago, 1968).
2 Franz Neumann, "The Social Sciences," *The Cultural Migration: The European Scholar in America* (Philadelphia, 1953), 4–26.
3 H. Stuart Hughes, *The Sea Change: The Migration of Social Thought, 1930–65* (New York, 1975); and Lewis A. Coser, *Refugee Scholars in America: Their Impact and Their Experiences* (New Haven, Conn., 1984). See also H. Stuart Hughes, "Social Theory in a New Context," in Jarrell Jackman and Carl M. Borden, eds., *The Muses Flee Hitler: Cultural Transfer and Adaptation, 1930–1945* (Washington, D.C., 1983).

273

analysis. First is the issue of perspective. Recently, Barry Katz, who acknowledged the validity of seeing "creative binding" as a mark of success,
pointed to the difficulty involved in using the émigrés themselves as reliable
chroniclers of this migration.[4] Their perspectives, he suggested, might benefit from a more distanced viewpoint. Another equally significant problem
of perspective is the timing of Neumann's seminal essay. When he wrote
"The Social Sciences," the intellectual migration was at the chronological
midway point. After two decades, it is possible that the actual patterns of
intellectual accommodation had yet to emerge.

As the last of the émigrés depart from the universities and their articles
cease to appear in the leading journals, it seems that some reexamination of
Neumann's categories is warranted. Was there, rather than a set of static
categories, a discernible paradigmatic sequence to the story of acculturation,
a process of integrating one's ideas into a new intellectual content? Did that
process find that individuals often fit into all of Neumann's categories, one
at each stage of their acculturation to the American context? In sum, when
the migration is viewed from a comprehensive perspective, do Neumann's
categories still apply? Or is it possible that the timing of Neumann's analysis
necessarily resulted in conclusions that were premature and therefore in
need of reconsideration?

The theologian Paul Tillich offers an appropriate focus from which
to bring new light to the study of migration. He was without a doubt
a "successful" émigré, admired by both the American public and the
American academic world. He occupied prestigious chairs at Union
Theological Seminary and at Harvard; his book *The Courage to Be* was a
bestseller. He arrived with sufficient ties to the German intellectual
world and Neumann's realm of the "old" to make him a strong and de-
vout representative of that tradition. As a youth, Tillich had believed
that Shakespeare, given his stature and excellence, was German. Upon
emigration, Tillich described his allegiance to Germany in the following
way: "Berlin was not only [a] homeland but also a religious concept."[5]
Second, he reflected at length and at many different times during his
thirty years in the United States on the refugee experience. Not only
did he leave several autobiographical pieces, one written at the outset
of his life in America, the other just before his death, but he referred
frequently in his lectures and his essays to the significance of leaving

---

4   Barry Katz, "The Acculturation of Thought: Transformations of the Refugee Scholar in America"
    [rev. art.], *Journal of Modern History* 63, no. 4 (1991): 740–52.
5   Paul Tillich, "My Travel Diary: 1936," in Jerald C. Brauer, ed., *Between Two Worlds* (New York,
    1970), and Paul Tillich, "Frontiers," *The Future of Religions* (New York, 1966), 56.

one culture to live in another.[6] Surprisingly, a sustained study of the way in which he fit into the intellectual migration has not yet been attempted. Symbolically, both Hughes and Coser end their studies of the migration with essays on Tillich. Although Tillich somehow defies conclusive categorization in their terms, he cannot be left out of their analyses.

The incompleteness of the portrait of Tillich is strengthened by disagreements between those who view him within the context of migration and those who study his life and thought within the discipline of theology. According to Hughes, Tillich "was perhaps the one who embraced America most whole-heartedly . . . yet . . . he too remained more German than his American admirers suspected." Coser agrees. "Tillich's mind was essentially fixed before he came here." Yet he found ways, according to both Coser and Hughes, to bring together his Germanic cast of mind and the American intellectual milieu. Hughes sees the American affection for Tillich as a case of "misunderstanding or half-understanding." Tillich's biographers, Wilhelm and Mary Pauck, disagree. They point to the fact that Tillich altered his language and "learned how to relate himself to the American way of thinking." The Paucks add another element as well in understanding the degree of success a refugee intellectual encountered. As they point out, changes in American society affected the careers of the refugees. Nineteen-fifties America, they assert, "in its own postwar doldrums, no longer bustling with utopian optimism, now gave ear to Tillichian themes to which it had been tone-deaf in the early years of his immigration." Baruch concurs: "Prior to the end of World War Two, America was not ready for or open to Tillich's type of theology. The anxieties of the postwar era changed that. Here was a philosopher who could provide solace to a society on the brink."[7]

The question inadvertently raised by the varying views of Tillich – how did the refugee experience affect the development of his thought – provides an apt springboard for delving further into his story. Elusive and pivotal, Tillich provides significant territory for exploration in an effort to understand the intellectual migration. His own intellectual acculturation occurred over a series of stages and suggests a pattern that one might discern among other émigrés.

6 Paul Tillich, "On the Boundary," *The Interpretation of History* (New York, 1936); "Autobiographical Reflection," in Charles W. Kegley and R. W. Bretall, eds., *The Theology of Paul Tillich* (New York, 1964); "My Travel Diary: 1936"; and *My Search for Absolutes* (New York, 1967).
7 Hughes, *The Sea Change*, 265–8; Coser, *The Refugee Scholar in America*, 318; Wilhelm Pauck and Marion Pauck, *Paul Tillich: His Life and Thought* (New York, 1976), vol. 1; Jerald C. Brauer, "Paul Tillich's Impact on America," in Tillich, ed., *The Future of Religions*, 15–22.

THE EARLY PERIOD: LOOKING BACKWARD

Tillich came to the United States reluctantly, indecisively, and at the behest of his American colleague, Reinhold Niebuhr. Both his reluctance and Niebuhr's invitation were understandable. The European refugee intellectuals for the most part hardly relished the idea of leaving Europe behind. Many, including historian Hajo Holborn, who ventured first to England, and Renaissance scholar Paul Kristeller, who spent time in Italy, hoped along with the American press and diplomatic service that Hitler's rule would come to a precipitous end.[8] As a group, they sensed at the outset the difficulties they would encounter should they come to the United States. First, they would of necessity have to learn a new language. For them, this was not just a matter of skill; it was by definition an exchange of philosophical orientation. Embedded in the German language, many insisted, was a terminology and a structure of thought that seemed untranslatable.[9] A second difficulty was the lack of access to sources, the medium of their occupations. The libraries and archives of Europe constituted their stock in trade. In the United States, they could not rely on such provision.[10] A third difficulty, to their minds, was the loss of a community in which to conduct their dialogues.

For Tillich, the loss of dialogue, and its origins in the use of language, were pivotal problems. At the age of forty-seven, he was not in a position to begin his career anew. Nor did his early years here presage success for him on the order that he experienced it. Language remained an issue for him throughout his life in the United States. For him, verbal communication had a religious dimension. "Only in a community of language," wrote Tillich, "can one actualize his faith." Struggling as he did with language in his early classroom and public encounters, he faced difficulties caused by the structures of the American academy as well. In 1934, when the Philosophy Department at Columbia pondered the question of whether or not to try and secure a place for him in their midst, they found themselves

---

8   Otto Pflanze, "The Americanization of Hajo Holborn," in Hartmut Lehmann and James J. Sheehan, eds., *An Interrupted Past: German-Speaking Refugee Historians in the United States after 1933* (New York, 1991); and author's interview with Paul Oskar Kristeller, April 12, 1982.

9   See, e.g., Louise W. Holborn, "Deutsche Wissenschaftler in den Vereinigten Staaten in den Jahren nach 1933," *Jahrbuch für Amerikastudien* 10 (1963): 19; and the interviews collected in Radio Bremen, *Auszug des Geistes: Bericht über eine Sendereihe* (Bremen, 1962), 32–3, 39, 41–2, 63, 155.

10 A particularly poignant expression of the loss of printed materials occurs in Paul Oskar Kristeller and John Herman Randall, "The Study of the Philosophies of the Renaissance," *Journal of the History of Ideas* 2 (1941): 495–6, where the authors expressed their hope that the United States would some day possess the libraries and therefore the scholarship to match those of Europe.

in a quandary. The chairman of the department, John Jacob Coss, considered Tillich to be a scholar who was "as thoroughly informed in the philosophy of religion as anybody in America." But the members of the department, including Coss, did not think they could offer this philosopher of religion a position. The recent émigré from Germany, they concluded, had not made "an outstanding contribution to philosophy" and seemed unlikely to do so. Meanwhile, at Union Theological Seminary, there was concern that Tillich was too philosophically oriented and not theological enough for the seminary curriculum. The members of the Theological Discussion Group to which he was elected in 1934 found themselves "baffled" by Tillich's ideas, although the chairman of the department had a lifelong acquaintance with European philosophy.[11]

Despite his legitimate feelings of loss, Tillich was not entering totally uncharted territory. There was by the 1930s a solid connection between German and American academics. That connection underlay the majority of invitations extended on behalf of American universities to German refugee scholars in the period between 1933 and 1941, and presupposed some formative dialogue. Tillich had met Niebuhr in Germany the summer before his emigration. Niebuhr had translated Tillich's work into English in the 1920s. Sometimes, as in the case of Franz Boas, who chaired the faculty Fellowship Committee at Columbia that issued invitations to refugees, or in the case of Carl J. Friedrich at Harvard or Nicholas Spykman at Yale, American faculty interested in the refugees were European or German by birth and had positioned themselves to know scholars in Europe as well as in the United States.

Other connections had grown out of American philanthropic investments in German science and learning during the interwar years. The Rockefeller Foundation, to give the leading example, had brought American and German scholars into contact with one another in a series of research and teaching fellowships in Germany and in the United States. Some refugee scholars – for example, the mathematician Felix Bernstein – found themselves in the United States when Hitler came to power. Bernstein was helped by the Rockefeller Foundation, which was supporting him at the time, in his endeavors to stay. International publishing projects such as E.R.A. Seligman's and Alvin Johnson's *International Encyclopedia of the Social*

---

11 Paul Tillich, "What Faith Is," in *Dynamics of Faith* (New York, 1957), 24; Leslie C. Dunn to Edward R. Murrow, March 23, 1934, Papers of the Emergency Committee in Aid of Displaced Foreign Scholars, box 156, "L.C. Dunn"; Pauck and Pauck, *The Life and Thought of Paul Tillich*, 160–1.

Sciences and the Carnegie Endowment's multivolume study of World War I had helped to foster a sense of scholarly comradery among American and German scholars.[12]

Once the refugee scholars were in the United States, the importance of former contacts and of the network of refugees grew geometrically. Not surprisingly, Paul Lazarsfeld was on Columbia University's Committee of Instruction when the committee oversaw the appointments of Arthur Nussbaum and Franz Neumann in public law and of Karl Polanyi as a visiting faculty member in economics. Albert Solomon arranged for Alfred Schutz to come to the New School for Social Research. Friedrich helped open doors at Harvard as did Arnold Wolfers at Yale, from which the latter had received a stipend in 1933.[13]

Ultimately, the political expediency of coming to the United States made the issue of reluctance moot, practically if not psychologically. Tillich remained in the United States for three years before returning home for a visit, only to discover that Germany was no longer a viable country in which to live. He likened his return to the United States to the dramatic exile of Abraham who was told by the Lord, "Go out from thy country into a land that I shall show thee."[14] The sense of loss and disorientation remained. The more courageous refugees wandered around in their new surroundings, whether they were in Gambier, Ohio, or New York City. Age was not necessarily a deterrent to such explorations. Ernst Cassirer prided himself on the fact that at the age of seventy he took it upon himself to master the New York subway system.[15] Tillich too immersed himself in the museums and avenues of the city.[16]

But learning about the physical environment was only a beginning for the refugee scholars. They needed as well to survey and find a point of entry into the intellectual landscape of their new home. Toward that end, they participated frequently in conferences and discussion clubs; they wrote and visited individuals who might bring them into contact with others in their fields; and they struggled with their heavy accents, inappropriate idi-

12 See Karen J. Greenberg, "The Mentor Within: The German Refugee Scholars of the Nazi Period and Their American Context," Ph.D. diss., Yale University, 1987.
13 Faculty of Political Science, minutes, April 18, 1947 and Nov. 21, 1947, Columbia University; Department of Political Science, general papers, minutes, 1913–56, Columbia University Archives; Franz Boas et al., "To the members of the faculties," n.d., John Dewey Collection, Columbia University Microfilm Collection, Columbia University; "American Committee, 1938," Carl J. Friedrich papers, Harvard University archives; Helmut R. Wagner, *Alfred Schütz: An Intellectual Biography* (Chicago, 1983).
14 Paul Tillich, *The Interpretation of History*, 67.
15 Toni Cassirer, *Aus Meinem Leben mit Ernst Cassier* (New York, 1950).
16 Hannah Tillich, *From Time to Time* (New York, 1973), 170–1.

oms, and mixed metaphors to find an audience. Tillich, for example, joined the prestigious New York Philosophy Club and taught seminars jointly with Columbia philosophy professor John Herman Randall. Most important from their point of view, the refugees, Tillich among them, began to write.

These early essays and books, written between 1933 and 1945, reflected in their style and content the nostalgia that the refugee scholars felt as a group. Commonly, the articles took the shape of odes to the past, to the German heritage, and to the essential cultural orientation that lay behind the German language. Often, as in the case of Tillich, the articles were written in German. These essays, constituting the first stage of intellectual accommodation for the refugees, thus commonly dwelled upon the past; they took the form of historiographical surveys of specific disciplines or areas of inquiry. The political scientist Hans Morgenthau, for example, devoted a book to the nature of the study of politics in Germany. Holborn described in detail the craft of history as it had developed under the tutelage of Rousseau, Herder, and others into German neoclassicism and beyond.[17]

Tillich adapted initially in similar fashion. In *The Interpretation of History*, his first American book, he chronicled the history of theological reasoning from the Greeks to the present day. His essays in the 1930s and 1940s, notably his "Existential Philosophy,"[18] often surveyed philosophical and theological trends. In a similar vein, his decision to write *Systematic Theology*, a comprehensive study of theological reasoning, appeared during this early phase of his adjustment to the United States, a phase marked more by thinking about the past than by living in the present or looking into the future.

These early works, in their emphases upon the historical and philosophical, were at times quite direct in their criticism of American empirical approaches to the study of the social sciences. Morgenthau's *Scientific Man vs. Political Man* counsels against the dangers of a social science based on numbers, statistics, and measurements. Holborn warned his adopted audience that "the historical and scientific methods are as different as the physical and the human world." Tillich, by contrast, was not eager to find fault, at least not publicly, with his new colleagues. He confessed to fears that he would "make angry" his new friends. Tillich's initial instincts counseled him to stay away from such clear attacks. Approached in 1935 by Edward R. Murrow, who was then working with the Emergency Committee in

---

17   Hajo Holborn, "Greek and Modern Concepts of History," *Journal of the History of Ideas* 12 (1949): 3–13; Hans Morgenthau, *Scientific Man vs. Power Politics* (Chicago, 1946).

18   Paul Tillich, "Existential Philosophy," *Journal of the History of Ideas* 5 (1944): 44–70. See also, e.g., Paul Tillich, "Nietzsche and the Bourgeois Spirit," *Journal of the History of Ideas* 6 (1945): 307–9.

Aid of Displaced German Scholars (later called the Emergency Committee for Displaced Foreign Scholars), Tillich refused to contribute to a symposium on refugee views of American scholarship.[19] Elsewhere, however, he did express his views on "the empiricist and positivistic trend of the Anglo-Saxon mind." He confessed to a disappointment with logical positivism and metaphysical naturalism, neither of which gave sufficient room to the assumptions of existentialism, both of which he associated with the Anglo-American tradition. "And even pragmatism," he wrote, "which is more closely related to existential thinking, has surrendered itself as 'instrumentalism' to the objective process of nature and society, producing means for ends which are finite and, consequently, not a matter of infinite, passionate concern."[20]

THE MOBILE PERIOD: CONSTRUCTING
A DIALOGUE

However much they might distinguish, either explicitly or implicitly, between the cultures they straddled, the refugee scholars were not blind to the necessity of building a bridge to the American environment. The question was, how were they to do that? Having laid out the cast of characters and theories that inspired their own work, how could they foster that constructive dialogue with their new colleagues and intellectual context? They devised for themselves a number of strategies, the earliest of which appeared in the form of allusions to the American intellectual tradition.

Whenever they could, many of the refugees included Americans in surveys of their disciplines. Eugene Rosenstock-Huessey, for example, brought Kant into dialogue with Santayana. He wrote that "Kant has no interest in pragmatic history. Yet he cares for tradition; he could have said, like Santayana: 'Those who can not remember the past are condemned to repeat it.' "[21] With one stroke, Rosenstock-Huessey dismissed the pragmatists and found something in the American tradition to salvage – namely, Santayana's quotation. Elsewhere, the refugee scholars also found more legitimate places for American thinkers, as the educational historian Robert Ulich did when he saw Mann and Dewey as successors to Pestalozzi and Froebel or as

---

19　Paul Tillich to Edward R. Murrow, Jan. 26, 1935, Papers of the Emergency Committee in Aid of Displaced German Scholars, box 153, "Symposium, 1935."

20　Paul Tillich, "Kierkegaard in English," *American-Scandinavian Review* 30 (1942): 256–7. James Luther Adams provides an insightful discussion of Paul Tillich's views toward Anglo-American thought by presenting those views in the context of the relationship between the thought of Tillich and Kierkegaard.

21　Eugene Rosenstock-Huessey, "The Predicament of History," *Journal of Philosophy* 32 (1935): 93–100.

Arnold Wolfers did when he rejected an article for *The American Political Science Review* on grounds that the author, "apparently of German origin," failed to include Americans in his source material. "I don't see how the 'evolution' of geopolitics can stop short of MacKinder, Spykman, Sprout, Gottman, and others, and yet be of interest to American political scientists." Holborn accomplished a dialogue between American thinkers in part by the texts he chose for his intellectual history courses such as his 1940–41 syllabus in which one third of the texts were written by Americans, including Dewey and Henry Adams. At the New School for Social Research, Schutz substituted Husserl for readings in James, Dewey, Whitehead, Mead, Colley, and Thomas.[22]

Tillich was likewise determined to emphasize similarities, even if he only felt justified in doing so to a minimal degree. In the beginning of "Existential Philosophy," Tillich pointed to connections between existential philosophers and other philosophers, including Americans. "Like Bergson, Bradley, James, and Dewey, the existential philosophers are appealing from the conclusion of rationalistic thinking, which equates reality with the object of thought." Throughout his years in America, Tillich insisted that the European heritage had a clear relevance for understanding the relationship between the individual and society in America. Tillich wrote that "the Neo-Stoics of the Renaissance, by transforming the courage to accept fate personally . . . into an active wrestling with fate, actually prepared the way for the courage to be in the democratic conformism of America."[23]

In addition, Tillich, a man who craved intimacy and developed close ties to the men and women who surrounded him, attested to a sense of intellectual closeness with his colleagues. As he wrote to John Herman Randall at Columbia, "I don't see that there is much difference between you and me." When he found himself unable to find points to praise, he often stayed his pen from expressing overt judgments as he did, for example, when he found himself unable to find existentialists to his liking in the United States. While excoriating Sartre and Heidegger for their pessimism, he glossed over the strands of negativist thought, which he had noticed in American pragmatism, but on which he chose not to dwell.[24]

22   Richard Grathoff, ed., *The Theory of Social Action: The Correspondence of Alfred Schutz and Talcott Parsons* (Bloomington, Ind., 1974), xiii–xiv; Arnold Wolfers to Harvey C. Mansfield, June 1956, "Selected Letters," 1933–1947, Arnold Wolfers papers, box 1, Yale University Archives; Hajo Holborn, "References on the Idea of Progress," Hajo Holborn papers, series I, box 2, Yale University Archives; Robert Ulich, *A Sequence of Educational Influences Traced through Unpublished Writings of Pestalozzi, Diesterweg, Horace Mann, and Henry Barnard* (Cambridge, 1935).

23   Paul Tillich, "Existential Philosophy," 44–5; and Paul Tillich, *The Courage To Be* (New Haven, Conn., 1952), 104.

24   Paul Tillich to Jack Randall, Feb. 20, 1957, John H. Randall papers, Columbia University Archives. See also Paul Tillich, "The Political Meaning of Utopia," in Tillich, ed., *Political Expectation* (New

Accordingly, rather than set himself apart from Americans in an explicit way, Tillich searched during his first two decades in the United States for points of intersection between the European philosophical past and his new environment. The first such nexus he located was himself. He prided himself on being able to stand in the middle of dialectical oppositions. Thus he found it fitting that he had alternately occupied positions in philosophy and theology in his five positions in Germany between the years 1919 and 1933. On a more substantive level, he appealed for the revitalization of Protestantism, and saw the need to bring together the theory and the practice of religion.

When he finally came to the realization in 1936 that he would remain in the United States, Tillich wrote an autobiographical piece that became the introduction to *The Interpretation of History*. Entitled "On the Boundary," the autobiographical portion of the book described a series of dialectical situations that defined Tillich as a thinker and in which he saw himself as existing at the point of intersection between the opposing states of being or thought. He lived, as his chapter headings indicated, between city and country, between social classes, between reality and imagination, between theory and practice, between heteronomy and autonomy, between theology and philosophy, between church and society, between religion and culture, between Lutheranism and socialism, between idealism and Marxism, and finally, between home and an alien land.[25]

Presented in this fashion, Tillich's status as a refugee became a capstone position for the man who lived in between, a state of being Tillich had admired even during his life in Germany. In fact, during his Weimar years he had identified himself as a champion of the "human border situation," an existence lying between a concrete state of being and acting (*logos*) and the eternal realm, between the limited human condition and the unlimited sphere of divinity (*kairos*).[26]

As a refugee, he became an even better spokesman for the human border situation and thus for making Protestantism speak to the modern consciousness. While still in Germany, Tillich had called for a new language for Protestant theology in the twentieth century, and thus it seemed only ap-

---

York, 1971), 137–8, a series of four lectures delivered originally at the Deutsche Hochschule für Politik, Berlin, in 1951.

25 Paul Tillich, *The Interpretation of History*, 3–76.

26 In Tillichian terms, this differs from the highly abstract use of the terms used by Ritschl, Harnack, and others. *Logos* is both the ground of being and the origin of being (God). In opposition to *kairos*, it is used to mean that which is concrete but which is able to intersect with that which is universal. See, e.g., Paul Tillich, *Die Religiöse Lage der Gegenwart* (Berlin, 1926); Tillich's *Religiöse Verwirklichungsphilosophie* presents a comprehensive and reliable treatment of Tillich's early thought.

propriate that he would himself have to learn a new language once he
became a refugee. Like the individual poised between the past and the
future, he existed between Germany and America. Like the individual al-
ienated from his roots and searching for a place of refuge, he had come to
reside in a new land. Tillich, a representative modern man, had always been
a refugee.

The alien land is not the geographically different one, but the temporally future
one, the "beyond the present." Finally in speaking of the alike, we can point to
the feeling that even the nearest and most familiar has an element of strangeness
for us. I mean that metaphysical experience of strangeness in our world, which the
philosophy of existence takes an outstanding expression of human finiteness. In all
these respects, I always stood between home and alien land.[27]

To Tillich, all men who existed in the human border situation were refugees:

To stand on many border lines means to experience in many forms the unrest,
insecurity, and inner limitation of existence, and to know the inability of attaining
serenity, security, and perfection. That is true of life as well as of thought . . . In
its presence, even the very center of our being is only a boundary . . . [28]

This form of intellectual accomodation – in which the very fact of being
a refugee became an explanatory paradigm for the refugee's philosophy –
appeared particularly during the middle of second stage of accomodation
in the writings of other refugee scholars as well, most notably those of
Hannah Arendt. For Arendt, the situation of the Jew in Western bourgeois
culture was aptly symbolized by the refugee. The refugee was either pariah
or parvenu, either outsider or insider, as the Jew in Europe had been. That
choice between alienation and membership was the choice of modern man.
To a lesser extent, Morgenthau followed a similar strategy. His theory of
the balance of power found uncanny illustration in the position of the
European refugee intellectual in the United States. The struggle over geographical territory between nations in the world had its counterpart in the
struggle over intellectual territory between the European and the American
way of thinking.

The border situation was central not only to Tillich's vision of himself
but to his theology as well. During his years in Germany, he had devoted
himself to the defense and explanation of religious socialism. Christianity
and socialism, Tillich had explained, existed in a dialectical relationship to
one another. Religious socialism attempted to overcome the tension be-

tween the two modes of thought and being. The opposition existed largely because of the emphasis on materialism as opposed to spiritualism in Christian humanism. "This adoption of the materialistic element of bourgeois society led to the struggle between religion and socialism. . . ." Religious socialism would unite the belief in God within the Marxist interpretation of society and culture. Religion would combat the sense of alienation and restore a sense of community. All peoples could belong and share in that community based on God.

Identifying himself as a religious socialist, Tillich sought to enable the individual to find himself, to discover his essence, while at the same time being able to communicate and sense a part of the larger divine entity, God. In philosophical terms, Tillich's religious socialism coincided, with the theological notion of theogeny. Theogeny was the unification of *kairos* and *logos*, toward which Tillich hoped to guide modern man. Within the religious community, Tillich's theogeny signified a diversion, indeed a point of opposition, to transcendent Lutheranism. His respect for *logos*, for the specific moment, the "right time," clashed fundamentally with the idea that one's life should be lived with an eye toward God. His opponents within the Lutheran church in Germany had insisted that the regard for *kairos* would of necessity weaken the measure of faith in the transcendent Being.

THE FINAL PERIOD; THE UNITED STATES AT CENTER STAGE

In the United States, Tillich's theogeny, his insistence that *kairos* and *logos* coexist in a constructive unit, made sense. First, America, in its own mind and in that of the European refugees, often represented empiricism, pragmatism, and the practical side of thought as well as of life, which Tillich emphasized as a necessary component of religion. Second, Tillich recognized the way in which Americans naturally welcomed the focus on the individual, the particular event, the concrete moment.[29] In the United States, Tillich's focus on the materialist aspects of bourgeois society, his dwelling on a Marxist critique of work and labor faded before the preoccupation with the individual, the particular, the concrete as a conceptual term, free of socialist connotation. As Tillich explained it in *The Courage to Be*, Americans were peculiarly set to understand what he meant by theo-

---

29 For some interesting discussion on this point, see Pauck and Pauck, *The Life and Thought*, 161.

geny. In that book, he took the concept of theogeny and translated them into categories of courage. In the United States, the individual was encouraged both to be true to his essence, to be an individual, and to feel a sense of belonging to a large entity, the group, or the nation. In Tillich's view, Americans are evidence of the courage to be oneself and of the courage to belong. That tendency toward conformism seen in its most positive light as an urge toward community, toward identification with a larger entity than the self, opened up Americans to the possibility of identifying with the divine entity. The individual and the collective came together in constructive form in the United States.[30]

In finding a modern-day expression of theogeny in the United States, Tillich also discovered the importance of a spiritual sensibility that he found unique in the United States – an irrepressible sense of Hope. Americans displayed, according to Tillich, "something astonishing" for a European – the "affirmation of oneself as a participant of mankind." For Americans, means and ends, *kairos* and *logos*, overlapped. For Tillich, the "courage to be" was a point of bringing together the European and American traditions and a beginning point for moving in the direction of sensibilities that to his mind were peculiarly American. The American faith in new beginnings. In the United States, hope could replace the pull of despair that had characterized his past.

Like a sufficiently receptive audience for his concept of theogeny, Tillich's sense of Hope had eluded him prior to his emigration. Indeed, a lack of hope had been for Tillich a major problem inherent in contemporary existentialist philosophy. In Heidegger and in Sartre, who, like Tillich, grappled with the questions of anxiety and alienation in the individual, there was a tendency not to find a message of hope, but to learn instead to live with anxiety rather than to overcome it. Although, as Tillich admitted, certain American pragmatists shared that tendency, the more prevalent response of Americans to the anxiety of modern times, to existential angst, was to develop a philosophy of affirmation.

The key to being able to overcome the despair over existence lay in the future-oriented nature of America. Tillich had always been a yea-sayer, one who in the Nietzschean fashion would act and think constructively in spite of the anguish suitable to the modern predicament. But in the United States, Tillich began to see just how counterproductive the pull of the past that he had glorified in his early émigré writing actually was. This transformation

30 Paul Tillich, *The Courage To Be*, 113–23.

in his thought is particularly apparent in his essays and lectures on the topic of utopia, the earliest of which he delivered in postwar Germany.[31]

Tillich depicts a utopia in which both positive and negative scenarios may follow. The positive vision stands on the stage of theogeny. Within each human being there is a character of being, one that presents a universe of possibilities. Utopia lies in the future that the individual can realize through the intersection of his essential self and the real world. Utopia, in other words, has a "foundation in man's being," and looks forward. For Tillich, the notion of utopia as forward-looking coincided directly with his description of the United States as forward-looking. The more common view of utopia took as its focus the past rather than the future. The Stoics, the Christians, the Renaissance philosophers, and even some of Marx's followers equated utopia with restoration of a state of perfection that had once existed in the past.

In championing the cause of utopia as necessarily forward-looking, and in criticizing the utopian vision that embraced the past, Tillich began to exchange an American vision for a European one. *The Courage To Be*, as well as his writings on utopia, revealed the change of emphasis and signaled a newfound independence from the German intellectual tradition, from the heritage that he had once felt to be the very essence of his mind and being. As Tillich pointed out, the German language itself emphasized the "phenomenon of the backward-looking utopia." In the distinction between *Wesen* (essence) and *Gewesen* (was or has been), it was clear "that essence is that form which we become and have always been." The better life at the heart of German utopian dramas assumed that the reality of the better life lay in the past. For Americans, the better life, according to Tillich, lay in the future.

Tillich preferred the style of utopian thinking that was progressive in its orientation to one that envisioned an ultimate – and ultimately static – state of perfection. Tillich wrote that "progress is a moderated utopia that is no longer sure of itself but nonetheless determined to give it up." Quoting Goethe to a German audience, he assented to the great German's observation that "In America this [progressive] conception is widely held." By contrast, Tillich feared the notion of a permanent and perfect utopia.[32]

This criticism of Germany – and Tillich's declaration of independence

---

31 Paul Tillich, "The Political Meaning of Utopia," 125–80. Nietzsche also recognizes the need to be future oriented. His yea-saying is indeed an invitation to the future; his nay-saying, a rejection of the past.

32 Paul Tillich, "The Political Meaning of Utopia," 140, 154–67; and Paul Tillich, "Decline and Validity of the Idea of Progress," in *The Future of Religions*, 64–79.

from that tradition – involved a transformation in Tillich's thinking not only in regard to the past but also in regard to the border situation. In the final years of his life, Tillich began to refine his notion of being on the boundary. Whereas in *The Interpretation of History* he had denied the border situation as existing in the middle of two situations, two states of being, he began in the 1960s to emphasize the need to "cross over" into the existences which were joined at the border. "Only he who participates on both sides of a border line can serve the Comprehensive and thereby peace." This involved "crossing and return, a repetition of return and crossing, a back-and-forth." Although Tillich's life – as a member of theological and philosophy faculties, in Germany and the United States – had illustrated departure and return, his definition of the boundary had once been a more static one in which the individual positioned himself between states of being without necessarily immersing himself in one side and then the other.

For Tillich, the change of emphasis involved further renunciation of his ties with Germany, in this case with present-day Germany. During the Nazi period, Tillich reminded a German audience that the German church had retreated from the border between the church and the state. At a time when advancement was necessary, the church along with the nation, had turned inward. This was an endemic German problem, according to Tillich, one in which the lack of respect for boundaries coincided with the "demonic urge . . . to wipe out one's frontier in order to be the whole thing by one's self." In retreat and in advancement, the German nation saw itself as a singular actor with a singular goal and a lack of acceptance of the nation's proper finiteness, its true essence. For Tillich, the admirable country, like the respectable individual, understood its own essential being, replete with possibilities and limitations, and acted accordingly.[33]

Tillich underscored the relationship between his fears about the dominant character of Germany and his appreciation of the United States at the 1965 meeting of the Marketing Union of the German Book Trade, where he was awarded the organization's peace prize. In his acceptance speech, the German-born American theologian contrasted his two homes explicitly. "In the United States, the consciousness of calling has created faith in a new beginning and the spirit of a crusade for its universal accomplishment." In the United States, "a people found its essential limits and sought to make them into factual limits." Theogeny, Tillich reiterated, made sense in the United States. It had not made sense to Weimar leaders of the church; it did not make sense to present-day Germans. Throughout his life, Tillich

33   Paul Tillich, "Frontiers," 53.

held onto the notion that Germany should have heeded his call in the 1920s and should heed his call in the postwar era. But his hopes and advice for Germany aside, he had come to see the cultural essence of America as a parallel to his own self-described essence – hopeful, future-oriented, understanding of the border situation, respectful of its true self. Germany still lagged in these respects. Tillich addressed his former countrymen accordingly, "And my wish is this for the German people, from whom I come . . . that it keep itself open, recognize its essential frontier and its calling, and fulfill progressively its factual frontier." Germany, Tillich was suggesting, should adopt some of the characteristics he associated with the United States.[34]

Over time, as Tillich embraced the future at the expense of the hold of the past, as he substituted the open and changing border for the static one, as he distanced himself from Germany and complimented America, he found a reason for his exile. He had come to reside in the land that made sense for the thinker and person he was. Unlike Abraham, Tillich would not return home, for the home he sought had always been that of the United States. Other émigrés, even those who eventually returned to Europe, similarly found an intellectual home in the United States.

Kurt Weill embraced the world of American music as providing the appropriate arena for bringing popular idioms to a serious audience, his lifelong goal. Arendt saw the United States as the land where the author of "The Jew as Pariah" could build a constructive home. Thomas Mann tried, although less convincingly, to see the United States as a logical home for his attraction to modernist forms.

There was for Tillich, however, a strong undercurrent of loss in finding a new home. In the process of bidding farewell to his religious attachment to Germany, Tillich revealed at least one moment of recognition that his status as a refugee would deprive him ultimately of having a significant say for future minds; that the dialectic he respected would supersede him; that progress as he defined it would leave him behind. In a sermon delivered in 1955, Tillich confessed to a recognition that the refugees and the tradition they represented constituted "a generation of the end." He and his compatriots had lost, by virtue of their attachment to a culture that bred mass destruction and death, the ability to survive spiritually in the atmosphere of hope that he had identified as uniquely American. He wrote that the refugees carried "in their souls . . . the traces of death" and would "never

34   Ibid., 63.

completely lose them." He and his generation could only be "symbols of death," participants in an ending.[35]

Viewed over the course of his entire career, Tillich's life and thought does seem to call for some reconsideration of Neumann's categories. At different stages of his life in the United States, Tillich would have fit into all three of those categories. In his early American career, he, like the majority of his colleagues, sought stability in portraying his heritage to his American audience. In the early 1950s, Tillich's middle years in the United States, he self-consciously tried to bring together old and new. A similar attempt underlay the essays collected in *The Cultural Migration*, the volume in which Neumann's essay on the social sciences appeared. In his later years, Paul Tillich recognized that the old would be lost in the formation of new syntheses; the new, albeit the European heritage deeply embedded within it, would survive on its own grounds, its own territory. The "creative blending" would exist but in an altered form often indiscernible from the American intellectual milieu. At the very least, an irreversible change in emphasis had occurred where the identification with the American context took precedence over a focus on the European heritage. Perhaps this sequential paradigm of intellectual acculturation can open up new avenues of thought about migration, avenues that will underscore the ways in which individuals seek to find for themselves, for the essential structure of their minds, and for their personal, intellectual needs. There is of course some sense of loss entailed in recognizing this process, but it was a necessary and unavoidable loss. For as Tillich, who had once thought Shakespeare to be German, had discovered, the new synthesis might bear an imprint of Germany only in invisible ways.

35   Paul Tillich, "Love is Stronger than Death," in Tillich, *The New Being* (New York, 1955), 172.

Index